# Research Foundations in Object-Oriented and Semantic Database Systems

*Editors:*



**Alfonso F. Cárdenas**
*Computer Science Department*
*University of California, Los Angeles*
*and*
*Computomata International Corp*

**Dennis McLeod**
*Computer Science Department*
*University of Southern California*

**Prentice Hall Series in Data and Knowledge Base Systems**
**Dennis McLeod, Series Editor**

**Prentice Hall,** Upper Saddle River, New Jersey 07458

Library of Congress Cataloging-in-Publication Data

Research foundations in object-oriented and semantic database systems / editors,
Alfonso F. Cardenas, Dennis McLeod.
p. cm. – (Prentice Hall series in data and knowledge base
systems)
Includes bibliographical references.
ISBN 0-13-806340-0
1. Data base management. 2. Object-oriented programming (Computer
science) I. Cardenas, Alfonso F. II. McLeod, Dennis.
III. Series.
QA76.9.D3R47 1990 89-72130
005.75—dc20 CIP

Editorial/production supervision and
interior design: Joe Scordato
Cover design: Lundgren Graphics
Cover art: The Image Bank
Cover illustration by Pierre Peyrolle
Manufacturing buyer: Lori Bulwin



Printed in the United States of America

10 9 8 7 6 5 4 3 2 1

ISBN 0-13-456476-6

Prentice-Hall International (UK) Limited, London
Prentice-Hall of Australia Pty. Limited, Sydney
Prentice-Hall Canada Inc., Toronto
Prentice-Hall Hispanoamericana, S.A., Mexico
Prentice-Hall of India Private Limited, New Delhi
Prentice-Hall of Japan, Inc., Tokyo
Pearson Education Asia Pte. Ltd., Singapore
Editoria Prentice-Hall do Brasil, Ltda., Rio De Janeiro

*To my wife,*
*Fandy, and*
*to my children,*
*Christian and Amanda*

*A.C.*

*To my parents,*
*James and Virginia, and*
*to Marte Post*

*D.M.*

# Contents

# Preface

This book brings together a number of papers which represent seminal contributions underlying semantic and object-oriented database systems. An overview of semantic (structurally object-oriented) and behaviorally object-oriented databases examines the main principles, concepts, mechanisms, and techniques underlying this technology, and provides a historical perspective. The subsequent contributed chapters are structured into three major selctions: Concepts and Techniques, Systems and Implementation, and Applications.

A chapter by Hull and King provides an overview of semantic (structurally object-oriented) database models and systems. A chapter by Hammer and McLeod presents a rich semantic data model (SDM), the philosophy underlying it, and its intended applications. The chapter on Bobrow et al. examines the merging of a programming language (LISP) with object-oriented concepts; to a large extent, this chapter examines the behaviorally object-oriented approach. The chapter by Rowe and Stonebraker describes the data model underlying POSTGRES, which incorporates some important object-oriented capabilities. The Lyngbaek and McLeod work examines the sharing of objects in a distributed environment. Finally, the Concepts and Techniques section concludes with a chapter by Skarra and Zdonik focusing on the importance of managing evolution in object-oriented databases.

The Systems and Implementation section of the book begins with a chapter by Kim et al., describing important aspects of the comprehensive ORION object-oriented database management system developed at MCC. Key aspects of the IRIS database management developed at Hewlett-Packard Research Laboratories are described in a chapter by Fishman et al. The chapter by Maier et al. examines the Gemstone object-oriented DBMS, which is to a large extent a persistent version of SmallTalk with important extensions. The chapter by Andrews explores the VBase DBMS, which combines structurally object-oriented and behaviorally object-oriented concepts into a single framework. The SIM DBMS, an implementation of a structurally object-oriented data model is described by Fritchman et al. in the final chapter of the Systems and Implementation section.

The third section of the book contains three chapters which describe selected issues in the application and use of object-oriented database concepts. The first chapter, by Katz and Chang, describes a rich object version mechanism for computer-aided design (CAD) databases. The chapter by Joseph and Cárdenas examines the management of pictorial objects in a DBMS. Finally, Dittrich et al. describe the management of complex objects in engineering database applications.

# About the Editors

**ALFONSO F. CÁRDENAS** Dr. Cárdenas is Professor, Computer Science Department, School of Engineering and Applied Science, UCLA, and consultant in computer science and management, Computomata International Corporation. He obtained the B.S. degree from San Diego State University and the M.S. and Ph.D. degrees in Computer Science, at the University of California, Los Angeles, 1969. His major areas of interest include database management, distributed heterogeneous (text, image/picture, voice) systems, information systems planning and development methodologies, and software engineering automation. Dr. Cárdenas has offered seminars and consulted for IBM Corporation, The Rand Corporation, Arthur Young and Company, TTI/Citicorp, Tandem Computers, Banco Nacional de Mexico, Petroleos Mexicanos, Jet Propulsion Laboratory, Goodyear Atomic Corporation, General Dynamics, Hughes aircraft, and other major organizations. He was visiting scientist/consultant to IBM Corporation in 1972–1975, on future database and applications generation technology.

He has served as chairman and member of organizations and program committees for many conferences, and has led seminars and has spoken at conferences in many countries. He is past-president (1984–1989) and member of the board of trustees of the Very Large Data Base Endowment, which conducts the annual International Conference on Very Large Data Bases. He is the author of the book **Data Base Management Systems**, Allyn and Bacon Incorporated, 1979 and 1984; co-editor and co-author of **Computer Science**, John Wiley & Sons Incorporated, 1972; and author of many other publications. He is a member of the Association for Computing Machinery and the Society for Information Management, and editor of *Information Systems*.

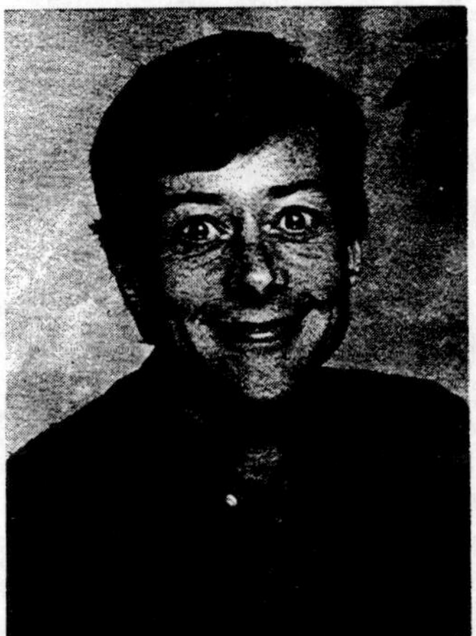

**DENNIS MCLEOD** Dr. Dennis McLeod received his B.S., M.S., and Ph.D. degrees in Computer Science from the Massachusetts Institute of Technology in 1974, 1976, and 1978 (respectively). He joined the faculty of the University of Southern California in 1978, where he is currently an Associate Professor of Computer Science. His principal research interests include: database system modeling, design, and evolution; distributed databases and database networks; information protection and security; knowledge managment; applied machine learning; personal information management systems; and information management environments for engineering design, scientific data, and computer-supported cooperative work. Dr. McLeod has published widely in the areas of database systems, knowledge management, and office information systems; he is particularly noted for his work on semantic data modeling and federated databases. He has lectured widely on an international basis, and has served as an advisor and consultant to a variety of private and public sector organizations. He has served as chairman and member of program and organizational committees for numerous technical conferences and workshops, is a member of the VLDB Endowment board of trustees, and an editor of the *ACM Transactions on Information Systems*, the *International Journal on Very Large Databases*, and *IEEE Office Knowledge Engineering*.

# Research Foundations In Object-Oriented and Semantic Database Systems

# An Overview of Object-Oriented and Semantic Database Systems

**Alfonso F. Cárdenas**

*Computer Science Department, University of California, Los Angeles*

**Dennis McLeod**

*Computer Science Department, University of Southern California*

## 1. INTRODUCTION

Beginning in the late 1960s, and particularly in the late 1970s to the present, a diverse body of technology has emerged for structuring and managing integrated databases and database-intensive information systems and applications. Knowledge, tools, practices, and commercial software systems have emerged whose focus is on supporting the organization, control, and manipulation of collections of structured/formatted data.

The late 1970s and 1980s witnessed a number of milestones in data management through the appearance and successful application of generalized file and generalized database management systems (DBMSs). A growing number of users are now exploiting the benefits of the available, evolving, and fast-growing database technology and know-how. This technology has now been reaching the masses of non-database professionals, and finding applications now at the level of personal computer users and everyday tasks of small companies, and even households. The 1970s witnessed the emergence of hierarchical and network types of DBMS, widely used today. In the 1980s, relational database management systems emerged, and now dominate more of the marketplace, particularly at the level of less sophisticated users requiring accessible database facilities.

With the advance of information systems and applications, existing users are now demanding more capabilities from the commercial DBMSs. Moreover, new areas of endeavor are now challenging the applicability and effectiveness of information systems technology for automation. Before us are these challenges of additional capabilities for existing computerized applications as well as the ability to meet requirements not well supported by current systems or not supported at all by current systems. This has led to a diffused, growing, promising, and exciting body of knowledge, prototypes and now commercial products that we will refer to as object-oriented and semantic database systems.

## 2. OBJECT-ORIENTED AND SEMANTIC DATABASES

The concepts, principles, techniques, and mechanisms underlying "object-oriented" and "semantic" databases are best examined in the context of general-purpose database management systems (DBMSs). A general-purpose DBMS can be viewed as a generalized collection of integrated mechanisms and tools to support the definition, manipulation, and control of databases for a variety of application environments. The functional capabilities a general-purpose DBMS is intended to provide include the following:

- Support the independent existence of a database, apart from the application programs and systems that manipulate it;
- Provide a conceptual/logical level of data abstraction;
- Support the query and modification of databases;
- Accommodate the evolvability of both the conceptual structure and internal (physical) organization of a database, in response to changing information, usage, and performance requirements;
- Control a database, which involves the four aspects of semantic integrity (making sure the database is an accurate model of its application environment), security (authorization), concurrency (handling multiple simultaneous users), and recovery (restoring the database in the event of a failure of some type).

While the emphasis here is on discussing the capabilities of general-purpose database management systems, it should be noted that the concepts examined here also apply to database systems tailored to specific application environments.

At the core of any database management system is a database model (data model), which is a mechanism for specifying the structure of a database and operations that can be performed on the data in that database. As such, a database model should allow databases to be viewed in a manner that is based upon the meaning of data as seen by its users; accommodate various levels of abstraction and detail; support both anticipated and unanticipated database uses; accommodate multiple viewpoints; and be free of implementation and physical optimization detail (physical data independence).

Abstractly speaking, a database model is a collection of generic structures, (semantic integrity) constraints, and primitive operations. The structures of a database model must support the specification of objects, object classifications, and inter-object relationships. The semantic integrity constraints of the database model specify restrictions on states of a database or transitions between such states, in order that the database accurately reflect its application environment. Some constraints are embedded within the structural component of a database model, while others may be expressed separately and enforced externally to the DBMS. We can refer to the specification of a particular database constructed using these general-purpose structures and constraints as a (conceptual) schema.

The operational component of a database model consists of a general-purpose collection of primitives that support the query and modification of a database; viz., given a database with an associated conceptual schema, the operations facilitate the manipulation of that database in terms of the schema. Such primitives may be embodied in a stand-alone end-user interface or a specialized language, or embedded within a general-purpose programming language. Database-specific operations (transactions) can be constructed utilizing the primitives of the database model as building blocks.

Record-oriented database models, which dominate the database systems in practical use today, include the relational model as well as partially relational models (pseudo-relational models), and hierarchical and network models. While there is considerable variation among the versions of these models embodied in particular DBMSs, the key point they have in common is the use of the record construct as the foundation of the model.

The variety of DBMSs which embody hierarchical and network type database models offer inter-record link types in addition to the record as a basic modeling construct; these link types explicitly express inter-record relationships. Traditionally, such systems suffer from a lack of physical data independence, but this need not be the case in principle. By contrast, DBMSs based upon the relational model capture inter-record relationships in a uniform manner: by means of common data values. In fact, the simplicity and uniformity of the relational database model is a fundamental goal of that model. Other important aspects of the relational approach are also quite significant, although these are not necessarily tied to the model itself; these include the importance of physical data independence, high-level general-purpose operational primitives, set-at-a-time (as opposed to record-at-a-time) orientation, and a firm mathematical foundation[Cod70, Cod79, Dat82].

When applied to database models, the terms "object-oriented" and "semantic" are used to refer to many characteristics and mechanisms [Abi87, Afs86, And87, Ban87, Fis87, Gib83, Hum81, Hul87, Jag88, Zdo84]. We shall attempt here to use them somewhat precisely; specifically, we use the term object-oriented to refer to the following characteristics, as exhibited by a database model and a database management system that embodies that model:

- *Individual object identity*: Objects in a database can include not only primitive types of data items, such as strings and numbers, but also abstract objects representing physical entities in the real world, as well as intangible things. Relationships among and classifications of such objects can themselves be considered as abstract objects in the database. Graphical, image, pictorial, and voice objects can also be accommodated. Such abstract objects can be directly represented and manipulated in a database[Cod79, Ham81, Ken79, Smi87].

- *Explicit semantic primitives*: Primitives are provided to support object classification, structuring, semantic integrity constraints, and derived data. These primitive abstraction mechanisms support such features as aggregation, classification, instantiation, and inheritance. The roots of these semantic primitives are in "semantic data models"[Cod79,Ham81,Kin85a,Myl80a,Shi81,Smi77] and in artificial intelligence knowledge representation techniques[Bra85,Bro86,Woo75].
- *Object behavior and encapsulation*: Database objects can be active as well as passive, in the sense that they can exhibit behavior. Various specific approaches to the modeling of object behavior can be adopted, such as an inter-object message passing paradigm (e.g., as described in[Pur87,Ste86b]), or abstract datatype encapsulation (e.g., [And87]). The important point is that behavioral abstraction and encapsulation are supported. Behavioral encapsulation can also be used to define new (application-specific) abstractions.
- *Object uniformity*: All information (or nearly all) in a database is described using the same object model[Afs85a,Ban87a]. Thus, descriptive information about objects, referred to here as meta-data, is conceptually represented in the same way as specific "fact" objects.

Since practical semantic and object-oriented DBMSs are now only beginning to appear, it is logical that only some of the above aspects of object-orientation are handled by them. The first two, object identity and explicit semantic primitives, can be ascribed to a "semantic DBMS" which has a structural object-orientation; the last aspect, object uniformity, is also addressed to some extent by these new systems. Behaviorally object-oriented systems also address the issue of active objects, viz., accommodating application-specific methods or procedures on objects in the database itself [Banc88,Pur87].

## 3. THE ROOTS OF OBJECT-ORIENTED AND SEMANTIC DATABASE TECHNOLOGY

To provide a historical perspective on state-of-the-art semantic and object-oriented database models and systems, Figure 1 shows a twenty year perspective with descriptive terms highlighting some of the most significant developments and the major conceptual trends underlying them.

In Figure 1, we note on the top left of the upper portion of the figure the introduction and subsequent development of the relational database model. Work on normalization focused on the design of "good" relational conceptual schemas, while work on constraints for the relational model addressed the problem of adding additional semantics to the simple relational structures. Following to the right, we see RM/T, the structural model, SAM/SAM*, and GEM, which are extensions of the relational model to capture more meaning.

Functional models explored the use of mappings from one data set to another, and are related to the binary relational models. The data semantics model was an early binary semantic model. The entity-relationship model was originally introduced as a design

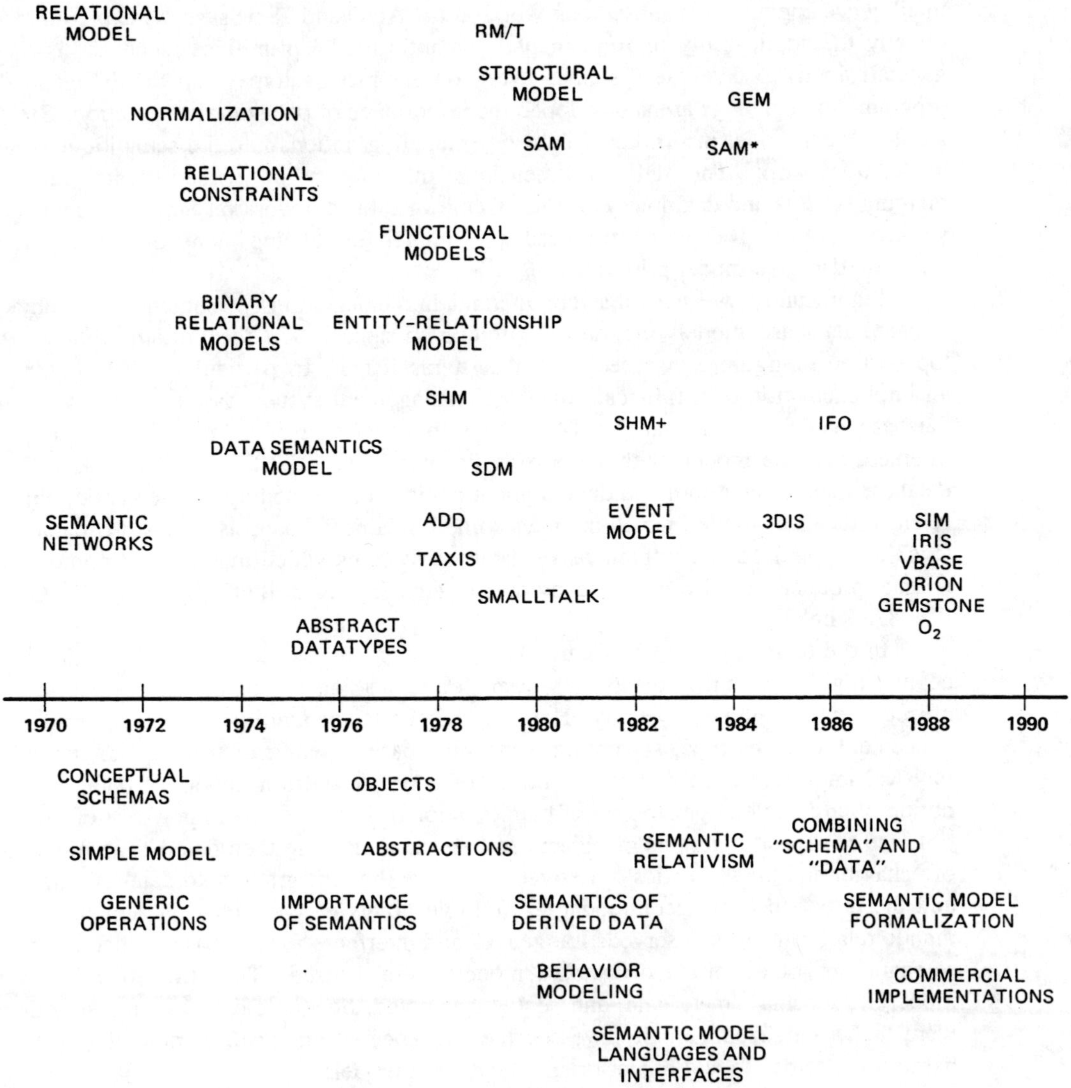


**Figure 1** 20 Year Research and Development Trends.

tool for record-oriented databases (as were many of the semantic database models), and the SHM (semantic hierarchy model) focused on the importance of aggregation and generalization primitives. SDM was a complex semantic database model, containing a rich collection of modeling primitives, and supporting a variety of semantic integrity constraints and derived data specifications.

On the bottom left of the upper portion of Figure 1, we see work on semantic networks which represented a significant step in the structuring of knowledge for artificial intelligence applications; subsequent work on the ADD and Taxis systems explored more directly the applicability of fundamental semantic model primitives (such as "is-a" or generalization) to database systems. Work on abstract datatypes and SmallTalk in the programming language arena developed the importance of behavioral abstraction. SHM+ and the event model incorporated behavior modeling notions into the semantic database model framework. The 3DIS (3-dimensional information space) incorporated ideas of merging schema and data into a uniform framework (as did work on SmallTalk and early work on Orion). IFO was introduced as a model formalizing many of the important semantic database model primitives.

Significantly, we note that commercial implementations of semantic and object-oriented database models are now beginning to appear. In the bottom right of the top portion of figure 1, we see several systems listed. In particular, SIM [Jag88] is an implementation of a full-scale database management system based upon a semantic database model. Gemstone [Pur87] is an implementation of a SmallTalk-like object-oriented database model, with supporting database server facilities. Vbase [And87] is database management tool and development environment based upon a semantic, object-oriented database model, which includes some fundamental aspects of abstract datatypes [Lis77]. Several other comprehensive database systems which may soon become commercial products are also under development (e.g., Iris [Fis87], O2 [Banc88], and Orion [Ban87a,Kim87]).

In the bottom portion of Figure 1, we see a summary of some of the major conceptual highlights during the twenty year period leading to commercial semantic and object-oriented database systems. Here, we see early recognition of the importance of conceptual schemas (viz., separating a meaning-based specification of a database from physical implementation detail), the utility of a simple uniform model of data, and the notion of a (complete) generic set of manipulation operations. The importance of semantics, and the specific notions of objects and abstractions were then noted. The modeling of behavior and the semantics of derived data were then integrated into database models, and the importance of accommodating multiple points of view on data semantics (semantic relativism) was observed. Languages and interfaces for databases structured with semantic and object-oriented database models were devised. The utility of a uniform model of "schema" (meta-data) and "data" was noted. Semantic database model notions were then formalized. Finally, we see the existence of practical, commercial systems based upon semantic and object-oriented database models.

## 4. APPROACHES TO OBJECT-ORIENTED AND SEMANTIC DATABASE SYSTEMS

A major part of the thrust of research and development in object-oriented and semantic database systems sets aside the use or extension of current DBMSs. The reason is that the requirements of object-oriented approaches are considered by many to be not well matched by the requirements that gave rise to current record-oriented DBMS technology. Efforts that take this approach, as described in chapters in this book, include the following:

- the ORION object-oriented database management system developed at MCC;
- the Ontologic VBase system, now commercially available;
- the Servio Logic Gemstone system, a commercial product;
- the CERM/Damokles system of the University of Karlsruhe;
- the UCLA Pictorial Database Management System.

Among these efforts are those that have been heavily influenced by advances in programming languages such as Simula and SmallTalk, and abstract data types. The Gemstone effort is a good example of this, in which the SmallTalk environment is extended to include complete database management system facilities. This includes support for multiple users, the ability to accommodate large volumes of objects, and the user-transparent unification of object management in the large-volume, slow-access storage world with that in the low-volume, high-speed main memory world. Further, objects and their allowed operations are closely integrated in such an approach.

By contrast, a portion of the effort towards object-oriented and semantic database systems is based in some sense on the evolution or extension of existing DBMSs. In this work, current record-oriented DBMSs are upgraded, extended, or otherwise utilized as building blocks to meet the object-oriented and semantic database challenge.

In the POSTGRES system of the University of California, Berkeley (as described in a chapter of this book), an existing relational DBMS is extended to accommodate important object-oriented database concepts. This exemplifies the strategy of building rather directly upon existing record-oriented technology.

In a somewhat different approach to utilizing existing database technology, the IRIS system (also detailed in this book) being developed at Hewlett-Packard Research Laboratories utilizes a relational DBMS as a storage subsystem. IRIS provides a very significant layer on top of the relational DBMS, insulating users from details of record-oriented database structuring and manipulation. The SIM (Semantic Information Manager) system of Unisys similarly utilizes an existing DBMS as a storage manager; in this case it is the DMS-II CODASYL-type system. SIM incorporates a semantic database model similar to SDM, and provides database manipulation facilities for this model.

Another approach that has been taken is to attempt to stretch the applicability of commercial record-oriented DBMSs to significantly new types of applications. An example of this, described in this book, is the the UCLA Pictorial Database Management System.

Part of the justification for extending or building upon existing DBMSs, rather than building a new object-oriented or semantic DBMS from scratch, includes the following:

- It is possible to avoid rebuilding lower layers of database software, e.g., those that support physical storage structure and access method management, concurrency control, recovery, etc. A very substantial investment has been made in producing such software, and to rebuild it can be very costly indeed.
- An evolutionary continuum can be provided for users, in order to preserve their investment and commitment to existing DBMSs. In this way, conversion and transition to new technology can be eased.

Of course, when extending or building upon an existing system one may well be faced with limitations that impact on the functional capabilities of the new DBMS.

## 5. A SNAPSHOT OF THE STATE-OF-THE-ART IN OBJECT-ORIENTED AND SEMANTIC DATABASE SYSTEMS

In this book, we have attempted to bring together a number of papers which represent seminal contributions to the state-of-the-art of semantic and object-oriented database systems. Many of these papers have been previously published and appear here in (possibly revised) form; there are also several new papers included. We have not attempted to be exhaustive of all important work in the field, but rather have assembled a selective collection of chapters which emphasize what in our view are the most important aspects of structurally and behaviorally object-oriented databases.

We have structured the book in three major sections or parts: concepts and techniques, systems and implementation, and applications. It is important to note that our classification of a given work into one of these categories is not intended to characterize the sole contribution of it, but rather to accentuate its contributions within the framework of this edited volume.

The concepts and techniques section begins with a chapter by Hull and King, which serves as a brief tutorial and survey of the principal aspects of semantic (structurally object-oriented) databases. This is followed by a chapter by Hammer and McLeod, which describes a rich semantic data model (SDM), the philosophy underlying it, and its intended applications. The next chapter by Bobrow et. al. examines the merging of a programming language (LISP) with object-oriented concepts; to a large extent, this chapter examines the behaviorally object-oriented approach.

The chapter by Stonebraker and Rowe describes the data model underlying POSTGRES, which is a follow-on to the INGRES relational database management system; POSTGRES incorporates some important object-oriented capabilities. The Lyngbaek and McLeod work examines the sharing of objects in a distributed environment. Finally, the concepts and techniques section concludes with a chapter by Skarra and Zdonik focusing on the importance of managing evolution in object-oriented databases.

The systems and implementation section of the book begins with a chapter by Kim et. al., describing important aspects of the comprehensive ORION object-oriented database management systems developed at MCC. Key aspects of the IRIS database management developed at Hewlett-Packard Research Laboratories are described in a chapter by Fishman et. al. The chapter by Maier et. al. examines the Gemstone object-oriented DBMS, which is to a large extent a persistent version of SmallTalk with important extensions. The chapter by Andrews and Harris explores the VBase DBMS, which combines structurally object-oriented and behaviorally object-oriented concepts into a single framework. The SIM DBMS, an implementation of a structurally object-oriented data model is described by Tolbert et. al. in the final chapter of the systems and implementation section.

The third section of the book contains three chapters which describe selected issues in the application and use of object-oriented database concepts. The first chapter, by Katz and Chang, describes a rich object version mechanism for computer-aided design (CAD) databases. The chapter by Cárdenas et. al. examines the management of pictorial objects in a DBMS. Finally, Dittrich et. al. describe the management of complex objects in engineering database applications.

Each of the chapters that follow contain extensive references to additional material, should the reader be interested in more detail. The area of object-oriented databases is a rapidly evolving one, and new developments should lead to exciting new commercial products and applications of this technology in the near future.

# 1

# A Tutorial on Semantic Database Modeling

**Richard Hull***

*Computer Science Department, University of Southern California*

**Roger King****

*Computer Science Department, University of Colorado*

This is an updated version of the article originally published in ACM Computing Sciences, Vol. 19, No. 3, Sept. 1987.

## ABSTRACT

Most common database management systems represent information in a simple record-based format. Semantic modeling provides richer data structuring capabilities for data base applications. In particular, research in this area has articulated a number of constructs which provide mechanisms for representing structurally complex interrelations between data typically arising in commercial applications. In general terms, semantic modeling compliments work on knowledge representation (in Artificial Intelligence), and the new generation of database models based on the object-oriented paradigm of programming languages.

*This researcher was supported in part by NSF under grants IST-83-06517 and IST-85-11541.

**This researcher was supported in part by ONR under contract number N00014-86-K-0054 and by NSF under grant DMC-8505164

This chapter presents a tutorial on semantic data modeling. It reviews the philosophic motivations of semantic models, including the need for high-level modeling abstractions and the reduction of semantic overloading of data type constructors. The chapter then provides an introduction to the primary components of semantic models, which are the explicit representation of objects, attributes of and relationships between objects, type constructors for building complex types, ISA relationships, and derived schema components.

# 1. INTRODUCTION

Commercial database management systems have been available for two decades, originally in the form of the hierarchical and network models. Two opposing research directions in databases were initiated in the early 70s, namely the introduction of the relational model and the development of semantic database models. The relational model revolutionized the field by separating logical data representation from physical implementation. Significantly, the inherent simplicity in the model permitted the development of powerful, non-procedural query languages and a variety of useful theoretical results.

The history of semantic modeling research is quite different. Semantic models were introduced primarily as schema design tools: a schema could first be designed in a high level semantic model, and then translated into one of the traditional models for ultimate implementation. The emphasis of the initial semantic models was to accurately model data relationships which arise frequently in typical database applications. Consequently, semantic models are more complex than the relational model, and encourage a more navigational view of data relationships. The field of semantic models is continuing to evolve. There has been increasing interest in using these models as the basis for full-fledged database management systems, or at least as complete front-ends to existing systems.

The first published semantic model appeared in 1974 [Abr74]. The area matured during the subsequent decade, with the development of several prominent models and a large body of related research efforts. The central result of semantic modeling research has been the development of powerful mechanisms for representing the structural aspects of business data. In recent years, database researchers have turned their attention toward incorporating the behavioral (or dynamic) aspects of data into modeling formalisms; this work is being heavily influenced by the object-oriented paradigm from programming languages.

This chapter provides an introduction to and a tutorial on semantic modeling. In keeping with the historical emphasis of the field, the primary focus is on the structural aspects of semantic models; their behavioral aspects are also briefly discussed. We begin by giving a broad overview of the fundamental components and the philosophical roots of semantic modeling (Section 2). We also discuss the relationship of semantic modeling to other research areas of computer science. In particular, we discuss important differences between the constructs found in semantic models and in object-oriented programming languages.

Semantic data models and related issues are described in the survey article [Ker76b], the text [Tsi82b], and the collection of articles which comprise [Bro84b]. Also, [Af584, Kin85b, Mar86] present taxonomies of the more prominent models; and [Urb86] surveys several semantic models, with an emphasis on features in support of temporal information. The dynamic aspects of semantic modeling are emphasized in [Bor85a]. This chapter is a slightly revised version of the first half of [Hud87], which also provides a detailed survey of several specific semantic models from the literature. Unlike previous surveys, that paper focuses on both the prominent semantic models, and the research directions which they have spawned.

## 2. PHILOSOPHICAL CONSIDERATIONS

There is an analogy between the motivations behind semantic models and those behind high level programming languages. The ALGOL-like languages were developed in an attempt to provide richer, more convenient programming abstractions; they buffer the user from low-level machine considerations. Similarly, semantic models attempt to provide more powerful abstractions for the specification of database schemas than are supported by the relational, hierarchical, and network models. Of course, more complex abstraction mechanisms introduce implementation issues. The construction of efficient semantic databases is an interesting problem - and largely an open research area.

In this section, we focus on the major motivations and advantages of semantic database modeling, as described in the literature. These were originally proposed in, e.g., [Ham81, Ken78, Ken79, Smi77], and have since been echoed and extended in works such as [Abi87, Bro84a, Kin85b, Tsi82b].

Historically, semantic database models were first developed to facilitate the design of database schemas [Che76, Ham81, Smi77]. In the 70s, the traditional models (relational, hierarchical, and network) were gaining wide acceptance as efficient data management tools. The data structures used in these models are relatively close to those used for the physical representation of data in computers, ultimately viewing data as collections of records with printable or pointer field values. Indeed, these models are often referred to as being *record-based*. Semantic models were developed to provide a higher level of abstraction for modeling data, allowing database designers to think of data in ways which correlate more directly to how data arise in the world. Unlike the traditional models, the constructs of most semantic models naturally support a top-down, modular view of the schema, thus simplifying both schema design and database usage. Indeed, although the semantic models were first introduced as design tools, there is increasing interest and research directed towards developing them into full-fledged database management systems.

To present the philosophy and advantages of semantic database models in more detail, we begin by introducing a simple example using a generic semantic data model, along with a corresponding third normal form (3NF) relational schema. The example is used for several purposes. First, the fundamental differences between semantic models and the object-oriented paradigm from programming languages are presented. Next, we illustrate the primary advantages often cited in the literature of semantic data models over the record-oriented models. We then show how these advantages relate to the process of schema design. We conclude by comparing semantic models with the related field of knowledge representation in AI.

## 2.1 An Example

The sample schema shown in Figure 1.2.1 will be used to provide an informal introduction to many of the fundamental components of semantic data models. This schema is based on a generic model, called the Generic Semantic Model (GSM), which was developed for this survey.

The primary components of semantic models are the explicit representation of objects, attributes of and relationships between objects, type constructors for building complex types, ISA relationships, and derived schema components. The example schema provides a brief introduction to each of these. The schema corresponds to a mythical database, called the "World Traveler Database", which contains information about both business and pleasure travelers. It is necessarily simplistic, but highlights the primary features common to the prominent semantic database models.

The World Traveler schema represents two fundamental object or entity types, corresponding to the types `PERSON` and `BUSINESS`. These are depicted using triangle nodes, indicating that they correspond to *abstract* data types in the world. Speaking conceptually, in an *instance* of this schema, a set of objects of type `PERSON` is associated with the `PERSON` node. In typical implementations of semantic data models [Atk83, Kin84d, Smi81b], these abstract objects are referenced using internal identifiers which are not visible to the user. A primary reason for this is that objects in a semantic data model may not be uniquely identifiable using printable attributes which are directly associated with them. In contrast with abstract types, *printable* types such as `PNAME` (person-name) are depicted using ovals. (In [Ver82], which considers the design of information systems, printable types are called 'lexical object types' (LOT) and abstract types are called 'non-lexical object types' (`NOLOT`).)

The schema also represents three subtypes of the type `PERSON`, namely `TOURIST`, `BUSINESS-TRAVELER`, and `LINGUIST`. Such subtype/supertype relationships are also called *ISA* relationships, for example, each tourist "is-a" person. In the schema, the three subtypes are depicted using circular nodes (indicating that their underlying type is given elsewhere in the schema), along with double-shafted ISA arrows indicating the ISA relationships. In an instance of this schema, subsets of the set of persons (i.e., the set of internal identifiers associated with `PERSON` node) would be associated with each of the three subtype nodes. Note that in the absence of any restrictions, the sets corresponding to these subtypes may overlap.

The sample schema illustrates two fundamental uses of subtyping in semantic models, these being to form *user-specified* and *derived* subtypes. For example, the subtypes `TOURIST` and `BUSINESS-TRAVELER` are viewed here as being user-specified, because a person will take on either (or both) of these roles only if this is specified by a database operation. In contrast, we assume here (again simplistically) that a person is a

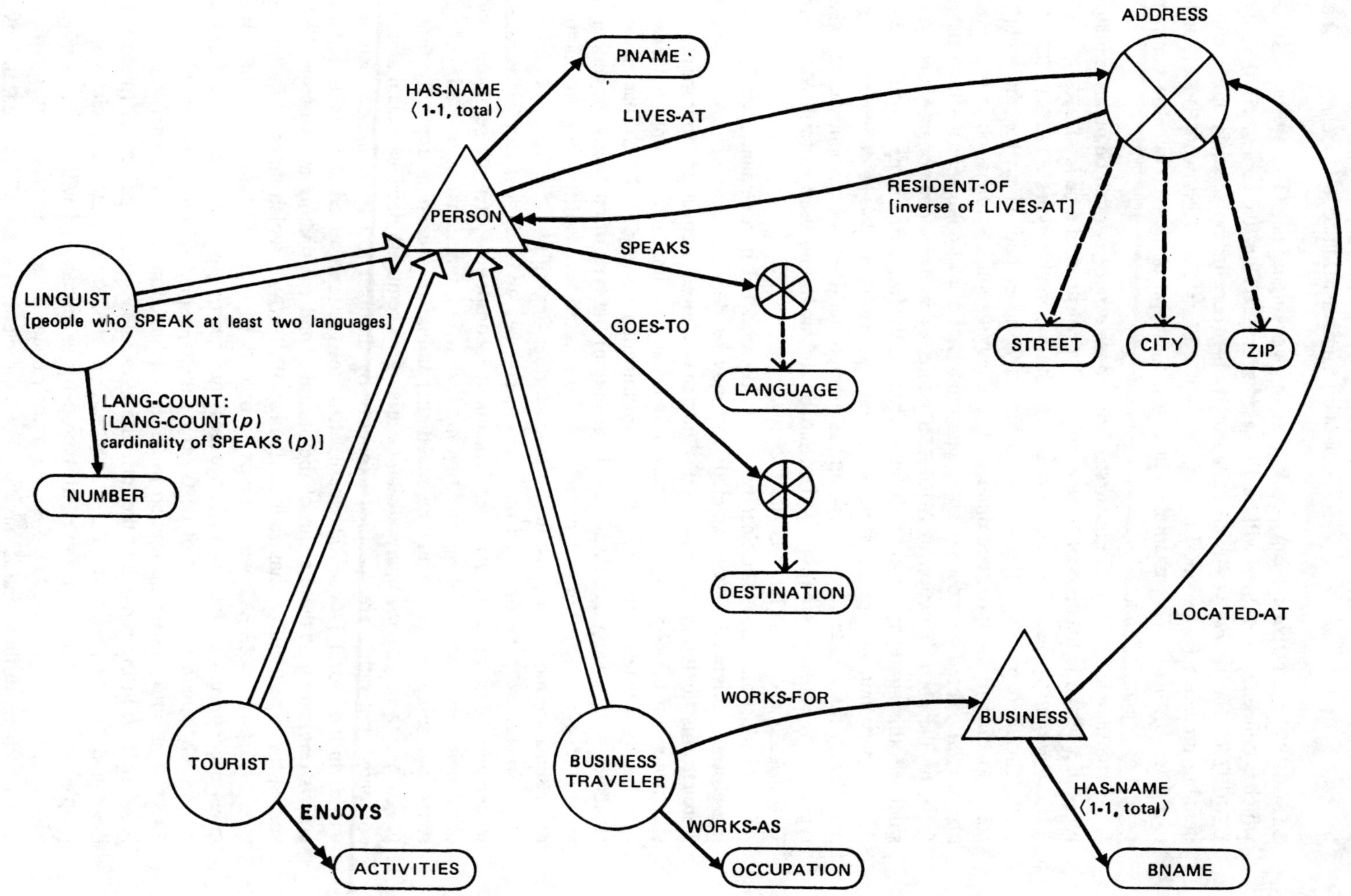


**Figure 1.2.1** Schema of World Traveler Database.

LINGUIST if that person can speak at least two languages. (The attribute SPEAKS which is defined on PERSON will be discussed shortly.) Thus, the contents of the subtype LINGUIST can be *derived* from data stored elsewhere in the schema, along with the defining predicate (in pseudo-English) "LINGUIST := PERSONs who SPEAK at least two LANGUAGEs". This example illustrates one type of derived schema component typical of semantic models.

The sample schema also illustrates how *constructed types* can be built from atomic types in a semantic data model. One example of a constructed type is ADDRESS, which is an *aggregation* (i.e., Cartesian product) of three printable types STREET, CITY and ZIP. This is depicted in the schema using an X-node, and which has three children corresponding to the three coordinates of the aggregation. Aggregation is one form of *abstraction* offered by most semantic data models. For example, here it allows users to focus on the abstract notion of ADDRESS while ignoring its component parts. As we shall see, this aggregate object will be referenced by two different parts of the schema. A second prominent type constructor in many semantic models is called *grouping*, or *association* (i.e., finitary powerset), and is used to build sets of elements of an existing type. In the schema, grouping is depicted by a *-node and used to form, e.g., sets of LANGUAGEs and DESTINATIONs.

As illustrated above, object types can be modeled in a semantic schema as being abstract, printable, or constructed; and may be defined using an ISA relationship. Through this flexibility the schema designer may choose a construct appropriate to the significance of the object type in the particular application environment. For example, in a situation where cities play a more prominent role (e.g., if CITY had associated attributes such as language or climate information) the type of city could be modeled as an abstract type instead of as a printable. As discussed below, different combinations of other semantic modeling constructs provide further flexibility.

So far, we have focussed on how object types and subtypes can be represented in semantic data models. Another fundamental component of most semantic models consists in mechanisms for representing *attributes* (i.e., functions) associated with these types and subtypes. It should be noted that unlike the functions typically found in programming languages, many attributes arising in semantic database schemas are not computed, but rather are specified explicitly by the user to correspond to facts in the world. In the World Traveler Database, attributes are represented using (single-shafted) arrows originating at the domain of the attribute, and terminating at its range. For example, the type PERSON has four attributes: HAS-NAME which maps to the printable type PNAME; LIVES-AT which maps to objects of type ADDRESS; SPEAKS which maps each person to the set of languages that person speaks; and GOES-TO which maps each person to the set of destinations that person frequents. In the schema, the HAS-NAME attribute is constrained to be a 1-1, total function. The attribute SPEAKS is *set-valued,* in the sense that the attribute associates a set of languages (indicated by the *-node) to each person. RESIDENT-OF is similar, in that it associates a set of people with an address; however, this property is represented with a *multi-valued* attribute. ENJOYS of TOURIST is also multi-valued. In several models it is typical to depict both an attribute and its inverse. For example, in the sample schema, the inverse of the LIVES-AT attribute from PERSON to ADDRESS is the multi-valued attribute RESIDENT-OF.

As shown in the schema, the subtype BUSINESS-TRAVELER has two attributes, WORKS-FOR and WORKS-AS. Because business-travelers are people, the members of this subtype also *inherit* the four attributes of the type PERSON. Similarly, the other two subtypes of PERSON inherit these attributes of type PERSON.

The schema also illustrates how attributes can serve as derived schema components. One example is the attribute RESIDENT-OF; another is the attribute LANG-COUNT of the (derived) subtype LINGUIST, which is specified completely by the predicate "LANG-COUNT is cardinality of SPEAKS" and other parts of the schema.

To conclude this subsection, Figure 1.2.2 shows a 3NF [Ull82] relational schema corresponding to the World Traveler schema. In order to capture most of the semantics of the original schema, key and inclusion dependencies are included in the relational schema. (Briefly, a *key dependency* states that the value of one (or several) field(s) of a tuple determines the remaining field values of that tuple; an *inclusion dependency* states that all of the values occurring in one (or more) column(s) of one relation also occur in some column(s) of another relation.) For example, PNAME is the key of PERSON indicating that each person has only one address; and the PNAME column of TOURIST is contained in the PNAME column of PERSON, indicating that each tourist is a person. In this schema, one or more relations is used for each of the object types in the semantic schema. For example, even ignoring the subtypes of the type PERSON, information about persons is stored in the three relations PERSON, PERSPEAKS and PERGOES. (In principle, a single relation could be used for this information, but in the presence of set-valued and/or multi-valued attributes such relations will not be in 3NF.)

## 2.2 Semantic Models vs. Object-Oriented Programming Languages

Now that we have briefly introduced the essentials of semantic modeling, we are in a position to describe the fundamental distinctions between semantic models and object-oriented programming [Bha86, Goi83, Moo86a]. This is crucial in light of current database research thrusts, which are largely focused on data models which embody the object-oriented paradigm.

Essentially, semantic models encapsulate structural aspects of objects, while object-oriented languages encapsulate behavioral aspects of objects. Historically, object-oriented languages stem from research on abstract data types [Gut77, Lis77]. There are three principle features of object-oriented languages. The first is the explicit representation of object classes (or types). Objects are identified by surrogates rather than by their values. The second feature is the encapsulation of "methods" or operations within objects. For example, the object type GEOMETRIC_OBJECT may have the method "display_self". Users are free to ignore the implementation details of methods. The final feature of object-oriented languages is the inheritance of methods from one class to another.

There are two central distinctions between this approach and semantic models. First, object-oriented models do not typically embody the rich type constructors of semantic models. From the structural point of view, object-oriented models support only

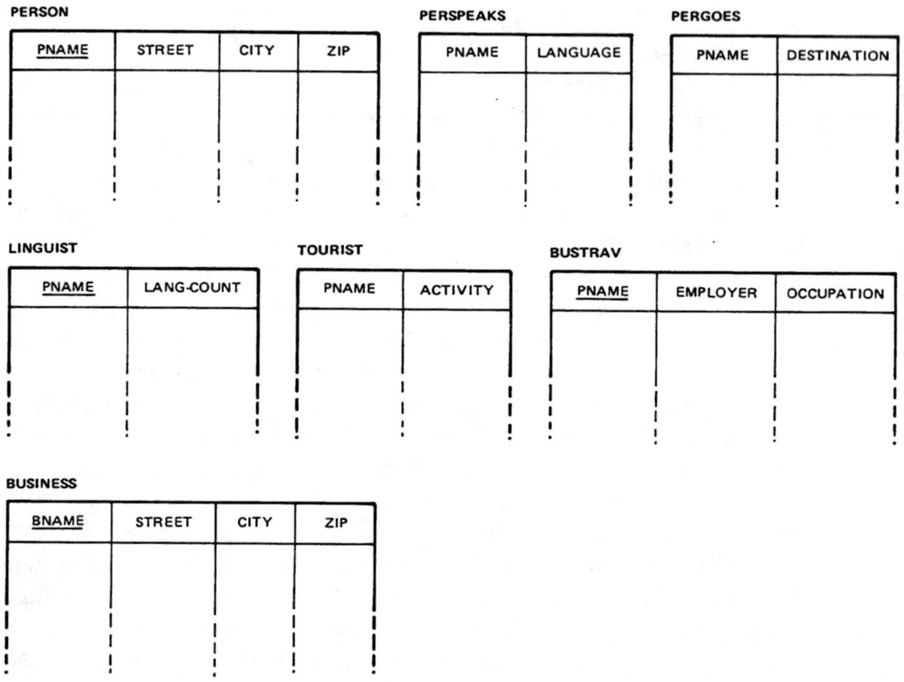


(a) Relations

PERSPEAKS[PNAME] $\subseteq$ PERSON[PNAME]
PERGOES[PNAME] $\subseteq$ PERSON[PNAME]
LINGUIST[PNAME] $\subseteq$ PERSON[PNAME]
TOURIST[PNAME] $\subseteq$ PERSON[PNAME]
BUSTRAV[PNAME] $\subseteq$ PERSON[PNAME]
BUSTRAV[EMPLOYER] $\subseteq$ BUSINESS[BNAME]

(b) Inclusion Dependencies

**Figure 1.2.2** 3NF relational schema corresponding to the World Traveler schema.

the ability to define single- and set-valued attributes. Second, the inheritance of methods is strictly different than the inheritance of attributes (as in semantic models). In a semantic model, attributes are inherited only between types where one is a subset of the other. A method, as it is a behavioral—and not a structural—property, can be inherited between seemingly unlike types. Thus, the object type `TEXT` might be able to inherit the "display_self" method of `GEOMETRIC_OBJECT`.

## 2.3 Advantages of Semantic Data Models

In this subsection we summarize the motivations often cited in the literature in support of semantic data models over the traditional data models. It was noted above that semantic data models were first introduced primarily as schema design tools, and embody the fundamental kinds of relationships arising in typical database applications. As a result of this philosophic foundation, semantically-based data models and systems will provide the following advantages over traditional, record-oriented systems:

**1.** increased separation of conceptual and physical components;
**2.** decreased semantic overloading of relationship types;
**3.** availability of convenient abstraction mechanisms.

Abstraction mechanisms are the means by which the first two advantages of semantic models are obtained. We discuss abstraction separately because of the significant effort researchers have put into developing these mechanisms. Each of the three advantages is discussed below.

***Increased separation of logical and physical components:*** In record- oriented models, the access paths available to end users tend to directly mimic the logical structure of the database schema [Che76, Ham81, Ken79, Ker76a, Shi81, Smi77]. This phenomenon exhibits itself in different ways in the relational and the hierarchical/network models. In the relational model, a user must simulate pointers by comparing identifiers in order to traverse from one relation to another (typically using the join operator). In contrast, the attributes of semantic models may be used as direct conceptual pointers. Thus, users must consciously traverse through an extra level of indirection imposed by the relational model, making it more difficult to form complex objects out of simpler ones. For this reason, the relational model has been referred to as being *value-oriented* [Kho86, Ull87] as opposed to object oriented.

In the hierarchical and network models a similar situation occurs. Users must navigate through the database, constructing larger objects out of flat record structures by associating records of different types. In contrast, semantic models allow users to focus their attention directly on abstract objects. Thus, in a hierarchical/network model, the access paths correspond directly to the low-level physical links between records, and not to the conceptual relationships modeled in a semantic schema.

To illustrate this point using the relational model, suppose in the World Traveler database that Mary is a business-traveler. Using attributes, the city of Mary's employer can be obtained with the simple query:

```
print LOCATED-AT(WORKS-FOR('Mary')).CITY
```

This query operates as follows: Mary's employer is obtained by `WORKS-FOR('Mary')`; applying `LOCATED-AT` yields the address of that employer; and the '`.CITY`' construct isolates the second coordinate of the address. (We assume as syntactic sugar that because `HAS-NAME` is 1-1, the string 'Mary' can be used to denote the person Mary; if not, in the above query, 'Mary' would have to be replaced by `HAS-NAME[-1]('Mary')`.) Thus, the semantic model permits users to refer to an object (in this case using a printable surrogate identifier), and to "navigate" through the schema by applying attributes directly to that object. In the relational model, on the other hand, users must navigate through the schema within the provided record structure using joins.

In the SEQUEL language, for example, the analogous query directed at the schema of Figure 1.2.2 would be:

```
select CITY
from BUSINESS
where BNAME  in
    select EMPLOYER
    from BUSTRAV
    where PNAME = 'Mary'
```

In essence, the user first obtains the name of Mary's employer by selecting the record about Mary in the relation `BUSTRAV` and retrieving the `EMPLOYER` attribute; finds the record in the relation `BUSINESS` which has that value in its `BNAME` field; and then reads the `CITY` attribute of that record. Thus, the linkage between the `BUSTRAV` and `BUSINESS` relations is obtained by explicitly comparing business identifiers (the `EMPLOYER` coordinate of `BUSTRAV` and the `BNAME` coordinate of `BUSINESS`).

***Semantic Overloading:*** The second fundamental advantage cited for the semantic models focuses on the fact that the record-oriented models provide only two or three constructs for representing data interrelationships, while semantic models typically provide several such constructs. As a result, constructs in record-oriented models are *semantically overloaded,* in the sense that several different types of relationship must be represented using the same constructs [Ham81, Ken78, Ken79, Smi77, Sus83]. In the relational model, for example, there are only two ways to represent relationships between objects: (1) within a relation, and (2) by using the same values in two or more relations.

To illustrate this point, we briefly compare the relational and semantic schemas of the World Traveler database. In the relational schema, at least three different types of relationships are represented structurally within individual relations:

1. the functional relationship between `PNAME` and `STREET`;
2. the many-many association between `PNAME`s and `LANGUAGE`s; and
3. the clustering of `STREET`, `CITY`, and `ZIP` values as addresses.

At least three other types of relationship are represented by pairs of relations:

a. the type/subtype relationship between `PERSON` and `TOURIST`;
b. the fact that `PERSON`, `PERSPEAKS`, and `PERGOES` all describe the same set of objects; and
c. the fact that the employers of `BUSTRAV`s are described in the `BUSINESS` relation.

In contrast, each of these types of relationship has a different representation in the semantic schema.

As indicated in the above paragraph, in the absence of integrity constraints the data structuring primitives of the relational model (and the other record-oriented models) are not sufficient to accurately model the different types of commonly arising data relationships. This is one reason that integrity constraints such as key and inclusion dependencies are commonly used in conjunction with the relational model. While these do provide a more accurate representation of the data, they are typically expressed in a text-based language; it is therefore difficult to comprehend their combined significance. A primary objective of many semantic models has been to provide a coherent family of constructs for representing in a structural manner the kinds of information which the relational model can represent only through constraints. Indeed, semantic modeling could be viewed as having shifted a substantial amount of schema information from the constraint side to the structure side.

***Abstraction Mechanisms:*** Semantic models provide a variety of convenient mechanisms for viewing and accessing the schema at different levels of abstraction [Ham81, Kin85a, Smi77, Sus83, Tsi82b]. One dimension of abstraction provided by these models concerns the level of detail at which portions of a schema can be viewed. In the most abstract level, only object types and ISA relationships are considered. At this level the structure of objects is ignored, for example, the X-node ADDRESS would be shown without its children. A more detailed view includes the structure of complex objects; the further detail includes attributes; and the rules governing derived schema components. A second dimension of the abstraction provided by semantic models is the degree of modularity which they provide. It is easy to isolate information about a given type, its subtypes, and its attributes. Furthermore, it is easy to follow semantic connections (e.g., attribute and ISA relationships) to find closely associated object types. Both of the above dimensions of abstraction are very useful in schema design, and for *schema browsing*, that is, the ad hoc perusal of a schema to determine what and how things are modeled. Interactive, graphics-based systems have been developed which utilize these properties of semantic models [Bry86, Gol85, Kin84c, Won82]; comparable systems for the record-oriented models have not been developed.

An interesting question is why the central components of semantic models—objects, attributes, ISA relationships—are necessarily the best mechanisms to use to enrich a data model. While of course there can be no clear-cut choice of modeling constructs, there are two reasons to support the selection of these particular primitives. First, practice has shown that schemas constructed with traditional record-oriented models tend to simulate objects and attributes by interrelating records of different types with logical and physical pointers. The second point is that computer science researchers in AI and programming languages have selected similar constructs to enhance the usability of other software tools. It is thus interesting that researchers with somewhat different goals have found semantic model-like mechanisms useful. This latter point is discussed in more detail later in this section.

A third dimension of abstraction is provided by derived schema components which are supported by a few semantic models [Ham81, Kin85a, Shi81], and also by some relational implementations [Sto76]. These schema components allow users to define new portions of a schema in terms of existing portions of a schema. Derived schema components permit the user to identify a specific subset of the data, possibly perform computations on it, and then structure it in a new format. The "new" data is then given a name, and can subsequently be used while ignoring the details of the computation and re-formatting. In the relational model, derived schema components must be either new relations or new columns in existing relations. Semantic models provide a much richer framework for defining derived schema components. For example, a derived subtype specifies both a new type and an ISA relationship; similarly, a derived single-valued attribute specifies both a piece of data and a constraint on it. Therefore, semantic models give the user considerably more power for abstracting data in this way.

Derived data is closely related to the notion of a *user view* (or external schema) [Cha75, Tsi77], except that derived data is incorporated directly into the original schema rather than used to form a separate new schema. Another difference is that a view may contain raw or non-derived components as well as derived information.

## 2.4 Database Design with a Semantic Model

In general, the advantages of semantic models, as described in the literature, are oriented toward the support of database design and evolution [Bro84c, Che76, Kin85a, Smi77]. At the present time the practical use of semantic models has been generally limited to the design of record-oriented schemas. Designers often find it easier to express the high-level structure of an application in a semantic model, and then map the semantic schema into a lower-level model. One prominent semantic model, the Entity Relationship model, has been used to design relational and network schemas for over a decade [Teo86]. Interestingly, relational schemas designed using the ER model are typically in third normal form, an indication of the naturalness of using a semantic model as a design tool for traditional DBMS's.

A number of features of semantic models contribute to their utility in both the design and the eventual evolution of database schemas. They provide constructs which closely parallel the kinds of relationships typically arising in database application areas; this makes the design process easier and lessens the likelihood of design errors. This is in contrast to record-oriented models, which force the designer to concentrate on many low-level details. Semantic models also provide a variety of abstraction mechanisms which researchers have used to develop structured design methodologies. A detailed and fairly comprehensive design methodology appears in [Rou84]. After requirements analysis is performed, the authors advise the use of a semantic model as a means of integrating and formalizing the requirements. A semantic model serves nicely as a buffer between the form of requirements collected from non-computer specialists and the low-level, computer-oriented form of record-oriented models. Several methodologies have also addressed the issue of integrating schema and transaction design, in order to simplify the collection and formalization of database dynamic requirements; see [Bro84c, Kin85a] for examples.

Semantic models are a convenient mechanism for allowing database specifications to evolve incrementally in a natural, controlled fashion [Bro84c, Che76, Kin85a, Teo86]. This is because semantic models provide a framework for top-down schema design, beginning with the specification of the major object types arising in the application environment, then specifying subsidiary object types. Referring to the World Traveler schema, the design might begin with the specification of the `PERSON` and `BUSINESS` nodes; the `LINGUIST`, `TOURIST`, and `BUSINESS-TRAVELER` nodes would follow;

and finally the various attributes would be defined. The constructed type ADDRESS might be introduced when it is realized that both PERSON and BUSINESS share the identical attributes STREET, CITY and ZIP.

In conclusion, significant research has been directed at applying specific semantic models to the design of either semantic or traditional database schemas. However, little work has been directed at providing methodological support for selecting an appropriate semantic model, or for integrating the various modeling capabilities found in semantic models. Rather, methodological approaches are typically tied to one model and to one prescriptive approach at producing a semantic schema.

## 2.5 Related Work in Artificial Intelligence

We now consider the relationship between semantic data modeling and research on knowledge representation in artificial intelligence. While having different goals, these two areas have developed similar conceptual tools.

Early research on knowledge representation focused on *semantic networks* [Fin79, Isr84, Myl80b] and *frames* [Bra85, Fik85, Min84]. In a semantic network, real world knowledge is represented as a graph formed of data items connected by edges. The graph edges can be used to recursively construct complex items and to place items in categories according to similar properties. The important relationship types of *ISA*, *is-instance-of*, and *is-part-of* (which is closely related to aggregation) are naturally modeled in this context. Unlike semantic data models, semantic networks mix schema and data, in the sense that they do not typically provide convenient ways to abstract the *structure* of data from the data itself. As a consequence, each object modeled in a semantic network is represented using a node of the semantic network; these networks can be quite large if many objects are modeled. One of the earliest semantic database models, the Semantic Binary Data Model [Abr74], is closely related to semantic networks; schemas from this model are essentially semantic networks which focus exclusively on object classes.

Frame-based approaches provide a much more structured representation for object classes and relationships between them. Indeed, there are several rough parallels between the frame-based approach and semantic data models. The frame-based analog of the abstract object types is called a *frame*. A frame generally consists of a list of *properties* of objects in the type (e.g., that elephants have four legs), and a tuple of *slots*, which are essentially equivalent to the attributes of semantic data models. Frames are typically organized using ISA relationships, and slots are inherited along ISA paths in a manner similar to the semantic data models. In general, properties of a type are inherited by a subtype, but exceptions to this inheritance can also be expressed within the framework (e.g., three-legged elephants are elephants, but have only three legs). Exception-handling mechanisms may also be provided for the inheritance of slot values. For example, referring to the World Traveler Database, in a frame-based approach the HAS-NAME attribute of a given person might be different in his role as PERSON and his role as TOURIST (e.g., his nick-name). (Although the terminology used by the KL-ONE model [Bra85] differs from that just given, essentially the same concepts are incorporated there.)

In general, frame-based approaches do not permit explicit mechanisms such as aggregation and grouping for object construction. In recent research and commercial systems [Aik85, Keh83, Ste83], frames have been extended so that slots can hold methods in the sense of object-oriented programming languages; this development parallels current research in object-oriented databases (e.g., [Ban87a, Mai86b]).

Because frame-based systems are generally in-memory tools, the sorts of research efforts that have been directed at implementing semantic databases have not been applied to them. For example, considerable research effort has focussed on the efficient implementation of semantic schemas and derived schema components [Cha82, Far85, Hud86, Hud87, Smi81b].

## 3. TUTORIAL

This section provides an in-depth discussion of the fundamental features and components common to most semantic database models. The various building blocks used in semantic models are described and illustrated; and subtle and not-so-subtle differences between similar components are highlighted. Philosophic implications of the overall approaches to modeling taken by different models are also considered.

To provide a basis for our discussion we use the Generic Semantic Model (GSM). This was developed expressly for this survey, and is based largely on three of the most prominent models found in the literature (the Entity-Relationship Model, the Functional Data Model, and the Semantic Data Model). The GSM is derived in large part from the IFO model [Abi87], which itself was developed as a theoretical framework for studying the prominent semantic models [Abr74, Bro84c, Ham81, Ker76a, Kin85a, Shi81, Sib77]. While the GSM incorporates many of the constructs and features of these models, it cannot be a true integration of all semantic models, because of the very different approaches they take. Specifically, the approach taken by GSM is closest to the Functional Data Model. Because the primary purpose of GSM has been to serve as a tool for exposition, it is not completely specified in this chapter.

In some cases the literature taken as a whole uses a given term ambiguously. Perhaps the most common example of this is the term 'aggregation'. At a philosophical level, this term is used universally to indicate object types which are formed by combining a group of other objects, e.g., `ADDRESS` might be modeled as an aggregation of `STREET`, `CITY`, and `ZIP`. At a more technical level, some models support this using a construction based on Cartesian product, while others use a construction based on attributes. In the discussion of this section we adopt specific, somewhat technical definitions for various terms. For example, we use the term 'aggregation' to refer to Cartesian-product based constructions. These more restrictive definitions will permit a clear articulation of the different concepts arising in the literature.

This section has four major subsections. The first briefly compares two broad philosophical approaches which many models choose between. This provides a useful perspective before delving into detailed discussion of the different building blocks of semantic models. The second subsection defines the specific constructs used for describing the *structure* of data in semantic models, and presents examples which highlight similarities and differences between them. The third subsection considers how these constructs are combined and augmented to form data base schemas in semantic models. The fourth subsection discusses languages for accessing and manipulating data, and for specifying semantic schemas.

## 3.1 Two Philosophical Approaches

GSM is meant to be representative of a wide class of semantic models; as a result of being somewhat eclectic, it blurs an important philosophical distinction arising in semantic modeling literature. Historically, there have been two general approaches taken in constructing semantic models. This distinction is not black-and-white, but models have had a tendency to adopt one approach or the other. Essentially, various models place different emphasis on the various constructs for interrelating object classes. One approach stresses the use of attributes to interrelate objects; the other places an emphasis on explicit type constructors. As a result, different data models may yield somewhat different schemas for the same underlying application. This difference is most pronounced in modeling situations which cannot be represented using single-argument, single-valued attributes. In these instances, a semantic model typically provides either more complex attribute constructs (such as multi-argument or multi-valued attributes) or explicit type constructors (such as aggregation or grouping).

To illustrate this point, we compare two schemas for the same underlying data which give very different prominence to attributes and type constructors. The comparison is particularly salient because the schemas reflect the underlying philosophies of two early influential semantic models, namely the Functional Data and the Entity-Relationship Models (respectively).

Figure 1.3.1 shows the two GSM schemas, both representing the same data underlying a portion of the World Traveler Database application. The schema of part (a) loosely follows the Functional Data Model, and emphasizes the use of attributes for relating abstract object types with other abstract object types. The schema of part (b) loosely follows the philosophy of the Entity-Relationship (ER) Model, in that it emphasizes the use of the type constructors aggregation (called *relationship* in the ER model) and grouping for relating abstract object types. With both schemas, an instance will include a set of PERSONs and a set of BUSINESSes (both considered as sets of abstract objects), along with attributes specifying person and business names and the languages spoken by PERSONs.

Interestingly, in an instance of the first schema the relationship of people and their business is represented by the attribute (i.e., function) WORKS-FOR and its inverse $\texttt{WORKS-FOR}^{-1}$; in the second, the aggregation EMPLOYMENT (which is a set of ordered pairs) is used. Both schemas represent the constraint that many people work for the same business, but not the reverse: in the first schema, this is accomplished using a single-valued attribute and a multi-valued attribute, and in the second schema by the N:1 constraint. Further, in the first schema, a multi-valued attribute is used to represent the languages spoken by a person, while in the second, a grouping construct is used.

The choice of emphasis—attribute-based or type constructor-based—affects the language mechanisms which seem natural for manipulating semantic databases. Consider Figure 1.3.1(a). If a user wanted to know the business of a particular person, the attribute WORKS-FOR may be used to directly reference the business. In 1.3.1(b), the type constructor representing ordered pairs of PERSONs and BUSINESSes must be manipulated in order to obtain the desired data. On the other hand, the type constructor approach gives the user the flexibility of directly referencing, by name, ordered pairs in EMPLOYMENT.

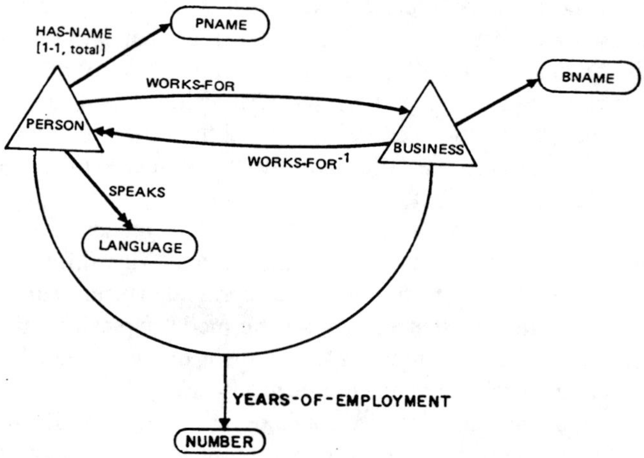


(a) Schema emphasizing attributes

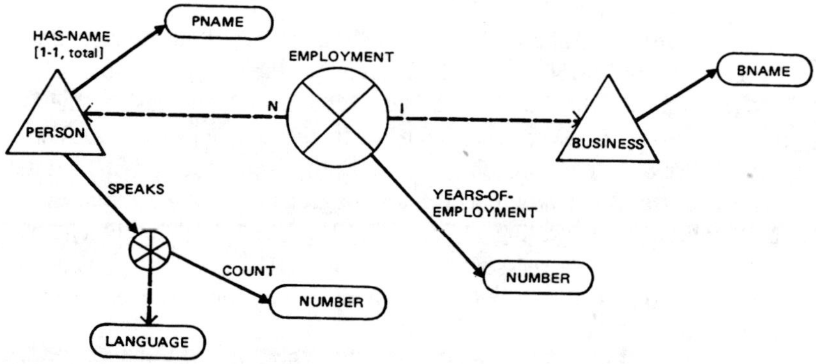


(b) Schema emphasizing type constructors

**Figure 1.3.1** Two schemas for the same underlying data.

The use of type constructors also allows information to be associated directly with schema abstractions. As one illustration, the bottom subschema includes an attribute on EMPLOYMENT which describes the length of time an individual has been employed at a particular company. (Essentially the same information is represented in the first schema with the two-argument attribute YEARS-OF-EMPLOYMENT; although the relationship EMPLOYMENT and this attribute are not linked together.) Analogously, in the second schema, the grouping construct for LANGUAGES is augmented with an attribute giving the cardinality of each set of languages. (No analog for this exists in the attribute-based approach.) In a model which stresses type constructors, relationships between types are essentially viewed as types in their own right; thus it makes perfect sense to allow these types to have attributes which further describe them.

## 3.2 Local Constructs

This subsection presents detailed descriptions of the building blocks semantic models use to represent the structure of data. The discussion is broken into three parts, which focus on types, attributes, and ISA relationships, respectively. Importantly, in the subsection on attributes we compare the notions of attributes and aggregations.

**3.2.1 Atomic and constructed types.** A fundamental aspect of all semantic models is the direct representation of object types, distinct from their attributes and sub- or super-types. Most models provide mechanisms to represent atomic or non-constructed object types, and many models also provide type constructors. In the discussion below we focus on the use of object types in semantic models, and on the two most prominent type constructors, namely aggregation and grouping.

A semantic model typically provides the ability to specify a number of *atomic types*. Intuitively, each of these types corresponds to a class of non-aggregate objects in the world, such as PERSONs or ZIP-codes. (Of course, the type PERSON has many attributes.) Many semantic models distinguish between atomic types which are *abstract*, and those which are *printable* (or *representable*). The abstract types are typically used for physical objects in the world, such as PERSONs, and for conceptual (or legal) objects, such as BUSINESSes. Atomic printable types are typically alpha-numeric strings, but in some graphics-based systems might include icons as well. It is often convenient to articulate subclasses of these, such as ZIP-codes, Person-NAMEs, or Business-NAMEs; and most models associate operators with them, such as addition for numbers. As shown in the World Traveler schema, in GSM abstract types are depicted with triangles, atomic printable types are depicted with flattened ovals, and subtypes are depicted with circles.

In instances of a semantic schema, abstract objects are viewed conceptually to correspond directly to physical or conceptual objects in the world. In some implementations of semantic models, these are represented using internal identifiers which are not directly accessible to the user. This corresponds to the intuition that such objects cannot be "printed" or "displayed" on paper or on a monitor.

When defining an instance of a semantic schema, an *active domain* is associated with each node of the schema. The active domain of an atomic type holds all objects of that type which are currently present in the database. This notion of active domain is extended to type constructor nodes below.

We now turn to *type constructors*. The most prominent of these in the semantic literature are *aggregation* (called *relationship* in the ER model) and *grouping* (also known as *association* [Bro84c]). An aggregation is a composite object constructed from other objects in the database. For example, each object associated with the aggregation type EMPLOYMENT of Figure 1.3.2(a) is an ordered pair of PERSON and BUSINESS values. Mathematically, an aggregation is an ordered n-tuple. In an instance, the active domain of an aggregation type will be a *subset* of the Cartesian product of the active domains assigned to the underlying nodes. For example, the active domain of EMPLOYMENT will be the set of pair corresponding to the set of employee-employer relationships currently true in the database application. According to our definition, the identity of an aggregation object is completely determined by its component values. Figure 1.3.2(b) highlights the use of aggregation for encapsulating information.

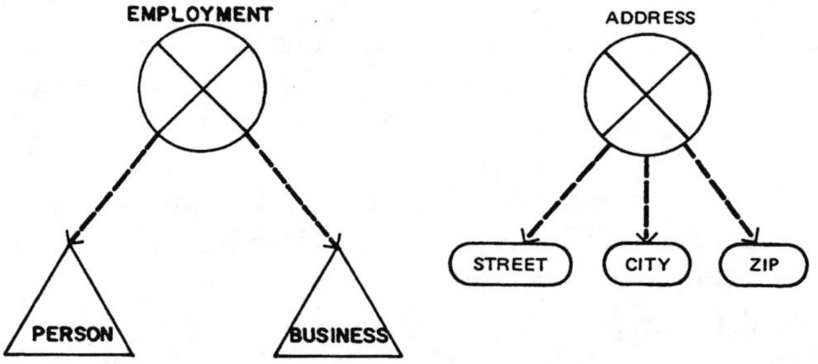


**Figure 1.3.2** Object types constructed with aggregation.

Before continuing, we reiterate that the definition of 'aggregation' used here is deliberately somewhat narrow, and differs from the usage of that term in some models, including SDM and TAXIS. The representation of aggregations used in those models is generally based on attributes, and is discussed in the next subsection. It should also be noted that some models, including FDM, emphasize the use of attributes but also support the use of aggregations in attribute domains.

The grouping construct is used to represent sets of objects of the same type. Figure 1.3.3(a) shows the GSM depiction of the grouping construct to form a type whose objects are sets of languages. Mathematically, a grouping is a finite set. In an instance, the active domain of a grouping type will hold a set of objects, each of which is a finite subset of the active domain of the underlying node. In a constructed object, a *-node will also have exactly one child.

As defined here, a grouping object is a set of objects. Technically, then, the *identity* of a grouping object is determined completely by that set. To emphasize the significance of this, we consider how committees might be modeled in a semantic schema. One approach is to define the type COMMITTEE as a grouping of PERSON, because each committee is basically a set of people. This is probably not accurate in most cases, because the identity of a committee is separate from its membership at a particular time. Figure 1.3.3(b) shows a more appropriate approach. COMMITTEE is modeled as an abstract type, and has an attribute MEMBERSHIP whose range is a grouping type.

As illustrated in Figure 1.3.4, the type constructors can be applied recursively. In this example, we view a VISIT to be a triple consisting of a TOURIST-TRAP, a GUIDE (viewed as a subtype of PERSON), and a set of TOURISTs (also a subtype of person).

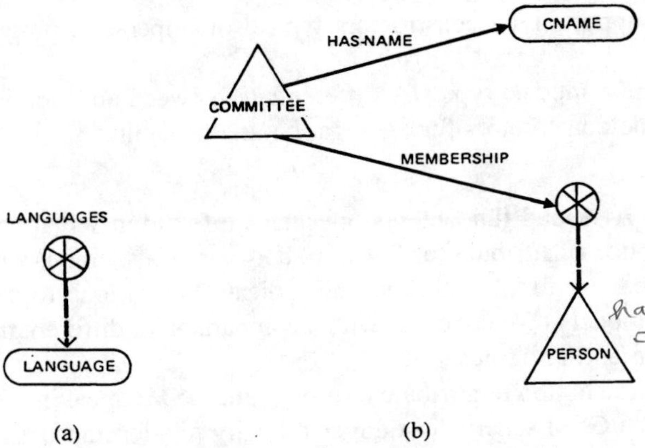


**Figure 1.3.3** Object types constructed with grouping.

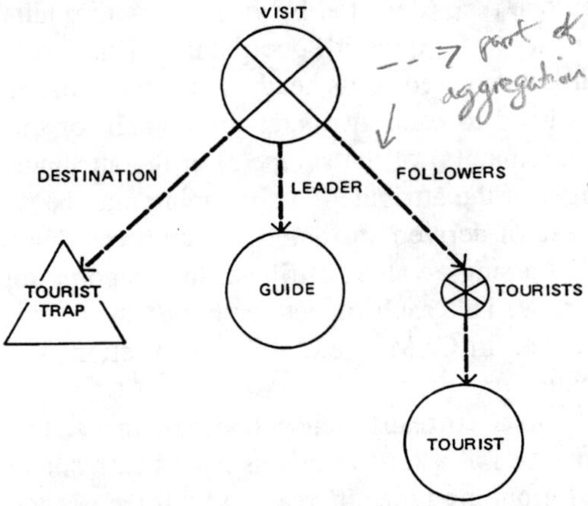


**Figure 1.3.4** Recursive application of aggregation and grouping constructs.

As indicated in the figure, edges originating from an aggregation node can be labeled by a role; this is important if more than one child of an aggregation is of the same type.

We close this subsection by mentioning other kinds of type constructors found in the literature. The TAXIS and Galileo models support *metatypes*, i.e., types whose elements are themselves types. For example, in the World Traveler example, a metatype `TYPE-OF-PERSON` might contain the types `PERSON`, `LINGUIST`, `TOURIST`, and `BUSINESS-TRAVELER`. This metatype could have attributes such as `SIZE` or `AVERAGE-AGE`, which describe characteristics of the populations of the underlying types. A comparison of metatypes with both subtypes and grouping construct is presented in subsection 3.3.2 below.

In principle, a data model can support essentially any type constructor, in much the same way that some programming languages do. Historically, almost all semantic models have focussed almost exclusively on aggregation and grouping. Notable exceptions include SAM*, TAXIS and Galileo. These models permit a variety of type constructors which may be applied to atomic printable types. SAM* is oriented in part towards scientific and statistical applications, and supports sets, vectors, ordered sets, and matrices; TAXIS and Galileo supports type constructors typical of imperative programming languages.

To summarize, semantic models typically differentiate between abstract and printable types, and provide type constructors for aggregation and grouping.

**3.2.2 Attributes.** A second fundamental mechanism found in semantic models for relating objects is the notion of attribute (or function) between types. In this subsection we articulate a specific meaning for this notion, and indicate the various forms that it takes in different semantic models. We conclude with a comparison of different modeling strategies using aggregation and attributes.

We begin by defining the notion of attribute as used in the GSM. Speaking formally, a *one-argument attribute* in a GSM schema is a directed binary relationship between two types (depicted by an arrow); and an *n-argument attribute* is a directed relationship between a set of n types and one type (depicted by an arrow with n tails). Attributes can be *single-valued*, depicted using an arrow with one pointer at its head, or *multi-valued*, depicted using an arrow with two pointers at its head. In an instance, a mapping (a binary or (n+1)-ary relation) is assigned to each attribute; the domain of this mapping is the (cross product of the) active domain(s) of the source(s) of the attribute, and the range is the active domain of the target of the attribute. The mapping may be specified explicitly through updates, or in the case of derived attributes, it may be computed according to a derivation rule. In the case of a single-valued attribute, the mapping must be a function in the strict mathematical sense, i.e., each object (or tuple) in the domain is assigned at most one object in the range. In GSM, there are no restrictions on the types of the source or target of an attribute.

Of course, there is a close correspondence between the semantics of a multi-valued attribute, and the semantics of a *set-valued* attribute, i.e., a single-valued attribute whose range is a constructed grouping type. In keeping with the general philosophy that GSM incorporate prominent features from several representative semantic models, both of these possibilities have been included. Most models in the literature support multi-valued attributes, and do not permit set-valued attributes. Also, some models, including SDM and INSYDE, view all attributes to be multi-valued, and use a constraint if one of them is to be single-valued. Similarly, there is also a close relationship between a one-argument attribute whose domain is an aggregation, and an n-argument attribute.

We now briefly mention another kind of attribute, called here a *type-attribute*. This is supported in several models, including SDM, TAXIS, and SAM*. Type-attributes associate a value with an entire type, rather than associating a value to each object in the active domain. For example, the type-attribute `COUNT` might be associated with the type `PERSON`, and would hold one value: the number of people currently "in" the database. Other type-attributes might hold more complex statistics about a type, e.g., the average salary, or the standard deviation of those salaries. The value associated with an type-attribute is generally prescribed in the schema; such attributes thus form a special kind of derived data.

We conclude the section by comparing four different ways to represent essentially the same data interrelationships using the aggregation and attribute constructs. Figure 1.3.5 shows four subschemas which be used to model tye type ENROLLMENT. To simplify the pictures, we depict all atomic nodes as circular. In the first subschema, ENROLLMENT is viewed as an aggregation of COURSE and STUDENT. Each object of type ENROLLMENT will be an ordered pair; and a GRADE is associated to it be the attribute shown. The IFO and Galileo models provide explicit mechanisms for this representation. The second approach might be taken in models such as SAM* and SHM+ which do not provide an explicit attribute construct. In this case, ENROLLMENT is viewed as a ternary aggregation of COURSE, STUDENT, and GRADE. As suggested in the diagram, a key constraint is typically incorporated into this schema, to ensure that each course-student pair has only one associated grade. The third approach shown in Figure 1.3.5 might be taken in models which do not provide an explicit type constructor for aggregation. Many semantic models fall into this category, including SBDM, SDM, TAXIS, and INSYDE (and the object-oriented programming language SMALLTALK, for that matter). Under this approach ENROLLMENT is viewed as an atomic type with three attributes defined on it. Although now shown here, a constraint might be included so that no course-student pair has more than one grade. The fourth approach is especially interesting in that it does not require that the construct ENROLLMENT be explicitly named or defined, if it is not in itself relevant to the application. In this case, HAS-GRADE would be a function with two arguments. FDM has this capability.

We now compare the first three of these approaches from the perspective of object identity. In part (a), each enrollment is an ordered pair. Thus, the grade associated with an enrollment can change without affecting the identity of the enrollment. Technically speaking, in the absence of the key dependency, this is not true in part (b), where an enrollment is an ordered triple. In part (c), the underlying identity is independent of any of the associated course, student and grade values. An enrollment *e* with values CS101, Mary, and 'A' might be modified to have values Math2, Mary, 'B' without losing its underlying identity. Also, in the absence of a constraint, the structure does not preclude the possibility that two distinct enrollments *e* and *e'* have the same course, the same student, and the same grade.

**3.2.3 ISA relationships.** The third fundamental component of virtually all semantic models is the ability to represent *ISA* or supertype/subtype relationships. In this subsection we review the basic intuitions underlying these relationships, and describe different variations of the concept found in the literature. The focus of this subsection is on the local properties of ISA relationships; global restrictions on how they may be combined are discussed in subsection 3.3.1. In several models subtypes arise almost exclusively as derived subtypes; this aspect of subtypes is considered in subsection 3.3.2.

Intuitively, an ISA relationship from a type SUB to a type SUPER indicates that each object associated with SUB is associated with the type SUPER. For example, in the World Traveler schema the ISA edge from TOURIST to PERSON indicates that each tourist is a person. More formally, in each instance of the schema, the active domain of TOURIST must be contained in the active domain of PERSON. In most semantic models each attribute defined on the type SUPER is automatically defined on SUB, that is, attributes of SUPER are *inherited* by SUB. It is also generally true that a subtype may have attributes not shared by the parent type.

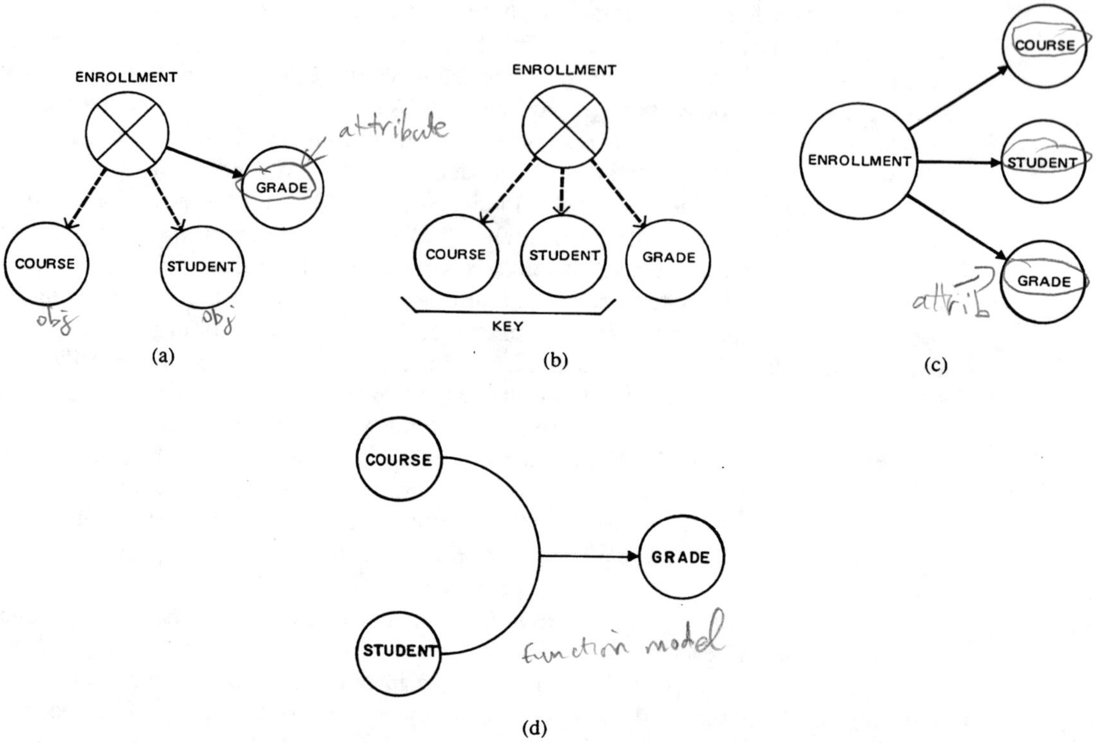


**Figure 1.3.5** Four alternative representations for ENROLLMENT.

The family of ISA relationships in a schema forms a directed graph. In the literature this has been widely termed the ISA 'hierarchy'. However, as suggested in Figure 1.3.6, most semantic models permit undirected (or weak) cycles in this graph. For this reason we follow [Atz86, Len87] in adopting the term *ISA network*. Although ISA relationships are transitive, it is customary to specify the fundamental ISA relationships explicitly, and view the links due to transitivity as specified implicitly.

Speaking informally, ISA relationships might be used in a semantic schema for two closely related purposes. The first is to represent one or more possibly overlapping subtypes of a type, as with the subtypes of `PERSON` shown in the World Traveler schema. The second purpose is to form a type which contains the union of types already present in a schema. For example, a type `VEHICLE` might be defined to be the union of the types `CAR`, `BOAT` and `PLANE`; or the type `LEGAL-ENTITY` might be the union of `PERSON`, `CORPORATION`, and `LIMITED-PARTNERSHIP`. When using ISA for forming a union, it is common to include a *covering constraint*, which states that the (active domain of the) super-type is contained in the union of the (active domains of the) sub-types.

Historically, semantic models have used a single ISA relationship for both of these purposes. Furthermore, several early papers on semantic modeling (including FDM and SDM) provide schema definition primitives which favor the specification of ISA networks

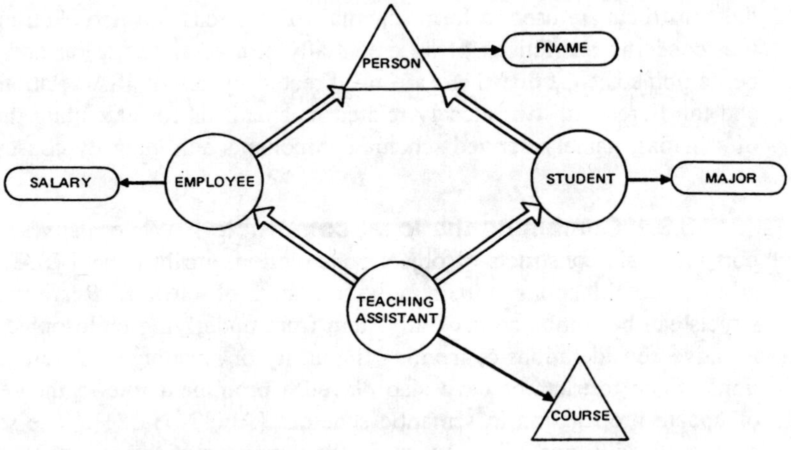


**Figure 1.3.6** ISA network with undirected cycle.

from top-to-bottom. For example, in these models the type `VEHICLE` would be specified first, and subtypes `CAR`, `BOAT` and `PLANE` would be specified subsequently.

More recent research on semantic modeling has differentiated several kinds of ISA relationship; and some models, including IFO, RM/T, Galileo, and extensions of the Entity-Relationship model, incorporate more than one type of ISA into the same model. For example, in the extension of the Entity-Relationship model described in [Teo86], *subset* and *generalization* ISA relationships are supported. A subset ISA relationship arises when one type is contained in another; this is the notion already discussed in connection with the GSM. Generalization ISA relationships arise when one type is *partitioned* by its subtypes, that is, when the subtypes are disjoint and together cover the supertype. Generalization ISA relationships could thus be used for the `VEHICLE` and `LEGAL-ENTITY` types mentioned above. As noted in [Abi87, Teo86], the update semantics of these two constructs are different. For example, in the first case deletion of and object from a subtype has no impact on the supertype; in the second case deletion from a subtype also requires deletion from the supertype.

A second broad motivation for distinguishing kinds of ISA relationships, stems from studies of schema integration [Boti86, Day84, Nav86]. For example, [Day84] studies the problem of integrating two or more FDM schemas. Suppose that two FDM schemas contain types EMP1 and EMP2, respectively, for employees. To integrate these, a new type EMPLOYEE can be formed as the generalization of EMP1 and EMP2. This generalization may have overlapping subtypes, but must be covered by them. Interestingly, [Day84] also permits ISA relationships between attributes.

## 3.3 Global Considerations

In the preceding section we discussed the constructs used in semantic models largely in isolation. This section takes a broader perspective, and examines the larger issue of how the constructs are used to form schemas. The discussion is broken into three areas. The first concerns restrictions of an essentially structural nature on how the constructs can be combined, e.g., that there are no directed cycles of ISA relationships. The second and third areas are two closely related mechanisms for extending the expressive power of schemas, namely derived schema components and integrity constraints.

**3.3.1 Combining the local constructs.** While many semantic models support the basic constructs of object construction, attribute, and ISA, they do not permit arbitrary combinations of them in the formation of schemas. Restrictions on how the constructs can be combined generally stem from underlying philosophic principles, or from intuitive considerations concerning the utility or meaning of different possible combinations. Such restrictions have also played a prominent role in theoretical investigations of update propagation in semantic schemas [Abi87, Hec81]. The restrictions are typically realized in one of two ways: in the definition of the constructs themselves (e.g., in the original ER model, all attribute ranges are printable types); or as global restrictions on schema formation (e.g., that there be no directed cycles of ISA relationships). The following discussion surveys some of the intuitions and restrictions arising in construct definitions, and then considers global restrictions on schema formation.

In the description of the local constructs given in the previous subsection, relatively few restrictions were placed on their combination. For example, aggregation and grouping can be used recursively; and attributes can have arbitrary domain and range types. Indeed, part of the design philosophy of the GSM was to present the underlying constructs in as unrestricted a form as feasible, in order to separate fundamental aspects of the constructs from their usage in the various semantic models of the literature. In contrast with the GSM, many semantic models in the literature present constructs in restricted forms. As an example, some models permit aggregations in attribute domains, but not as attribute ranges or in ISA relationships.

Restrictions explicitly included in the definition of constructs are essentially local. However, these restrictions can affect the overall or global structure of the family of schemas of a given model. A dramatic illustration of this is provided by the original Entity-Relationship model [Che76]. In that model, aggregation can be used only to combine abstract types. As a result, schemas from the model have a two-tier character; with abstract types in one level and aggregations in the second. Attributes may be defined on both abstract types or aggregations, but must have ranges of printable types.

We conclude our discussion of local constructs by attempting to indicate why certain models introduce restrained versions of constructs. Intuitively, a model designer tries to construct a simple, yet comprehensive model that can represent a large family of naturally-occurring applications. Thus, for example, FDM allows grouping only in attribute ranges. As illustrated in the discussion of `COMMITTEE`s around Figure 1.3.3(b), grouping objects are rarely of interest in isolation.

In addition to restricting the use of constructs at the local level, many semantic models specify global restrictions on how they may be combined (including notably [Abi87, Bro84c, Bro83, Day84, Hec81]). The most prominent restrictions of this kind concern how ISA relationships can be combined. More recently, the interplay of constructed types and ISA relationships has also been studied. To give the flavor of this aspect of semantic models we present a representative family of global restrictions on ISA relationships. It should also be noted that several models [Alb85, Ham81, Kin85a, Shi81, Sus83]) do not explicitly state global rules of this sort, but nevertheless imply them in the definitions of the underlying constructs.

To focus our discussion of ISA restrictions we consider only abstract types. This coincides with most early semantic models, including FDM and SDM. In schemas for those models, a family of *base types* is viewed as being defined first, and subtypes are subsequently defined from these in a top-to-bottom fashion. The World Traveler schema follows this philosophy, as does the example of Figure 1.3.6. In GSM subtypes are depicted using a subtype (circle) node, indicating that they are not base types. To enforce this philosophy, we might insist that: the tail of each specialization edge is a subtype node; and the head of each specialization edge is an abstract or subtype node.

A second general restriction on ISA involves directed cycles. Consider the "schema" of Figure 1.3.7(a). (We use quotes, because this graph does not satisfy the global restriction we are about to state.) It suggests that `TOURIST` is a subtype of `BUSINESS-TRAVELER`, which is a subtype of `LINGUIST`, which is a subtype of `TOURIST`. Intuitively, this cycle implies that the three types are *redundant*, i.e., in every instance, the three types will contain the same set of objects. Furthermore, if the cycle is not connected via ISA relationships to some abstract type, there is no way to determine the underlying type (e.g., `PERSON`) of any of the three types. Thus, we might insist that: there is no directed cycle of ISA edges.

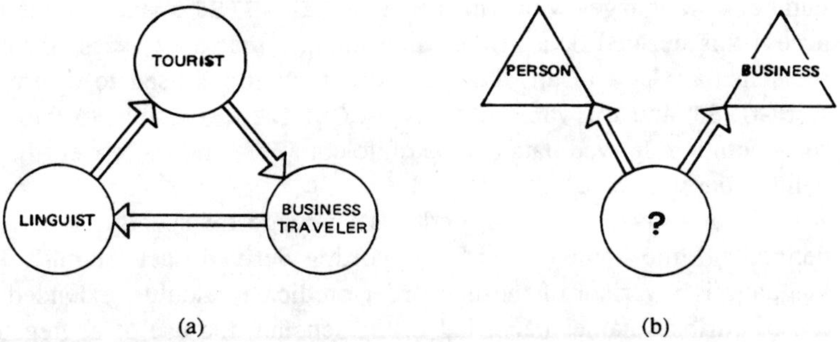


**Figure 1.3.7** "Schemas" violating intuitions concerning ISA.

In the "schema" of Figure 1.3.7(b), the type labeled '?' is supposed to be a subtype of the abstract type `PERSON`, and also of the abstract type `BUSINESS`. If we suppose that the underlying domains of `PERSON` and `BUSINESS` are disjoint, then in every instance the node labeled '?' will be assigned the empty set. Speaking intuitively, the '?' node cannot hold useful information. So, we might insist that: any pair of directed paths of ISA edges originating at a given node can be extended to a common node.

The above discussion provides a *complete* family of restrictions on ISA relationships for the GSM, considered without type constructors. Speaking informally, the rules are complete because they capture all of the basic natural intuitions concerning how ISA relationships (of the top to bottom variety) must be restricted in order to be meaningful. On a more formal level, it can be shown that if a schema satisfies these rules, then every node will have an unambiguous underlying type; no pair of nodes will be redundant; and every node will be satisfiable, in the sense that some instance will assign a non-empty active domain to that node. The set of rules given above applies to the special case of abstract types and top-to-bottom ISA relationships. As discussed in subsection 3.2.3, some models support different kinds of ISA relationships. Furthermore, in some models constructed types can participate in ISA relationships. Specification of global rules in these cases is more involved; the IFO model presents one such set of rules [Abi87].

**3.3.2 Derived schema components.** *Derived schema components* are one of the fundamental mechanisms in semantic models for data abstraction and encapsulation. A derived schema component consists of two elements, a structural specification for holding the derived information and a mechanism for specifying how that structure is to be filled, called a *derivation rule.* (Keeping with common terminology, we will refer to derived schema components simply as "derived data".) Derived data thus allows computed information to be incorporated into a database schema.

In published semantic models, the most commonly arising kinds of derived data are *derived subtypes* and *derived attributes*. Each of these is illustrated in the World Traveler schema: `LINGUIST` is a derived subtype of `PERSON` which contains all persons who speak at least two languages and `LANG-COUNT` is a derived attribute which gives the number of languages which members of `LINGUIST` speak. In queries, users may freely access this derived data in the same manner that they access data from other parts of the schema. As a result, the specific computations used to determine the members of `LINGUIST` and the value of `LANG-COUNT` are invisible to the user. The derivation rules defining derived data can be quite complex, and moreover, they can use previously defined derived data.

In any given semantic model, a language for specifying derivation rules must be defined. In the notable models supporting derived data [Ham81, Kin85a, Shi81], this language is a variant of the first-order predicate calculus, extended to permit the direct use of attribute names occurring in the schema; the use of aggregate attributes; and the use of set operators (such as set-membership and set-inclusion). This is discussed further in Section 3.4. (Although not traditionally done, the language for specifying derivation rules can, in principle, allow side-effects.)

To illustrate the potential power of a derived data mechanism, we present an example which could be supported in the DBMS CACTIS [Hud86]. Figure 1.3.8 shows a schema involving `BUSINESS-TRAVELER`s and `TRIPS` they have taken. The derived attribute `TOTAL-MILES-TRAVELED` is also defined on business travelers. This attribute uses two pieces of information, the `TRIP` attribute of `BUSINESS-TRAVELER` and the `ADDRESS` attribute of `BUSINESS`. `TRIP` consists of ordered pairs of `DATE` and `CITY`, each representing one business trip. The definition of `TOTAL-MILES-TRAVELED` is based on a derivation rule which is a relatively complex function. For each city traveled to on a trip, this function computes the distance between that city and the city the individual works in. Then, the distances are summed and multiplied by 2, to give the total miles traveled per individual. This distance information may be stored elsewhere in the database or elsewhere in the system.

To further illustrate the power of derived data, we present an example showing the interplay of derived data with schema structures. The example also provides a useful comparison of the notions of grouping, subtype and metatype. Figure 1.3.9 shows three related ways to model categorizations of people based on the languages which they can speak. Part (a) is taken from SDM, and uses the grouping construct in conjunction with a derivation rule stating that the node should include sets of people grouped by the languages which they speak. In an instance, this type would include the set of persons who speak French, the set of persons who speak Chinese, and more generally, a set of persons for each of the languages in the database. These sets are accessed in queries by referring to languages. (This construction is closely related to forming the inverse function SPEAKS$^{-1}$.) In the example, we also define a (non-derived) attribute on the grouping type.

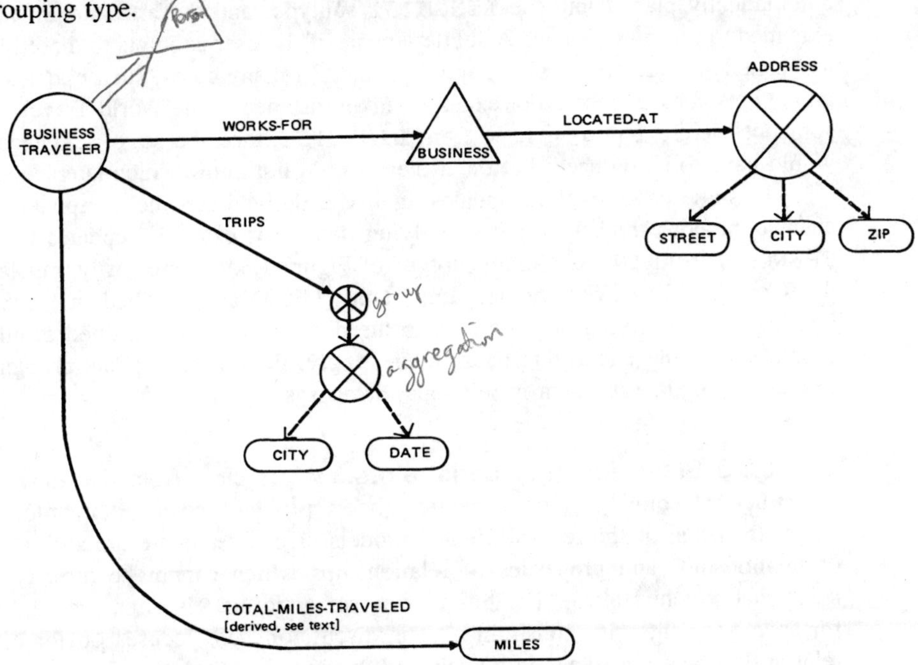


**Figure 1.3.8** Schema used in example of derived attribute.

The schema of Figure 1.3.9(b) includes a derived subtype for each of the languages which arise. In this representation, different attributes can be associated with each of the subtypes. Importantly, the number of subtypes is equal to the number of languages arising in the underlying instance, while in the schema of part (a), only one additional type is used. Although not shown here, type-attributes could be defined on the subtypes to record information on the number of speakers of each language.

The schema of part (b) could be extended to include the graph of part (c), which shows the use of a *metatype*, as found in TAXIS. The elements of this metatype are types from elsewhere in the schema. The derived attribute `NUMBER-OF-SPEAKERS` defined on this metatype shows a third way to obtain this cardinality information.

Several models including FDM and SDM view the specification of derived data as part of the schema design and/or evolution process, while others support a much more dynamic view. For example, in the implementation of INSYDE described in [Kin84b], users can specify derived data at any time and incorporate it as permanent in the schema. Indeed, in the graphics-based interface to this model [Kin84b], database queries are formed through the iterative specification of derived data.

We close the subsection with a discussion of the interaction of derived data with database updates. Speaking in general terms, derived data is automatically updated as required by updates to other parts of the schema. For example, in the World Traveler database, if a person who speaks one language learns a second one, that person is automatically placed into the `LINGUIST` subtype, and the attribute `LANG-COUNT` is extended to this new person. A subtlety arises if the user attempts to directly update data associated with a derived schema component. In many cases, such updates would have ambiguous consequences. For example, in an instance of the World Traveler database, if someone were explicitly deleted from `LINGUIST`, then the set of languages he speaks would have to be reduced; but the system would not know which languages to remove.

In some cases explicit updates against a derived schema component might have an unambiguous impact on the underlying data. For example, updates on the subtype `FRENCH-SPEAKING-PERSON` subtype of Figure 1.3.9(b) are easily translated into updates on the SPEAKS attribute. Importantly, FDM as described in [Shi81] provides facilities for specifying how updates to the derived data, if permitted at all, should be propagated to the underlying data. Interestingly, the derived update problem is related to the view update problem in relational databases [Cos84].

**3.3.3 Static integrity constraints.** As is clear from the above discussion, the structural component of semantic models provides considerably more expressive power than that of the record-oriented models. However, there are still a wide variety of relationships and properties of relationships which cannot be directly represented using that structure alone. For this reason, semantic models often provide mechanisms for specifying integrity constraints. The discussion here focuses on three topics: the relationship between semantic models and the prominent relational integrity constraints; prominent types of integrity constraints found in semantic models; and the differences between integrity constraints and derived data. While integrity constraints can in principle focus on both the static and dynamic aspects of data [Tsi82b, Via87], little research on dynamic constraints has been done relative to semantic models. For this reason, we focus on static integrity constraints here.

Broadly speaking, semantic models express in a structural manner the most important types of relational integrity constraints, namely key dependencies and inclusion dependencies. As suggested by the World Traveler schema in Figure 1.2.1 and the associated relational schema in Figure 1.2.2, relational key dependencies can be represented

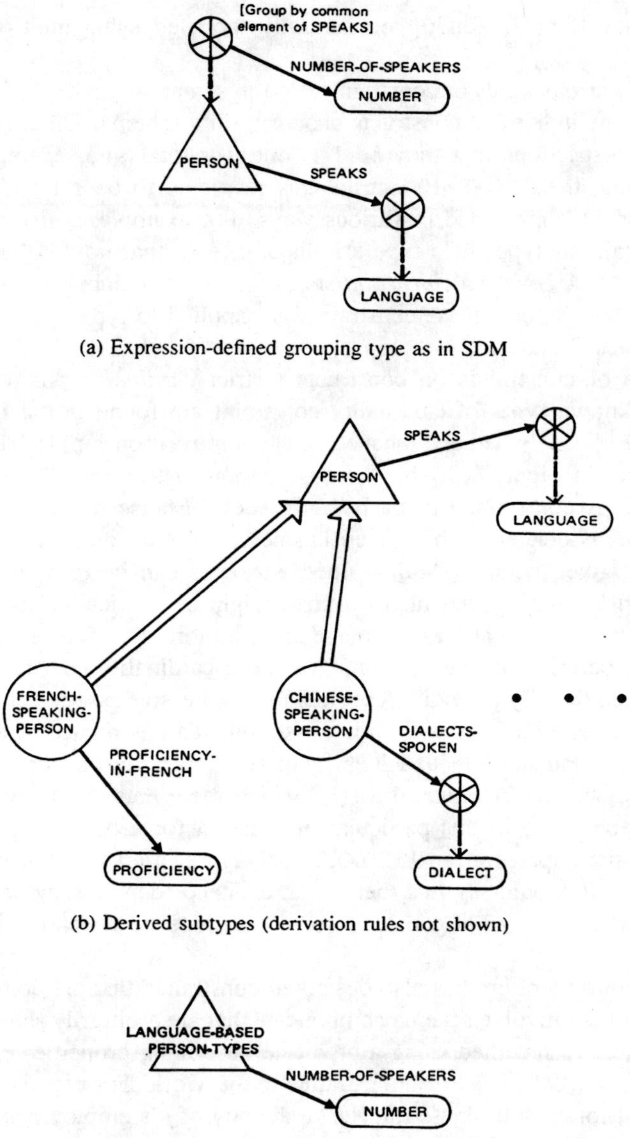


(a) Expression-defined grouping type as in SDM

(b) Derived subtypes (derivation rules not shown)

(c) Meta-types whose elements are types, as in TAXIS

**Figure 1.3.9** Related uses of derived schema components.

using single-valued attributes. Inclusion dependencies arising from subtyping can be represented using ISA relationships. Inclusion dependencies which serve as *referential constraints* are typically modeled in an implicit manner in semantic schemas. For example, the dependency BUSTRAV[EMPLOYER] $\subseteq$ BUSINESS[BNAME] in the relational schema is represented in the semantic schema by the fact that the attribute edge WORKS-FOR points directly to the BUSINESS node as its range. Interestingly, some examples of multivalued dependency [Fag77, Zan76] are naturally modeled using multi-valued attributes.

We now turn to the various kinds of constraints used in semantic models. Many of these focus on restricting the individual constructs occurring in a schema. On attributes, such constraints include restrictions that they be 1-1, onto, or total. For example, in the World Traveler schema, the `HAS-NAME` attribute is restricted to be 1-1 and total. ISA relationships can also be constrained in various ways. For example, a *disjointness constraint* states that certain subtypes of a type are disjoint (e.g., that no `TOURIST` is a `BUSINESS-TRAVELER`). A *covering constraint* states that a set of subtypes together cover a type. In some investigations, these constraints are applied to types which need not be related by ISA edges [Len87].

An important class of constraints on constructs restrict *cardinalities* in various ways. Perhaps the best known types of cardinality constraint are found in the Entity-Relationship model: these specify whether a binary aggregation (relationship) is 1:1, 1:N, N:1 or M:N. For example, in Figure 1.3.1(b), the aggregation `EMPLOYMENT` between `PERSON` and `BUSINESS` is constrained to be N:1. In each instance of this schema, several (N) people can be associated with a given business, but only one (1) business can be associated with a given person. Multi-valued attributes can be restricted in a similar manner: an attribute mapping students to courses might be restricted to be [1:6], meaning that each student must take at least 1 course and no more than 6 courses. The IRIS data model [Lyn86] permits the specification of several cardinality constraints on the same n-ary aggregation, thereby providing considerable expressive power.

Another prominent constraint is an *existence* constraint. This is related to a relational inclusion dependency, and states that each entity of some type must occur in some aggregation. Consider the schema of Figure 1.3.1(b), which represents the aggregation `EMPLOYMENT`. It makes no sense in this particular application for a business to exist in the database unless it participates in an `EMPLOYMENT` aggregation for at least one employee. To enforce this we would say that there is an existence dependency between `BUSINESS` and `EMPLOYMENT`. It is also natural to place existence dependencies on attribute ranges.

The semantic modeling literature has also described constraints that are computed in nature; such constraints may involve schema components that are arbitrarily separated. These constraints are generally specified using a predicate describing properties of data taken from disparate parts of a schema. Such constraints in the World Traveler database, for example, can state that for each business-traveler *p*, the city of *p*'s employer is equal to the city where *p* lives; or that the number of persons living in a given zip-code area is no greater than 10,000. Although several authors have suggested the utility of computed constraints in principle [Ham81, Kin85a, Tsi82b], no models in the literature support for them formally.

There is a close relationship between integrity constraints and derived schema components. Both require that data associated with different parts of a schema be consistent according to some criteria. The essential difference is that an integrity constraint does not extend the database with any new information, whereas derived data truly augments the database.

## 3.4 Manipulation Languages

Up to this point we have overviewed the data structuring mechanisms supported by typical semantic models. These capabilities would normally be supported by a *data definition language* associated with a specific model. No data model is complete without a corresponding *data manipulation language*, which allows the database user to create, update, and delete data which corresponds to a given schema. In this subsection, we describe the general structure of a data manipulation language for the GSM, and use it as a means for discussing the general nature of semantic data manipulation.

There are three fundamental capabilities that differentiate a semantic data manipulation language from a manipulation language for a traditional record-oriented model. First, the language must be able to query abstract types. Second, it must provide facilities for referencing and manipulating attributes. In this way, abstract, non-printable information may be manipulated. Third, semantic manipulation languages often allow the user to manage derived data, in the form of subtypes and functions constructed from existing (sub)types and functions. Thus, the specification of derived data is not reserved for the user of the data definition languages, but may also be performed at run time. This blurs to some degree the traditional boundary between schema and data; the user's view of the world may now be extended dynamically with new information constructed from existing data. This provides a marked contrast with approaches taken in record-oriented models, where the data definition and data manipulation languages are quite distinct.

Semantic data manipulation languages represent diverse programming language paradigms, but there are strong commonalities in terms of their functionality. Essentially, a semantic manipulation language typically takes the form of an extension to a language resembling a relational query language. Some semantic manipulation languages also include the flow-of-control and computational capabilities of general-purpose imperative programming languages. The GSM data manipulation language is a simple SEQUEL-like language.

Below is a query. It lists the names of all linguists who speak three or more languages, and illustrates the basic capabilities of a semantic access language to manipulate types and functions.

```
for each X in LINGUIST
      such that LANGCOUNT ≥ 3
print (PNAME(X))
```

The next query prints any address such that more than one person resides at the given address. Note that the "." notation is used to reference the various components of an aggregation. It is also true that if, for example, an address could have two components of the same type (e.g., two ZIP's), this notation would create an ambiguity. In general it is necessary to be able to given names to the components of an aggregation, and to reference them by those names, rather than by their types.

```
for each X in ADDRESS
      such that for some Y in PERSON
      and for some Z in PERSON
```

```
          Y ≠ Z and
          ADDRESS(Y) = X and ADDRESS(Z) = X
print X.STREET,X.CITY,X.ZIP
```

The next query illustrates the capability of a semantic language to manipulate derived information. The query creates a subtype, called ROMANCE-LINGUIST of all linguists who speak French, Italian, Spanish, Portuguese, Rumanian, and Sardinian. Then the names of all romance linguists are printed and the subtype is permanently recorded in the data-base schema. When a query specifies a derived subtype, it must be possible to name the subtype in order to reference it later. Again, we note that as a direct result of their rich modeling capabilities, semantic models require the creation of names that would not exist in a corresponding relational schema. Since such things as aggregations and subtypes may be created and referenced, they need names. This can be viewed as a limitation to the casual user who might feel that a semantic model causes a proliferation of names and therefore creates confusing schemas.

```
create subtype ROMANCE-LINGUIST  of LINGUIST
    where SPEAKS  includes French, Italian, Spanish, Portuguese,
                    Rumanian, Sardinian
for each X in ROMANCE-LINGUIST  print PNAME(X)
record ROMANCE-LINGUIST
```

In the examples presented above, the output of the queries was a list of objects or values, not instances of semantic types. This is quite different than relational queries, which take relations as input, and produce relations as output. As a result, in most semantic languages operations cannot be composed. Notably, the language FQL [Bun82] does not suffer from this limitation.

Research has also been performed on transaction languages for semantic models. One approach, embodied by the TAXIS [Myl80a] and Galileo [Alb85] systems, synthesizes semantic modeling constructs with control and typing mechanisms from imperative programming languages. In contrast, SHM+[Bro84c] and INSYDE [Kin85a] develop control mechanisms that closely follow the structure of semantic schemas. These systems are described in more detail in [Hud87].

## 4. CONCLUDING REMARKS

In this paper, we presented an introduction to semantic database models, providing both the fundamental motivations for these models and a tutorial on them. Over the past decade semantic models have provided the basis for research in a number of directions, including semantic data access languages, graphics-based interfaces based on semantic models, physical implementations of semantic DBM's, and theoretical investigations of semantic models [Hud87]. There are several other important research issues relating to semantic models which could be investigated, such as the integration of temporal reasoning into semantic models, the optimization of semantic database queries, the development of semantic database machines, and the construction of expert database systems which use semantic models (such databases would be capable of making inferences about complex, semantic data).

We conclude this chapter by mentioning a rapidly growing area of database research which is related to semantic modeling. Recently, a number of research projects have focused on the development of data models which are more expressive than conventional models, but use techniques different from semantic models. Experimental systems based on these *object-oriented* models are typically centered around the concepts of large objects and extensible type structures, as arise in engineering design applications, and the concept of local behavior stemming from object-oriented programming languages.

Object-oriented database models are fundamentally different from semantic models in that they support forms of local behavior in a manner similar to object-oriented programming languages. This means that a database entity may locally encapsulate a complex procedure or function for specifying the calculation of a data operation. This gives the database user the capability to express, in an elegant fashion, a wider class of derived information than semantic models. For example, in the system Postgres [Sto86a] a data item may have an attribute which is a database query or an application program. This project is an experiment in extending already-developed relational techniques to handle complex data. In the system Cactis [Hud86] an object may have attribute values which are computed by arbitrary computable functions. This project focuses on the design of formalisms which may be used to efficiently implement complex derived data, and uses attributed graphs as an underlying physical construct. The Gemstone [Mai86b], ORION [Ban87a] and $O_2$ [Lec88] projects focus on providing database users with message passing and inheritance mechanisms similar to those of Smalltalk. Thus, generalized methods may be defined for specifying how an object should react to messages from another object.

## ACKNOWLEDGMENTS

This paper consists of essentially the first three sections of [Hud87]; we would like to acknowledge Salvatore March, editor-in-chief of *ACM Computing Surveys*, for his help in preparing that paper.

# 2

# Database Description with SDM: A Semantic Database Model*

**Michael Hammer**

*Laboratory for Computer Science, Massachusetts Institute of Technology*

**Dennis McLeod**

*Computer Science Department, University of Southern California*

## ABSTRACT

SDM is a high-level semantics-based database description and structuring formalism (database model) for databases. This database model is designed to capture more of the meaning of an application environment than is possible with contemporary database models. An SDM specification describes a database in terms of the kinds of entities that exist in the application environment, the classifications and groupings of those entities, and the structural interconnections among them. SDM provides a collection of high-level



This research was supported in part by the Joint Services Electronics Program through the Air Force Office of Scientific Research (AFSC) under Contract F44620-76-C-0061, and, in part by the Advanced Research Projects Agency of the Department of Defense through the Office of Naval Research under Contract N00014-76-C-0944. The alphabetical listing of the authors indicates indistinguishably equal contributions and associated funding support.

Authors' addresses: M. Hammer, Laboratory for Computer Science, Massachusetts Institute of Technology, Cambridge, MA 02139; D. McLeod, Computer Science Department, University of Southern California, University Park, Los Angeles, CA 90007. 

*Source*: Adapted from "Database Description with SDM: A Semantic Database Model", ACM Transactions on Database Systems, Volume 6, Number 3, September 1981, Pages 351–386. Copyright 1981, Association for Computing Machinery, Inc., reprinted by permission.

modeling primitives to capture the semantics of an application environment. By accommodating derived information in a database structural specification, SDM allows the same information to be viewed in several ways; this makes it possible to directly accommodate the variety of needs and processing requirements typically present in database applications. The design of the present SDM is based on our experience in using a preliminary version of it.

SDM is designed to enhance the effectiveness and usability of database systems. An SDM database description can serve as a formal specification and documentation tool for a database; it can provide a basis for supporting a variety of powerful user interface facilities, it can serve as a conceptual database model in the database design process; and, it can be used as the database model for a new kind of database management system.

Key Words and Phrases: database management, database models, database semantics, database definition, database modeling, logical database design
CR Categories: 3.73, 3.74, 4.33

## 1. INTRODUCTION

Every database is a *model* of some real world system. At all times, the contents of a database are intended to represent a snapshot of the state of an *application environment*, and each change to the database should reflect an event (or sequence of events) occurring in that environment. Therefore, it is appropriate that the structure of a database mirror the structure of the system that it models. A database whose organization is based on naturally occurring structures will be easier for a database designer to construct and modify than one that forces him to translate the primitives of his problem domain into artificial specification constructs. Similarly, a database user should find it easier to understand and employ a database if it can be described to him using concepts with which he is already familiar.

The global user view of a database, as specified by the database designer, is known as its *(logical) schema*. A schema is specified in terms of a database description and structuring formalism and associated operations, called a *database model*. We believe that the data structures provided by contemporary database models do not adequately support the design, evolution, and use of complex databases. These database models have significantly limited capabilities for expressing the meaning of a database and to relate a database to its corresponding application environment. The *semantics* of a database defined in terms of these mechanisms are not readily apparent from the schema; instead, the semantics must be separately specified by the database designer and consciously applied by the user.

Our goal is the design of a higher-level database model, which will enable the database designer to naturally and directly incorporate more of the semantics of a database into its schema. Such a semantics-based database description and structuring formalism is intended to serve as a natural application modeling mechanism to capture and express the structure of the application environment in the structure of the database.

## 1.1 The Design of SDM

This paper describes *SDM*, a database description and structuring formalism that is intended to allow a database schema to capture much more of the meaning of a database than is possible with contemporary database models. SDM is designed to provide features for the natural modeling of database application environments. In designing SDM, we analyzed many database applications, in order to determine the structures that occur and recur in them, assessed the shortcomings of contemporary database models in capturing the semantics of these applications, and developed strategies to address the problems uncovered. This design process was iterative, in that features were removed, added, and modified during various stages of design. A preliminary version of SDM was discussed in [Ham78]; however, this initial database model has been further revised and restructured based on experience with its use. This paper presents a detailed specification of SDM, examines its applications, and discusses its underlying principles.

SDM has been designed with a number of specific kinds of uses in mind. First, SDM is meant to serve as a formal specification mechanism for describing the meaning of a database; an SDM schema provides a precise documentation and communication medium for database users. In particular, a new user of a large and complex database should find its SDM schema of use in determining what information is contained in the database. Second, SDM provides the basis for a variety of high level, semantics-based user interfaces to a database; these interface facilities can be constructed as front-ends to existing database management systems, or as the query language of a new database management system. Such interfaces improve the process of identifying and retrieving relevant information from the database. For example, SDM has been used to construct a user interface facility for nonprogrammers [Mcl80a]. Finally, SDM provides a foundation for supporting the effective and structured design of databases and database-intensive application systems.

SDM has been designed to satisfy a number of criteria that are not met by contemporary database models, but which we believe to be essential in an effective database description and structuring formalism [Ham80b]. They are as follows:

1. The constructs of the database model should provide for the explicit specification of a large portion of the *meaning* of a database. Many contemporary database models (such as the CODASYL DBTG network model [Coda71, Tay76] and the hierarchical model [Tsi76]) exhibit compromises between the desire to provide a user-oriented database organization and the need to support efficient database storage and manipulation facilities. By contrast, the relational database model [Cod70,Cod71] stresses the separation of user-level database specifications and underlying implementation detail (data independence). Moreover, the relational database model emphasizes the importance of understandable modeling constructs (specifically, the nonhierarchic relation), and user-oriented database system interfaces [Chan75,Cha76].

However, the *semantic expressiveness* of the hierarchical, network, and relational models is limited; they do not provide sufficient mechanism to allow a database schema to describe the meaning of a database. Such models employ overly simple data structures to model an application environment. In so doing, they inevitably lose information about the database; they provide for the expression of only a limited range of a designer's knowledge of the application environment [Bil78,Sch75,Wie77]. This is a consequence of the fact that their structures are essentially all record-oriented constructs; the appropriateness and adequacy of the record construct for expressing database semantics is highly limited [Ham79,Ham79,Ken78,Ken79,Mcl78]. We believe that it is necessary to break with the tradition of record-based modeling, and to base a database model on structural constructs that are highly user-oriented and expressive of the application environment. To this end, it is essential that the database model provide a rich set of features to allow the direct modeling of application environment semantics.

2. A database model must support a *relativist* view of the meaning of a database, and allow the structure of a database to support alternative ways of looking at the same information. In order to accommodate multiple views of the same data and to enable the evolution of new perspectives on the data, a database model must support schemas that are flexible, potentially logically redundant, and integrated. *Flexibility* is essential in order to allow for multiple and co-equal views of the data. In a *logically redundant* database schema, the values of some database components can be algorithmically derived from others. Incorporating such derived information into a schema can simplify the user's manipulation of a database, by statically embedding in the schema data values that would otherwise have to be dynamically and repeatedly computed. Furthermore, the use of derived data can ease the development of new applications of the database, since new data required by these applications can often be readily adjoined to the existing schema. Finally, an *integrated* schema explicitly describes the relationships and similarities between multiple ways of viewing the same information. Without a degree of this critical integration, it is difficult to control the redundancy and to specify that the various alternative interpretations of the database are equivalent.

Contemporary, record-oriented database models do not adequately support relativism. In these models, it is generally necessary to impose a single structural organization of the data, one which inevitably carries along with it a particular interpretation of the data's meaning. This meaning may not be appropriate for all users of the database and may furthermore become entirely obsolete over time. For example, an association between two entities can legitimately be viewed as an attribute of the first entity, as an attribute of the second entity, or as an entity itself; thus, the fact that an officer is currently assigned as the captain of a ship could be expressed as an attribute of the ship (its current captain), as an attribute of the officer (his current ship), or as an independent (assignment) entity. A schema should make all three of these interpretations equally natural and direct. Therefore, the conceptual database model must provide a specification mechanism that simultaneously accommodates and integrates these three ways of looking at an assignment. Conventional database models fail to adequately achieve these goals.

Similarly, another consequence of the primacy of the principle of relativism is that, in general, the database model should not make rigid distinctions between such concepts as entity, association, and attribute. Higher-level database models that do require the database schema designer to sharply distinguish among these concepts (such as [Che76,Pir77]) are thus considered somewhat lacking in their support of relativism.

3. A database model must support the definition of schemas that are *based on abstract entities*. Specifically, this means that a database model must facilitate the description of relevant *entities* in the application environment, *collections* of such entities, *relationships* (associations) among entities, and *structural interconnections* among the collections. Moreover, the entities themselves must be distinguished from their syntactic identifiers (*names*); the user-level view of a database should be based on actual entities rather than on artificial entity names.

Allowing entities to represent themselves makes it possible to directly reference an entity from a related one. In record-oriented database models, it is necessary to cross reference between related entities by means of their identifiers. While it is of course necessary to eventually represent "abstract" entities as symbols inside a computer, the point is that users (and application programs) should be able to reference and manipulate abstractions as well as symbols; internal representations to facilitate computer processing should be hidden from users.

Suppose, for example, that the schema should allow a user to obtain the entity that models a ship's current captain from the ship entity. To accomplish this, it would be desirable to define an attribute "Captain" that applies to every ship, and whose value is an officer. To model this information using a record-oriented database model, it is necessary to select some identifier of an officer record (e.g., last name or identification number) to stand as the value of the "Captain" attribute of a ship. For example, using the relational database model, we might have a relation SHIPS, one of whose attributes is Officer_name, and a relation OFFICERS, which has Officer_name as a logical key. Then, in order to find the information about the captain of a given ship, it would be necessary to join relations SHIPS and OFFICERS on Officer_name; an explicit cross reference via identifiers is required. This forces the user to deal with an extra level of indirection, and to consciously apply a join to retrieve a simple item of information.

In consequence of the fact that contemporary database models require such surrogates to be used in connections among entities, important types of semantic integrity constraints on a database are not directly captured in its schema. If these semantic constraints are to be expressed and enforced, additional mechanisms must be provided to supplement contemporary database models [Bun77,Esw75,Ham75,Ham76,Sto74]. The problem with this approach is that these supplemental constraints are at best ad hoc, and do not integrate all available information into a simple structure. For example, it is desirable to require that only captains who are known in the database be assigned as officers of ships. To accomplish this in the relational database model, it is necessary to impose the supplemental constraint that each value of attribute Captain_name of SHIPS must be present in the Captain_name column of relation OFFICERS. If it were possible to simply state that each ship has a captain attribute whose value is an officer, this supplemental constraint would not be necessary.

The design of SDM has been based on the principles outlined above, which are discussed at greater length in [Ham79].

## 2. A SPECIFICATION OF SDM

The following general principles of database organization underlie the design of SDM:

1. A database is to be viewed as a collection of *entities*, which correspond to the actual objects in the application environment.
2. The entities in a database are organized into *classes*, which are meaningful collections of entities.
3. The classes of a database are not in general independent, but rather are logically related by means of *interclass connections.*
4. Database entities and classes have *attributes*, which describe their characteristics and relate them to other database entities. An attribute value may be derived from other values in the database.
5. There are several primitive ways of defining interclass connections and derived attributes, corresponding to the most common types of information redundancy appearing in database applications. These facilities integrate multiple ways of viewing the same basic information, and provide building blocks for describing complex attributes and interclass relationships.

### 2.1 Classes

An *SDM database* is a collection of entities, which are organized into classes. The structure and organization of an SDM database is specified by an *SDM schema*, which identifies the classes in the database. Appendix I contains an example SDM schema for a portion of the "tanker monitoring application environment"; a specific syntax (detailed in Appendix II), is used for expressing this schema. Examples in this paper are based on this application domain, which is concerned with monitoring and controlling ships with potentially hazardous cargos (such as oil tankers), as they enter U.S. coastal waters and ports. A database supporting this application would contain information on ships and their positions, oil tankers and their inspections, oil spills, ships that are banned from U.S. waters, and so forth.

Each class in an SDM schema has the following features:

1. A *class name* identifies the class. Multiple synonymous names are also permitted. Each class name must be unique with respect to all class names used in a schema. For notational convenience in this paper, class names are strings of upper case letters and special characters (e.g., `OIL_TANKERS`), as shown in Appendix I.

2. The class has a collection of *members*: the entities that comprise it. The phrases "the members of a class" and "the entities in a class" are thus synonymous. Each class in an SDM schema is a homogeneous collection of one type of entity, at an appropriate level of abstraction.

The entities in a class may correspond to various kinds of objects in the application environment. These include objects that may be viewed by users as:

a. concrete objects, such as ships, oil tankers, and ports (in Appendix I, these are classes SHIPS, OIL_TANKERS, and PORTS, respectively),
b. events, such as ship accidents (INCIDENTS) and assignments of captains to ships (ASSIGNMENTS),
c. higher-level entities, such as categorizations (e.g., SHIP_TYPES) and aggregations (e.g., CONVOYS) of entities,
d. names, which are syntactic identifiers (strings), such as the class of all possible ship names (SHIP_NAMES) and the class of all possible calendar dates (DATES).

Although it is useful in certain circumstances to label a class as containing "concrete objects" or "events" [Ham78], in general the principle of relativism requires that no such fixed specification be included in the schema; for example, inspections of ships (INSPECTIONS) could be considered to be either an event or an object, depending upon the user's point of view. In consequence, such distinctions are not directly supported in SDM. Only name classes (classes whose members are names) contain data items that can be transmitted into and out of a database, e.g., names are the values that may be entered by, or displayed to, a user. Non-name classes represent abstract entities from the application environment.

3. An (optional) textual *class description* describes the meaning and contents of the class. A class description should be used to describe the specific nature of the entities that constitute a class, and to indicate their significance and role in the application environment. For example, in Appendix I, class SHIPS has a description indicating that the class contains ships with potentially hazardous cargos that may enter U.S. coastal waters. Tying this documentation directly to schema entries makes it accessible and consequently more valuable.
4. The class has a collection of attributes that describe the members of that class or the class as a whole. There are two types of attributes, classified according to *applicability*.
   a. A *member attribute* describes an aspect of each member of a class, by logically connecting the member to one or more related entities in the same or another class. Thus, a member attribute is used to describe each member of some class. For example, each member of class SHIPS has attributes Name, Captain, and Engines, which identify the ship's name, its current captain, and its engines (respectively).

**b.** A *class attribute* describes a property of a class taken as a whole. For example, the class INSPECTIONS has the attribute Number, which identifies the number of inspections currently in the class; the class OIL_TANKERS has the attribute Absolute_legal_top_speed, which indicates the absolute maximum speed any tanker is allowed to sail.

5. The class is either a *base class* or a *nonbase class*. A base class is one that is defined independently of all other classes in the database; it can be thought of as modeling a primitive entity in the application environment, e.g., SHIPS. Base classes are mutually disjoint, in that every entity is a member of exactly one base class. Of course, at some level of abstraction all entities are members of class "THINGS"; SDM provides the notion of base class to explicitly support cutting off the abstraction below that most general level. (If it is desired that all entities in a database be members of some class, then a single base class would be defined in the schema.)

A nonbase class is one that does not have independent existence; rather, it is defined in terms of one or more other classes. In SDM, classes are structurally related by means of *interclass connections*. Each nonbase class has associated with it one interclass connection. In the schema definition syntax shown in Appendix I, the existence of an interclass connection for a class means that it is nonbase; if no interclass connection is present, the class is a base class. In Appendix A, OIL_TANKERS is an example of a nonbase class; it is defined to be a subclass of SHIPS, which means that its membership is always a subset of the members of SHIPS.

6. If the class is a base class, it has an associated list of groups of member attributes; each of these groups serves as a logical key to uniquely identify the members of a class (*identifiers*). That is, there is a one-to-one correspondence between the values of each identifying attribute or attribute group and the entities in a class. For example, class SHIPS has the unique identifier Name, as well as the (alternative) unique identifier Hull_number.
7. If the class is a base class, it is specified as either *containing duplicates* or *not containing duplicates*. (The default is that duplicates are allowed; in the schema syntax used in Appendix I, "duplicates not allowed" is explicitly stated to indicate that a class may not contain duplicate members.) Stating that duplicates are not allowed amounts to requiring the members of the class to have some difference in their attribute values; "duplicates not allowed" is explicit shorthand for requiring all of the member attributes of a class taken together to constitute a unique identifier.

## 2.2 Interclass Connections

As specified above, a nonbase class has an associated interclass connection that defines it. There are two main types of interclass connections in SDM: the first allows subclasses to be defined, and the second supports grouping classes. These interclass connection types are detailed as follows.

**2.2.1 The subclass connection.** The first type of interclass connection specifies that the members of a nonbase class ($S$) are of the same basic entity type as those in the class to which $S$ is related (via the interclass connection). This type of interclass connection is used to define a subclass of a given class. A *subclass* $S$ of a class $C$ (called the *parent class*) is a class that contains some, but not necessarily all, of the members of $C$. The very same entity can thus be a member of many classes, e.g., a given entity may simultaneously be a member of the classes `SHIPS`, `OIL_TANKERS`, and `MERCHANT_SHIPS`. (However, only one of these may be a base class.) This is the concept of "subtype" [Ham78,Lee78,Myl78,Pal78,Smi77], which is missing from most database models (in which a record belongs to exactly one file).

In SDM, a subclass $S$ is defined by specifying a class $C$ and a predicate $P$ on the members of $C$; $S$ consists of just those members of $C$ that satisfy $P$. Several types of predicates are permissible:

1. A predicate on the member attributes of $C$ can be used to indicate which members of $C$ are also members of $S$. A subclass defined by this technique is called an *attribute-defined subclass*. For example, the class `MERCHANT_SHIPS` is defined (in Appendix A) as a subclass of SHIPS by the member attribute predicate "where Type = 'merchant'"; that is, a member of `SHIPS` is a member of `MERCHANT_SHIPS` if the value of its attribute Type is "merchant". (A detailed discussion of member attribute predicates is provided below. The usual comparison operators and Boolean connectives are allowed.)
2. The predicate "where specified" can be used to define $S$ as a *user-controllable subclass* of $C$. This means that $S$ contains at all times only entities that are members of $C$. However, unlike an attribute-defined subclass, the definition of $S$ does not identify which members of $C$ are in $S$; rather, database users "manually" add to (and delete from) $S$, so long as the subclass limitation is observed. For example, `BANNED_SHIPS` is defined as a "where specified" subclass of "SHIPS"; this allows some authority to ban a ship from U.S. waters (and possibly later rescind that ban).

An essential difference between attribute-defined subclasses and user-controllable subclasses is that the membership of the former type of subclass is determined by other information in the database, while the membership of the latter type of subclass is directly and explicitly controlled by users. It would be possible to simulate the effect of a user-controllable subclass by an attribute-defined subclass, through the introduction of a dummy member attribute of the parent class, whose sole purpose is to specify whether or not the entity is in the subclass. Subclass membership could then be predicated on the value of this attribute. However, this would be a confusing and indirect method of capturing the semantics of the application environment; in particular, there are cases in which the method of determining subclass membership is beyond the scope of the database schema (e.g., by virtue of being complex).

3. A subclass definition predicate can specify that the members of subclass $S$ are just those members of $C$ that also belong to two other specified database classes ($C_1$

and $C_2$); this provides a class *intersection* capability. To insure a type-compatible intersection, $C_1$ and $C_2$ must both be subclasses of $C$, either directly or through a series of subclass relationships. For example, the class BANNED_OIL_TANKERS is defined as the subclass of SHIPS that contains those members common to the classes OIL_TANKERS and BANNED_SHIPS.

In addition to an intersection capability, a subclass can be defined by class *union* and *difference*. A union subclass contains those members of $C$ in either $C_1$ or $C_2$. For example, class SHIPS_TO_BE_MONITORED is defined as a subclass of SHIPS with the predicate "where is in BANNED_SHIPS or is in OIL_TANKERS_REQUIRING_INSPECTION." A difference subclass contains those members of $C$ that are not in $C_1$. For example, class SAFE_SHIPS is defined as the subclass of SHIPS with the predicate "where is not in BANNED_SHIPS."

The intersection, union, and difference subclass definition primitives allow *set-operator-defined subclasses* to be specified; these primitives are provided because they often represent the most natural means of defining a subclass. Moreover, these operations are needed to effectively define subclasses of user-controllable subclasses. For example, class intersection (rather than a member attribute predicate) must be used to define class SHIPS_TO_BE_MONITORED; since BANNED_SHIPS and OIL_TANKERS_REQUIRING_INSPECTION are both user-controllable subclasses, no natural member attributes of either of these classes could be used to state an appropriate defining member attribute predicate for SHIPS_TO_BE_MONITORED.

4. The final type of subclass definition allows a subclass $S$ to be defined as consisting of all of the members of $C$ that are currently values of some attribute $A$ of another class $C_1$. That is, class $S$ contains all of the members of $C$ that are a value of $A$. This type of class is called an *existence subclass*. For example, class DANGEROUS_CAPTAINS is defined as the subclass of OFFICERS satisfying the predicate "where is a value of Involved_captain of INCIDENTS"; this specifies that DANGEROUS_CAPTAINS contains all officers who have been involved in an incident.

**2.2.2 The grouping connection.** The other type of interclass connection allows for the definition of a nonbase class, called a *grouping class* ($G$), whose members are of a higher-order entity type than those in the underlying class ($U$). A grouping class is *second order*, in the sense that its members can themselves be viewed as classes; in particular, they are classes whose members are taken from $U$.

The following options are available for defining a grouping class:

1. The grouping class $G$ can be defined as consisting of all classes formed by collecting the members of $U$ into classes based on having a common value for one or more designated member attributes of $U$ (an *expression-defined grouping class*). A *grouping expression* specifies how the members of $U$ are to be placed into these groups. The groups formed in this way become the members of $G$, and the members

of a member of $G$ are called its *contents*. For example, class SHIP_TYPES in Appendix I is defined as a grouping class of SHIPS with the grouping expression "on common value of Type". The members of SHIP_TYPES are not ships, but rather are groups of ships. In particular, the intended interpretation of SHIP_TYPES is as a collection of types of ships, whose instances are the contents (members) of the groups that constitute SHIP_TYPES. This kind of grouping class represents an abstraction of the underlying class. That is, the elements of the grouping class correspond in a sense to the shared property of the entities that are its contents, rather than to the collection of entities itself.

If the grouping expression used to define a grouping class involves only a single-valued attribute, then the groups partition the underlying class; this is the case for SHIP_TYPES. However, if a multi-valued attribute is involved, then the groups may have overlapping contents. For example, the class CARGO_TYPE_GROUPS can be defined as a grouping class on SHIPS with the grouping expression "on common value of Cargo_types"; since Cargo_types is multi-valued, a given ship may be in more than one cargo-type category. Although the grouping mechanism is limited to single grouping expressions (viz., on common value of one or more member attributes), complex grouping criteria are possible via derived attributes (as discussed below).

It should be clear that the contents of a group are a subclass of the class underlying the grouping. The grouping expression used to define a grouping class thus corresponds to a collection of attribute-defined subclass definitions. For example, for SHIP_TYPES, the grouping expression "on common value of Type" corresponds to the collection of subclass member attribute predicates (on SHIPS) "Type = 'merchant'," "Type = 'fishing'," and "Type = 'military'." Some or all of these subclasses may be independently and explicitly defined in the schema. In Appendix I, the class MERCHANT_SHIPS is defined as a subclass of SHIPS, and it is also listed in the definition of SHIP_TYPES as a class that is explicitly defined in the database ("groups defined as classes are MERCHANT_SHIPS"). In general, when a grouping class is defined, a list of the names of the groups that are explicitly defined in the schema is to be included in the specification of the interclass connection; the purpose of this list is to relate the groups to their corresponding subclasses in the schema.

2. A second way to define a grouping class $G$ is by providing a list of classes ($C_1$, $C_2$, ... $C_n$) that are defined in the schema; these classes are the members of the grouping class (an *enumerated grouping class*). Each of the classes ($C_1$, $C_2$, ..., $C_n$) must be explicitly defined in the schema as an (eventual) subclass of the class $U$ that is specified as the class underlying the grouping. This grouping class definition capability is useful when no appropriate attribute is available for defining the grouping, and when all of the groups are themselves defined as classes in the schema. For example, a class TYPES_OF_HAZARDOUS_SHIPS can be defined as "grouping of SHIPS consisting of classes BANNED_SHIPS, BANNED_OIL_TANKERS, and SHIPS_TO_BE_MONITORED."

3. A grouping class $G$ can be defined to consist of user-controllable subclasses of some underlying class (a *user-controllable grouping class*). In effect, a user-controllable grouping class consists of a collection of user-controllable subclasses. For example, class CONVOYS is defined as a grouping class of SHIPS "as specified." In this case, no attribute exists to allow the grouping of ships into convoys, and individual convoys are not themselves defined as classes in the schema; rather, each member of CONVOYS is a user-controllable group of ships, that users may add to or delete from. This kind of grouping class models simple "aggregates" over a base class: arbitrary collections of entities manipulated by users.

**2.2.3 Multiple interclass connections.** As specified above, each nonbase class in an SDM schema has a single interclass connection associated with it. While it is meaningful and reasonable in some cases to associate more than one interclass connection with a nonbase class, the uncontrolled use of such multiple interclass connections could introduce undesirable complexity into a schema. In consequence, only a single interclass connection (the most natural one) should be used to define a nonbase class.

To illustrate this point, consider for example the class RURITANIAN_OIL_TANKERS. Clearly, this class could be specified as an attribute-defined subclass of OIL_TANKERS (by the interclass connection "subclass of OIL_TANKERS where Country.Name='Ruritania'"), or as a subclass of RURITANIAN_SHIPS (by the interclass connection "subclass of RURITANIAN_SHIPS where Cargo_types contains 'oil'"); these definitions are, in a sense, semantically equivalent. The possibility of allowing multiple (semantically equivalent) interclass connections to be specified for a nonbase class was considered, but it was determined that such a feature could introduce considerable complexity: the mechanism could be used to force two class definitions that are not semantically equivalent to define classes with the same members. For example, one could associate the sets of members of these two possibly independent collections to be the same. In sum, without a carefully formulated and powerful notion of semantic equivalence [McK79], it was determined that multiple interclass connections for a nonbase class should not be allowed in SDM. Of course, multiple class names and judiciously selected class descriptions can be used to convey additional definitions, e.g., naming a class BANNED_SHIPS and RURITANIAN_OIL_TANKERS to indicate that the two sets of ships are intended to be one and the same.

## 2.3 Name Classes

Entities are application constructs that are directly modeled in an SDM schema. In the real world, entities can be denoted in a number of ways; e.g., a particular ship can be identified by giving its name or its hull number, by exhibiting a picture of it, or by pointing one's finger at the ship itself. Operating entirely within SDM, the typical way of referencing an entity is by means of an entity-valued attribute that gives access to the entity itself. However, there must also be some mechanism that allows for the outside world (i.e., users) to communicate with an SDM database. This will typically be accomplished by data being entered or displayed on a computer terminal. However, one cannot enter or display a real entity on such a terminal; it is necessary to employ representations of them for that purpose. These representations are called SDM *names*. A name is any string of symbols that denotes an actual value encountered in the application environment; the strings "red", "128", "8/21/78", and "321-004" are all names. A name class in SDM is a collection of strings, viz., a subclass of the built-in class `STRINGS` (which consists of all strings over the basic set of alphanumeric characters).

Every SDM name class is defined by means of the interclass connection "subclass". The following methods of defining a class $S$ of names are available:

1. The class $S$ can be defined as the intersection, union, or difference of two other name classes.
2. The class $S$ can be defined as a subclass of some other name class $C$ with the predicate "where specified", which means that the members of $S$ belong to $C$, but must be explicitly enumerated. In Appendix I, class `COUNTRY_NAMES` is defined in this way.
3. A predicate can be used to define $S$ as a subclass of $C$. The predicate specifies the subset of $C$ that constitutes $S$ by indicating constraints on the format of the acceptable data values. In Appendix I, classes `ENGINE_SERIAL_NUMBERS`, `DATES`, and `CARGO_TYPE_NAMES` are defined in this way. `CARGO_TYPE_NAMES` has no format constraints, indicating that all strings are valid cargo type names. `ENGINE_SERIAL_NUMBERS` and `DATES` do have constraints that indicate the patterns defining legal members of these classes. Note that for convenience, the particular name classes `NUMBERS`, `INTEGERS`, `REALS`, and `YES/NO` (Booleans) are also built into SDM; these classes have obvious definitions. (Further details of the format specification language used here are presented in [Mcl77].)

## 2.4 Attributes

As stated above, each class has an associated collection of attributes. Each attribute has the following features:

1. An *attribute name* identifies the attribute. An attribute name must be unique with respect to the set of all attribute names used in the class, the class's underlying base class, and all eventual subclasses of that base class. (As described in [Mcl79], this means that attribute names must be unique within a "family" of classes; this is necessary to support the attribute inheritance rules described below.) As with class names, multiple synonymous attribute names are permitted. For notational convenience in this paper, attribute names are written as one upper case letter followed by a sequence of lower case letters and special characters (e.g., the attribute Cargo_types of class SHIPS), as shown in Appendix A.
2. The attribute has a *value*, which is either an entity in the database (a member of some class), or a collection of such entities. The value of an attribute is selected from its underlying *value class*, which contains the permissible values of the attribute. Any class in the schema may be specified to be the value class of an

attribute. For example, the value class of member attribute Captain of SHIPS is the class OFFICERS. The value of an attribute may also be the special value *null* (i.e., no value).

3. The *applicability* of the attribute is specified by indicating that the attribute is either:
   a. a member attribute, which applies to each member of the class, and so has a value for each member (e.g., Name of SHIPS), or
   b. a class attribute, which applies to a class as a whole and has only one value for the class (e.g., Number of INSPECTIONS).
4. An (optional) *attribute description* is text that describes the meaning and purpose of the attribute. For example, in Appendix I, the description of Captain of SHIPS indicates that the value of the attribute is the current captain of the ship. (This serves as an integrated form of database documentation.)
5. The attribute is specified as either *single-valued* or *multi-valued*. The value of a single-valued attribute is a member of the value class of the attribute, while the value of a multi-valued attribute is a subclass of the value class. Thus, a multi-valued attribute itself defines a class, i.e., a collection of entities. In Appendix I, the class OIL_TANKERS has the single-valued member attribute Hull_type, and the multi-valued member attribute Inspections. (In the schema definition syntax used in Appendix I, the default is single-valued.) It is possible to place a constraint on the size of a multi-valued attribute, by specifying "multi-valued with size between $X$ and $Y$", where $X$ and $Y$ are integers; this means that the attribute must have between $X$ and $Y$ values. For example, attribute Engines of SHIPS is specified as "multi-valued with size between 0 and 10"; this means that a SHIP has between zero and ten engines.
6. An attribute can be specified as *mandatory*, which means that a null value is not allowed for it. For example, attribute Hull_number of SHIPS is specified as "may not be null"; this models the fact that every SHIP has a Hull_number.
7. An attribute can be specified as *not changeable*, which means that once set to a non-null value, this value cannot be altered except to correct an error. For example, attribute Hull_number of SHIPS is specified as "not changeable."
8. A member attribute can be required to be *exhaustive* of its value class. This means that every member of the value class of the attribute (call it $A$) must be the $A$ value of some entity. For example, attribute Engines of SHIPS "exhausts value class," which means that every engine entity must be an engine of some ship.
9. A multivalued member attribute can be specified as *nonoverlapping* which means that the values of the attribute for two different entities have no entities in common; that is, each member of the value class of the attribute is used at most once. For example, Engines of SHIPS is specified as having "no overlap values," which means that any engine can be in only one ship.
10. The attribute may be related to other attributes, and/or defined in terms of other information in the schema. The possible types of such relationships are different for member and class attributes, and are detailed in what follows.

**2.4.1 Member attribute interrelationships.** The first way in which a pair of member attributes can be related is by means of inversion. Member attribute $A_1$ of class $C_1$ can be specified as the *inverse* of member attribute $A_2$ of $C_2$, which means that the value of $A_1$ for a member $M_1$ of $C_1$ consists of those members of $C_2$ whose value of $A_2$ is $M_1$. The inversion inter-attribute relationship is specified symmetrically, in that both an attribute and its inverse contain a description of the inversion relationship. A pair of inverse attributes in effect establish a binary association between the members of the classes that the attributes modify. (Although all attribute inverses could theoretically be specified, if only one of a pair of such attributes is relevant, then it is the only one that is defined in the schema, viz., no inverse specification is provided.) For example, attribute Ships_registered_here of `COUNTRIES` is specified in Appendix I as the inverse of attribute Country_of_registry of `SHIPS`; this establishes the fact that both are ways of expressing in what country a ship is registered. This is accomplished by:

1. specifying that the value class of attribute Country_of_registry of `SHIPS` is `COUNTRIES`, and that its inverse is Ships_registered_here (of `COUNTRIES`),
2. specifying that the value class of attribute Ships_registered_here of `COUNTRIES` is `SHIPS`, and that its inverse is Country_of_registry (of `SHIPS`).

The second way in which a member attribute can be related to other information in the database is by *matching* the value of the attribute with some member(s) of a specified class. In particular, the value of the match attribute $A_1$ for the member $M_1$ of class $C_1$ is determined as follows:

1. A member $M_2$ of some (specified) class $C_2$ is found that has $M_1$ as its value of (specified) member attribute $A_2$.
2. The value of (specified) member attribute $A_3$ for $M_2$ is used as the value of $A_1$ for $M_1$.

If $A_1$ is a multi-valued attribute, then it is permissible for each member of $C_1$ to match to several members of $C_2$; in this case, the collection of $A_3$ values is the value of attribute $A_1$. For example, a matching specification indicates that the value of the attribute Captain for a member $S$ of class `SHIPS` is equal to the value of attribute Officer of the member $A$ of class `ASSIGNMENTS` whose Ship value is $S$.

Inversion and matching provide multiple ways of viewing $n$-ary associations among entities. Inversion permits the specification of binary associations, while matching is capable of supporting binary and higher degree associations. For example, suppose it is necessary to establish a ternary association among oil tankers, countries, and dates, to indicate that a given tanker was inspected in a specified country on a particular date. To accomplish this, a class could be defined (say, `COUNTRY_INSPECTIONS`) with three attributes: Tanker_inspected, Country, and Date_inspected. Matching would then be used to relate these to appropriate attributes of `OIL_TANKERS`, `COUNTRIES`, and `DATES` that also express this information. Inversions could also be specified to relate the relevant member attributes of `OIL_TANKERS` (e.g., Countries_in_which_inspected),

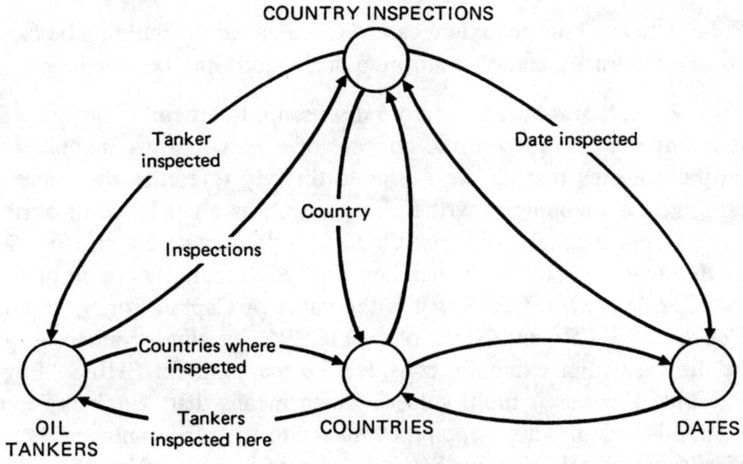


**Figure 2.1** Multiple perspectives on the "Country Inspections" association. Circles denote classes and are labeled with class names. Arrows denote member attributes, labeled by name, with the arrowhead pointing to the attribute's value class. For brevity, only some of the possible attributes are named (as would be the case in many real SDM schemata).

COUNTRIES (e.g., Tankers_inspected_here), DATES, and COUNTRY_INSPECTIONS (see Figure 2.1).

The combined use of inversion and matching allows an SDM schema to accommodate relative viewpoints of an association. For instance, one may view the ternary relationship in the above example as an inspection entity (a member of class COUNTRY_INSPECTIONS ), or as a collection of attributes of the entities that participate in the association. Similarly, a binary relationship defined as a pair of inverse attributes could also be viewed as an association entity, with matching used to relate that entity to the relevant attributes of the associated entities [Mcl79].

***2.4.1.1 Member Attribute Derivations.*** As described above, inversion and matching are mechanisms for establishing the equivalence of different ways of viewing the same essential relationships among entities. SDM also provides the ability to define an attribute whose value is calculated from other information in the database. Such an attribute is called *derived*, and the specification of its computation is its associated *derivation*.

The approach we take to defining derived attributes is to provide a small vocabulary of high level attribute derivation primitives, which directly model the most common types of derived information. Each of these primitives provides a way of specifying one method of computing a derived attribute. More general facilities are available for describing attributes that do not match any of these cases: a complex derived attribute is defined by first describing other attributes that are used as building blocks in its definition, and then applying one of the primitives to these building blocks. For example, attribute Superiors of OFFICERS is defined by a derivation primitive applied to attribute Commander, and in turn, attribute Contacts is defined by a derivation primitive applied to Superiors and

Subordinates. This procedure can be repeated for the building block attributes themselves, so that arbitrarily complex attribute derivations can be developed.

***2.4.1.2 Mappings.*** Before discussing the member attribute derivation primitives, it is important to present the concept of a *mapping*. A mapping is a concatenation of attribute names that allows a user to directly reference the value of an attribute of an attribute. A mapping is written, in general, as a sequence of attribute names separated by "."s. For example, consider the mapping "Captain.Name" for class SHIPS. The value of this mapping, for each member $S$ of SHIPS, is the value of attribute Name of that member $O$ of OFFICERS that is the value of Captain for $S$. In this case, the attributes Captain of SHIPS and Name of OFFICERS are single-valued; in general, this need not be the case. For example, consider the mapping for SHIPS "Engines.Serial_number". Attribute Engines is multi-valued, which means that "Engines.Serial_number" may also be multi-valued. This mapping evaluates to the serial numbers of the engines of a ship. Similarly, the mapping for SHIPS "Captain.Superiors.Name" evaluates to the names of all of the superiors of the captain of a ship. This mapping is multi-valued, since at least one of the steps in the mapping involves a multi-valued attribute. The value of a mapping "$X.Y.Z$", where $X$, $Y$, and $Z$ are multi-valued attributes, is the class containing each value of $Z$ that corresponds to a value of $Y$ for some value of $X$.

***2.4.1.3 Member Derivation Primitives.*** The following primitives are provided to express the derivation of the value of a member attribute; here, attribute $A_1$ of member $M_1$ of class $C_1$ is being defined in terms of the relationship of $M_1$ to other information in the database:

1. $A_1$ can be defined as an *ordering* attribute. In this case, the value of $A_1$ denotes the sequential position of $M_1$ in $C_1$, when $C_1$ is ordered by one or more other specified (single-valued) member attributes (or mappings) of $C_1$. Ordering is by increasing or decreasing value (the default is increasing). For example, the attribute Seniority of `OFFICERS` has the derivation "order by Date_commissioned". The `OFFICER` with the earliest date commissioned will then have Seniority value of 1. Ordering within groups is also possible: "order by $A_2$ within $A_3$" specifies that the value of $A_1$ is the sequential position of $M_1$ within the group of entitics that have the same value of $A_1$ as $M_1$, as ordered by the value of $A_2$. ($A_2$ and $A_3$ may be mappings as well as attributes.) For example, attribute Order_for_tanker of `INSPECTIONS` has the derivation "order by decreasing Date within Tanker", which orders the inspections for each tanker. The value class of an ordering attribute is `INTEGERS`.
2. The value of attribute $A_1$ can be declared to be a Boolean value that is "yes" (true) if $M_1$ is a member of some other specified class $C_2$, and "no" (false) otherwise. Thus, the value class of this *existence* attribute is `YES/NO`. For example, attribute Is_tanker_banned? of class `OIL_TANKERS` has the derivation "if in `BANNED_SHIPS` ".
3. The value of attribute $A_1$ can be defined as the result of combining all the entities obtained by recursively tracing the values of some attribute $A_2$. For instance, attribute Superiors of `OFFICERS` has the derivation "all levels of values of Com-

mander"; the value of the attribute includes the immediate commander of the officer, his commander's superiors, and so on. Note that the value class of commander is OFFICERS; this must be true for this kind of recursive attribute derivation to be meaningful. It is also possible to specify a maximum number of levels over which to repeat the recursion, viz., "up to $N$ levels" where $N$ is an integer constant; this would be useful, for example, to relate an officer to his subordinates and their subordinates.

4. When a grouping class is defined, the derived, multi-valued member attribute *Contents* is automatically established. The value of this attribute is the collection of members (of the class underlying the grouping) that form the contents of that member. For example, each member of the grouping class SHIP_TYPES has as the value of its Contents attribute the class of all ships of the type in question.
5. The value of a member attribute can be specified to be derived from and equal to the value of some other attribute or mapping. For instance, attribute Date_last_examined of OIL_TANKERS has the derivation "same as Last_inspection.Date". (Note that this in effect introduces a member attribute as shorthand for a mapping.)
6. Attribute $A_1$ can be defined as a *subvalue* attribute of some other (multi-valued) member attribute or mapping ($A_2$). The value of $A_2$ is specified as consisting of a subclass of the value of $A_1$ that satisfies some specified predicate. For example, attribute Last_two_inspections of class OIL_TANKERS is defined as "subvalue of Inspections where Order_for_tanker $\leq$ 2".
7. The value of a member attribute can be specified as the intersection, union, or difference of two other (multi-valued) member attributes or mappings. For example, attribute Contacts of OFFICERS has the definition "where is in Superiors or is in Subordinates", indicating that its value consists of an officer's superiors and subordinates.
8. A member attribute derivation can specify that the value of the attribute is given by an arithmetic expression that involves the values of other member attributes or mappings. The involved attributes/mappings must have numeric values, i.e., they must have value classes that are (eventual) subclasses of NUMBERS. The arithmetic operators allowed are addition ("+"), subtraction ("−"), multiplication ("*"), division ("/"), and exponentiation ("!"). For example, attribute Top_speed_in_miles_per_hour of OIL_TANKERS has the derivation "= Absolute_top_speed / 1.1" (to convert from knots).
9. The operators "maximum", "minimum", "average", "sum" can be applied to a member attribute or mapping that is multi-valued; the value class of the attributes involved must be an (eventual) subclass of NUMBERS. The maximum, minimum, average, or sum is taken over the collection of entities that comprise the current value of the attribute or mapping.
10. A member attribute can be defined to have its value equal to the number of members in a multi-valued attribute or mapping. For example, attribute Number_of_instances of SHIP_TYPES has the derivation "number of members in Contents". "Number of unique members" is used similarly. "Number of members" and "number of unique

members" differ only when duplicates are present in the multi-valued attribute involved.

*2.4.1.4 The Definition of Member Attributes.* We now specify how these derivation mechanisms for derived attributes may be applied. The following rules are formulated in order to allow the use of derivations while avoiding the danger of inconsistent attribute specifications:

1. Every attribute may or may not have an inverse; if it does, the inverse must be defined consistently with the attribute.
2. Every member attribute $A_1$ satisfies one of the following cases:
   a. $A_1$ has exactly one derivation. In this case, the value $A_1$ is completely specified by the derivation. The inverse of $A_1$ (call it $A_2$), if it exists, may not have a derivation or a matching specification.
   b. $A_1$ has exactly one matching specification. In this case, the value of $A_1$ is completely specified by its relationships with an entity (or entities) to which it is matched (viz., member(s) of some class $C$). The inverse of $A_1$ (call it $A_2$), if it exists, may not have a derivation. It can have a matching specification, but this must match $A_2$ to $C$ in a manner consistent with the matching specification of $A_1$.
   c. $A_1$ has neither a matching specification nor a derivation. In this case, it may be the case that the inverse of $A_1$ (call it $A_2$) has a matching specification or a derivation; if so, then one of the above two cases (a or b) applies. Otherwise, $A_1$ and $A_2$ form a pair of primitive values that are defined in terms of one another, but which are independent of all other information in the database.

   With regard to updating the database, we note that in case c, a user can explicitly provide a value for $A_1$ or for $A_2$ (and thereby establish values for both of them). In cases a and b, neither $A_1$ nor $A_2$ can be directly modified; their values are changed by modifying other parts of the database.

**2.4.2 Class attribute interrelationships.** Attribute derivation primitives analogous to primitives 5 through 10 for member attributes can be used to define derived class attributes, as these primitives derive attribute values from those of other attributes. Of course, instead of deriving the value of a member attribute from the value of other member attributes, the class attribute primitives will derive the value of a class attribute from the value of other class attributes. In addition, there are two other primitives that can be used in the definition of derived class attributes:

1. An attribute can be defined so that its value equals the number of members in the class it modifies. For example, attribute Number of `INSPECTIONS` has the derivation "number of members in this class".
2. An attribute can be defined whose value is a function of a numeric member attribute of a class; the functions supported are "maximum", "minimum", "average", and "sum" taken over a member attribute. The computation of the function is made

over the members of the class. For example, the class attribute Total_spilled of OIL_SPILLS has the derivation "sum of Amount_spilled over members of this class".

**2.4.3 Attribute predicates for subclass definition.** As stated earlier, a subclass can be defined by means of a predicate on the member attributes of its parent class. Having described the specifics of attributes, it is now possible to detail the permissible types of attribute predicates. In particular, an attribute predicate is a simple predicate or a Boolean combination of simple predicates; the operators used to form such a Boolean combination are "and", "or", "not", and "( )". A simple predicate has one of the following forms:

1. MAPPING SCALAR_COMPARATOR CONSTANT,
2. MAPPING SCALAR_COMPARATOR MAPPING,
3. MAPPING SET_COMPARATOR CONSTANT,
4. MAPPING SET_COMPARATOR CLASS_NAME,
5. MAPPING SET_COMPARATOR MAPPING.

Here, MAPPING is any mapping (including an attribute name as a special case); SCALAR_COMPARATOR is one of "$=$", "$\neq$", "$>$", "$\geq$", "$<$", and "$\leq$"; CONSTANT is a string or number constant; SET_COMPARATOR is one of: "is contained in", "is properly contained in", "contains", and "properly contains"; CLASS_NAME is the name of some class defined in the schema. For illustration, an example of each of these five forms is provided below along with an indication of its meaning; the first two predicates define subclasses of class OFFICERS, while the third, fourth, and fifth apply to class SHIPS:

1. Country_of_license = 'Panama' (officers licensed in Panama),
2. Commander.Date_commissioned > Date_commissioned (officers commissioned before their commander),
3. Cargo_types contains 'oil' (ships that can carry oil),
4. Captain is contained in DANGEROUS_CAPTAINS (ships whose captain is in the class containing officers that are bad risks),
5. Captain.Country_of_license is contained in Captain.Superior.Country_of_license (ships commanded by an officer who has a superior licensed in the same country as he).

**2.4.4 Attribute inheritance.** As noted earlier, it may often be the case that an entity in an SDM database belongs to more than one class. SDM classes can and frequently do share members, e.g., a member of OIL_TANKERS is also a member of SHIPS; a member of OIL_SPILLS is also in INCIDENTS. As a member of a class $C$, a given entity $E$ has values for each member attribute associated with $C$. But in addition, when viewed as a member of $C$, $E$ may have additional attributes that are not directly associated with $C$, but which are *inherited* from other classes. For example, since all oil tankers are ships, each member $T$ of the class OIL_TANKERS inherits the member attributes of SHIPS. In addition to the attributes Hull_type, Is_tanker_banned, Inspections, Number_of_times_inspected, Last_inspection, Last_two_inspections, Date_last_examined, and Oil_spills_involved_in, which are explicitly associated with OIL_TANKERS, $T$ also has the attributes Name, Hull_number, Type, etc.; these are not mentioned in the definition of OIL_TANKERS, but are inherited from SHIPS (a superclass of OIL_TANKERS). The value of each inherited attribute of tanker $T$ is simply the value of that attribute of T when it is viewed as a member of SHIPS; the very same ship entity that belongs to OIL_TANKERS belongs also to SHIPS, so that the value of each such inherited attribute is well-defined.

The following specific rules of attribute inheritance are applied in SDM:

**1.** A class $S$ that is an attribute-defined subclass of a class $U$, or a user-controllable subclass of $U$, inherits all of the member attributes of $U$. For example, since RURITANIAN_OIL_TANKERS is an attribute-defined subclass of OIL_TANKERS, RURITANIAN_OIL_TANKERS inherits all of the member attributes of OIL_TANKERS; in turn, members of OIL_TANKERS inherit all of the member attributes of SHIPS.

Class attributes describe properties of a class taken as a whole, and so are not inherited by an attribute-defined or user-controllable subclass. In order for an attribute to be inherited from class $U$ by class $S$, both its meaning and its value must be the same for $U$ and $S$. This is not true in general for class attributes. Although a subclass may have a similar class attribute to one defined for its parent class, e.g., Number_of_members, their values will in general not be equal.

**2.** A class $S$ defined as an intersection subclass of classes $U_1$ and $U_2$ inherits all of the member attributes of $U_1$ and all of the member attributes of $U_2$. For example, the class BANNED_OIL_TANKERS, defined as containing all members of SHIP that are in both BANNED_SHIPS and OIL_TANKERS, inherits all attributes of BANNED_SHIPS as well as all of the attributes of OIL_TANKERS. This follows since each member of BANNED_OIL_TANKERS is both an oil tanker and a banned ship and so must have the attributes of both. Note that since BANNED_SHIPS and OIL_TANKERS are themselves defined as subclasses, they may inherit attributes from their parent classes, which are in turn inherited by BANNED_OIL_TANKERS.

**3.** A class $S$ defined as the union of classes $U_1$ and $U_2$ inherits all of the member attributes shared by $U_1$ and $U_2$. For example, the class SHIPS_TO_BE_MONITORED inherits the member attributes shared by BANNED_SHIPS and OIL_TANKERS_REQUIRING_INSPECTION (which turn out to be all of the member attributes of SHIPS).

**4.** A subclass $S$ defined as the difference of classes, viz., consisting of all of the members in a class $U$ that are not in class $U_1$ inherits all of the member attributes of $U$. This case is similar to 1, since $S$ is a subclass of $U$.

These inheritance rules determine the attributes associated with classes that are defined in terms of interclass connections. These rules need not be explicitly applied by the SDM user; they are an integral part of SDM and are automatically applied wherever appropriate.

*2.4.4.1 Further Constraining an Inherited Member Attribute.* An important constraint may be placed on inherited attributes in an SDM schema. This constraint requires that the value of an attribute $A$ inherited from class $C_1$ by class $C_2$ be a member of a class $C_3$ ($C_3$ is a subclass of the value class of $A$). To specify such a constraint, the name of the inherited attribute is repeated in the definition of the member attributes of the subclass, and its constrained value class is specified. For example, attribute Cargo_types is inherited by `MERCHANT_SHIPS` from `SHIPS`; its repetition in the definition of `MERCHANT_SHIPS` indicates that the value class of Cargo_types for `MERCHANT_SHIPS` is restricted to `MERCHANT_CARGO_TYPE_NAMES`. Values of attribute Cargo_types of `SHIPS` must satisfy this constraint. If the value being inherited does not satisfy this constraint, then the attribute's value is null.

## 2.5 Duplicates and Null Values

As specified above, an SDM class is either a set or a multiset: it may or may not contain duplicates. If a class has unique identifiers, then it obviously cannot have duplicates. If unique identifiers are not present, then the default is that duplicates are allowed. However, a class can be explicitly defined with "duplicates not allowed". Duplicates may also be present in attribute values, since attribute derivation specifications and mappings can yield duplicates.

In point of fact, the existence or nonexistence of duplicates is only of importance when considering the number of members in a class or the size of a multi-valued attribute. On most occasions, the user need not be concerned with whether or not duplicates are present. Consequently, the only SDM primitives that are affected by duplicates are those that concern the number of members in a class and the size of an attribute. The SDM interclass connections and attribute derivation primitives are defined so as to propagate duplicates in an intuitive manner. For example, attribute-defined and user-controllable subclasses contain duplicates if and only if their parent class contains duplicates; and, if the class underlying a grouping class has duplicates, the contents of the groups will similarly contain duplicates. Further details of this approach to handling duplicates are provided in [Mcl78].

As stated above, any attribute not defined as "mandatory" may have "null" as its value. While the treatment of null values is not a simple issue, we state that for the purposes here null is treated just like any other data value. A detailed discussion of null value handling is beyond the scope of this paper (see [Cod79] for such a discussion).

## 2.6 SDM Data Definition Language

As noted above, this paper provides a specific *database definition language (DDL)* for SDM. The foregoing description of SDM did not rely on a specific DDL syntax, although the discussion proceeded through numerous examples expressed in a particular sample

DDL syntax. Many forms of DDL syntax could be used to describe SDM schemas, and we have selected one of them in order to make the specification of SDM precise.

The syntax of SDM DDL is presented in Appendix B, expressed in Backus-Naur Form style. The particular conventions used are described at the beginning of Appendix II. For the most part, the syntax description is self-explanatory; however, the following points are worthy of note:

1. Syntactic categories are capitalized (with no interspersed spaces, but possibly including "_"s). All lower-case strings are in the language itself, except those enclosed in "*"s; the latter are descriptions of syntactic categories whose details are obvious.
2. Indentation is an essential part of the SDM DDL syntax. In Appendix II, the first level of indentation is used for presentation, while all others indicate indentation in the syntax itself. For example, `MEMBER_ATTRIBUTES` is defined as consisting of "member attributes", followed by a group of one or more member attribute items (placed vertically below "member attributes").
3. Many rules that constrain the set of legal SDM schemata are not included in the syntax shown in the figure. For example, in SDM, the rule that attributes of different applicability (member attributes and class attributes) must not be mixed is not included in the syntax, as its incorporation therein would be too cumbersome. A similar statement can be made for the rules that arithmetic expressions must be computed on attributes whose values are numbers, that a common underlying class must exist for classes defined by multiset operator interclass connections, and so forth.

### 2.7 Operations on an SDM Database

An important part of any database model is the set of operations that can be performed on it. The operations defined for SDM allow a user to derive information from a database, to update a database (adding new information to it or correcting information in it), and to include new structural information in it (change an SDM schema) [Mcl78]. Note that operations to derive information from an SDM schema are closely related to SDM primitives for describing derived information (e.g., nonbase classes and derived attributes). There is a vocabulary of basic SDM operations, which are application environment independent and pre-defined. The set of permissible operations is designed to permit only semantically meaningful manipulations of an SDM database. User-defined operations can be constructed using the primitives. A detailed specification of the SDM operations is beyond the scope of this paper.

## 3. DISCUSSION

In this paper, we have presented the major features of SDM, a high-level data modeling mechanism. The goal of SDM is to provide the designer and user of a database with a formalism whereby a substantial portion of the semantic structure of the application environment can be clearly and precisely expressed. Contemporary database models do not support such direct conceptual modeling, for a number of reasons that are summarized above and explored in greater detail in [Ham80]. In brief, these conventional database models are too oriented towards computer data structures to allow for the natural expression of application semantics. SDM, on the other hand, is based on the high-level concepts of entities, attributes, and classes.

In several ways, SDM is analogous to a number of recent proposals in database modeling, including [Abr74, Bac77, Bun79, Che76, Cod79, Pir77, Rou77, Shi81, Smi77, Smi77, Smi79, Sus79]. Where SDM principally differs from these is in the extent of the structure of the application domain that it can capture and in its emphasis on relativism, flexibility, and redundancy. An SDM schema does more than just describe the kinds of objects that are captured in the database; it allows for substantial amounts of structural information that specifies how the entities and their classes are related to one another. Furthermore, it is a fundamental premise of SDM that a semantic schema for a database should directly support multiple ways of viewing the same information, since different users inevitably will have differing slants on the database and even a single user's perspective will evolve over time. Consequently, redundant information (in the form of nonbase classes and derived attributes) plays an important role in an SDM schema, and provides the principal mechanism for expressing multiple versions of the same information.

## 3.1 The Design of SDM

In the design of SDM, we have sought to provide a higher-level and richer modeling language than that of conventional database models, without developing a large and complex facility containing a great many features (as exemplified by some of the knowledge representation and world modeling systems developed by the artificial intelligence community, e.g., [Sch73, Won77]). We have sought neither absolute minimality, with a small number of mutually orthogonal constructs, nor a profusion of special case facilities to precisely model each slightly different type of application. There is a significant trade-off between the complexity of a modeling facility and its power, naturalness, and precision. If a database model contains a large number of features, then it will likely be difficult to learn and to apply; however, it will have the potential of realizing schemas that are very sharp and precise models of their application domains. On the other hand, a model with a fairly minimal set of features will be easier to learn and employ, but a schema constructed with it will capture less of the particular characteristics of its application. We have sought a middle road between these two extremes, with a relatively small number of basic features, augmented by a set of special features that are particularly useful in a large number of instances. We adhere to the principle of the well-known "80-20" rule; in this context, this rule would suggest that 80 percent of the modeling cases can be handled with 20 percent of the total number of special features that would be required by a fully detailed modeling formalism. Thus, a user of SDM should find that the application constructs that he most frequently encounters are directly provided by SDM, while he will have to represent the less common ones by means of more generic features. To this end, we have included such special facilities as the inverse and matching mechanisms for attribute derivation, but have not, for example, sought to taxonomize entity types more fully (since to do so in a meaningful and useful way would greatly expand the size and complexity of SDM). We have also avoided the introduction of a huge number of attribute derivation primitives, limiting ourselves to the ones that should be of most critical importance. For example, there does not exist a derivation primitive for class attributes to determine what percentage the members of the class constitute of another class. Such special cases would be most usefully handled by means of a general-purpose computational mechanism.

SDM as presented in this paper is neither complete nor final. SDM as a whole is open to any number of extensions. The most significant omission in this paper is that of the operations that can be applied to an SDM database: the database manipulation facility associated with the database definition facility presented here. Such a presentation would be too lengthy for this paper, and can be found in [Mcl78]. In brief, however, the design of SDM is strongly based on the duality principle between schema and procedure, as developed in [Ham78]. From this perspective, any query against the database can be seen as a reference to a particular virtual data item; whether that item can easily be accessed in the database, or whether it can only be located by means of the application of a number of database manipulation operations, depends on what information has been included in the schema by the database designer. Frequently retrieved data items would most likely be present in the schema, often as derived data, while less commonly requested information would have to be dynamically computed. In both cases, however, the same sets of primitives should be employed to describe the data item(s) in question, since dynamic data retrieval and static definitions of derived data are fundamentally equivalent, differing only in the occasions of their binding. Thus, the SDM database manipulation facility strongly resembles the facilities described above for computing nonbase classes and derived attributes. Among other beneficial consequences, this duality allows for a natural evolution of the semantic schema to reflect changing patterns of use and access: as certain kinds of requests become more common, they can be incorporated as derived data into the schema and thereby greatly simplify their retrieval.

### 3.2 Extensions

Numerous extensions can be made to SDM as presented here. These include extending SDM by means of additional general facilities, as well as tailoring special versions of it (by adding application environment specific facilities). For example, as it currently is defined, derived data is continuously updated so as always to be consistent with the primitive data from which it is computed. Alternative, less dynamic modes of computation could be provided, so that in some cases derived data might represent a snapshot of some other aspect of the database at a certain time. Similarly, a richer set of attribute inheritance rules, possibly under user control, might be provided to enable more complex relationships between classes and their subclasses. In the other direction, a current investigation is being conducted with the goal of simplifying SDM and accommodating more relativism [Mcl79]. Further, an attempt is currently under way to construct a version of SDM that contains primitives especially relevant to the office environment (such as documents, events, and organization hierarchies), to facilitate the natural modeling and description of office structures and procedures.

### 3.3 Applications

We envision a variety of potential uses and applications for SDM. As described in this paper, SDM is simply an abstract database modeling mechanism and language, which is not dependent on any supporting computer system. One set of applications uses SDM in precisely this mode to support the process of defining and designing a database, as well as in facilitating its subsequent evolution. It is well known that the process of logical database design, wherein the database administrator (DBA) must construct a schema using the database model of the database management system (DBMS) to be employed, is a difficult and error-prone procedure [Che78,Mcl79,Myl78,Sen75,Sen77,Smi78,Sol79,Wie79]. A primary reason for this difficulty is the distance between the semantic level of the application and the data structures of the database model; the DBA must bridge this gap in a single step, simultaneously conducting an information requirements analysis and expressing the results of his analysis in terms of the database model. What is lacking is a formalism in which to express the information content of the database in a way that is independent of the details of the database model associated with the underlying DBMS. SDM can be used as a higher-level database model in which the DBA describes the database prior to designing a logical schema for it. There are a number of advantages to using the SDM in this way:

1. An SDM schema will serve as a specification of the information that the database will contain. All too often, only the most vague and amorphous English language descriptions of a database exist prior to the database design process. A formal specification can more accurately, completely, and consistently communicate to the actual designer the prescribed contents of the database. SDM provides some structure for the logical database design process. The DBA can first seek to describe the database in high level, semantic terms, and then reduce that schema to a more conventional logical design. By decomposing the design problem in this way, its difficulty as a whole can be reduced.
2. SDM supports a basic methodology that can guide the DBA in the design process by providing him with a set of natural design templates. That is, the DBA can approach the application in question with the intent of identifying its classes, subclasses, and so on. Having done so, he can select representations for these constructs in a routine, if not algorithmic, fashion.
3. SDM provides an effective base for accommodating the evolution of the content, structure, and use of a database. Relativism, logical redundancy, and derived information support this natural evolution of schemas.

A related use of SDM is as a medium for documenting a database. One of the more serious problems facing a novice user of a large database is determining the information content of the database, and locating in the schema the information of use to him. An SDM schema for a database can serve as a readable description of its contents, organized in terms that a user is likely to be able to comprehend and identify. A cross-index of the schema would amount to a semantic data dictionary, identifying the principal features of the application environment and cataloguing their relationships. Such specifications and documentation would also be independent of the DBMS being employed to actually manage the data, and so could be of particular use in the context of DBMS selection or of a conversion from one DBMS to another. An example of the use of the SDM for specification and documentation is [Com79].

On another plane are a number of applications that require that the SDM schema for a database be processed and utilized by a computer system. One such application would be to employ the SDM as the conceptual schema database model for a DBMS within the three-schema architecture of the ANSI/SPARC proposal [Ans75]. In such a system, the conceptual schema is a representation of the fundamental semantics of the database. The external views of the data (those employed by programmers and end-users) are defined in terms of it, while a mapping from it to physical file structures establishes the database's internal schema (storage and representation). Because of its high level and support for multiple views, SDM could be effectively employed in this role. Once occupying such a central position in the DBMS, the SDM schema could also be used to support any number of "intelligent" database applications that depend on a rich understanding of the semantics of the data in question. For example, an SDM schema could drive an automatic semantic integrity checker, which would examine incoming data and test its plausibility and likelihood of error in the context of a semantic model of the database. A number of such systems have been proposed [Esw75,Ham75,Ham76,Sto74], but they are generally based on the use of expressions in the first-order predicate calculus that are added to a relational schema. This approach introduces a number of problems, ranging from the efficiency of the checking to the modularity and reliability of the resulting model. By directly capturing the semantics in the schema rather than in some external mechanism, SDM might more directly support such data checking. Another "semantics-based" application to which SDM has been applied is an interactive system that assists a naive user, unfamiliar with the information content of the database, in formulating a query against it [Mcl79].

It might even be desirable to employ SDM as the database model in terms of which all database users see the database. This would entail building an SDM DBMS. Of course, a high level database model raises serious problems of efficiency of representation and processing. However, it can also result in easier and more effective use of the data, which may in the aggregate dominate the performance issues. Furthermore, SDM can be additionally extended to be more than just a database model; it can serve as the foundation for a total integrated database programming language, in which both the facilities for accessing a database and those for computing with the data so accessed are combined in a coherent and consistent fashion [Ham80a]. And, SDM can provide a basis for describing and structuring logically decentralized and physically distributed database systems [Ham79,Mcl80b].

## ACKNOWLEDGMENTS

The authors are most grateful to the following persons who have commented on the current or earlier versions of this paper, SDM, and related work: Antonio Albano, Arvola Chan, Peter Chen, Ted Codd, Dennis Heimbigner, Roger King, Peter Kreps, Frank Manola, Paula Newman, Diane and John Smith. In particular, Diane and John Smith helped the authors realize some of the weaknesses of an earlier version of SDM vis-a-vis relativism. Ted Codd's RM/T model has also provided many ideas concerning the specifics of SDM. DAPLEX (of Dave Shipman) and FQL (of Peter Buneman and Robert Frankel) have aided us in formulating various SDM constructs (e.g., mapping). Work performed at the Computer Corporation of America (under Frank Manola) and at the Lockheed California Company (under Don Kawamoto) have provided valuable input regarding the practical use of SDM. Finally, the referees provided many helpful comments concerning both the substance and presentation of this paper; their observations and suggestions are gratefully acknowledged.

Note: Because of the lack of neuter personal pronouns in English, the terms "he", "his", etc., are used throughout this paper to refer to an individual who may be either male or female.

## APPENDIX A - AN SDM SCHEMA FOR THE TANKER MONITORING APPLICATION ENVIRONMENT

```
SHIPS
   description: all ships with potentially hazardous cargos that
      may enter U.S. coastal waters
   member attributes:
      Name
         value class: SHIP_NAMES
      Hull_number
         value class: HULL_NUMBERS
         may not be null
         not changeable
      Type
         description: the kind of ship, e.g., merchant or fishing
         value class: SHIP_TYPE_NAMES
      Country_of_registry
         value class: COUNTRIES
         inverse: Ships_registered_here
      Name_of_home_port
         value class: PORT_NAMES
      Cargo_types
         description: the type(s) of cargo the ship can carry
         value class: CARGO_TYPE_NAMES
         multi-valued
      Captain
         description: the current captain of the ship
         value class: OFFICERS
         match: Officer of ASSIGNMENTS on Ship
      Engines
         value class: ENGINES
```

```
            multi-valued with size between 0 and 10
            exhausts value class
            no overlap in values
         Incidents_involved_in
            value class: INCIDENTS
            inverse: Involved_ship
            multi-valued
      identifiers:
         Name
         Hull_number
   INSPECTIONS
      description: inspections of oil tankers
      member attributes:
         Tanker
            description: the tanker inspected
            value class: OIL_TANKERS
            inverse: Inspections
         Date
            value class: DATES
         Order_for_tanker
            description: the ordering of the inspections for a tanker
               with the most recent inspection having value 1
            value class: INTEGERS
            derivation: order by decreasing Date within Tanker
      class attributes:
         Number
            description: the number of inspections in the database
            value class: INTEGERS
            derivation: number of members in this class
      identifiers:
         Tanker + Date
   COUNTRIES
      description: countries of registry for ships
      member attributes:
         Name
            value class: COUNTRY_NAMES
         Ships_registered_here
            value class: SHIPS
            inverse: Country_of_registry
            multi-valued
      identifiers:
         Name
   OFFICERS
      description: all certified officers of ships
      member attributes:
         Name
            value class: PERSON_NAMES
         Country_of_license
            value class: COUNTRIES
         Date_commissioned
            value class: DATES
         Seniority
            value class: INTEGERS
            derivation: order by Date_commissioned
         Commander
            description: the officer in direct command of this officer
            value class: OFFICERS
         Superiors
            value class: OFFICERS
```

```
            derivation: all levels of values of Commander
            inverse: Subordinates
            multi-valued
         Subordinates
            value class: OFFICERS
            inverse: Superiors
            multi-valued
         Contacts
            value class: OFFICERS
            derivation: where is in Superiors or is in Subordinates
      identifiers:
         Name
   ENGINES
      description: ship engines
      member attributes:
         Serial_number
            value class: ENGINE_SERIAL_NUMBERS
         Kind_of_engine
            value class: ENGINE_TYPE_NAMES
         identifiers:
            Serial_number
   INCIDENTS
      description: accidents involving ships
      member attributes:
         Involved_ship
            value class: SHIPS
            inverse: Incidents_involved_in
         Date
            value class: DATES
         Description
            description: textual explanation of the accident
            value class: INCIDENT_DESCRIPTIONS
         Involved_captain
            value class: OFFICERS
         identifiers:
            Involved_ship + Date + Description
   ASSIGNMENTS
      description: assignments of captains to ships
      member attributes:
         Officer
            value class: OFFICERS
         Ship
            value class: SHIPS
         identifiers:
            Officer + Ship
   OIL_TANKERS
      description: oil-carrying ships
      interclass connection: subclass of SHIPS where Cargo_types
         contains 'oil'
      member attributes:
         Hull_type
            description: specification of single or double hull
            value class: HULL_TYPE_NAMES
         Is_tanker_banned?
            value class: YES/NO
            derivation: if in BANNED_SHIPS
         Inspections
            value class: INSPECTIONS
            inverse: Tanker
```

```
            multi-valued
         Number_of_times_inspected
            value class: INTEGERS
            derivation: number of unique members in Inspections
         Last_inspection
            value class: MOST_RECENT_INSPECTIONS
            inverse: Tanker
         Last_two_inspections
            value class: INSPECTIONS
            derivation: subvalue of Inspections where
               Order_for_tanker ≤ 2
            multi-valued
         Date_last_examined
            value class: DATES
            derivation: same as Last_inspection.Date
         Oil_spills_involved_in
            value class: INCIDENTS
            derivation: subvalue of Incidents_involved_in
               where is in OIL_SPILLS
            multi-valued
      class attributes:
         Absolute_top_legal_speed
            value class: KNOTS
         Top_legal_speed_in_miles_per_hour
            value class: MILES_PER_HOUR
            derivation: = Absolute_top_legal_speed / 1.1
   RURITANIAN_SHIPS
      interclass connection: subclass of SHIPS where
         Country.Name = 'Ruritania'
   RURITANIAN_OIL_TANKERS
      interclass connection: subclass of OIL_TANKERS where
         Country.Name = 'Ruritania'
   MERCHANT_SHIPS
      interclass connection: subclass of SHIPS where Type = 'merchant'
      member attributes:
         Cargo_types
           value class: MERCHANT_CARGO_TYPE_NAMES
   OIL_SPILLS
      interclass connection: subclass of INCIDENTS where
         Description = 'oil spill'
      member attributes:
         Amount_spilled
            value class: GALLONS
         Severity
            derivation: = Amount_spilled / 100000
      class attributes:
         Total_spilled
            value class: GALLONS
            derivation: sum of Amount_spilled over members of this class
   MOST_RECENT_INSPECTIONS
      interclass connection: subclass of INSPECTIONS where
         Order_for_tanker = 1
   DANGEROUS_CAPTAINS
      description: captains who have been involved in an accident
      interclass connection: subclass of OFFICERS where is a value of
         Involved_captain of INCIDENTS
   BANNED_SHIPS
      description: ships banned from U.S. coastal waters
      interclass connection: subclass of SHIPS where specified
```

```
    member attributes:
       Date_banned
          value class: DATES
 OIL_TANKERS_REQUIRING_INSPECTION
    interclass connection: subclass of OIL_TANKERS where specified
 BANNED_OIL_TANKERS
    interclass connection: subclass of SHIPS where
       is in BANNED_SHIPS and is in OIL_TANKERS
 SAFE_SHIPS
    description: ships that are considered good risks
    interclass connection: subclass of SHIPS where is not in BANNED_SHIPS
 SHIPS_TO_BE_MONITORED
    description: ships that are considered bad risks
    interclass connection: subclass of SHIPS where is in BANNED_SHIPS
       or is in OIL_TANKERS_REQUIRING_INSPECTION
 SHIP_TYPES
    description: types of ships
    interclass connection: grouping of SHIPS on common value of Type
       groups defined as classes are MERCHANT_SHIPS
    member attributes:
       Instances
          description: the instances of the type of ship
          value class: SHIPS
          derivation: same as Contents
          multi-valued
       Number_of_ships_of_this_type
          value class: INTEGERS
          derivation: number of members in Contents
 CARGO_TYPE_GROUPS
    interclass connection: grouping of SHIPS on common value of
       Cargo_types
 TYPES_OF_HAZARDOUS_SHIPS
    interclass connection: grouping of SHIPS consisting of classes
       BANNED_SHIPS, BANNED_OIL_TANKERS,
       SHIPS_TO_BE_MONITORED
 CONVOYS
    interclass connection: grouping of SHIPS as specified
    member attributes:
       Oil_tanker_constituents
          description: the oil tankers that are in the convoy (if any)
          value class: SHIPS
          derivation: subvalue of Contents where is in OIL_TANKERS
          multi-valued
 CARGO_TYPE_NAMES
    description: the types of cargo
    interclass connection: subclass of STRINGS
 MERCHANT_CARGO_TYPE_NAMES
    interclass connection: subclass of CARGO_TYPE_NAMES where specified
 COUNTRY_NAMES
    interclass connection: subclass of STRINGS where specified
 ENGINE_SERIAL_NUMBERS
    interclass connection: subclass of STRINGS where format is
    "H"
    number where integer and ≥ 1 and ≤ 999
    "-"
    number where integer and ≥ 0 and ≤ 999999
 DATES
    description: calendar dates in the range "1/1/75" to "12/31/79"
    interclass connection: subclass of STRINGS where format is
```

```
        month: number where ≥ 1 and ≤ 12
        "/"
        day: number where integer and ≥ 1 and ≤ 31
        "/"
        year: number where integer and ≥ 1970 and ≤ 2000
        where (if (month = 4 or = 5 or = 9 or = 11) then day ≤ 30)
           and (if month = 2 then day ≤ 29)
        ordering by year, month, day
ENGINE_TYPE_NAMES
   interclass connection: subclass of STRINGS where specified
GALLONS
   interclass connection: subclass of STRINGS where format is number
      where integer
HULL_NUMBERS
   interclass connection: subclass of STRINGS where format is number
      where integer
HULL_TYPE_NAMES
   description: single or double
   interclass connection: subclass of STRINGS where specified
INCIDENT_DESCRIPTIONS
   description: textual description of an accident
   interclass connection: subclass of STRINGS
KNOTS
   interclass connection: subclass of STRINGS where format is
      number where integer
MILES_PER_HOUR
   interclass connection: subclass of STRINGS where format is
      number where integer
PORT_NAMES
   interclass connection: subclass of STRINGS
PERSON_NAMES
   interclass connection: subclass of STRINGS
SHIP_NAMES
   interclass connection: subclass of STRINGS
SHIP_TYPE_NAMES
   description: the names of the ship types, e.g., merchant
   interclass connection: subclass of STRINGS where specified
```

## APPENDIX B - SYNTAX OF THE SDM DATA DEFINITION LANGUAGE

The following list is given to clarify and define some of the items and terms used in this appendix.

1. The left side of a production is separated from the right by a "←".
2. The first level of indentation in the syntax description is used to help separate the left and right sides of a production; all other indentation is in the SDM data definition language.
3. Syntactic categories are capitalized, while all literals are in lowercase.
4. { } - means optional
5. [ ] - means one of the enclosed choices must appear; choices are separated by a ";" (when used with "{ }" one of the choices may optionally appear).

6. ⟨ ⟩ - means one or more of the enclosed can appear, separated by spaces with optional commas and an optional "and" at the end.
7. ⟨⟨ ⟩⟩ - means one or more of the enclosed can appear, vertically appended.
8. * * - encloses a "meta"-description of a syntactic category (to informally explain it).

```
SCHEMA ←
   ⟨⟨CLASS⟩⟩
CLASS ←
   ⟨CLASS_NAME⟩
      {description: CLASS_DESCRIPTION}
      {[BASE_CLASS_FEATURES; INTERCLASS_CONNECTION]}
      {MEMBER_ATTRIBUTES}
      {CLASS_ATTRIBUTES}
CLASS_NAME ←
   *string of capitals possibly including special characters*
CLASS_DESCRIPTION ←
  *string*
BASE_CLASS_FEATURES ←
   {[duplicates allowed; duplicates not allowed]}
   {⟨⟨IDENTIFIERS⟩⟩}
IDENTIFIERS ←
   [ATTRIBUTE_NAME; ATTRIBUTE_NAME + IDENTIFIERS]
MEMBER_ATTRIBUTES ←
   member attributes:
      ⟨⟨MEMBER_ATTRIBUTE⟩⟩
CLASS_ATTRIBUTES ←
   class attributes:
      ⟨⟨CLASS_ATTRIBUTE⟩⟩
INTERCLASS_CONNECTION ←
   [SUBCLASS; GROUPING_CLASS]
SUBCLASS ←
   subclass of CLASS_NAME where SUBCLASS_PREDICATE
GROUPING ←
   [grouping of CLASS_NAME on common value of ⟨ATTRIBUTE_NAME⟩
      {groups defined as classes are ⟨CLASS_NAME⟩};
   grouping of CLASS_NAME consisting of classes ⟨CLASS_NAME⟩;
   grouping of CLASS_NAME as specified]
SUBCLASS_PREDICATE ←
   [ATTRIBUTE_PREDICATE;
   specified;
   is in CLASS_NAME and is in CLASS_NAME;
   is not in CLASS_NAME;
   is in CLASS_NAME or is in CLASS_NAME;
   is a value of ATTRIBUTE_NAME of CLASS_NAME;
   format is FORMAT]
ATTRIBUTE_PREDICATE ←
   [SIMPLE_PREDICATE; (ATTRIBUTE_PREDICATE);
   not ATTRIBUTE_PREDICATE;
   ATTRIBUTE_PREDICATE and ATTRIBUTE_PREDICATE;
   ATTRIBUTE_PREDICATE or ATTRIBUTE_PREDICATE]
SIMPLE_PREDICATE ←
   [MAPPING SCALAR_COMPARATOR [CONSTANT; MAPPING];
   MAPPING SET_COMPARATOR [CONSTANT; CLASS_NAME; MAPPING]]
MAPPING ←
   [ATTRIBUTE_NAME; MAPPING.ATTRIBUTE_NAME]
SCALAR_COMPARATOR ←
```

```
    [EQUAL_COMPARATOR; >; ≥; <; ≤]
EQUAL_COMPARATOR ←
    [=; ≠]
SET_COMPARATOR ←
    [is {properly} contained in; {properly} contains]
CONSTANT ←
    *a string or number constant*
FORMAT ←
    *a name class definition pattern*
    (see [McLeod 1977])
MEMBER_ATTRIBUTE ←
    ⟨ATTRIBUTE_NAME⟩
        {ATTRIBUTE_DESCRIPTION}
        value class: CLASS_NAME
        {inverse: ATTRIBUTE_NAME}
        {[match: ATTRIBUTE_NAME of CLASS_NAME on ATTRIBUTE_NAME;
        derivation: MEMBER_ATTRIBUTE_DERIVATION]}
        {single-valued; multi-valued {with size between CONSTANT and CONSTANT}}
        {may not be null}
        {not changeable}
        {exhausts value class}
        {no overlap in values}
CLASS_ATTRIBUTE ←
    ⟨ATTRIBUTE_NAME⟩
        {ATTRIBUTE_DESCRIPTION}
        value class: CLASS_NAME
        {[derivation: CLASS_ATTRIBUTE_DERIVATION]}
        {single-valued; multi-valued {with size between CONSTANT and CONSTANT}}
        {may not be null}
        {not changeable}
ATTRIBUTE_NAME ←
    *string of lowercase letters beginning with a capital and possibly
    including special characters*
ATTRIBUTE_DESCRIPTION ←
    "*string*"
MEMBER_ATTRIBUTE_DERIVATION ←
    [INTER-ATTRIBUTE_DERIVATION;
    MEMBER-SPECIFIC_DERIVATION]
CLASS_ATTRIBUTE_DERIVATION ←
    [INTER-ATTRIBUTE_DERIVATION;
    CLASS-SPECIFIC_DERIVATION]
INTER-ATTRIBUTE_DERIVATION ←
    [same as MAPPING;
    subvalue of MAPPING where [is in CLASS_NAME; ATTRIBUTE_PREDICATE];
    where [is in MAPPING and is in MAPPING; is in MAPPING or is in
    MAPPING; is in MAPPING and is not in MAPPING];
    = MAPPING_EXPRESSION;
    [maximum; minimum; average; sum] of MAPPING;
    number of {unique} members in MAPPING]
MEMBER-SPECIFIC_DERIVATION ←
    [order by [increasing; decreasing] ⟨MAPPING⟩
    {within ⟨MAPPING⟩};
    if in CLASS_NAME;
    [up to CONSTANT; all] levels of values of ATTRIBUTE_NAME;
    contents]
CLASS-SPECIFIC_DERIVATION ←
    [number of {unique} members in this class;
    [maximum; minimum; average; sum] of ATTRIBUTE_NAME over
    members of this class]
```

```
MAPPING_EXPRESSION ←
   [MAPPING; (MAPPING); MAPPING NUMBER_OPERATOR MAPPING]
NUMBER_OPERATOR ←
   [+; -; *; /; !]
```

# 3

# CommonLoops: Merging Lisp and Object-Oriented Programming*

**Daniel G. Bobrow, Kenneth Kahn, Gregor Kiczales, Larry Masinter, Mark Stefik, and Frank Zdybel**

*Xerox Palo Alto Research Center*
*Palo Alto, California 94304*

## ABSTRACT

CommonLoops blends object-oriented programming smoothly and tightly with the procedure-oriented design of Lisp. Functions and methods are combined in a more general abstraction. Message passing is invoked via normal Lisp function call. Methods are viewed as partial descriptions of procedures. Lisp data types are integrated with object classes. With these integrations, it is easy to incrementally move a program between the procedure and object-oriented styles.

One of the most important properties of CommonLoops is its extensive use of meta-objects. We discuss three kinds of meta-objects: objects for classes, objects for methods, and objects for discriminators. We argue that these meta-objects make practical both efficient implementation and experimentation with new ideas for object-oriented programming.



Source: Adapted From Bobrow, D., K. Kahn, G. Kiczales, L. Masinter, M. Stefik, and F. Zdybel, "CommonLoops: Merging Lisp and Object-Oriented Programming", Proceedings of the ACM Conference on Object-Oriented Programming Systems, Languages, and Applications, September 1986, pp. 17–29. Copyright 1986, Association for Computing Machinery, Inc., reprinted by permission.

CommonLoops' small kernel is powerful enough to implement the major object-oriented systems in use today.

## INTRODUCTION

Over the last decade many systems have been written that add objects to Lisp (e.g., Flavors, Loops, ObjectLisp). Each of these has attracted a group of users that recognize the benefits of message sending and specialization and have endorsed an object-oriented style. The object languages in these systems have been embedded in Lisp with different degrees of integration.

Lisp continues to be an important and powerful language for symbol manipulation and is widely used for programming in artificial intelligence applications. One of Lisp's interesting strengths is its ability to absorb other languages, that is, its use as a base for implementing experimental languages.

Within the procedure-oriented paradigm, Lisp provides an important approach for factoring programs that is different from common practice in object-oriented programming. In this paper we present the linguistic mechanisms that we have developed for integrating these styles. We argue that the unification results in something greater than the sum of the parts, that is, that the mechanisms needed for integrating object-oriented and procedure-oriented approaches give CommonLoops surprising strength.

We describe a smooth integration of these ideas that can work efficiently in Lisp systems implemented on a wide variety of machines. We chose the Common Lisp dialect as a base on which to build CommonLoops (a Common Lisp Object-Oriented Programming System) because Common Lisp is supported on almost all commercial Lisp workstations. A portable implementation of CommonLoops is available and is being used in many Common Lisp implementations.

With respect to Lisp, CommonLoops has tried to satisfy a number of different, sometimes conflicting goals:

**Compatibility.** CommonLoops is compatible with Lisp's functional programming style. Message sending uses the same syntax as function call. Method definition is an extension of Lisp function definition. This is described in section I. Object space is defined as a natural extension of the Common Lisp type space. This is described in section II. Integrated syntax and type spaces allow incremental conversion of programs from a functional to an object-oriented style.

**Powerful base.** CommonLoops is rich enough for building interesting applications without the need for higher level object languages. It also provides several desirable extensions to object-oriented programming. Method lookup can be based on the class of more than one argument ( a "multi- method"). Behavior for an individual object can be specified.

**Portability.** CommonLoops provides a small kernel that is easy to integrate into Common Lisp implementations. CommonLoops is currently running in five different implementations of CommonLisp.

**Flexibility.** CommonLoops can be used to implement the major object languages in use today (e.g., Flavors, Smalltalk and Loops) as well as new languages like ObjectLisp. CommonLoops supports intercallability among objects from these different languages. The use of meta-objects in CommonLoops supports variations in object representation, method syntax, combination and optimization. This makes CommonLoops open-ended enough to support research and experimentation with future object and knowledge representation languages, while providing a base for standardization.

**Efficiency.** Using proven software techniques, described in section III, CommonLoops can run efficiently without special hardware support. This is important because Common Lisp runs on a wide variety of hardware bases.

## 1. METHODS AND FUNCTIONS

In Lisp, functions are applied to arguments. The code that is run is determined only by the name of the function. The lisp form

```
(foo a b)
```

can be interpreted in terms of a function calling primitive, funcall as:

```
(funcall (function-specified-by 'foo).
         a b).
```

In object-oriented systems one "sends messages" to objects. The code that is run is determined by both the name of the message and the type (class) of the object. Methods defined for a particular selector are associated with a class. In the next section we will indicate how we merge the ideas of Lisp datatypes and object classes. The following message using selector `sel`:

```
(send a 'sel b)
```

can be interpreted as the function call:

```
(funcall
 (method-specified-by 'sel (type-of a))
  a b).
```

The collection of all methods defined for `sel` define the "generic" function for that selector. Which method is run when a generic function is invoked is determined by the type of the first argument. Thus a method is a partial description of a generic function restricted to objects of a particular type. With this understanding of method invocation, we can reinterpret all standard Lisp calls:

```
(foo a b)
```

as meaning

```
(funcall
  (method-specified-by 'foo (type-of a))
  a b).
```

if there is a method defined for `foo` and `(type-of a)`. Some of the ideas described here were independently invented and implemented in New Flavors [Moo86b]. Because of their similarity, we will contrast CommonLoops with New Flavors where appropriate. We adapted their term, generic function, to describe the collection of methods for a selector.

A method for move applicable only when the first argument is of type block is defined in CommonLoops as follows:

```
(defmeth move ((obj block) x y)
  ⟨code for moving a block⟩)
```

The code for this method is added to the generic function for move, and is invoked for objects of type block, or any subtype. If there was an existing method for the same selector and type, `defmeth` replaces that method. To invoke this method, one simply writes:

```
(move block1 x-pos y-pos)
```

Given that `block1` is of type `block`, the code above will be invoked. Other methods for move could be defined for first argument being a window, a sketch, etc. If more than one method is applicable (because of subclassing), the most specific method is used.

## 1.1 Default Methods

If one uses the `defmeth` form without specifying any type as in:

```
(defmeth move (thing x y)  ...)
```

this code is run when no more specific method of the generic function for `move` is applicable. When only such a default method is supplied, it is like defining an ordinary Lisp function. There is no speed penalty for using such default methods instead of functions.

The difference between defining a default method and defining an ordinary Lisp function is that the latter is not allowed to be augmented by specialized method definitions. This protects users from inadvertently overriding or specializing predefined functions where perhaps special compilation optimizations have been used. For example, in most Lisp implementations calls to the primitives `car`, `cdr`, and `cons` are compiled specially for efficiency. Specializing these functions could either have disastrous effect on system efficiency, or no effect on previously compiled code.

However, it is often useful to be able to define methods which specialize existing Lisp functions. To make the Lisp function print specializable, one uses:

```
(make-specializable 'print
                    '(thing stream))
```

This declares that the pre-existing lisp function `print` is to become the default method for the generic function, and that additional methods can be added.

## 1.2 Multi-Methods

CommonLoops extends Lisp's function call even further. It allows the method to be specified in terms of the types of any number of arguments to the form. It interprets the form:

```
(foo a b)
```

as

```
(funcall (method-specified-by 'foo
                              (type-of a)
                              (type-of b)) a b)
```

Thus, unlike most other object-oriented schemes, CommonLoops allows method-lookup to be based on more than the class of the first argument. For example,

```
(defmeth insidep
   ((w window) (x integer) (y integer))
   ... )
```

defines the method for `insidep` when the first argument is a window and the second and third arguments are integers.

For any set of arguments, there may be several methods whose type specifications match. The most specific applicable method is called. Method specificity is determined by the specificity of the leftmost type specifiers which differ. However, as discussed below, other regimes can be implemented using the meta-objects facility.

## 1.3 Method and Discriminator Objects

In CommonLoops all the data-structures used to implement the system are objects. In particular, defining a method creates three objects, the *method*, the *discriminator* and the *discriminating-function.*

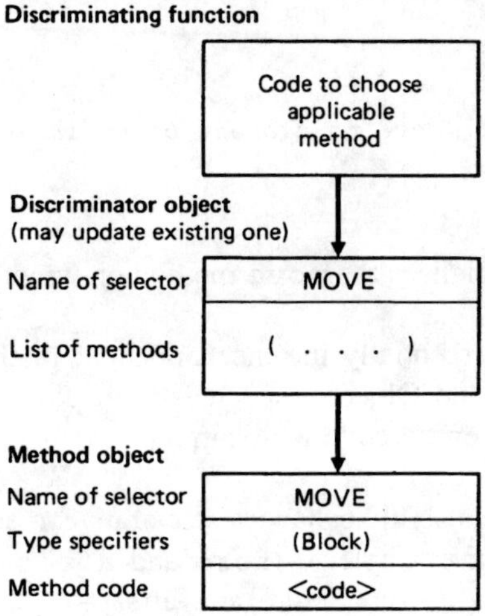


**Figure 3.1** These three objects are used for interpretation of a call. The discriminating function is the code object that selects the method to be called. The discriminator object describes the generic function and is used to construct the discriminating function. It uses the information in the method object; the method object is also used in the compilation of the code for the specific method.

The method object represents the method being defined. The method object contains the type-specifiers and the code for the method. The discriminator object contains a list of all the methods defined on a particular selector. Hence, it describes the generic function. Together, the discriminator and all of its methods produce the discriminating function, a piece of Lisp code which is called when the selector is invoked to determine which method to call. Because the method-lookup and calling mechanisms are under control of the discriminator and method objects, specialized method-lookup and method-combination mechanisms can be implemented by defining new classes of discriminators and methods which specialize parts of the method-lookup protocol.

One such special class are methods which are specialized to individuals. By this we mean that some methods are applicable only if called with a specific object as argument. For example, this would allow a special-case for a connection to a particular host on a network for some period of time when special rerouting needs to be done. Standard protocol makes a method applicable to an individual more specific than any method just specified on types.

## 1.4 Method Combination

Frequently, when one specializes behavior for a given class of object, the desire is to add only a little behavior to the methods of the super-classes.

The primary mechanism for method combination in CommonLoops is `run-super` which is defined to run the most specific method matching the arguments of the current method that is more general than the method in which the `run-super` occurs. If there is no such method an error is signaled.

For example,

```
(defmeth move
  ((w bounded-window)
   (x integer)
   (y integer))
  (cond ((in-bounds-p w x y)
(run-super))
        (t ...     ;; move to closest point inside
          (run-super))))
```

defines a method which specializes the move method on window so that it always moves in-bounds.

The `run-super` is essentially the mechanism of method combination found in Smalltalk, Loops, Director and Object-Lisp. It is both powerful and simple. It allows arbitrary combination of inherited code with current code using Lisp as the combination language.

Sometimes it is more useful to have a declarative means of specifying method combination. In Flavors, for example, `before` and `after` parts can be specified for any method, and these will be run before and after any directly specialized method without requiring any statement in the specialized method. `Before` and `after` parts can be attached any place in the inheritance chain, and are combined in a single method at definition time. In CommonLoops we implement this feature using a special discriminator object that indexes these parts and does the method combination. We have implemented in CommonLoops the interface for user defined method combination specified for New Flavors.

Method and discriminator objects are used to implement both `run-super` and the user defined method combination mechanism. This provides the flexibility of choosing either of the standard kinds of combination in use today. In addition, the existence of these meta-objects allows experimentation with other kinds of combination and invocation. We are currently looking at integrating logic programming into the CommonLoops framework. Logic programming requires specialized method and discriminator objects to combine method clauses using backtracking search.

## 1.5 Processing of Method Code

The code that implements a method is interpreted and compiled in a context in which the method object is available. The method can use information from the type-specifiers to optimize parts of the method body, or to provide special syntax within the body of the method to access the slots of arguments to the method. Because this processing is done using a defined protocol of messages to the method object, it can be extended by users.

## 2. DEFINING CLASSES

CommonLoops uses `defstruct` to define its classes, extending the syntax of the construct found in Common Lisp for defining composite structures.

```
(defstruct position
  (x-coord 0)
  (y-coord 0))
```

defines a class named `position`, and specifies that instances of that class should have two slots, `x-coord` and `y-coord`, each initialized to 0. As a side effect of defining this structure, `defstruct` also defines a function to make instances of type `position`, and functions `position-x-coord` and `position-y-coord` to access the slots of an instance. An updating form using `setf` and these access functions is used to change the values in the slots, e.g.:

```
(setf  (position-x-coord  i-1) 13)
```

In addition, `defstruct` can define an extension of a previously defined class.

```
(defstruct  (3d-position
              (:include position))
  (z-coord 0))
```

The new structure is a subclass of the old, and includes all of its slots and may add slots of its own. Thus `3d-position` has slots `x-coord`, `y-coord`, and `z-coord`, and inherits all methods defined on `position`.

### 2.1 Meta-classes

In CommonLoops, as in Smalltalk, classes are themselves instances of other classes. These special classes are known as meta-classes. The figure below indicates the relationships of the classes defined above, and their meta-class `structures-class`.

Meta-classes control the behavior of the class as a whole, and the class-related behavior of the instances such as initialization, as do Smalltalk meta-classes. In Flavors, the Flavors themselves are not instances of any Flavor, and hence their behavior is uniform.

In CommonLoops, meta-classes have important additional roles. A meta-class controls the interpretation of the defstruct form; it also controls the representation of instances of the class; it specifies the order of inheritance for classes; finally, it controls allocation and access to instance slots.

### 2.2 Interpreting the Defstruct Form

Because some meta-classes need to provide defstruct options not provided by other meta-classes, CommonLoops separates the interpretation of the defstruct form into two parts.

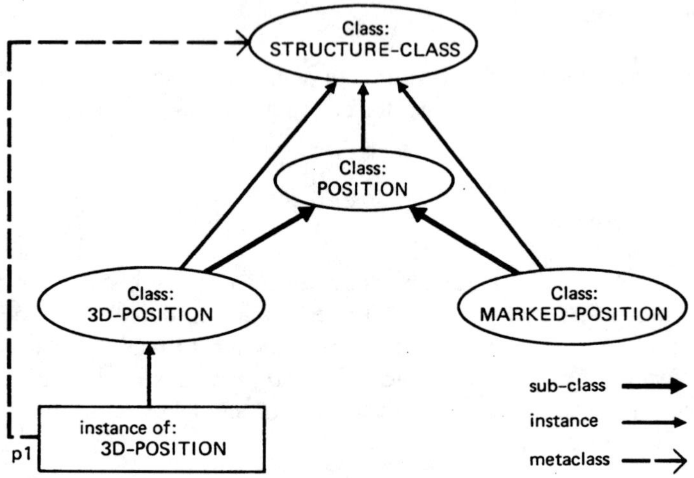


**Figure 3.2** Three different relations are illustrated in this diagram. 3d-position and marked-position are both subclasses of position, and inherit its structure and behavior. p1 is an instance of 3d-position, the three position classes are instances of structure-class. We call structure-class the "meta-class" of p1, since it is the class of its class.

In the first part, the defstruct is checked to make sure it conforms to basic `defstruct` syntax and the meta-class is determined by looking for a class option. Then `expand-defstruct` is called on the meta-class and the `defstruct` form. This allows the meta-class to process the `defstruct` form and interpret the options as it chooses.

## 2.3 Representation of Objects

Meta-classes control the representation of instances. Consider the following definitions of the class position:

```
(defstruct (position
             (:class structure-class))
  (x-coord 0)
  (y-coord 0)
(defstruct (position (:class class))
  (x-coord 0)
  (y-coord 0)
```

In the first definition, the `structure-class` meta-class is specified. An instance of position created using this definition will be represented as a linear block of storage with two data items. This is very efficient in space. The second definition specifies the meta-class `class` which causes the instances to be represented in a more flexible way, with a level of indirection between a header and the storage for the data. This allows such an instance to track any changes in its class (adding or deleting instance variables) without users of the instance needing to do anything to update the instance. Automatic updating occurs when access to slots is requested. The instance can even change its class, and invisibly update its structure. Because the meta-class is responsible for the implementation of the instance, it is also responsible for access to slots of the instance. We return to this below.

## 2.4 Multiple Inheritance

Many meta-classes allow multiple inheritance. These meta-classes extend the syntax of the `:include defstruct` option to allow a list of included classes. For example,

```
(defstruct
  (titled-window
    (:include (window titled-thing))))
```

defines a new-class, `titled-window`, which includes both `window` and `titled-thing` as super-classes. Under control of the meta-class, the new class will inherit slots from the super-classes. Although the usual inheritance for slots is to take the union of those specified in the included-classes, some meta-classes could signal an error if there were an overlap in names.

The class being defined is the root of a sub-lattice from which descriptions are inherited. The specified order of the included classes determines a local precedence among the classes. This is used as the basis of the precedence relation for specificity. The specificity of classes with respect to this new one is cached in the class as an ordered list that we call the *class precedence list*.

The meta-class determines the algorithm for computing the class precedence list from the local precedences. The algorithm used by the meta-class `class` is left to right, depth first up to joins, with the constraint that the local ordering of any local precedence list must be maintained. Except for the last constraint, this is the same as the algorithm used in Loops. The constraint is violated when a local precedence list contains C1 before C2, and C1 is somehow a super of C2. In this case, CommonLoops signals an error. This algorithm produces the same ordering as the one used in New Flavors.

## 2.5 Initial Classes in Common Loops

CommonLoops uses the flexibility provided by meta-classes to define classes which correspond to the primitive Lisp types. These classes are part of the same class lattice as all other CommonLoops classes. Thus the Lisp data-type space is included in the CommonLoops class lattice. This means that methods can be defined on the Lisp built-in classes as well as on types defined by defstruct. This is a significant difference from New Flavors.

As shown in Figure 3.3, CommonLoops provides several pre-defined meta-classes which provide functionality for structures of CommonLisp, the built-in types, and the meta-class `class` designed to facilitate exploratory programming [She84]. The user can define a new meta-class to provide other functionality for a different object system. For example, with Gary Drescher, we have looked at defining a meta-class that supports ObjectLisp [Drexx] inheritance and behavior.

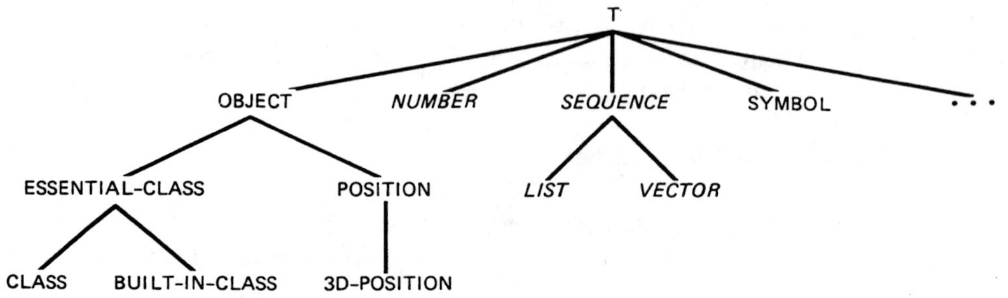


**Figure 3.3** Classes in italics are instances of `built-in-class`, all others are instances of `class`. `t` is the super-class of everything in CommonLoops. It corresponds to the Common Lisp type specifier of the same name. `essential-class` is a primitive class used to implement meta-classes. All meta-classes have `essential-class` as a super-class. It defines default behavior which all metaclasses must have.

## 2.6 Slot-Options in Class

The representation of instances used by `class` allows three additional allocation strategies for slots in addition to the usual direct allocation of storage in the instance. These provide facilities that have been found useful in a number of object systems. In each case, the user of the class does not need to change the form of access to change the form of allocation.

A `:class` allocation specifies that the slot is stored only in the class; no storage is allocated for it in the instances. Thus, the slot is shared by all instances of the structure. Updating the value in one instance is seen by all. This option provides functionality similar to class variables in Smalltalk and Loops, except that CommonLoops class variables share the same name space with instance variables.

A `:dynamic` allocation specifies that storage for this slot should be allocated in the instance, but only when the slot is first used. If the first access is a fetch, then storage is allocated, the `default-init` form is evaluated, the value is stored in the slot and returned. If the first access is a `setf`, then storage is allocated, the value is stored in the slot, and returned. This allows infrequently used slots to have initialization declarations, but take storage only if needed.

An allocation option of `:none` means that the slot should not exist in this instance. This is used to override inheritance of slots defined by a super class.

The meta-class `class` also allows objects to have slots that do not appear in the defstruct declaration. This gives objects their own property lists: this is analogous to Flavor's plist-mixin flavor. It differs from a plist-mixin in that there is uniform access to slots independent of whether they were declared.

# 3. COMMON LOOPS IMPLEMENTATION

CommonLoops can be implemented efficiently, even on conventional machines. The most important cases for time-critical applications are well understood and have been implemented in several object-oriented sytems.

### 3.1 Method Lookup

Implementation of method lookup can be specialized with respect to four cases: where there is only one method defined for a particular selector, where the only method has no type specification, where all the methods have specifiers only on their first argument, and the general case.

**Single method.** In this case there is only one non-default method defined on the selector. A static analysis of Loops and Flavors code shows that approximately 50% of the selectors fall in this category. In this case the method can be compiled with a type check to make sure it is applicable. The method-lookup time is only the time required to check the types of the arguments.

**Default method only.** This case is similar to the single method case except that the method has no type specifiers at all, so it is always applicable. In this case there is no type check required. It is implemented as if it were defined as a function.

**Classical methods only.** When there are multiple methods, all of which only have type specifiers on their first argument the situation is the same as in Smalltalk and Flavors. We call this "classical" to stress its equivalence to classical object programming systems. On stock hardware this can be implemented using any of the proven method-lookup caching schemes. The cache can either be a global cache, a selector-specific cache, a callee cache, or a caller cache. Variations have been used in Smalltalk-80 systems [Kra83], Loops, and Flavors. On specialized hardware this can be implemented using the same mechanisms as in Flavors. A default method can easily be combined with a set of classical methods, calling it instead of a standard error.

**Multiple multi-methods.** In the remaining case, a selector has more than one method, and at least one of them has a type specifier on other than the first argument. A standard case might have type specifiers for the first two arguments, e.g., where the types for show could be

```
(square, display-stream)
(square, print-stream)
(circle, display-stream)
...
```

In our current implementation of multi-method invocation, we have implemented a straightforward extension of the caching techniques used for classical method lookup. We do not have enough experience with multi-methods to know what other common patterns should be optimized.

In classical object-oriented programming, this example could be handled by introducing a second level of message sending. Instead of having separate multi-methods for each case, one could (by convention) write two methods for each case. Thus, the `show` message for square would send a second message to the stream (`show-square-on`) that would embed the type information about square implicitly in the selector.

Multi-method lookup in CommonLoops is faster than multiple sequential method lookups. The overhead for doing lookup is the time of an extra function call (a call to the discriminator function which then calls the chosen method) plus the time of a type check for each specialized argument.

### 3.2 Slot Access and Meta-classes

Slot access can be implemented in a variety of ways. The meta-class `class` uses a caching technique similar to that used in Smalltalk. The meta-class `structure-class`, because it does not allow multiple inheritance, can compile out the slot lookups in the standard way. Another meta-class could use the self-mapping-table technique used in Flavors.

We have also experimented with ways to compile out the cost of method lookup and slot lookup entirely. Having meta-classes and discriminator objects allows the specification of special ways of accomplishing a call to a selector when the types of some of the arguments are known at compile-time. In certain cases the appropriate method can be determined at compile-time so that no method lookup need occur at run-time. The body of the method can even be compiled in-line.

Compilation of calls to accessor functions is a common case where in-line expansion works well. The resulting code can access the slot directly. Meta-classes which do this kind of optimization are useful in production versions of applications where the time to change a program vs. program execution speed tradeoffs can be pushed completely towards execution speed.

Flexibility to use different slot-access or method-lookup schemes based on the meta-class is an important feature of CommonLoops. Efficiency is a matter of tradeoffs. Object systems without meta-classes must choose one set of tradeoffs and implement it as well as possible. Then, users have to live with it. In CommonLoops, several different sets of tradeoffs can be implemented as well as allowing users to choose which set of tradeoffs is appropriate for a given situation.

## 4. COMMONLOOPS AND OTHER SYSTEMS

In this section we consider several important object-oriented languages. All of these languages have been influential in the design of CommonLoops, and we try to note similarities and differences. A general overview of features of object languages and multi-paradigm systems can be found in [Ste86b].

### 4.1 Loops

Loops [Bob83] is a multi-paradigm system for knowledge programming implemented in Interlisp-D. It is integrated into the interactive environment provided by Interlisp-D. It also provides special environmental capabilities, such as classbrowsers and object inspectors. The design of CommonLoops draws on our experience with Loops, but is a major departure from it.

CommonLoops provides new functionality but also introduces many minor incompatibilities and lacks some functionality of Loops as discussed below. Features of Loops such as composite-objects that are appropriately implemented in terms of the CommonLoops kernel are not discussed. Modifying Loops to run on top of CommonLoops will require a substantial programming effort.

***Class variables.*** Loops supports the notion of class variables that are accessed via special functions. CommonLoops provides class variables which provide nearly equivalent functionality. There are not, however, different name spaces for instance variables and class variables as there are in Loops. We now believe that the advantages for modifiability of a program outweigh the advantages of multiple name spaces.

***Default values.*** Loops supports the notion of a default value which at slot access time finds the default value in the class or the super classes of the class. CommonLoops provides init-forms in slot-descriptions that specify how to compute the default value at creation time. The Loops behavior can be implemented in CommonLoops using annotated values as described in the section on open design questions. In our experience, initial values are satisfactory for most of the applications of default values.

***Slot properties.*** In Loops a slot can have named properties in addition to a value. This provides a convenient way to store more information about a value without interfering with access of the value. This can be supported using annotated values.

***Active values.*** In Loops a value can be active, so that specified functions can be run when a slot containing an active value is accessed. CommonLoops can provide comparable capabilities, as discussed below in the section on open design questions.

## 4.2 Smalltalk-80 System

The Smalltalk-80 system [Gol83] is both an object-oriented programming language and a vertically integrated programming environment that is uniformly object structured. The strength and importance of the Smalltalk-80 system rests not only with its object-oriented programming style, but also in the careful engineering of the set of kernel classes and their behavior that define the Smalltalk-80 image.

In terms of its provisions for class definition, name lookup, method discrimination, and method combination CommonLoops can be viewed as a superset of Smalltalk-80, with some notable exceptions:

The Smalltalk-80 virtual machine directly supports only single superclass inheritance. Nevertheless, additional inheritance schemes can be implemented (by changing the manner in which new classes are defined) and multiple superclass inheritance is included as part of the standard Smalltalk-80 environment. It operates substantially the same as in CommonLoops, except that multiple inherited methods for the same selector must be redefined at the common subclass, or else an error will result when the method is invoked. This Smalltalk-80 feature is inconvenient for mixin classes that specialize standard methods as used in Flavors and Loops.

The Smalltalk-80 multiple inheritance scheme provides an explicit scheme for method combination: objects can send messages to themselves in a way that specifies from which superclass method lookup is to proceed. This is done by composing the name of the superclass with the selector, e.g., an instance of ReadWriteStream may send itself the message ReadStream next to indicate that the ReadStream superclass is to supply the method. This explicitness can cause problems because methods build in as constants information about the class hierarchy, which may change.

Classes and meta-classes bear the same relationship to each other and there is some overlap of function in both systems. However, there are some significant differences in functionality. Instances of all Smalltalk classes (except for the compiled method class) are realized in terms of just three basic implementations: pointer objects, word objects, and byte objects. The class definition is to be used. By convention in Smalltalk each class has a unique meta-class.

In Smalltalk enumerating the instances of a class is intended to be computationally bearable (just how bearable depends on implementation dependent factors, e.g., whether and how virtual memory is implemented.) As a result, Smalltalk classes can broadcast to their instances. This makes them extensional, as well as intensional, characterizations of sets of objects. Since even integers have a class in CommonLoops, it is not generally useful to enumerate all instances of every class. It is straightforward in CommonLoops to implement a meta-class that allows a class to keep a list of instances it has created.

In the Smalltalk-80 system, one can find all references to most types of objects. It is even possible to interchange all the references to an object with all the references to some other object, regardless of their respective classes. In effect, the two objects exchange identities. This operation is inexpensive if the object memory indirects references via an object table, which is the standard practice. This capability enables, among other things, cheap re-sizing of instances of variable length classes. In CommonLoops, instances of classes created by the meta-class `class` can easily modify their contents and class pointers to achieve the same functionality.

Smalltalk provides class variables, which are shared by all the instances of a class and its subclasses, and pool variables, which are shared by all instances of some set of classes and their subclasses. The effect of class variables is directly achieved in CommonLoops through the allocation class slot option. The effect of Smalltalk's pool variables can be achieved through the expedient of defining a common superclass among the classes to be "pooled", which contributes nothing but a shared slot.

Smalltalk differs more fundamentally from CommonLoops in that Smalltalk objects are encapsulated, and control primitives are based upon message passing. In Smalltalk, unlike CommonLoops, only methods of an object can access and update the state directly (this is not strictly true, but the operations provided for breaking encapsulation are viewed as just that, and used primarily for building debuggers, viewers, etc.). All other methods must send messages.

Conditionals, iteration, and the like in Smalltalk are done via message passing, and contexts (stack frames) are first-class objects. CommonLoops relies upon the Common Lisp control constructs which in general are special forms and cannot be specialized.

## 4.3 New Flavors

CommonLoops is practically a superset of New Flavors. CommonLoops and Flavors share the notion of generic function. In developing CommonLoops we have included the Flavors mechanism for user-defined method combination.

The New Flavors algorithm for computing class-precedence is a refinement of the old Flavors algorithm which solves problems found in old Flavors, Loops and earlier versions of CommonLoops. We have described our equivalent to the New Flavors algorithm.

To be entirely compatible with New Flavors, CommonLoops would need to provide some syntactic support for the mechanisms for defining classes and methods. Machine dependent support is also necessary (and easily added) to provide the performance on microcoded machines.

The important difference between CommonLoops and New Flavors is the existence of meta-objects in CommonLoops. Meta-objects make CommonLoops much more extensible. Meta-objects allow experimentation with other kinds of object systems. They allow CommonLoops to treat primitive Lisp types as classes. Methods can be defined on those types, and the standard CommonLoops mechanisms for accessing the slots of a structure can be used to access the fields of primitive Lisp objects.

### 4.4 Other Object Languages

ObjectLisp [Drexx] also integrates objects and Lisp. Unlike CommonLoops, ObjectLisp distinguishes fundamentally between Lisp types and ObjectLisp objects. This means that one cannot define methods on existing types. Another difference is that ObjectLisp supports only classical methods.

T shares with CommonLoops the common syntax for message sending and function call. Like ObjectLisp, T supports only classical methods and there is no integration of Lisp types with objects. [Ree82]

## 5. OPEN DESIGN QUESTIONS

In this section we present some extensions to CommonLoops which seem attractive, and which suggest directions for future research.

### 5.1 Complex Type Specifiers

Extending CommonLoops to handle more complex type specifiers is attractive. The simplest extension is to allow logical combinations of the simpler type specifiers, for example

```
(or block window)
```

Another extension would be to allow an arbitrary predicate to be used. Yet another extension would allow specification based on the number of arguments.

The problem occurs when there are ambiguities about which method to use. For example, which of the two:

```
(or block window) (or block house)
```

is more specific with respect to `block`.

For this reason, we have chosen to disallow method type-specifiers which cannot be ordered by specificity in the kernel of CommonLoops. A user who wants to add such methods to CommonLoops can do so by defining a special method class and using the method-lookup protocol to specify different method-lookup rules.

We believe that handling incomplete type specifiers and the possible resolutions (backtracing, unification, production system rules) is a fertile area for language design and research, and perhaps a foundation for a graceful merger of Lisp, Prolog and production systems.

## 5.2 Structural versus Procedural Views of Objects

The object-oriented programming community is split on the issue of whether the specification or interface description of a class of objects should be strictly procedural, or whether it should be split into procedural and structural parts. In the procedural view an object is defined by its message protocols. As a matter of principle, programs that interact with an object should make no assumptions about the internal representations of the object. A procedural view of a complex number is defined in terms of its response to messages such as, `x`, `y`, `rho`, `theta`, `plus`, `print`, etc. CommonLoops continues the Common Lisp convention by usually generating access methods for structural components.

A description which includes a structural description could include the fact that `x`, `y`, `rho`, and `theta` are structural components of a complex number, that is, these named pieces are intended to have memory-cell semantics. Notice that the structural description need not be isomorphic with the implementation structure. For example, a complex number may be implemented as a pair `x` and `y`, with `rho` and `theta` computed.

Those that favor including a structural description argue that language forms should support this way of thinking. In CommonLoops, a uniform procedure `ref` is available to access structural parts by name, e.g.,

```
(ref some-complex 'theta),
```

instead requiring the use of an access function for each

```
(complex-number-theta some-complex).
```

Use of the `ref` form allows one to write code that can iterate through the slots of a structure, for example, as in a comparison routine. Also, in CommonLoops, the developmental meta-class supports slots in instances that are not declared in the class. The `ref` form provides a uniform way of accessing both declared and undeclared slots. The `ref` form has some advantages with respect to expressivity.

```
(ref x y)
```

is equivalent to the wordier

```
(funcall
  (find-accessor-function
    (class-of x)
     y)
   x y).
```

A `ref` form is also generally an appropriate first argument for `setf`, unlike `funcall`, because `ref` is used with memory-cell semantics.

A shortcoming with a structural description is that sometimes one wants procedures to be invoked upon access to a structural component. A way to achieve this within the structural framework uses annotated values as described below.

## 5.3 Annotated Values—Views and Implementations

Access-oriented programming is one of the popular features of Loops and several frame languages such as KEE, UNITS, and STROBE. The merits of this feature are often confounded with the merits of its various implementations. In this section, we try to separate these issues, and indicate alternative implementations available in CommonLoops.

In access-oriented programming, fetching from or storing in an object can cause user-defined operations to be invoked. *Procedural annotations* (*or active values*) associate objects with slots so that methods are invoked when values are fetched and stored. It is also useful to associate other information with a slot in addition to its value. *Structural* (*or property*) *annotations* associate arbitrary extendible property lists with a value in an object. Collectively these kinds of annotations are called annotated values. These annotations can be installed on slots and can be nested recursively.

Annotated values reify the notion of storage cell and are a valuable abstraction for organizing programs. Structural annotations can be used for in-core documentation. They are also used for attaching records for different purposes. For example, such annotations can record histories of changes, dependencies on other slots, or degrees of belief. Procedural annotations can be used as interfaces between programs that compute and programs that monitor those computations. For example, they can represent probes that connect slots in a simulation program to viewers and gauges in a display program.

Annotated values are conveniently represented as objects, and must satisfy a number of criteria for efficiency of operation and non-interference [Ste86a]. When multiple annotations are installed on the same value, the access operations must compose in the same order as the nesting. Annotated values can be implemented in different ways that optimize performance depending on the expected patterns of common use.

One implementation of annotated values in CommonLoops would require the slot-access primitives of the meta-class check whether the value is an active value object. The active value check can be made fast if the active value objects are wrapped in a unique data type. This technique for implementing active values has been used sucessfully in Loops. Hardware or microcode support of this fast check would allow the use of annotated values in ordinary Lisp structures (e.g., in cons-cells), greatly extending the utility of this abstraction.

Alternatively, a procedural implementation of annotated values could be built upon the ability in CommonLoops to specialize methods with respect to individuals. For those slots for which a special action is desired upon access, one can define methods for those accessors and objects that do the special action.

CommonLoops is capable of supporting either implementation. In addition, we believe that it is appropriate in CommonLoops to provide meta-classes that can support annotated values according to the needs of optimization. If active values are to be attached and detached frequently, checking dynamically for annotated values may be preferable to changing the discriminator frequently. If probes are usually installed only once, then one may prefer the lower overhead of the procedural implementation. If access to properties is relatively rare compared with the access to values, then differentiating property access at compile-time might be preferred.

It is useful to be able to view a program that uses annotations in terms of that abstraction, rather than in implementation terms. The issue of supporting views of programs is discussed more generally in the next section.

## 5.4 Programming Environment Support

Programming environments must provide computational support for particular views (or perspectives) of programs [Bob86d]. A view is said to support a particular programming abstraction when the elements of the view are in the terminology of the abstraction and the operations possible within that viewer are those appropriate for the abstraction.

For example, a viewer that supports the view of a program in terms of annotated values would show annotated values, not methods or wrappers that make up their implementation. The installation and nesting of annotated values are the appropriate actions available in the viewer.

Another important and popular view of object-oriented programs is that classes are defined by their slots and methods. While program listings often show structure and methods separated, it is useful to view such programs as organized in terms of classes with access to slot and method descriptions. CommonLoops viewers in definition groups [Bob86] also provide access to any multi-method from all of its associated classes. Thus, CommonLoops supports the classical view with appropriate extensions.

Views of classes can be organized around semantic categories, as in the standard Smalltalk-80 browser, or around a graph of the class inheritance lattice of some portion of the system, as in Loops, and CommonLoops. In the latter case, certain operations become natural to perform directly through the lattice browser—for example, promoting methods or slots to more general classes, or changing the inheritance structure. Changing the name of a slot or selector through a browser can invoke analysis routines that can find and change all occurrences of the name in code.

Viewers on CommonLoops also support a procedural abstraction. For example, they provide static browsers of program calling structure, where each discriminator is considered as a single function. However, through these browsers, one can get access to individual method definitions from the corresponding discriminator.

To provide viable support for programming with an abstraction, the viewers must be integrated with the debugging system. For example, to support a view of program in terms of methods, it should not be necessary to understand how methods are implemented or to refer to methods created automatically by the system. Rather, debugging should use the same terms that the programmer uses in writing the program.

## 6. SUMMARY AND CONCLUSIONS

Over the last ten years many systems have been written that add object-oriented programming to Lisp (e.g., Flavors, Loops, Object-LISP). Each of these has attracted a group of users that recognizes the benefits of message sending and specialization and has endorsed the object-oriented style. The object-languages in these systems have been embedded in Lisp with different degrees of integration.

Interest in object-oriented programming has also been spurred by work in expert systems. Several knowledge programming systems (ABE, ART, KEE, Strobe, UNITS, etc.) have emerged. These systems have included variations and extensions on object-oriented programming and tools for creating knowledge bases in terms of objects. As research continues, additional knowledge programming systems will emerge. Each of these will have their advocates and perhaps their niche in the range of applications and computer architectures. All of these systems can benefit from an object-oriented base that is efficient and extensible.

The creation of a good base involves both theoretical language design and engineering concerns. CommonLoops has attempted to respond to several kinds of pressure on the design of such a system.

The applications community wants to use a system for its work. The language must be suitable for state-of-the-art applications and systems that they build on top of it. The language must have an efficient implementation. It is an advantage if the language is a graceful extension of Common Lisp because existing code and existing programming skills can be preserved.

Vendors share these interests. They want their systems to provide a suitable base for a large fraction of the applications. They want the kernel of the language to be lean, easy to maintain, and efficient; they want the kernel to be principled and free of idiosyncratic features with no enduring value beyond their history. Vendors don't want to implement multiple versions of object languages, gratuitously different and incompatible.

The research community has somewhat different interests. Like the application community, it needs to be able to share code, but it is concerned with being able to try out other ways of doing things. New ideas for languages come out of the experience of the research community. To build higher level languages, the base must provide mechanisms for open-ended experimentation.

CommonLoops has responded to these pressures by providing a base for experimentation through the use of meta-objects, while capturing in its kernel the ability to implement the features of current object-oriented systems. By integrating classes with the Lisp type system, and using a syntax for method invocation that is identical to Lisp function call, CommonLoops makes possible a smooth and incremental transition from using only the functional paradigm for user code to using the object paradigm. As a portable system implemented in a widely available base, it allows users the choice of hardware and environments, and a road to the future.

## ACKNOWLEDGMENTS

Many people read early drafts of this paper, helped us to sharpen the ideas and present them more coherently. Thanks to Eric Benson, John Seely Brown, Margaret Butler, Johan de Kleer, Peter Deutsch, Richard Gabriel, Stanley Lanning, Henry Lieberman, Mark S. Miller, Sanjay Mittal, Randy Trigg, Bill van Melle, Daniel Weld, and Jon L. White.

# 4

# The POSTGRES Data Model*

**Lawrence A. Rowe and Michael R. Stonebraker**

*Computer Science Division, EECS Department, University of California, Berkeley, California*

## ABSTRACT

The design of the POSTGRES data model is described. The data model is a relational model that has been extended with abstract data types including user-defined operators and procedures, relation attributes of type procedure, and attribute and procedure inheritance. These mechanisms can be used to simulate a wide variety of semantic and object-oriented data modeling constructs including aggregation and generalization, complex objects with shared subobjects, and attributes that reference tuples in other relations.

*This research was supported by the National Science Foundation under Grant DCR-8507256 at the Defense Advanced Research Projects Agency (DoD), Arpa Order No. 4871, monitored by Space and Naval Warfare Systems Command under Contract N00039-84-C-0089.



*Source*: Adapted from Rowe, L. and M. Stonebraker, "The POSTGRES Data Model", Proceedings of the International Conference on Very Large Databases, September 1987, pp. 83–96.

## 1. INTRODUCTION

This paper describes the data model for POSTGRES, a next-generation extensible database management system being developed at the University of California [Sto86d]. The data model is based on the idea of extending the relational model developed by Codd [Cod70] with general mechanisms that can be used to simulate a variety of semantic data modeling constructs. The mechanisms include: 1) abstract data types (ADT's), 2) data of type procedure, and 3) rules. These mechanisms can be used to support complex objects or to implement a shared object hierarchy for an object-oriented programming language [Row86]. Most of these ideas have appeared elsewhere [Sto84,Sto85,Sto86b,Sto86c].

We have discovered that some semantic constructs that were not directly supported can be easily added to the system. Consequently, we have made several changes to the data model and the syntax of the query language that are documented here. These changes include providing support for primary keys, inheritance of data and procedures, and attributes that reference tuples in other relations.

The major contribution of this paper is to show that inheritance can be added to a relational data model with only a modest number of changes to the model and the implementation of the system. The conclusion that we draw from this result is that the major concepts provided in an object-oriented data model (e.g., structured attribute types, inheritance, union type attributes, and support for shared subobjects) can be cleanly and efficiently supported in an extensible relational database management system. The features used to support these mechanisms are abstract data types and attributes of type procedure.

The remainder of the paper describes the POSTGRES data model and is organized as follows. Section 2 presents the data model. Section 3 describes the attribute type system. Section 4 describes how the query language can be extended with user-defined procedures. Section 5 compares the model with other data models and section 6 summarizes the paper.

## 2. DATA MODEL

A database is composed of a collection of *relations* that contain tuples which represent real-world entities (e.g., documents and people) or relationships (e.g., authorship). A relation has attributes of fixed types that represent properties of the entities and relationships (e.g., the title of a document) and a primary key. Attribute types can be atomic (e.g., integer, floating point, or boolean) or structured (e.g., array or procedure). The primary key is a sequence of attributes of the relation [which], when taken together, uniquely identify each tuple.

A simple university database will be used to illustrate the model. The following command defines a relation that represents people:

```
create PERSON ( Name = char[25],
   Birthdate = date, Height = int4,
   Weight = int4, StreetAddress = char[25],
   City = char[25], State = char[2])
```

This command defines a relation and creates a structure for storing the tuples.

The definition of a relation may optionally specify a primary key and other relations from which to inherit attributes. A primary key is a combination of attributes that uniquely identifies each tuple. The key is specified with a **key**-clause as follows:

```
create PERSON ( . . . )
key (Name)
```

Tuples must have a value for all key attributes. The specification of a key may optionally include the name of an operator that is to be used when comparing two tuples. For example, suppose a relation had a key whose type was a user-defined ADT. If an attribute of type *box* was part of the primary key, the comparison operator must be specified since different *box* operators could be used to distinguish the entries (e.g., area equals or box equality). The following example shows the definition of a relation with a key attribute of type *box* that uses the area equals operator (*AE*) to determine key value equality:

```
create PICTURE(Title = char[25], Item = box)
key (Item using AE)
```

Data inheritance is specified with an **inherits**-clause. Suppose, for example, that people in the university database are employees and/or students and that different attributes are to be defined for each category. The relation for each category includes the *PERSON* attributes and the attributes that are specific to the category. These relations can be defined by replicating the *PERSON* attributes in each relation definition or by inheriting them for the definition of *PERSON*. Figure 4.1 shows the relations and an inheritance hierarchy that could be used to share the definition of the attributes.

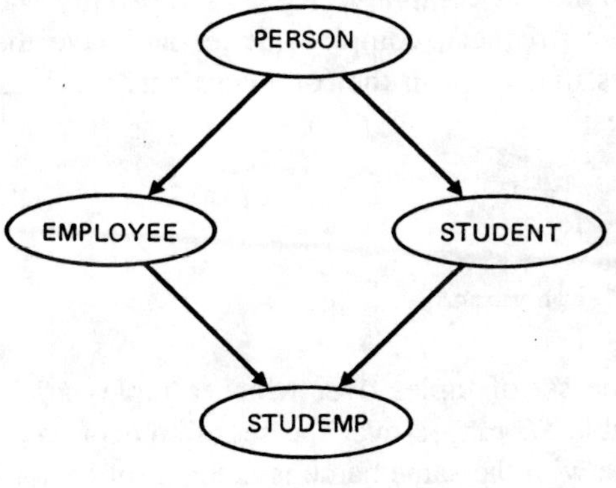


**Figure 4.1** Relation hierarchy.

The commands that define the relations other than the *PERSON* relation defined above are:

```
create EMPLOYEE (Dept = char[25],
   Status = int2, Mgr = char[25],
   JobTitle = char[25], Salary = money)
inherits (PERSON)
```

```
create STUDENT (Sno = char[12],
   Status = int2, Level = char[20])
inherits (PERSON)

create STUDEMP (IsWorkStudy = bool)
inherits (STUDENT, EMPLOYEE)
```

A relation inherits all attributes from its parent(s) unless an attribute is overriden in the definition. For example, the *EMPLOYEE* relation inherits the *PERSON* attributes *Name, Birthdate, Height, Weight, StreetAddress, City*, and *State*. Key specifications are also inherited so *Name* is also the key for EMPLOYEE.

Relations may inherit attributes from more than one parent. For example, *STUDEMP* inherits attributes from *STUDENT* and *EMPLOYEE*. An inheritance conflict occurs when the same attribute name is inherited from more than one parent (e.g., *STUDEMP* inherits *Status* from *EMPLOYEE* and *STUDENT*). If the inherited attributes have the same type, an attribute with the type is included in the relation that is being defined. Otherwise, the declaration is disallowed.[1]

The POSTGRES query language is a generalized version of QUEL [Hel75], called *POSTQUEL*. QUEL was extended in several directions. First, POSTQUEL has a **from**-clause to define tuple-variables rather than a **range** command. Second, arbitrary relation-valued expressions may appear any place that a relation name could appear in QUEL. Third, transitive closure and **execute** commands have been added to the language [Kun84]. And lastly, POSTGRES maintains historical data so POSTQUEL allows queries to be run on past database states or on any data that was in the database at any time. These extensions are described in the remainder of this section.

The **from**-clause was added to the language so that tuple-variable definitions for a query could be easily determined at compile-time. This capability was needed because POSTGRES will, at the user's request, compile queries and save them in the system catalogs. The **from**-clause is illustrated in the following query that lists all work-study students who are sophomores:

```
retrieve (SE.name)
from SE in STUDEMP
where SE.IsWorkStudy
  and SE.Status = "sophomore"
```

The **from**-clause specifies the set of tuples over which a tuple-variable will range. In this example, the tuple-variable *SE* ranges over the set of student employees.

A default tuple-variable with the same name is defined for each relation referenced in the target-list or **where**-clause of a query. For example, the query above could have been written:

[1]Most attribute inheritance models have a conflict resolution rule that selects one of the conflicting attributes. We chose to disallow inheritance because we could not discover an example where it made sense, except when the types were identical. On the other hand, procedure inheritance (discussed below) does use a conflict resolution rule because many examples exist in which one procedure is preferred.

```
retrieve (STUDEMP.name)
where STUDEMP.IsWorkStudy
  and STUDEMP.Status = "sophomore"
```

Notice that the attribute *IsWorkStudy* is a boolean-valued attribute so it does not require an explicit value test (e.g., *STUDEMP.IsWorkStudy = "true"*).

The set of tuples that a tuple-variable may range over can be a named relation or a relation-expression. For example, suppose the user wanted to retrieve all students in the database who live in Berkeley regardless of whether they are students or student employees. This query can be written as follows:

```
retrieve (S.name)
from S in STUDENT*
where S.city = "Berkeley"
```

The "*" operator specifies the relation formed by taking the union of the named relation (i.e., *STUDENT*) and all relations that inherit attributes from it (i.e., *STUDEMP*). If the "*" operator was not used, the query retrieves only tuples in the student relation (i.e., students who are not student employees). In most data models that support inheritance the relation name defaults to the union of relations over the inheritance hierarchy (i.e., the data described by *STUDENT** above). We chose a different default because queries that involve unions will be slower than queries on a single relation. By forcing the user to request the union explicitly with the "*" operator, he will be aware of this cost.

Relation expressions may include other set operators: union (∪), intersection (∩), and difference (−). For example, the following query retrieves the names of people who are students or employees but not student employees:

```
retrieve (S.name)
from S in (STUDENT ∪ EMPLOYEE)
```

Suppose a tuple does not have an attribute referenced elsewhere in the query. If the reference is in the target-list, the return tuple will not contain the attribute.[2] If the reference is in the qualification, the clause containing the qualification is "false".

POSTQUEL also provides set comparison operators and a relation-constructor that can be used to specify some difficult queries more easily than in a conventional query language. For example, suppose that students could have several majors. The natural representation for this data is to define a separate relation:

```
create MAJORS(Sname = char[25],
   Mname = char[25])
```

where *Sname* is the student's name and *Mname* is the major. With this representation, the following query retrieves the names of students with the same majors as Smith:

[2]The application program interface to POSTGRES allows the stream of tuples passed back to the program to have dynamically varying columns and types.

```
retrieve (M1.Sname)
from M1 in MAJORS
where {(x.Mname) from x in MAJORS
        where x.Sname = M1.Sname}
  ⊂ {(x.Mname) from x in MAJORS
      where x.Sname="Smith"}
```

The expressions enclosed in set symbols ("{...}") are relation-constructors.

The general form of a relation-constructor[3] is

```
{(target-list) from  from-clause
         where  where-clause}
```

which specifies the same relation as the query

```
retrieve (target-list)
from  from-clause
where  where-clause
```

Note that a tuple-variable defined in the outer query (e.g., M1 in the query above) can be used within a relation-constructor but that a tuple-variable defined in the relation-constructor cannot be used in the outer query. Redefinition of a tuple-variable in a relation constructor creates a distinct variable as in a block-structured programming language (e.g., PASCAL). Relation-valued expressions (including attributes of type procedure described in the next section) can be used any place in a query that a named relation can be used.

Database updates are specified with conventional update commands as shown in the following examples:

```
/* Add a new employee to the database.  */
append to EMPLOYEE(name = value,
  age =  value, ...)

/* Change state codes using
    MAP(OldCode, NewCode).  */
replace P(State = MAP.NewCode)
from P in PERSON*
where P.State = MAP.OldCode

/* Delete students born before today.  */
delete STUDENT
where STUDENT.Birthdate < "today"
```

Deferred update semantics are used for all updates commands.

POSTQUEL supports the transitive closure commands developed in QUEL* [Kun84]. A "*" command continues to execute until no tuples are retrieved (e.g., **retrieve***) or updated (e.g., **append***, **delete***, or **replace***). For example, the following query creates a relation that contains all employees who work for Smith:

[3]Relation constructors are really aggregate functions. We have designed a mechanism to support extensible aggregate functions, but have not yet worked out the query language syntax and semantics.

```
retrieve* into SUBORD(E.Name, E.Mgr)
from E in EMPLOYEE, S in SUBORD
where E.Name ="Smith"
  or E.Mgr = S.Name
```

This command continues to execute the **retrieve-into** command until there are no changes made to the *SUBORD* relation.

Lastly, POSTGRES saves data deleted from or modified in a relation so that queries can be executed on historical data. For example, the following query looks for students who lived in Berkeley on August 1, 1980:

```
retrieve (S.Name)
from S in STUDENT["August 1, 1980"]
where S.City = "Berkeley"
```

The date specified in the brackets following the relation name specifies the relation at the designated time. The date can be specified in many different formats and optionally may include a time of day. The query above only examines students who are not student employees. To search the set of all students, the **from**-clause would be

```
...from S in STUDENT*["August 1, 1980"]
```

Queries can also be executed on all data that is currently in the relation or was in it at some time in the past (i.e., all data). The following query retrieves all students who ever lived in Berkeley:

```
retrieve (S.Name)
from S in STUDENT[]
where S.City = "Berkeley"
```

The notation "[ ]" can be appended to any relation name.

Queries can also be specified on data that was in the relation during a given time period. The time period is specified by giving a start- and end-time as shown in the following query that retrieves students who lived in Berkeley at any time in August 1980:

```
retrieve (S.Name)
from S in STUDENT*["August 1, 1980",
                   "August 31, 1980"]
where S.City = "Berkeley"
```

Shorthand notations are supported for all tuples in a relation up to some date (e.g., *STUDENT*[, "August 1, 1980"]*) or from some date to the present (e.g., *STUDENT*["August 1, 1980",]*).

The POSTGRES default is to save all data unless the user explicitly requests that data be purged. Data can be purged before a specific data (e.g., before January 1, 1987) or before some time period (e.g., before six months ago). The user may also request that all historical data be purged so that only the current data in the relation is stored.

POSTGRES also supports versions of relations. A version of a relation can be created from a relation or a snapshot. A version is created by specifying the base relation as shown in the command

```
create version MYPEOPLE from PERSON
```

that creates a version, named *MYPEOPLE*, derived from the *PERSON* relation. Data can be retrieved from and updated in a version just like a relation. Updates to the version do not modify the base relation. However, updates to the base relation are propagated to the version unless the value has been modified. For example, if George's birthdate is changed in *MYPEOPLE*, a **replace** command that changes his birthdate in *PERSON* will not be propagated to *MYPEOPLE*.

If the user does not want updates to the base relation to propagate to the version, he can create a version of a snapshot. A snapshot is a copy of the current contents of a relation [Adi80]. A version of a snapshot is created by the following command:

```
create version YOURPEOPLE
from PERSON["now"]
```

The snapshot version can be updated directly by issuing update commands on the version. But, updates to the base relation are not propagated to the version.

A **merge** command is provided to merge changes made to a version back into the base relation. An example of this command is

```
merge YOURPEOPLE into PERSON
```

that will merge the changes made to *YOURPEOPLE* back into *PERSON*. The **merge** command uses a semi-automatic procedure to resolve updates to the underlying relation and the version that conflict [Gar84].

This section described most of the data definition and data manipulation commands in POSTQUEL. The commands that were not described are the commands for defining rules, utility commands that only affect the performance of the system (e.g., **define index** and **modify**), and other miscellaneous utility commands (e.g., **destroy** and **copy**). The next section describes the type system for relation attributes.

## 3. DATA TYPES

POSTGRES provides a collection of atomic and structured types. The predefined atomic types include: *int2*, *int4*, *float4*, *float8*, *bool*, *char*, and *date*. The standard arithmetic and comparison operators are provided for the numeric and date data types and the standard string and comparison operators for character arrays. Users can extend the system by adding new atomic types using an abstract data type (ADT) definition facility.

All atomic data types are defined to the system as ADT's. An ADT is defined by specifying the type name, the length of the internal representation in bytes, procedures for converting from an external to internal representation for a value and from an internal to external representation, and a default value. The command

```
define type int4 is (InternalLength = 4,
   InputProc = CharToInt4,
   OutputProc = Int4ToChar, Default = "0")
```

defines the type *int4* which is predefined in the system. *CharToInt4* and *Int4ToChar* are procedures that are coded in a conventional programming language (e.g., C) and defined to the system using the commands described in section 4.

Operators on ADT's are defined by specifying the number and type of operands, the return type, the precedence and associativity of the operator, and the procedure that implements it. For example, the command

```
define operator "+"(int4, int4) returns int4
   is (Proc = Plus, Precedence = 5,
       Associativity = "left")
```

defines the plus operator. Precedence is specified by a number. Larger numbers imply higher precedence. The predefined operators have the precedences shown in Figure 4.2. These precedences can be changed by changing the operator definitions. Associativity is either left or right depending on the semantics desired. This example defined an operator denoted by a symbol (i.e., "+"). Operators can also be denoted by identifiers as shown below.

| Precedence | Operators |
|---|---|
| 80 | ↑ |
| 70 | not – (unary) |
| 60 | * / |
| 50 | + – (binary) |
| 40 | < ≤ > ≥ |
| 30 | = ≠ |
| 20 | and |
| 10 | or |

**Figure 4.2** Predefined operators precedence.

Another example of an ADT definition is the following command that defines an ADT that represents boxes:

```
define type box is (InternalLength = 16,
   InputProc = CharToBox,
   OutputProc = BoxToChar, Default = "")
```

The external representation of a box is a character string that contains two points that represent the upper-left and lower-right corners of the box. With this representation, the constant

```
"20,50:10,70"
```

describes a box whose upper-left corner is at (20, 50) and lower-right corner is at (10, 70). *CharToBox* takes a character string like this one and returns a 16 byte representation of a box (e.g., 4 bytes per x- or y-coordinate value). *BoxToChar* is the inverse of *CharToBox*.

Comparison operators can be defined on ADT's that can be used in access methods or optimized in queries. For example, the definition

```
define operator AE(box, box) returns bool
   is (Proc = BoxAE, Precedence = 3,
       Associativity = "left", Sort = BoxArea,
       Hashes, Restrict = AERSelect,
        Join = AEJSelect, Negator = BoxAreaNE)
```

defines an operator "area equals" on boxes. In addition to the semantic information about the operator itself, this specification includes information used by POSTGRES to build indexes and to optimize queries using the operator. For example, suppose the *PICTURE* relation was defined by

```
create PICTURE(Title = char[], Item = box)
```

and the query

```
retrieve (PICTURE.all)
where PICTURE.Item AE "50,100:100,50"
```

was executed. The *Sort* property of the *AE* operator specifies the procedure to be used to sort the relation if a merge-sort join strategy was selected to implement the query. It also specifies the procedure to use when building an ordered index (e.g., B-Tree) on an attribute of type *box*. The *Hashes* property indicates that this operator can be used to build a hash index on a *box* attribute. Note that either type of index can be used to optimize the query above. The *Restrict* and *Join* properties specify the procedure that is to be called by the query optimizer to compute the restrict and join selectivities, respectively, of a clause involving the operator. These selectivity properties specify procedures that will return a floating point value between 0.0 and 1.0 that indicate the attribute selectivity given the operator. Lastly, the *Negator* property specifies the procedure that is to be used to compare two values when a query predicate requires the operator to be negated as in

```
retrieve (PICTURE.all)
where not (PICTURE.Item
             AE "50,100:100,50")
```

The **define operator** command also may specify a procedure that can be used if the query predicate includes an operator that is not commutative. For example, the commutator procedure for "area less than" (*ALT*) is the procedure that implements "area greater than or equal" (*AGE*). More details on the use of these properties is given elsewhere [Sto86a].

Type-constructors are provided to define structured types (e.g., arrays and procedures) that can be used to represent complex data. An *array* type-constructor can be used to define a variable- or fixed-size array. A fixed-size array is declared by specifying the element type and upper bound of the array as illustrated by

```
create PERSON(Name = char[25])
```

which defines an array of twenty-five characters. The elements of the array are referenced by indexing the attribute by an integer between 1 and 25 (e.g., "*PERSON.Name[4]*" references the fourth character in the person's name).

A variable-size array is specified by omitting the upper bound in the type constructor. For example, a variable-sized array of characters is specified by "char[]." Variable-size arrays are referenced by indexing the attribute by an integer between 1 and the current upper bound of the array. The predefined function *size* returns the current upper bound. POSTGRES does not impose a limit on the size of a variable-size array. Built-in functions are provided to append arrays and to fetch array slices. For example, two character arrays can be appended using the concatenate operator ("+") and an array slice containing characters 2 through 15 in an attribute named *x* can be fetched by the expression "x[2:15]."

The second type-constructor allows values of type procedure to be stored in an attribute. Procedure values are represented by a sequence of POSTQUEL commands. The value of an attribute of type procedure is a relation because that is what a **retrieve** command returns. Moreover, the value may include tuples from different relations (i.e., of different types) because a procedure composed of two **retrieve** commands returns the union of both commands. We call a relation with different tuple types a *multirelation.* The POSTGRES programming language interface provides a cursor-like mechanism, called a *portal*, to fetch values from multirelations [Sto86a]. However, they are not stored by the system (i.e., only relations are stored).

The system provides two kinds of procedure type-constructors: variable and parameterized. A variable procedure-type allows a different POSTQUEL procedure to be stored in each tuple while parameterized procedure-types store the same procedure in each tuple but with different parameters. We will illustrate the use of a variable procedure-type by showing another way to represent student majors. Suppose a *DEPARTMENT* relation was defined with the following command:

```
create DEPARTMENT(Name = char[25],
   Chair = char[25], ...)
```

A student's major(s) can then be represented by a procedure in the *STUDENT* relation that retrieves the appropriate *DEPARTMENT* tuple(s). The *Majors* attribute would be declared as follows:

```
create STUDENT(..., Majors = postquel, ...)
```

Data type *postquel* represents a procedure-type. The value in *Majors* will be a query that fetches the department relation tuples that represent the student's minors. The following command appends a student to the database who has a double major in mathematics and computer science:

```
append STUDENT( Name = "Smith", ...,
  Majors =
```

```
"retrieve (D.all)
from D in DEPARTMENT
where D.Name = "Math"
  or D.Name = "CS"")
```

A query that references the *Majors* attribute returns the string that contains the POSTQUEL commands. However, two notations are provided that will execute the query and return the result rather than the definition. First, nested-dot notation implicitly executes the query as illustrated by

```
retrieve (S.Name, S.Majors.Name)
from S in STUDENT
```

which prints a list of names and majors of students. The result of the query in *Majors* is implicitly joined with the tuple specified by the rest of the target-list. In other words, if a student has two majors, this query will return two tuples with the *Name* attribute repeated. The implicit join is performed to guarantee that a relation is returned.

The second way to execute the query is to use the **execute** command. For example, the query

```
execute (S.Majors)
from S in STUDENT
where S.Name = "Smith"
```

returns a relation that contains *DEPARTMENT* tuples for all of Smith's majors.

Parameterized procedure-types are used when the query to be stored in an attribute is nearly the same for every tuple. The query parameters can be taken from other attributes in the tuple or they may be explicitly specified. For example, suppose an attribute in *STUDENT* was to represent the student's current class list. Given the following definition for enrollments:

```
create ENROLLMENT(Student = char[25],
   Class = char[25])
```

Bill's class list can be retrieved by the query

```
retrieve (ClassName = E.Class)
from E in ENROLLMENT
where E.Student = "Bill"
```

This query will be the same for every student except for the constant that specifies the student's name.

A parameterized procedure-type could be defined to represent this query as follows:

```
define type classes is
   retrieve (ClassName = E.Class)
   from E in ENROLLMENT
   where E.Student = $.Name
end
```

The dollar-sign symbol ("$") refers to the tuple in which the query is stored (i.e., the current tuple). The parameter for each instance of this type (i.e., a query) is the *Name* attribute in the tuple in which the instance is stored. This type is then used in the **create** command as follows

```
create STUDENT(Name = char[25], ...,
   ClassList = classes)
```

to define an attribute that represents the student's current class list. This attribute can be used in a query to return a list of students and the classes they are taking:

```
retrieve (S.Name, S.ClassList.ClassName)
```

Notice that for a particular *STUDENT* tuple, the expression "$.*Name*" in the query refers to the name of that student. The symbol "$" can be thought of as a tuple-variable bound to the current tuple.

Parameterized procedure-types are extremely useful types, but sometimes it is inconvenient to store the parameters explicitly as attributes in the relation. Consequently, a notation is provided that allows the parameters to be stored in the procedure-type value. This mechanism can be used to simulate attribute types that reference tuples in other relations. For example, suppose you wanted a type that referenced a tuple in the *DEPARTMENT* relation defined above. This type can be defined as follows:

```
define type DEPARTMENT(int4) is
  retrieve (DEPARTMENT.all)
  where DEPARTMENT.oid = $1
end
```

The relation name can be used for the type name because relations, types, and procedures have separate name spaces. The query in type *DEPARTMENT* will retrieve a specific department tuple given a unique object identifier (*oid*) of the tuple. Each relation has an implicitly defined attribute named *oid* that contains the tuple's unique identifier. The *oid* attribute can be accessed but not updated by user queries. *Oid* values are created and maintained by the POSTGRES storage system [Sto87]. The formal argument to this procedure-type is the type of an object identifier. The parameter is referenced inside the definition by "$*n*" where *n* is the parameter number.

An actual argument is supplied when a value is assigned to an attribute of type *DEPARTMENT*. For example, a *COURSE* relation can be defined that represents information about a specific course including the department that offers it. The **create** command is:

```
create COURSE(Title = char[25],
   Dept = DEPARTMENT, ...)
```

The attribute *Dept* represents the department that offers the course. The following query adds a course to the database:

```
append COURSE(
  Title = "Introductory Programming",
```

```
   Dept = DEPARTMENT(D.oid))
from D in DEPARTMENT
where D.Name = "computer science"
```

The procedure *DEPARTMENT* called in the target-list is implicitly defined by the "**define type**" command. It constructs a value of the specified type given actual arguments that are type compatible with the formal arguments, in this case an *int4*.

Parameterized procedure-types that represent references to tuples in a specific relation are so commonly used that we plan to provide automatic support for them. First, every relation created will have a type that represents a reference to a tuple implicitly defined similar to the *DEPARTMENT* type above. And second, it will be possible to assign a tuple-variable directly to a tuple reference attribute. In other words, the assignment to the attribute *Dept* that is written in the query above as

```
... Dept = DEPARTMENT(D.oid) ...
```

can be written as

```
... Dept = D ...
```

Parameterized procedure-types can also be used to implement a type that references a tuple in an arbitrary relation. The type definition is:

```
define type tuple(char[], int4) is
   retrieve ($1.all)
   where $1.oid = $2
end
```

The first argument is the name of the relation and the second argument is the *oid* of the desired tuple in the relation. In effect, this type defines a reference to an arbitrary tuple in the database.

The procedure-type *tuple* can be used to create a relation that represents people who help with fund raising:

```
create VOLUNTEER(Person = tuple,
   TimeAvailable = integer, ...)
```

Because volunteers may be students, employees, or people who are neither students nor employees, the attribute *Person* must contain a reference to a tuple in an arbitrary relation. The following command appends all students to *VOLUNTEER*:

```
append VOLUNTEER(
   Person = tuple(relation(S), S.oid))
from S in STUDENT*
```

The predefined function *relation* returns the name of the relation to which the tuple-variable *S* is bound.

The type *tuple* will also be special-cased to make it more convenient. *Tuple* will be a predefined type and it will be possible to assign tuple-variables directly to attributes of the type. Consequently, the assignment to *Person* written above as

```
... Person = tuple(relation(S), S.oid) ...
```

can be written

```
... Person = S ...
```

We expect that as we get more experience with POSTGRES applications that more types may be special-cased.

## 4. USER-DEFINED PROCEDURES

This section describes language constructs for adding user-defined procedures to POSTQUEL. User-defined procedures are written in a conventional programming language and are used to implement ADT operators or to move a computation from a front-end application process to the back-end DBMS process.

Moving a computation to the back-end opens up possibilities for the DBMS to precompute a query that includes the computation. For example, suppose that a front-end application needed to fetch the definition of a form from a database and to construct a main-memory data structure that the run-time forms system used to display the form on the terminal screen for data entry or display. A conventional relation database design would store the form components (e.g., titles and field definitions for different types of fields such as scalar fields, table fields, and graphics fields) in many different relations. An example database design is:

```
create FORM(FormName, ...)

create FIELDS(FormName, FieldName,
   Origin, Height, Width,
   FieldKind, ...)

create SCALARFIELD(FormName,
   FieldName, DataType,
   DisplayFormat, ...)

create TABLEFIELD(FormName,
   FieldName, NumberOfRows, ...)

create TABLECOLUMNS(FormName,
   FieldName, ColumnName, Height,
   Width, FieldKind, ...)
```

The query that fetches the form from the database must execute at least one query per table and sort through the return tuples to construct the main-memory data structure. This operation must take less than two seconds for an interactive application. Conventional relational DBMS's cannot satisfy this time constraint.

Our approach to solving this problem is to move the computation that constructs the main-memory data structure to the database process. Suppose the procedure *MakeForm* built the data structure given the name of a form. Using the parameterized procedure-type mechanism defined above an attribute can be added to the *FORM* relation that stores the form representation computed by this procedure. The commands

```
define type formrep is
   retrieve (rep = MakeForm($.FormName))
end
addattribute (FormName, ...,
   FormDataStructure = formrep)
to FORM
```

define the procedure type and add an attribute to the *FORM* relation.

The advantage of this representation is that POSTGRES can precompute the answer to a procedure-type attribute and store it in the tuple. By precomputing the main-memory data structure representation, the form can be fetched from the database by a single-tuple retrieve:

```
retrieve (x = FORM.FormDataStructure)
where FORM.FormName = "foo"
```

The real-time constraint to fetch and display a form can be easily met if all the program must do is a single-tuple retrieve to fetch the data structure and call the library procedure to display it. This example illustrates the advantage of moving a computation (i.e., constructing a main-memory data structure) from the application process to the DBMS process.

A procedure is defined to the system by specifying the names and types of the arguments, the return type, the language it is written in, and where the source and object code is stored. For example, the definition

```
define procedure AgeInYears(date) returns int4
   is (language = "C", filename = "AgeInYears")
```

defines a procedure *AgeInYears* that takes a *date* value and returns the age of the person. The argument and return types are specified using POSTGRES types. When the procedure is called, it is passed the arguments in the POSTGRES internal representation for the type. We plan to allow procedures to be written in several different languages including C and Lisp which are the two languages being used to implement the system.

POSTGRES stores the information about a procedure in the system catalogs and dynamically loads the object code when it is called in a query. The following query uses the *AgeInYears* procedure to retrieve the names and ages of all people in the example database:

```
retrieve (P.Name,
      Age = AgeInYears(P.Birthdate))
from P in PERSON*
```

User-defined procedures can also take tuple-variable arguments. For example, the following command defines a procedure, called *Comp*, that takes an EMPLOYEE tuple and computes the person's compensation according to some formula that involves several attributes in the tuple (e.g., the employee's status, job title, and salary):

```
define procedure Comp(EMPLOYEE)
  returns int4 is (language = "C",
  filename = "Comp1")
```

Recall that a parameterized procedure-type is defined for each relation automatically so the type *EMPLOYEE* represents a reference to a tuple in the *EMPLOYEE* relation. This procedure is called in the following query:

```
retrieve (E.Name, Compensation = Comp(E))
from E in EMPLOYEE
```

The C function that implements this procedure is passed a data structure that contains the names, types, and values of the attributes in the tuple.

User-defined procedures can be passed tuples in other relations that inherit the attributes in the relation declared as the argument to the procedure. For example, the *Comp* procedure defined for the *EMPLOYEE* relation can be passed a *STUDEMP* tuple as in

```
retrieve (SE.Name,
     Compensation = Comp(SE))
from SE in STUDEMP
```

because *STUDEMP* inherits data attributes from *EMPLOYEE*.

The arguments to procedures that take relation tuples as arguments must be passed in a self-describing data structure because the procedure can be passed tuples from different relations. Attributes inherited from other relations may be in different positions in the relations. Moreover, the values passed for the same attribute name may be different types (e.g., the definition of an inherited attribute may be overridden with a different type). The self-describing data structure is a list of arguments, one per attribute in the tuple to be passed, with the following structure

```
(AttrName, AttrType, AttrValue)
```

The procedure code will have to search the list to find the desired attribute. A library of routines is provided that will hide this structure from the programmer. The library will include routines to get the type and value of an attribute given the name of the attribute. For example, the following code fetches the value of the *Birthdate* attribute:

```
GetValue("Birthdate")
```

The problem of variable argument lists arises in all object-oriented programming languages and similar solutions are used.

The model for procedure inheritance is nearly identical to method inheritance in object-oriented programming languages [Ste86b]. Procedure inheritance uses the data inheritance hierarchy and similar inheritance rules except that a rule is provided to select a procedure when an inheritance conflict arises. For example, suppose that a *Comp* procedure was defined for *STUDENT* as well as for *EMPLOYEE*. The definition of the second procedure might be:

```
define procedure Comp(STUDENT)
   returns int4 is (language = "C",
   filename = "Comp2")
```

A conflict arises when the query on *STUDEMP* above is executed because the system does not know which *Comp* procedure to call (i.e., the one for *EMPLOYEE* or the one for *STUDENT*). The procedure called is selected from among the procedures that take a tuple from the relation specified by the actual argument *STUDEMP* or any relation from which attributes in the actual argument are inherited (e.g., *PERSON*, *EMPLOYEE*, and *STUDENT*).

Each relation has an *inheritance precedence list* (IPL) that is used to resolve the conflict. The list is constructed by starting with the relation itself and doing a depth-first search up the inheritance hierarchy starting with the first relation specified in the **inherits**-clause. For example, the **inherits**-clause for *STUDEMP* is

```
... inherits (STUDENT, EMPLOYEE)
```

and its IPL is

```
(STUDEMP, STUDENT,
 EMPLOYEE, PERSON)
```

*PERSON* appears after *EMPLOYEE* rather than after *STUDENT* where it would appear in a depth-first search because both *STUDENT* and *EMPLOYEE* inherit attributes from *PERSON* (see Figure 4.1). In other words, all but the last occurrence of a relation in the depth-first ordering of the hierarchy is deleted.[4]

When a procedure is called and passed a tuple as the first argument, the actual procedure invoked is the first definition found with the same name when the procedures that take arguments from the relations in the ILP of the argument are searched in order. In the example above, the procedure defined for *STUDENT* is called because there is no procedure named *Comp* defined for *STUDEMP* and *STUDENT* is the next relation in the IPL.

The implementation of this procedure selection rule is relatively easy. Assume that two system catalogs are defined:

```
PROCDEF(ProcName, ArgName, ProcId)
IPL(RelationName, IPLEntry, SeqNo)
```

where *PROCDEF* has an entry for each procedure defined and *IPL* maintains the precedence lists for all relations. The attributes in *PROCDEF* represent the procedure name, the argument type name, and the unique identifier for the procedure code stored in another catalog. The attributes in *IPL* represent the relation, an IPL entry for the relation, and the sequence number for that entry in the IPL of the relation. With these two catalogs, the query to find the correct procedure for the call

```
Comp(STUDEMP)
```

[4]We are using a rule that is similar to the rule for the new Common Lisp object model [Bob+86b]. It is actually slightly more complicated than described here in order to eliminate some nasty cases that arise when there are cycles in the inheritance hierarchy.

is[5]

```
retrieve (P.ProcId)
from P in PROCDEF, I in IPL
where P.ProcName = "Comp"
 and I.RelationName = "STUDEMP"
 and I.IPLEntry = P.ArgName
 and I.SeqNo = MIN(I.SeqNo
  by I.RelationName
  where I.IPLEntry = P.ArgName
    and P.ProcName = "Comp"
    and I.RelationName = "STUDEMP")
```

This query can be precomputed to speed up procedure selection.

In summary, the major changes required to support procedure inheritance are as follows: 1) allow tuples as arguments to procedures, 2) define a representation for variable argument lists, and 3) implement a procedure selection mechanism. This extension to the relational model is relatively straightforward and only requires a small number of changes to the DBMS implementation.

## 5. OTHER DATA MODELS

This section compares the POSTGRES data model to semantic, functional, and object-oriented data models.

Semantic and functional data models [Day85,Ham81,Myl80a,Shi81,Smi77,Zan83] do not provide the flexibility provided by the model described here. They cannot easily represent data with uncertain structure (e.g., objects with shared subobjects that have different types).

Modeling ideas oriented toward complex objects [Has82,Lor83] cannot deal with objects that have a variety of shared subobjects. POSTGRES uses procedures to represent shared subobjects which does not have limitation on the types of subobjects that are shared. Moreover, the nested-dot notation allows convenient access to selected subobjects, a feature not present in these systems.

Several proposals have been made to support data models that contain non-first normal form relations [Bat86,Dad86,Dep86]. The POSTGRES data model can be used to support non-first normal form relations with procedure-types. Consequently, POSTGRES seems to contain a superset of the capabilities of these proposals.

Object-oriented data models [And86,Cop84] have modeling constructs to deal with uncertain structure. For example, GemStone supports union types which can be used to represent subobjects that have different types [Cop84]. Sharing of subobjects is represented by storing the subobjects as separate records and connecting them to a parent object with pointer-chains. Precomputed procedure values will, in our opinion, make POSTGRES performance competitive with pointer-chain proposals. The performance problem with pointer-chains will be most obvious when an object is composed of a

[5] This query uses a QUEL-style aggregate function.

large number of subobjects. POSTGRES will avoid this problem because the pointer-chain is represented as a relation and the system can use all of the query processing and storage structure techniques available in the system to represent it. Consequently, POSTGRES uses a different approach that supports the same modeling capabilities and an implementation that may have better performance.

Finally, the POSTGRES data model could claim to be object-oriented, though we prefer not to use this word because few people agree on exactly what it means. The data model provides the same capabilities as an object-oriented model, but it does so without discarding the relational model and without having to introduce a new confusing terminology.

## 6. SUMMARY

The POSTGRES data model uses the ideas of abstract data types, data of type procedure, and inheritance to extend the relational model. These ideas can be used to simulate a variety of semantic data modeling concepts (e.g., aggregation and generalization). In addition, the same ideas can be used to support complex objects that have unpredictable composition and shared subobjects.

# 5

# Object Management in Distributed Information Systems*

**Peter Lyngbaek, Dennis McLeod**

*Computer Science Department, University of Southern California*
*Los Angeles, California*

## ABSTRACT

A simple model for object sharing in distributed office information systems is described. The model provides a small set of operators for object definition, manipulation, and retrieval in a distributed environment, modeled as a logical network of workstations. Relationships among objects can be established across work station boundaries, objects are relocatable within the distributed environment, and mechanisms are provided for access control and the dynamic sharing of objects among individual work stations. An object naming convention supports location-transparent object references; that is, objects can be

*This work was supported in part by the Danish Natural Science Research Council under grant 11-4132, by a grant from the IBM Corporation, and by the Joint Services Electronics Program through the Air Force Office of Scientific Research under contract F49620-81-C-0070.

Authors' address: Computer Science Dept., University of Southern California, Los Angeles, CA 90089-0782.



*Source*: Adapted from Lyngbaek, P., and D. McLeod, "Object Management in Distributed Information Systems", ACM Transactions on Office Information Systems, Volume 2, Number 2, April 1984, pp. 96–122.

referenced by user-defined names rather than by addresses. The primitive operations introduced can be used as the basis for the specification and stepwise development of office information models and systems of increasing complexity. An experimental prototype implementation of the distributed object sharing model is described.

Categories and Subject Descriptors: H.2.1 [**Database Management**]: Logical Design—*data models*; H.2.4 [**Database Management**]: Systems—*distributed systems*; H.4.1 [**Information Systems Applications**]: Office Automation

General Terms: Design

Additional Keywords and Phrases: Office information systems, distributed office information management, semantic data modeling, nameservers

## 1. INTRODUCTION

Office information systems model real world situations that, by nature, are distributed [Ell82]. This is often reflected in the implementation of such systems: typically, an office information system consists of a number of workstations (personal computers, file servers, databases, printers, etc.) that are interconnected by a high bandwidth local-area communication network. The structure of such a network is highly dynamic. At any time, a new station may be added or an existing station removed from the network. Individual users of a distributed office system must be able to communicate with each other, dynamically share both hardware and software resources, and access information objects stored in remote "public" databases. Office objects, traditional formatted data, as well as unformatted data objects, such as text, audio, and images, are not permanently assigned to a single workstation; they might migrate in the network from workstation to workstation as real documents move from desk to desk in a traditional office [Tsi82a].

Many of the results and techniques from database research can be adapted to office information systems [Gib83]. However, most current approaches to distributed database management system design fail to adequately address issues concerning location transparency (the ability to reference data by name rather than by address), logical decentralization, catalog management, and the uniform handling of meta-data and user-data. Logically centralized database systems [And82,Rot80,Sto77] provide the users with a single integrated database schema describing all the data in the physically centralized or distributed environment. Recent research has also resulted in approaches to support the integration of heterogeneous as well as homogeneous (pre-existing) databases [Kim79,Lit81,Mot81,Smi81a]. However, a critical remaining problem is accommodating information sharing among individual, autonomous databases; this problem is critical in the context of distributed office information systems. Finally, existing distributed database system architectures that emphasize the autonomy of the individual databases [Hei82,Wil81,Tsi82c,Rab82] require centralized or complex catalog management.

The techniques and methodologies used to design a distributed database system are very specific to the conceptual model in which the distributed database is described. Most current distributed database research is carried out in the framework of either the relational model of data [Cod70] or some high-level semantic data model. For instance, the relational model of data has been adopted for SDD-1 [Rot80], Distributed INGRES [Sto77], R* [Wil81], the Multidatabase approach [Lit81], and the System for Managing Structured Messages [Tsi82c]. Many of the approaches and solutions to distributed database design are therefore specific to the relational data model.

The research described in this paper takes another approach. The object universe supports both coarser-grained and finer-grained organizations of information than is possible in systems based on the relational or a high-level semantic data model. Therefore, this research does not employ one of the traditional high-level database models, such as the hierarchical, network, relational, or functional database model; rather, it focuses on distributed information management at the finest possible level of data granularity, viz., the object level. This is done by introducing a simple model for interconnection and object sharing in distributed office information systems, and in terms of that model, proposing solutions to the distributed object management problems. The model is introduced by stepwise development of a series of object-oriented models.

First, a simple model called *ODM* (for *object-oriented database model*) is defined. ODM provides a user with the basic primitives for object definition, manipulation, and retrieval; it is straightforward to implement, but it lacks semantic expressiveness as well as mechanisms for integrity control and protection. Next, ODM is extended to provide object definition, manipulation, and retrieval facilities for a distributed environment. The distributed version of ODM, called *DODM*, supports object sharing among individual workstations, imposes access control, and allows relationships to be established among objects in different databases. Moreover, DODM provides location transparency, and can be implemented without introducing any central data structures or authorities. The ODM/DODM models were first introduced in [Lyn83].

DODM models the office environment as a logical network of *work stations*. Each work station has a unique name, and without loss of generality, contains a single collection of information (database). This convention is adopted to allow all resource sharing to be defined at the same level. In practice, several work stations may be grouped together at the same physical node of a computer network, but that is not reflected in this model, which describes the distributed office environment as a logical network of identical work stations. The work stations in the network need not implement the same database model; they are only required to be identical from a network point of view (i.e., they must all provide the same network interface). Thus, existing databases and information systems may be part of the network, if they are accommodated as virtual DODM work stations.

This paper focuses exclusively on ODM and DODM. Current research is in progress to explore object sharing in distributed databases that are modeled by higher-level semantic database models. These high-level models, based on the primitives of ODM and DODM, support abstractions such as object types (for object classification), supertypes/subtypes hierarchies (for generalization and specialization), and attributes (for inter-object mappings) [Abr74,Che76,Cod81,Ham81,Kin82,Kin84a,Mcl81,Smi77]. Section 2 of this paper defines ODM by describing its primitive operations and its implementation. Section 3 extends ODM to cover distributed office modeling: a naming convention is introduced for DODM, its operations are described, and the implementation is discussed. Finally, Section 4 presents a summary and concluding remarks.

## 2. ODM: AN OBJECT-ORIENTED DATABASE MODEL

ODM is a very simple object-oriented database model with a straightforward implementation. The main purpose of ODM is to provide a basic framework for object-oriented office information models and office information systems. ODM is based on a small number of simple concepts, and can be used as a tool for stepwise development of database models of increasing complexity and levels of abstraction.

### 2.1 The Modeling Elements of ODM

An ODM database is modeled as a collection of *objects*. Objects correspond to concepts that have an associated meaning (e.g., the legal contract #1754, the phone number "(213) 743-5501", the president of XYZ Corporation, and the assignment of a certain task to a certain employee). In addition to modeling the data content of a database, objects are used for modeling the structures imposed on the data as well as the operations defined on the data. Objects in an ODM database are unique in the sense that there is a single instance of each object. Each object is distinguished by a unique *object key* that serves as a handle on the object. In addition to the object key, an object may have a number of [external] user-defined *object identifiers*. Object identifiers are unique atomic strings of characters; they are displayable and serve as external object references.

ODM supports the following kinds of objects:

- *Descriptor objects* are atomic strings of characters. They are displayable and serve as symbolic identifiers in the database. The character string that constitutes a given descriptor object is also the object identifier for the object; the character string of a descriptor object is unique.
- *Abstract objects* are objects that do not carry any descriptive, behavioral, or structural information and, as such, they are neither displayable nor executable. Concepts modeled by abstract objects can only be described in terms of their relationships with other objects.[1]
- *Structural objects* are used to capture database semantics. A structural object models a relationship among three objects, say $x$, $y$, and $z$. The relationship is denoted by the 3-tuple $(x, y, z)$ in which the components are called *domain object*, *map object*, and *range object*, respectively. Relationships can be established among any three objects in a database. A structural object may have unique object identifiers.
- *Behavioral objects* embody database operations [Bro81,Kin82,Kin84a] and are executable. ODM includes behavioral objects to support data definition, manipulation, and retrieval; user-defined behavioral objects are also supported. The unique object identifiers of a behavioral object can be used to refer to a behavioral object when it is to be invoked.

[1]The only difference between abstract objects and descriptor objects is that a descriptor object has an object identifier and an abstract object does not.

- *Text objects* are used for variable length character strings. The byte string that constitutes a text object is uninterpreted by the ODM system. A text object may be referred to via its unique object identifiers or via its relationships with other objects.
- *Image objects* are used for digitized images for graphics devices. The byte string that constitutes an image object is uninterpreted by the ODM system. An image object may be referred to via its unique object identifiers or via its relationships with other objects.
- *Audio objects* are used for digitized voice. The byte string that constitutes an audio object is uninterpreted by the ODM system. An audio object may be referred to via its unique object identifiers or via its relationships with other objects.

Audio, behavioral, image, and text objects are used to support unformatted data. Such objects are normally not found in conventional database models, but they are needed in an office information model. Recent research [Has82,Sto83] has also suggested extensions to the relational model of data to accommodate unstructured objects. In ODM, unformatted data objects can be referred to via their unique object identifiers, and they can participate in relationships as any other object.

Abstract objects are used to model concepts that cannot naturally be represented in a database by a single identifier. For example, a given abstract object may represent the person John Smith. This abstract object does not itself contain any descriptive information about the person it denotes. Rather, such information is modeled by descriptive objects, e.g., the person name "John Smith" and the social security number "900-13-2607", which are related to the abstract object via appropriate mappings ("Has name" and "Has id"). When referring to an abstract object in this paper, an unquoted mnemonic name is used (e.g., Manager of Department K44); all other objects are referenced by their object identifier(s) for example, "Project 5443".

Objects and relationships are the basic concepts for information modeling in ODM. These concepts support *referential integrity* [Dat81a]. A relationship cannot exist unless all its components are existing database objects. When an object is removed from the database, all the relationships in which it participates cease to exist.

Mathematically, an ODM database can be thought of as a collection of relations. Each object in the database corresponds to a relation on the set of all database objects. Let $x$, $y$, and $z$ be objects. For each relationship $(x, y, z)$, y is a relation. In particular, $y = \{(x', z') \mid \text{the relationship } (x', \text{y}, z') \text{ exists}\}$.

An ODM database can be represented as a directed graph in which the nodes are boxes labeled with the object identifiers of the corresponding domain and range objects, and the edges are directed from domain objects to range objects and labeled with the object identifiers of the corresponding map objects. Objects without object identifiers are represented as empty boxes or unlabeled edges. Thus, the relationship ("John Smith", "Has phone", "(213) 452-1031") is represented graphically as shown in Figure 5-1.

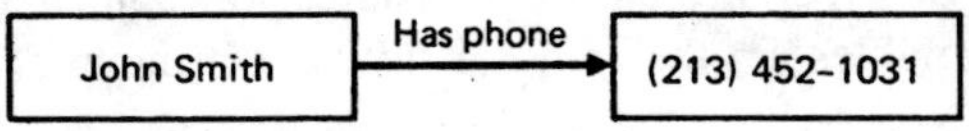


**Figure 5.1** Graphical representation of a relationship.

Since relationships may exist among any three objects in a database, a structural object (i.e., a relationship) may be part of another structural object. This capability supports what is *semantic relativism* [Mcl81], as illustrated by the example below.

Suppose John Smith is working on the Database Project, and that the task was assigned to him on November 11, 1983. These facts can be modeled by introducing an object representing a work assignment. The work assignment object is then related to "John Smith", "Database Project", and "11/11/83" via appropriate mappings (see Figure 5.2). The same information could also be modeled in ODM by treating the work assignment as a structural object related to the start date via an appropriate mapping. This way of modeling may be more natural or correct in the sense that the start date indeed is a property of the relationship between John Smith and Database Project. Figure 5.3 illustrates this approach.

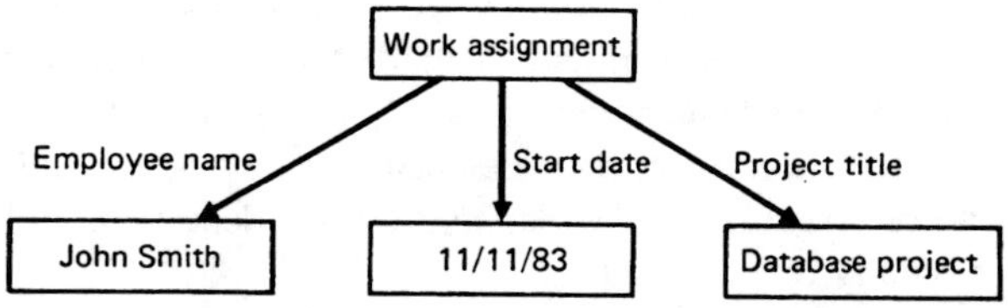


**Figure 5.2** Introducing an artificial object.

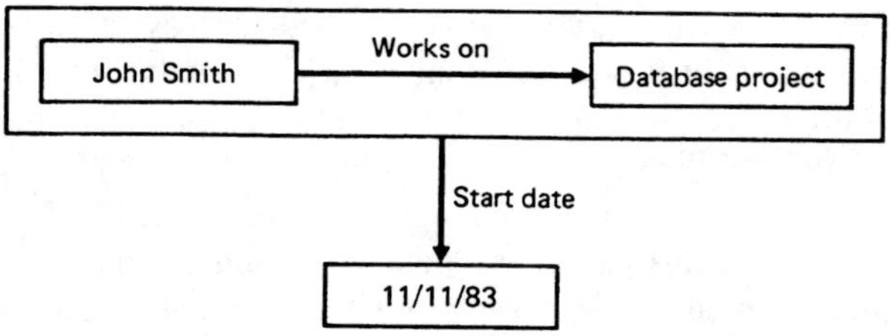


**Figure 5.3** Relating to a relationship.

## 2.2 The ODM Data Definition and Manipulation Language

The ODM data definition and manipulation language is described in this paper as a set of primitive operations that are embedded in a host programming language. The purpose here is not to propose a specific approach to host language embedding of data manipulation operations, but rather to define a set of primitive building blocks for a high-level, interactive user interface through which unsophisticated users can communicate with the database.

The host language must support the data types `objectid`, `objectkey`, `objectref`, and `set of objectref`, and the usual set operations. Variables can then be declared (in programs written in the host language) to be of these types. Values of variables of type objectid are object identifiers. Values of variables of type objectkey are object keys. Values of variables of type objectref are references to objects, internal as well as external; variables of this type are used as "handles" on objects in the database. At any given time, several variables (in the same or different programs) can denote the same object.

The primitive operations of ODM are themselves stored in the database (as behavioral objects). This approach enhances the flexibility and functionality of an office information system, treating the primitive operations of such a system as ordinary data. For example, operations may be added or modified as needed. The predefined operations allow a user to add new descriptor, audio, behavioral, image, text, and abstract objects to a database, to create relationships (structural objects) among existing database objects, to remove existing objects from a database, to test whether or not a given object reference denotes an existing database object, to rename objects, to define synonym object identifiers, to retrieve objects from the database, and to return (print) their unique object identifiers. A detailed description of the operations together with examples of their usage is given immediately below. A Pascal-like language is used here to illustrate the use of the operations.

**2.2.1** *`CREATE([id: objectid]): objectkey`.* The `CREATE` operation generates a new abstract or descriptor object,[2] adds it to the database, and returns its object key. If no identifier is specified, the new object is an abstract object, which can only be accessed via the reference returned. If an identifier is given that is not the object identifier of an existing database object, the new object is a descriptor object with the specified object identifier. An execution error occurs if the specified identifier denotes an existing database object.

Suppose that john, mary, mail, memo, has-name, has-phone, has-id, person1, and person2 are all variables of type objectref. Thus, the following operations would then create nine new objects:

```
john := CREATE("John Smith");
mary := CREATE("Mary Brown");
mail := CREATE("Incoming mail");
memo := CREATE("The committee is meeting at 3 p.m.");
has-name := CREATE("Has name");
has-phone := CREATE("Has phone");
has-id := CREATE("Has id");
person1 := CREATE();
person2 := CREATE();
```

First, the descriptor object "John Smith" is created; its object key is assigned to the program variable john. Six more descriptor objects are then created and their object keys are assigned to the variables mary, mail, memo, has-name, has-phone, and has-id, respectively. Finally, two abstract objects are created, and their object keys are assigned to the variables, person1 and person2.

**2.2.2** *`ISOBJECT(o: objectref, m: modality): boolean`.* The `ISOBJECT` operation returns the value true if the specified object reference denotes an existing object of the modality specified; otherwise it returns the value false. The modality specified can be one of the following: descriptor, abstract, structural, behavioral,

[2]Behavioral objects, text objects, image and audio objects are created using the `DEFINE` operation; structural objects are created using the `RELATE` operation.

text, image, audio, or "*" (don't care, denoting any modality). After the execution of the CREATE operations listed above, the operations ISOBJECT("Has name", descriptor) and ISOBJECT(person1, abstract) would return the value true, but the operation ISOBJECT("7", *) would return the value false.

**2.2.3** *DELETE(o: objectref).* The DELETE operation simply removes a given object from the database. If the specified object participates in relationships, those relationships are deleted recursively (see the DETACH operation below). After the execution of the CREATE operations listed above, the operation DELETE(john) would remove the object "John Smith" from the database.

**2.2.4** *RELATE(d, m, r: objectref): objectkey.* The RELATE operation returns the object key of the structural object denoted by $(d, m, r)$. If the relationship does not already exist, the RELATE operation will first create it and add it to the database. In ODM, any three objects can be related; consequently, it is the user's responsibility to avoid the creation of meaningless relationships (this problem is further discussed below).

The following example illustrates the use of the RELATE operation. Suppose that $r1$ through $r8$ are all variables of type objectref and that the CREATE operations listed above have been executed:

```
r1 := RELATE(person1, has-name, john);
r2 := RELATE(person2, has-name, mary);
r3 := RELATE(person1, mail, memo);
r4 := RELATE(person2, mail, memo);
r5 := RELATE(person1, has-phone, CREATE("(213) 452-1031"));
r6 := RELATE(person2, has-phone, CREATE("(213) 743-2438"));
r7 := RELATE(person1, has-id, CREATE("900-13-2607"));
r8 := RELATE(person2, has-id, CREATE("218-90-8146"));
```

First, the domain object denoted by the variable person1 is related to the descriptor object "John Smith" (denoted by the variable john) via the map object "Has name" (denoted by the variable has-name). The object key of the structural object is assigned to the variable $r1$. In the fifth line above, the abstract object denoted by person1 is related to the descriptor object "(213) 452-1031" (which is created inline) via the object denoted by has-phone; the object key of the relationship is assigned to the variable $r5$.

**2.2.5** *DETACH(d, m, r: objectref).* The DETACH operation deletes the relationship (d, m, r) from the database. If the specified relationship participates in relationships with other objects, those relationships are detached recursively. The DETACH operation has no effect if (d, m, r) is not an existing relationship. After the example CREATE and RELATE operations above have been executed, the operation DETACH(person1, mail, memo) would cause the abstract object modeling John Smith not to be related to the object "The committee is meeting at 3 p.m." via the (mapping) object "Incoming mail". The operation DETACH(memo, person1, mail) would have no effect, since the object "The committee is meeting at 3 p.m." is not related to the object "Incoming mail" via John Smith.

**2.2.6** *`ADDNAME(o: objectref, id: objectid).`* The ADDNAME operation defines a new object identifier for the specified object. The new object identifier must be unique, otherwise an execution error occurs. An object may be given any number of object identifiers.

After the CREATE operations above have been executed, the operations `ADDNAME("Mary Brown", "Brown, Mary")` and `ADDNAME("Mary Brown", "Mary")` would define the two identifiers "Brown, Mary" and "Mary" for the descriptor object "Mary Brown". The operation `ADDNAME("John Smith", "John")` would define the identifier "John" for the object "John Smith".

**2.2.7** *`DROPNAME(id: objectid).`* The DROPNAME operation drops the specified object identifier from the database. After an identifier has been dropped by the DROPNAME operation, it may be used as an identifier for another object. For example, the operation `DROPNAME("Mary")` removes the identifier "Mary" as a synonym for "Mary Brown".

**2.2.8** *`FIND(d-set, m-set, r-set: set of objectref): set of objectref.`* The `FIND` operation is used to retrieve objects from the database. The FIND operation returns a set of objects satisfying a predicate specified by the three parameters $d$-set, $m$-set, and $r$-set. Each parameter is either a question mark ("?") or a set of object references. The question mark denotes the objects in question. A single object reference may be used as a shorthand notation for the set containing only that one object reference. The "don't care" symbol "*" is the set containing the object references of all the objects in the database. The first parameter of the `FIND` operation corresponds to domain objects, the second to map objects, and the third to range objects. Thus, if the first parameter is a question mark and the two other parameters are sets of object references, the predicate specifies all the domain objects that have been related to some range object in the specified set of range objects via some map object in the specified set of map objects. If none of the parameters is a question mark, viz., if all three parameters are sets of object references, the predicate specifies all the structural objects that correspond to the relationships with domain, map, and range objects from the object sets denoted by the first, second, and third parameter, respectively.

In the following definition of the `FIND` operation, `OBJECTS` denotes the set of all objects in an ODM database; the sets $d$-set, $m$-set, and $r$-set are arbitrary subsets of `OBJECTS`:

- `FIND(`$d$`-set, `$m$`-set, `$r$`-set)` returns all the structural objects (i.e., relationships) with domain, map, and range objects from $d$-set, $m$-set, and $r$-set, respectively: `FIND(`$d$`-set, `$m$`-set, `$r$`-set)` $= \{(d, m, r) \in$ `OBJECTS` $\mid d \in d$-set $\wedge m \in m$-set $\wedge r \in r$-set$\}$
- `FIND(?, `$m$`-set, `$r$`-set)` returns all the objects that have been related to some range object in $r$-set via some map object in $m$-set: `FIND(?, `$m$`-set, `$r$`-set)` $= \{d \in$ `OBJECTS` $\mid$ the relationship $(d, m, r)$ exists for some $m \in m$-set $\wedge r \in r$-set$\}$.

- `FIND(`*d*`-set, ?, `*r*`-set)` returns all the objects that some domain object in *d*-set has been related to via some range object in *r*-set: `FIND(`*d*`-set, ?, `*r*`-set)` $= \{m \in$ `OBJECTS` $|$ the relationship $(d, m, r)$ exists for some $d \in d$-set $\wedge\ r \in r$-set$\}$.
- `FIND(`*d*`-set, `*m*`-set, ?)` returns all the objects that some domain object in *d*-set has been related to via some map object in *m*-set: `FIND(`*d*`-set, `*m*`-set, ?)` $= \{r \in$ `OBJECTS` $|$ the relationship $(d, m, r)$ exists for some $d \in d$-set $\wedge$ $m \in m$-set$\}$.
- `FIND(`*d*`-set, ?, ?)` returns all the map objects via which some object in *d*-set has been related and all the range objects to which some object in *d*-set has been related: `FIND(`*d*`-set, ?, ?)` = `FIND(`*d*`-set, ?, *)` ∪ `FIND(`*d*`-set, *, ?)`.
- `FIND(?, `*m*`-set, ?)` returns all the domain objects related via some object in *m*-set and all the range objects related via some object in *m*-set: `FIND(?, `*m*`-set, ?)` = `FIND(?, `*m*`-set, *)` ∪ `FIND(*, `*m*`-set, ?)`.
- `FIND(?, ?, `*r*`-set)` returns all the domain objects related to some object in *r*-set and all the map objects via which some object in *r*-set is related: `FIND(?, ?, `*r*`-set)` = `FIND(?, *, `*r*`-set)` ∪ `FIND(*, ?, `*r*`-set)`.
- `FIND(?, ?, ?)` returns all the objects that participate in a relationship, that is, all the domain objects, map objects, and range objects in the database: `FIND(?, ?, ?)` = `FIND(?, *, *)` ∪ `FIND(*, ?, *)` ∪ `FIND(*, *, ?)`.

After the execution of the `CREATE` and `RELATE` operations listed above, the operation `FIND(person1, *, ?)` would return the set {"John Smith", "The committee is meeting at 3 p.m.", "(213) 452-1031", "900-13-2607"}, that is, the set of all objects to which the domain object modeling John Smith is related via some map object. The operation `FIND(FIND(?, "Has name", "John Smith"), "Has phone", ?)` returns the set {"(213) 452-1031"}, that is, the phone numbers of persons with name John Smith.

**2.2.9** *`DEFINE(id: objectid, m: modality, fn: filename): objectkey`*. The DEFINE operation creates a new object of a specified modality of unformatted data, adds it to the database, and returns its object key. The object identifier must be unique; otherwise an execution error occurs. The modality specifies whether an audio, behavioral, image, or text object is to be created. Integrated tools that allow a user to create such complex objects within the framework of ODM are currently not available; however, such objects can be created by external text editors, graphics editors, compilers, and so on, and passed to the database as a file.

Behavioral objects are operations defined in the host programming language in terms of previously defined operations, as a procedure or function is defined in a Pascal program. While the specification of behavior is a very important issue [Bro81,Kim84], it is beyond the scope of this paper to directly address it. However, Figure 5.4 provides an example of a new operation called `PRINTINFO`, that will print the name and the phone numbers of a person with a given social security number.

```
operation PRINTINFO(id:  objectid)
var name, person, phone:  objectref
begin
  if ISOBJECT(id) then
    for each person in FIND(?, "Has id", id) do
      for each name in FIND(person, "Has name", ?)  do
        PRINT(name)
      end;
      for each phone in FIND(person, "Has phone", ?)  do
        PRINT(phone)
      end
    end
  end
end
```

**Figure 5.4** Definition of the PRINTINFO operation.

**2.2.10** *PRINT(o: objectref).* The PRINT operation prints the unique object identifier(s) for the specified object. An execution error occurs if the specified object has no object identifier. For example, the operation PRINT(memo) outputs the string "The Committee is meeting at 3 p.m.", and the operation PRINT("John Smith") outputs the string "John Smith".

**2.2.11** *INVOKE(o: objectref [, p1..pn: objectref]).* The INVOKE operation invokes the specified object which must be a behavioral object. The optional object references denote value parameters. If they are specified, they will be passed in the order indicated to the operation being invoked. The object identifier of an executable object can be used as a short-hand notation for the invocation of the object. This is how behavioral object invocations have been illustrated up to this point. For example, the PRINTINFO operation defined in Figure 5.4 is invoked by

```
PRINTINFO("John Smith")
```

The effect of that invocation is equivalent to the effect of the following invocation:

```
INVOKE("PRINTINFO", "John Smith")
```

### 2.3 Implementation of ODM

A straightforward implementation of ODM is possible using existing database technology. This section describes a simple prototype that has been built using the INGRES relational database management system [Sto76], running the UNIX[3] operating system.

The prototype maintains four relations to store an ODM database. Each ODM object is represented by a tuple in one of the relations. Figure 5.5 shows how an example database is represented in the prototype implementation.

- The DESCRIPTOR relation contains all the descriptor and abstract objects. An object is described by the two attributes KEY and IDENTIFIER, corresponding

[3]UNIX is a trademark of Bell Laboratories.

DESCRIPTOR

| Key | Identifier |
|---|---|
| 2435 | John Smith |
| 2435 | John |
| 2478 | Has name |
| 2494 | Has id |
| 2513 | 900-13-2607 |
| 34897 | |
| 34898 | |

RELATIONSHIP

| Key | Identifier | Dkey | Mkey | Rkey |
|---|---|---|---|---|
| −789 | | 34897 | 2478 | 2435 |
| −792 | | 34897 | 2494 | 2513 |

UNFORMATTED

| Key | Identifier | Modality | Address |
|---|---|---|---|
| −78965 | CREATE | behavioral | 22654 |
| −78974 | DETACH | behavioral | 22866 |
| −78987 | FIND | behavioral | 24188 |
| −30501 | PO 3465 | text | 73456 |
| −30718 | PO 3469 | text | 88152 |

**Figure 5.5** Relations in the ODM prototype.

to the unique object key and object identifier, respectively. A secondary index is defined on both the `KEY` attribute and the `IDENTIFIER` attribute.

- The `RELATIONSHIP` relation contains all the structural objects. A structural object is described by the attributes `KEY`, `IDENTIFIER`, `DKEY`, `MKEY`, and `RKEY`. The `KEY` attribute is the unique object key of the structural object. `DKEY`, `MKEY`, and `RKEY` are the object keys of the domain, map, and range objects (respectively) that participate in the relationship described by the structural object. A secondary index is defined on every attribute.
- The `UNFORMATTED` relation contains a description of all the unformatted objects. The objects themselves are stored in an object heap. An unformatted object is described by the attributes `KEY`, `MODALITY`, `IDENTIFIER`, and `ADDRESS`. `KEY` is the unique object identifier, `MODALITY` is the object modality (i.e., audio, behavioral, image, or text), `IDENTIFIER` is the object identifier, and `ADDRESS` is the address of the object in the object heap. Secondary indices are defined on the `KEY` and `IDENTIFIER` attributes.

There are several ways to support unique object keys. One approach is to use the object identifiers directly, as they are already unique. However, their arbitrary length causes problems. The prototype implements object keys as integers. All objects of a certain modality have object keys in a given subrange of the integers. In this way, it is easy to determine the modality of an object given its key, and the relation storing the description of the object can easily be selected.

The `DESCRIPTOR` relation of Figure 5.5 has seven tuples. The first five tuples describe descriptor objects, and the two last tuples describe abstract objects (they have no object identifiers). The `RELATIONSHIP` relation shows two tuples. The first tuple denotes the structural object with object key -789. The corresponding relationship has a domain object with object key 34897 (an abstract object), a map object with object key 2478 ("Has name"), and a range object with object key 2435 ("John Smith"). Although it is in general possible to provide identifiers for structural objects, in this example no such names are assigned. The `UNFORMATTED` relation contains five tuples. The first tuple describes the `CREATE` operation. This behavioral object, which has object key -78965, is stored at heap address 22654. If a given object has more than one object identifier, the relation describing the object will contain a tuple for each object identifier. For example, the `DESCRIPTOR` relation in Figure 5.5 has two tuples describing the same object. One tuple describes the object by the object identifier "John Smith", the other tuple describes the object by the object identifier "John".

Given an object identifier, the prototype implementation must support the fast retrieval of the tuple describing the object denoted by the given identifier. If all the objects were described in the same relation, the lookup procedure could be performed in a single task. Such a relation would have the following attributes: object key, object identifier, object modality, domain object key, map object key, range object key, and heap address. The domain object key, map object key, and range object key, however, only apply to structural objects, and the heap address only applies to unformatted objects. If more than one relation is used to describe objects that have object identifiers, as is the case in the prototype, the lookup procedure can be performed in parallel by concurrent processes; this potentially decreases both access time as well as storage requirements.

The object heap is implemented as a direct access file. The byte string that constitutes each unformatted object is preceded in the heap by a byte count, indicating the size of the object in number of bytes. When an unformatted object is deleted, its heap address is inserted in a free list together with its size. New objects are inserted in the heap on a first fit basis. When the percentage of free space in the heap exceeds a certain limit, the heap is automatically reorganized. Heap reorganization can also be explicitly initiated by the user.

The ODM operations are implemented as a collection of separately compiled EQUEL/C[4] [Woo81] programs. The executable programs implementing the ODM operations are stored as behavioral objects in the database, and documents describing the use of the operations are stored as text objects. A user-friendly interface to the ODM

[4]EQUEL/C is an extension of the programming language C to include the facilities of the INGRES database access and update language (QUEL).

system is provided by a command interpreter that guides the user through the process of selecting, specifying, and invoking ODM operations.

It is a major task to integrate the proposed ODM primitives with a host programming language on top of a relational database management system. Furthermore, due to limitations of UNIX, run-time invocation of the ODM operations is not elegantly implementable. However, the ad-hoc operation `EXECUTE` provided by the prototype allows existing operations to be invoked at run-time from user-defined operations (behavioral objects) written in the programming language C. The primitive operations of the current prototype are also easily extendible with new primitive operations written in C. The `EXECUTE` operation invokes a specified operation by calling the UNIX System Command. Parameter values are passed between the calling and the called operations via dedicated files. This solution is not very elegant, but given the limitations of the UNIX run-time system, it provides the facilities necessary to demonstrate the capabilities of ODM.

The prototype described does not support object identifiers of arbitrary length. This restriction is caused by the use of fixed-sized attributes to store the object identifiers. The problem would not have occurred in a prototype implementation that provides data structures to support data of varying length. In addition, the overhead introduced by using a very general relational database management system to implement a much simpler data model, may not be desirable from an efficiency point of view. To avoid the overhead of INGRES, a simple ad-hoc implementation can be built on top of a file system. Such an implementation would typically maintain four files corresponding to the four relations in the prototype described above. In order to provide fast access to the information in the files, B-tree indices would suffice.

### 2.4 Discussion of ODM

ODM is based on the two essential concepts of objects and relationships. All data in an ODM database is treated uniformly as objects; relationships among these objects allow semantic properties to be modeled. Operations on the data allow behavioral properties to be modeled. The implementation of ODM is straightforward. However, the simple model is not appropriate for a non-expert database user. It is easy to create meaningless relationships and operations, and no built-in mechanisms for data protection and integrity control are provided. However, the primitive operations of ODM can be used as the basic building blocks in the design and implementation of higher-level office information systems based on semantically richer data models.

## 3. DODM: AN OBJECT-ORIENTED DATABASE MODEL FOR DISTRIBUTED DATABASES

DODM is a simple extension of ODM; the purpose of DODM is to support object definition, manipulation, and retrieval in a distributed office environment. The distributed office system can be thought of as a logical network of communicating (active) databases. In DODM, relationships among objects can be established across database boundaries, objects may be copied or moved from one database to another, and mechanisms are provided for access control and the dynamic sharing of objects among individual databases.

### 3.1 Objects in a Distributed Environment

The single object instance rule of DODM states that in a network of databases, there is exactly one instance of a given object. However, objects stored in different databases may be identical; that is, they may have the same object identifier and the same "value" even though they are considered to be instances of different objects. When an object in a given database is copied to another database, the copy will be a completely new object owned by the database to which it is copied, but the copy and the original object are identical. In the distributed environment, a distinction is made between *local objects* and *global objects*. An object is said to be local to the database containing the object, and an object is said to be global to those databases that may access the object. Since a given database may access all its local objects, an object is always global to the database to which it is local.

Objects may be relocated from one database to another. Therefore, it is important to distinguish between the *creator* of the object and the *owner* of the object. The creator of a given object is the database creating the object; the owner of an object is the database currently containing the object. At object creation time the owner and the creator of the object are identical. The creator of an object remains the same throughout the life-time of the object, whereas the owner of the object changes every time the object is relocated.

If objects owned by different databases have the same object identifier, the objects are said to be *name equivalent* or just equivalent. Descriptor objects that are name equivalent are also value equivalent, that is, they are completely identical; however, DODM treats such objects as independent. This is because the consistency among equivalent objects is not guaranteed: if an object local to a given database is changed and that object is equivalent to a certain remote object, then the remote object is not changed correspondingly. The notion of equivalence is introduced to allow individual databases to coordinate their object naming if appropriate. Name equivalence makes most sense for descriptor objects; for unformatted and structural objects it only states whether or not the objects have identical identifiers. Value equivalence of unformatted and structural objects is beyond the scope of this paper (it is further addressed in [Lyn84]).

### 3.2 Database and Object Naming

Conventions for naming information objects and mechanisms to support name resolution are very crucial in a distributed information management system [Lin80,Lyn82,Opp83, Ter83]. In DODM, each database is uniquely identified by its *database identifier*, which is an atomic string of characters. A protocol that coordinates the naming of new databases joining the network has been developed [Lyn84]. The protocol does not violate the goal of site autonomy of the individual databases in the network.

It must be possible to reference databases from programs written in the host programming language. Therefore, the language must support the data types `databaseref` and `set of databaseref`, so that variables can be declared (in programs written in the host language) to be of these types. A database identifier is a database reference, and the "don't care" symbol "*", when used as a database reference, is an abbreviation for the set of references to all databases. A single database reference may be used as a shorthand notation for the set containing only that one reference.

Objects in DODM may be referred to by their user-defined object identifiers. There are three different kinds of *object identifiers*: local, global, and transparent object identifiers. As noted above, the object identifier of a descriptor object is the string that constitutes the object, and the object identifier of an unformatted object (i.e., an audio, behavioral, image, or text object) is the atomic string denoting the object.[5] A *local object identifier* is an object identifier as introduced in ODM. It uniquely identifies an object within the database that is local to the object reference. Each database in the network may contain an object denoted by the same local object identifier, but there can at most be one such object per database. Objects with identical local object identifiers are name equivalent. A *global object identifier* uniquely identifies an object within the entire network of databases. It is composed of a local object identifier, an "@", and a database identifier:

```
⟨object identifier⟩@⟨database identifier⟩
```

Note that the global object identifier of a given object depends on the owner of the object and not the creator (as is the case in R* [Lin80]). If an object is relocated from one database to another, its global object identifier is changed accordingly.

The presence of distribution-dependent information in a global object identifier may seem inconvenient, but location transparency can be attained by using transparent object identifiers. A *transparent object identifier* denotes every object in a given set of databases that has the same local object identifier (at most, one per database). In other words, a given transparent object identifier denotes all the objects in a given set of databases that are name equivalent based on the identifier. A transparent object identifier is composed of a local object identifier, an "@", and a set of database identifiers:

```
⟨object identifier⟩@{⟨database identifier⟩,..,⟨database identifier⟩}
```

A single database identifier may be used as a shorthand notation for the set containing only that one identifier. To avoid enumeration of all the databases in the network, the "don't care" symbol ("*") can be used. The following transparent object identifier simply denotes all the objects in the entire network that are name equivalent with the identifier specified:

```
⟨object identifier⟩@*
```

[5] As noted above, objects without object identifiers can be referenced only by their relationships with other objects.

If there is only one object in the global system with a given local object identifier, that object may be uniquely referenced with its transparent object identifier (i.e., the object reference is completely location transparent).

Suppose that a database network consists of the three databases (DB1, DB2, and DB3), and that each database contains the two descriptor objects "Employees" and "Has instances". Then the operation `FIND("Employees", "Has instances", ?)` returns references to every object in the network that has been related locally to the local objects "Employees" and "Has instances". The operation `FIND@DB2("Employees", "Has instances", ?)` returns references to every object in the network that has been related in DB2 to the two local (with respect to DB2) objects "Employees" and "Has instances". The operation `FIND@DB3("Employees"@"DB1", "Has instances", ?)` returns references to every object in the network that has been related in DB3 to the object "Employees" in DB1 and the local (with respect to DB3) object "Has instances". The operation `FIND@*("Employees", "Has instances"@*, ?)` returns references to every object in the network that has been related in some database to the local object "Employees" and the object "Has instances" in some database.

## 3.3 The Primitive Operations of DODM

DODM supports modified versions of the primitive operations of ODM. In order to maximize the autonomy of each individual database, the operations for object creation and deletion have been restricted to operate on only local objects. The `CREATE` operation creates a local object, and the `DELETE` operation deletes a local object. When an object is deleted from a given database, all the relationships throughout the database network in which the deleted object participated are detached recursively. The `ISOBJECT` operation tests if an object reference denotes an existing global object. The `RELATE` operation creates a local relationship among three global objects, and the DETACH operation deletes a local relationship. Like the `DELETE` operation, the `DETACH` operation notifies all other databases about the deletion. The `PRINT` operation prints the object identifier of a global object. In addition to printing the local object identifier of a given object, the PRINT operation can optionally print the global object identifier of the object. Finally, the DEFINE operation creates a new local audio, behavioral, image, or text object.

The `FIND`, `ADDNAME`, and `DROPNAME` operations are modified slightly in order to accommodate the distributed environment where objects of interest reside at many different sites. The new `FIND`, `ADDNAME`, and `DROPNAME` operations are described below. In addition to the primitive operations of ODM, DODM has primitive operations for object sharing and access control, and for copying and moving objects from database to database. These primitives are also described below.

### 3.3.1 *PERMIT(o: objectref, ds: set of databaseref [, INVOKE] [, MOVE]).*

Access control and object sharing among individual databases is controlled by the `PERMIT` operation. The `PERMIT` operation specifies an object, a set of remote databases, optionally an `INVOKE` right, and optionally a `MOVE` right. The `PERMIT` operation makes the specified object "known" to the specified set of databases.

More specifically, a database to which a remote object is known has the following rights to the object: it may FIND the object in the database containing it, PRINT the object identifier, RELATE the object to other (local or remote) objects, and make a COPY of the object (see below). In addition, the function ISOBJECT evaluates to true when applied to a known object, and the operation WHERE (see below) only applies to known objects. A structural object (a relationship) is used to evaluate a remote FIND operation, only if the object is known to the remote database issuing the FIND operation. A structural object cannot be known to a remote database unless the three objects participating in the relationship are known to the database.

If the INVOKE right is specified as a parameter to the PERMIT operation, the specified object may be invoked by the set of databases specified. The right to invoke an object can only be granted if the specified object is a behavioral object (it must be executable). If the behavioral object returns a set of object references, only references to objects that are known to the database invoking the operation will be returned. If the MOVE right is specified as a parameter to the PERMIT operation, the specified object may be moved by the set of databases specified. When an object is moved to another database, the MOVE right will not automatically be granted by that database. That first happens when the database explicitly executes a PERMIT operation with a MOVE right.

If the object specified as a parameter to the PERMIT operation is always known with the specified rights to the specified set of databases, the PERMIT operation has no effect. The PERMIT operation results in an execution error if the specified object is not a local object.

The operation PERMIT("John Smith", "Payroll") causes the local object "John Smith" to be known to the Payroll database. Moreover, the Payroll database is not granted the INVOKE right or the MOVE right. Figure 5.6 shows how information about the objects that have been related to "John Smith" is made known to the Personnel database.

```
var  p, m, r: objectref
begin
  for each  p in FIND(?, "Has name", "John Smith") do
    PERMIT( p, "Personnel");
    for each  m in FIND( p, ?, *) do
      PERMIT( m, "Personnel");
      for each  r in FIND( p, m, ?)  do
        PERMIT( r, "Personnel");
        PERMIT(FIND( p, m, r)., "Personnel");
      end
    end
  end
end
```

**Figure 5.6** An example of PERMIT operation usage.

**3.3.2** *REVOKE(o: objectref, ds: set of databaseref [,INVOKE] [,MOVE]).* The REVOKE operation revokes rights granted by the PERMIT operation. If the INVOKE option is present, the specified object (a behavioral object) remains known to the specified set of databases, but the right to invoke the object is revoked from those databases. If the MOVE option is present, the specified object remains known to the specified set of databases, but the right to move the object is revoked from those databases. If neither the INVOKE nor the MOVE option is present, the specified object will no longer be known to the specified set of databases. This implies that MOVE and INVOKE rights to the object (if such rights were granted) are also revoked. For example, REVOKE("(213) 452-1031", "Personnel") causes the phone number of John Smith ((213) 452-1031) to be "unknown" to the Personnel database.

**3.3.3** *ADDNAME(o: objectref, id: objectid [, ds: set of databaseref]).* The DODM ADDNAME operation supports object naming in a distributed environment. If the optional database specification is omitted, the ADDNAME operation defines a new local identifier for the object specified, as in ODM. If a database specification is given, the specified object will become known by the identifier given to the specified set of databases. The naming facility allows an object to be known by different names to different databases. As an example, the operation ADDNAME("John Smith", "Smith, John", *) makes the object "John Smith" known to every database as the object "Smith, John".

**3.3.4** *DROPNAME(id: objectid [, ds: set of databaseref]).* The DODM DROPNAME operation drops an object identifier from a specified set of databases. If the optional database specification is omitted, the DROPNAME operation drops the specified identifier from the local database; remote databases are not affected. If a database specification is given, the object identifier will be dropped from the specified set of databases. For example, the operation DROPNAME("Smith, John") drops the local object identifier "Smith, John". The operation DROPNAME("Smith, John", "DB4"), when executed in database DB1, prevents the object identifier "Smith, John" from being used by database DB4 as a denotation for an object in DB1.

**3.3.5** *FIND(d-set, m-set, r-set: set of objectref [, ds: set of databaseref]): set of objectref.* As is the case for the FIND operation of ODM, the DODM FIND operation returns a set of object references denoting those objects that correspond to the given predicate. The only difference is an optional specification of a set of databases that indicates where the predicate is to be applied. If the database specification is omitted, the predicate is applied to all the relationships that have been created locally, as in ODM. If a database specification is given, the predicate is applied to all the relationships that are stored in the specified databases and are known to the database executing the FIND operation.

The operation FIND(?, "Has name", "John Smith") will return the set of domain objects that have been related locally to "John Smith" via "Has name". This example is similar to the ODM usage of the FIND operation. The operation FIND(?, "Has name", "John Smith", "Personnel") returns the set of known domain objects that have been related to "John Smith" via "Has name" in those relationships in the Personnel database that are known to the database executing the FIND operation.

There are two different ways a given database (DB1) can allow its local objects to be queried by a remote database:

1. DB1 can make structural objects (relationships) known such that they can be used to resolve the predicate specified in a `FIND` operation issued by remote database(s).
2. DB1 can grant the `INVOKE` right to its `FIND` operation; in this case, a remote database can use all of DB1's relationships to resolve a `FIND` predicate.

For example, suppose that a local database (DB2) specifies the following `FIND` request:

```
FIND(?, "Has name", "John Smith", "Personnel")
```

This request returns references to all the objects that have been related to "John Smith" via "Has name" in those relationships of the Personnel database that are known to DB2. By contrast, suppose DB2 issues the following request:

```
FIND@Personnel(?, "Has name", "John Smith")
```

This returns references to all the objects in the Personnel database that have been related to "John Smith" via "Has name" and are known to the database issuing the `FIND` operation. (It is of course assumed here that the `INVOKE` right to the `FIND` operation has been granted to DB2 by the Personnel database.)

**3.3.6** *`COPY(o: objectref [, id: objectid]): objectkey`*. The `COPY` operation creates a local copy of the referenced remote object and returns its unique object key. The object copy is considered a new and independent object; it may optionally be renamed. The object identifier, if specified, will denote the new object copy. The original object and the copy have the same "value". If the object copy has not been renamed, the original object and the copy will be name equivalent. The `COPY` operation has no effect if the referenced object is a local object.

When a given remote object is known to a certain database, the database can query the object, ask for its object key, and print the object. In other words, the database can gather enough information about the object to recreate it locally. In many distributed applications, it is desirable to allow data to be seen or read by remote users, but to disallow the users to make their own local copies of the data. This is, for instance, the case when users pay for the right to read the data. The approach taken here, however, recognizes the fact that once a remote object can be printed it can also somehow be recreated; therefore, the `COPY` operation is provided.

**3.3.7** *`MOVE(o: objectref)`*. The `MOVE` operation moves the specified remote object to the local database. If the reference denotes a local object, the operation has no effect. The specified object must have been awarded (see below) by its owner to the database issuing the `MOVE` operation. The object reference remains the same after the object has been moved. (The section describing the implementation of DODM (below) explains how location transparency in object references can be achieved).

The result of executing a `MOVE` operation is different from the result of making a copy of the object and then deleting the original object, because all the relationships in which the object participates are preserved by the `MOVE` operation. This is important when an object is migrating in the office environment while being accessed and possibly even modified by different users. Examples of such objects might include legal documents, purchase orders, travel reimbursement forms, and so on. The `MOVE` operation thus eliminates the need for maintaining the consistency between several "identical" objects. As an example, the operation `MOVE`("PO 3465"@"Peter Lyngbaek") issued by DB1 moves the Purchase Order with number 3465 from the Peter Lyngbaek database to DB1.

**3.3.8** *`EQUIVALENCE(os: set of objectref): boolean`.* The `EQUIVALENCE` operation returns the value true if the set of objects specified are equivalent; otherwise it returns the value false. Suppose the two databases DB1 and DB2 each contain the two objects "employee" and "salary"; then, the operation `EQUIVALENCE({"employee", "employee"@"DB2"})` returns the value true, whereas the operation `EQUIVALENCE({"employee", "salary"})` returns the value false.

**3.3.9** *`WHERE(o: objectref): databaseref`.* The `WHERE` operation returns a database reference denoting the database that contains the object denoted by the specified object reference. If the object reference is specified as a local object identifier, the `WHERE` operation returns a reference to the local database if it contains the specified object. The `WHERE` operation only returns a reference to a remote database if that database has made the object known to the database executing the `WHERE` operation. Suppose, for example, that the three databases DB1, DB2, and DB3 each have an object denoted by the local object identifier "has mail". Furthermore, suppose that DB1 and DB3 have made their "has mail" objects known to every database, but DB2's "has mail" object is not known to any remote database. Then the operation `WHERE("has mail")`, when executed by DB1, will return references to DB1 and DB3. If the same operation is executed by DB2, it will return references to DB1, DB2, and DB3.

### 3.4 Implementation of DODM

Each database in a DODM database network contains its own objects and relationships in a way similar to an ODM database. As in ODM, objects are referenced by their unique object keys; but in order to be able to distinguish between objects from different databases, object keys must be unique within the entire network. This is achieved by using object keys that have two parts: a key that is unique within a given database (analogous to the ODM object key), and the database identifier of that database. This key format is similar to the format of a global object identifier. However, an object key will never change during the lifetime of an object; this is true even if the object is relocated from one database to another. The method of constructing object keys for DODM objects is similar to that used in other distributed systems such as R* [Lin80] and the Clearinghouse [Opp83].

Since object keys are unique within the entire database network, a relationship can be described by the keys of the three objects in the relationship. Thus, relationships may span database boundaries. Furthermore, a relationship is not affected by objects being relocated to other databases after the relationship has been established.

In the experimental implementation of DODM, each node in the database network consists of a *database*, a *catalog manager*, a *communication subsystem*, and a *database operation interpreter* (see Fig. 5.7). These components allow users and application programs at a given node to communicate, cooperate, and share objects with users and programs at other nodes in the network. In this architecture, the database stores all the objects and relationships as explained in the section describing the ODM implementation.

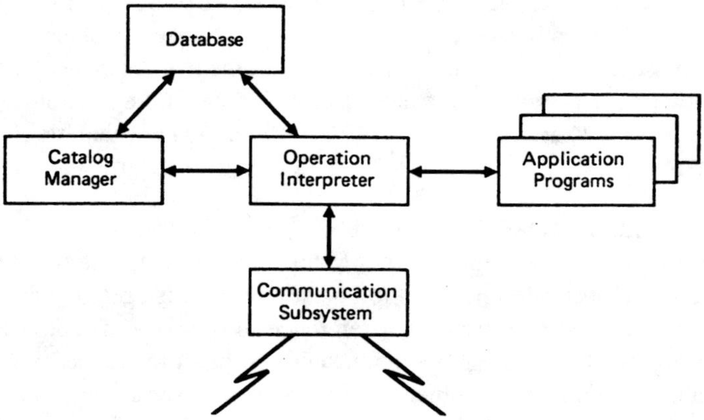


**Figure 5.7** DODM system structure.

The catalog manager describes access control and object sharing among the individual databases in the distributed environment. The catalog manager maintains an *external catalog* for each remote database to which access to objects is permitted. The prototype implementation of an external catalog contains four INGRES relations per remote database. Figure 5.8 shows how these relations are used to describe objects from the example database illustrated in Figure 5.5. Specifically, the four INGRES relations contain the following information:

- The `PERMITTED` relation describes all the objects that are known. A known object is described by the attribute `KEY` corresponding to the unique object key.
- The `INVOKE` relation describes all the behavioral objects that may be invoked. An invokable object is described by the attribute `KEY` corresponding to the unique object key.
- The `MOVE` relation describes all the objects that may be moved. A movable object is described by the attribute `KEY` corresponding to the unique object key.
- The `RENAMED` relation describes all the objects to which object identifiers have been added for the given remote database. A renamed object is described by the attributes `KEY` and `IDENTIFIER`, corresponding to the unique object key and the identifier by which the object is known, respectively. If an object is known by several identifiers, the `RENAMED` relation contains a tuple for each identifier.

PERMITTED

| Key |
|---|
| -789 |
| -30501 |
| -30718 |
| -78987 |
| -78965 |
| 2435 |
| 2513 |

INVOKE

| Key |
|---|
| -78965 |
| -78987 |

MOVE

| Key |
|---|
| -30501 |
| -30718 |

RENAMED

| Key | Identifier |
|---|---|
| 2435 | Smith, John |
| 2513 | 900132607 |

**Figure 5.8** Relations for object sharing in the DODM prototype.

When a database receives a request from a remote database to resolve an object reference, the following takes place. If the reference is an object identifier and is listed in the `RENAMED` relation corresponding to the remote database referencing the object, the object key is obtained; otherwise, the given object identifier is not known. If the reference is an object key, the key is looked up in the `PERMITTED` relation corresponding to the database referencing the object. If the `PERMITTED` relation contains the object key, the object is known by the remote database; otherwise, the object is not known and cannot be accessed by the remote database.

The database operation processor interprets database operations. If it is necessary to access remote objects in order to process a given operation, the databases containing the remote objects are activated via the communication subsystem. The communication subsystem provides the following three primitives:

*send*(set of database identifiers, message),
*broadcast*(message),
*receive*(database identifier, message)

The send primitive sends the message from the sender database to the specified set of databases, where it is queued. The broadcast primitive is a special case of the send primitive. It simply broadcasts the message to all the databases in the network without an explicit specification of all the databases. The receive primitive obtains from the queue of incoming messages the next message and the name of the database that sent it.

Broadcast communication is used to implement location transparency. An object reference in the form of an object key does not provide sufficient information to locate the corresponding object in the network.[6] In order to resolve such a reference the database operation processor broadcasts a request to every database in the network via the communication subsystem. Every remote database then attempts to resolve the object reference from the external catalog corresponding to the requesting database. The requesting database attempts to resolve the object reference from the local catalog. Finally, the requesting database is notified of the outcome of the catalog lookups.

This scheme for resolution of object references can be optimized by allowing each database to maintain a catalog describing remote objects that are frequently accessed. The catalog associates an object key with the identifier of the database that owns the object. Thus, rather than broadcasting a request to every database, a remote reference is looked up in the catalog. If the reference is described there, a request is sent directly to the database that was the owner of the object the last time it was accessed.

The operation of a distributed office information system must not be vulnerable to the failure of any particular workstation. But in a network with many work stations, it is reasonable to assume that some such failures will occur. It is therefore necessary to maintain a log of those operations that have a scope that is the entire network. One such operation is the `DELETE` operation. When an object is deleted, every relationship throughout the network in which it participates is detached (recursively). This is implemented by broadcasting a message from the database deleting the object. In this way, each database in the network is notified of the deletion, and can thus detach the appropriate relationships. However, if the deleted object participates in a relationship in a database that is not available at the time the deletion message is broadcast, it must be possible for that database to determine that the relationship is no longer valid (when the database becomes available). The solution taken here is to maintain a log at each database, which records all the messages that are broadcast. It is part of the "log-in procedure" for a database that has been unavailable to get a transcript of the log from one of the available databases and take the appropriate action.

As noted above, in order to provide location transparent object references, the communication subsystem must support broadcast communication. Ethernet [Met76] is a commercially available local area network that uses broadcast as the basic communication technique. In fact, the Ethernet hardware broadcasts a message, whether it is intended for every node in the network or just a single node. Therefore, the communication subsystem can perform a send and a broadcast operation as explained above for the same cost. If a broadcast is not supported directly by the network hardware, it can be implemented on networks of both the star and ring configurations.

### 3.5 Discussion of DODM

DODM is a very simple database model for the specification of objects and relationships in a logical network of databases. Mechanisms are provided to allow relationships to be established across database boundaries, objects are allowed to be copied and moved from database to database, and access control and object sharing among individual databases

[6] An object key indicates where an object is created and not where it is located.

are accommodated. The conventions for object naming in the distributed system allow objects to have different names for different purposes. DODM supports broadcast communication in addition to direct communication, both of which are important in a distributed system emphasizing efficiency as well as simplicity.

In DODM, the unit of access control and sharing is a single object. However, a concept or a "thing" being modeled is not always described by a single object, but by a collection of objects and relationships. For the purpose of access control and sharing as well as for other purposes,[7] it might therefore be desirable to treat as a unit the set of objects and relationships that best describe a given concept. Such a set is characterized by the *boundary* of the object that models the concept. For example, a person might be modeled as an abstract object, but that abstract object does not describe the person very well (in fact, not at all). The person is described by the relationships in which the abstract object participates. Such relationships might include "has name", "has phone", and "has father". Objects related to the abstract object might be described by their relationships to other objects, and so on. For example, the father of the person is modeled by another abstract object described by his father, and so forth. Thus, it should be possible to define different object boundaries for different purposes. However, a general approach to object boundaries is beyond the scope of this paper.

Like ODM, DODM is not a high-level model appropriate for unsophisticated database users; it lacks semantic expressiveness, mechanisms for integrity control, high-level operations for database integration, and so forth. However, the main purpose of DODM is not to define such a high-level database model but, on the contrary, to define a small set of fundamental concepts to be used as a vehicle in the design and implementation of distributed office information systems providing more expressive models.

## 4. CONCLUDING REMARKS

This paper describes a simple model for object manipulation in a distributed office environment. The model provides a small set of primitive operations for object definition, manipulation, and retrieval. Described first are the primitive operations and the implementation of ODM: a simple object-oriented data model for a single centralized system. A prototype implementation of this model is discussed, and the operations and implementation of the DODM model (an extended version of ODM for the modeling of distributed databases) is described. An experimental implementation of DODM and the associated support facilities required are also discussed.

Analysis, testing, and extensions of the research described in this paper are currently under study. In particular, the prototype DODM implementation will be used to further assess the adequacy and completeness of the primitives of the model. For example, further investigation in treating relationships as completely first-class objects, and in the semantics of object equivalence, is planned. Another important area concerns the use of broadcast communication. Finally, the concurrency and multiple copy control issues

[7] For example, for input and output purposes a user might want to see a number of the objects describing a given concept.

have been avoided in this paper, by assuming a single copy of each object and single-user systems at each node in the network. Results of current research in these areas will be utilized as this research progresses to address these limitations.

The work described in this paper is part of a current research effort at the University of Southern California to design and develop a "personal information management environment" and experimental tool called INFOBASE, which is intended to provide information management facilities to support a wide range of personal work station applications, including data management activities of a professional, manager, or home computer user. INFOBASE is also intended to provide a basis for the information management needs of engineering applications, including software engineering and CAD/VLSI design [Mcl83a].

## ACKNOWLEDGMENTS

The authors would like to thank the referees and Michael Brodie for their helpful comments on earlier versions of this paper.

# 6

# *Type Evolution in an Object-Oriented Database**

**Andrea H. Skarra and Stanley B. Zdonik**

*Department of Computer Science, Brown University*
*Providence, RI 02912*

## ABSTRACT

We address the problem of maintaining consistency between a set of persistent objects and a set of type definitions that can change. The context of the problem is an object-oriented database system. Our objective is to make a type's changes transparent with respect to programs that use the type. The solution involves the use of a version control mechanism and a set of error handlers associated with the versions of a type. We describe the structure of the version control and error handling mechanisms and demonstrate their use.

*This research was supported in part by the National Science Foundation under grant DCR8605567, by International Business Machines Corporation under contract 55916 with amendment contract 643513, by the office of Naval Research under contract N00014-86-K-0621, and by DARPA under ONR contract N000014-83-K-0146, ARPA order 4786.

*Source*: Adapted from Skarra, A., and S. Zdonik, "Type Evolution in an Object-Oriented Database", in Research Directions in Object-Oriented Programming, B. Shriver & P. Wegner (eds.), MIT Press 1987, pp. 1–15.

## 1. INTRODUCTION

Our research centers on the development of techniques for the use of database technology in advanced applications on high-performance workstations. We are particularly interested in the large class of applications involving design. These include programming environments, computer-aided design, logical database design, and office information systems. We are designing database tools that are well suited for these environments.

Design environments are characterized by constant change. Traditional database tools do not deal well with certain kinds of change. In particular, changing the database schema in arbitrary ways is a very difficult process. We feel that it is important for a design database to be able to deal with change at all levels, including the type level.

In this work we look at the problem of changes in type definitions (i.e., the database schema). It is natural to assume that in the course of a design, views of the world (i.e., type definitions) will change. A database stores objects for long periods of time. Each object was created as an instance of some type at some point in that type's evolution. The type described all of the assumptions about that object's behavior. What happens when that type definition changes? Old objects may be incompatible with a new definition of their type. Also, new objects may be incompatible with old definitions of their type for which programs have already been written.

Our general approach to the problem of changing types adopts the philosophy that type designers are sophisticated users. They modify type definitions because the design process requires it. They know that this is a dangerous process, and they would be willing to do extra work if they knew that the work would help avert disaster. Currently, this extra work is very unstructured: it is not clear what needs to be done when a type changes. Our solution gives type designers a framework for this task, and provides them with a structured approach to defining the correspondences between new types and old ones.

## 2. THE DATABASE MODEL

The database system that forms the basis for this work [Zdo86d] supports an object-oriented model of data. It is in the tradition of much of the work on high-level semantic models [Bee85,Che76,Cod79,Ham81,Myl80a,Shi81,Smi83,Smi77,Won77], but it takes a view of data that is very closely aligned with many of the object-oriented programming languages [Bob83,Fla85,Gol83]. It illustrates a new direction in database research characterized as object-oriented databases [Cop84,Dit86,Mai86a,Mai86b,Rud86,Zdo846].

Every object is an instance of some *type* which describes the behavior of its instances. A type $T$ is a specification of behavior. As such, it describes a set of operations *op* ($T$), a set of properties *pr* ($T$), and a set of constraints *con* ($T$) that pertain to any instance $t$ of $T$. Any operation $o$ in *op* ($T$) can legally be applied to $t$, any property $p$ in *pr* ($T$) is defined for $t$, and every constraint $c$ in *con* ($T$) must be satisfied by $t$.

Each type has an implementation that is hidden. The implementation of a type includes a representation for instances and some code that implements the operations and properties. No code outside of the type definition has access to the type's implementation. Type definitions may use only the exported interface of other types, including a type and its subtypes. No subtype can make use of the implementation of any of its supertypes, and no supertype can make use of the implementation of any of its subtypes.

Types, operations, and properties are all objects in their own right and as such have a type that describes their behavior. Operations are active objects that are supported by code. All operations have an *invoke* operation defined for them such that it is possible to invoke an operation defined on type $T$ on any object of type $T$. Properties are objects that are used to relate other objects [Zdo86c]. For example, a property called `works-for` might be defined on the type `Person` to relate a given person to the company object for which he or she works. As a first-class object, it is possible for a property to have properties. A property of the *`works-for`* property might be *`starting-date`*. A common constraint on property types limits the acceptable values for the property. We will call the set of all legal values for a property $p$ its *value class*.

Types can be related to each other by means of a special property called `is-a`. The `is-a` property induces an inheritance relationship between types. If `A is-a B`, then all operations, properties, and constraints that are defined on $B$ will also be defined on $A$. In this case, we say that $A$ is a *subtype* of $B$ and that $B$ is a *supertype* of $A$. The system enables a type to have more than one supertype (i.e., multiple inheritance). The set of *is-a* relationships may be represented as a directed acyclic graph with exactly one node containing no outgoing arcs. The graph is known as the *type lattice*.

The constraints defined on a type delimit the range of acceptable values for properties and operations. A single constraint may involve one or more properties or operation parameters. For example, two properties of `Student` might be *`year:{frsh, soph, jr, sr}`* and *`major : Majors`*. The domain of each property is constrained to a given set of values, and in addition there might be an interproperty constraint that all juniors and seniors must have a declared major. We may state the constraint as

`if student.year=jr or student.year=sr then student.major ≠ NULL.`

An equivalent Boolean expression using $\wedge$ (*AND*), $\vee$ (*OR*), and $\neg$ (*NOT*) for the constraint is

$$\neg\ (student.year{=}jr \vee student.year{=}sr) \vee student.major \neq NULL.$$

The individual property constraints may be described as a disjunction such as

$$student.year{=}frsh \vee \ldots \vee student.year{=}sr.$$

Our constraint language consists of expressions built from basis predicates of the following three forms:

```
⟨property value⟩  ⟨comparison operator⟩ ⟨constant⟩
⟨property value⟩  ⟨comparison operator⟩ ⟨property value⟩
⟨property value⟩  ⟨comparison operator⟩ ⟨property value⟩ + ⟨constant⟩
```

where *comparison operator* is in the set $\{=, \neq, <, >, \leq, \geq\}$.

We may use the constraint language to verify that a newly defined type is a legal subtype of the type(s) declared as its supertype(s). By the standard inheritance model, each property or operation defined on a type $T$ must be a supertype of the property and operation redefined on a subtype $T_{sub}$ [Zdo86c]. In addition, the constraints on $T$ must be consistent with the constraints on each of its subtypes. Consistency in this context means that the constraints on the subtype may only tighten the constraints on the supertype. We may define a predicate $C_T$ that consists of the conjunction of the constraint expressions defined on $T$. If we construct a similar predicate $C_{T_{sub}}$ for each subtype of $T$, we can compute whether the *is-a* relationship is consistent between $T$ and each of its subtypes. Specifically, $T_{sub}$ *is-a* $T$ if and only if the following expression is unsatisfiable:

$$C_{T_{sub}} \wedge \neg C_T$$

The satisfiability problem in the predicate calculus is in general unsolvable. However, when the basis predicates are defined as above for a fixed number of properties, satisfiability may be decided by a polynomial time algorithm [Hun79]. Thus, the system is able to prevent the definition of any type that violates the model of inheritance.

It is important to realize that the model of data described above is a part of a database system. As such, it governs the way in which persistent, sharable objects behave. Our system also addresses database notions of transaction, consistency, associative retrieval, and views.

## 3. THE APPROACH

Our solution has been driven by the observation that in a real application environment the simultaneous support of several consistent views of the type structures is necessary. These views are defined by the versions of types that are current when the application code is written. It is often not feasible to adjust this application code as the type definitions evolve.

### 3.1 Goal

We strive to provide *type change transparency*. That is, if $T_1$, $T_2$, ..., $T_n$ are versions of type $T$ and $f$ is an operation defined on instances of some $T_i$, then $f(t)$ is well defined for all $t$ such that $t$ is an instance of any $T_j$. Type change transparency is particularly useful for operations that iterate over all instances of a type, regardless of the type version under which the instances were created. Iteration of this sort occurs during associative retrieval, when we are interested in obtaining all instances of a type such that some predicate is satisfied.

The system supports type change transparency by supporting a version control mechanism for types and by allowing type designers to add error handlers to type versions. The handlers effectively expand the behavior defined by each version so that instances of different versions may be used interchangeably by programs. The handlers added to each version correspond to behavior not defined by that version but defined by other versions of the type. Thus, when a type $T$ is changed a new version $T_i$ is created. The new version $T_i$ carries handlers for any behavior that is not defined locally, but is defined by some other version of the type, $T_j$. Moreover, handlers may be required by former versions of the type for behavior uniquely defined by the new version.

### 3.2 Why Not Convert?

An alternative approach to managing change in types is to require with each change that all instances be converted to the new type version. Although there are situations in which conversion is reasonable or necessary (e.g., when a property is added to a type that applies uniformly to all instances of the type, both old and new, and has a value that must be stored with each instance), we have not chosen it as the general mechanism for the following reasons. First, it might not be practical. If there are a large number of objects, the conversion might be very expensive. Examples drawn from current database practice show that the conversion of millions of records may involve several hours of processing. Second, it might not be possible. If the information held in instances of one type version is significantly different from that held in those of another, conversion might require making guesses for values (generating information) or discarding values (destroying information) that might be useful later. Finally, it might not be desirable. If there are old programs that must operate with instances of old type versions, these programs would become inoperative if we converted the instances that they use. In many environments, the expense of converting all existing programs to be compatible with the new type definitions is prohibitive.

## 4. A FRAMEWORK FOR CHANGING TYPES

We may categorize type change as either change in the structure of a type lattice or change in the specification of an individual type. Individual types are changed by the addition, deletion, or modification of properties, operations, and constraints. Lattice changes, such as adding, deleting, or relocating a type, have an effect similar to the adding or deleting of properties, operations, and constraints to the type's subtypes. For the most part, lattice changes are managed by the same mechanisms as are type changes. For example, adding a type to a lattice has the effect on each subtype of adding properties. We may manage the change in the lattice by applying type change mechanisms to each subtype.

We will use the type definitions shown in Figure 6.1 to describe the problem. Each version of a type definition includes the name of the type and its version number, a list of its supertypes, and descriptions of the properties, operations, and constraints that are defined for the type's instances. The declaration of each property indicates a class that constrains the value of the property in all valid instances of the type. Although not shown in the figure, operations and their parameters are similarly declared.

The first version of `Car` defines a single property, `color`. The second adds the properties *epa_mpg* and `fuel`, and the third removes the `fuel` property and changes

| Type Definitions | | |
|---|---|---|
| **Define Type** $Car_1$<br>**Supertypes**<br>$Vehicle_1$<br>**Property Definitions**<br>color:$Carcolors_1$ | **Define Type** $Car_2$<br>**Supertypes**<br>$Vehicle_1$<br>**Property Definitions**<br>color:$Carcolors_1$<br>epa_mpg:{10..40}<br>fuel:{leaded, unleaded} | **Define Type** $Car_3$<br>**Supertypes**<br>$Vehicle_1$<br>**Property Definitions**<br>color:$Carcolors_1$<br>epa_mpg:{20..50} |

**Figure 6.1** The versions of `car` resulting from a sequence of first adding the properties `epa_mpg` and `fuel` and then removing `fuel` while changing the constraints on `epa_mpg`.

the constraints on *epa_mpg*. The example reflects the time during which all cars initially burned leaded gas and had no mileage rating set by the EPA (i.e., Environmental Protection Agency), then some burned leaded and some unleaded, and finally all cars burn unleaded gas.

The errors arising in a program using objects of a changed type occur in one of two ways. Either the program attempts to access a property or operation *undefined* on the type version under which the objects were created, or the program reads or writes a value that is *unknown*. The first kind of error results from the addition or deletion of properties or operations to a type. The second results from strengthening or relaxing the constraints defined by a type on its properties and operations. For the following discussion we use the symbol $car_i$ to denote an instance of `Car` that was created under version $Car_i$ A program that uses objects of type `Car` and was written under version $Car_i$ is denoted $P_i$. A $P_i$ may be used on instances of any version of `Car`, but the program expects all instances to have the behavior defined by $Car_i$.

## 4.1 Undefined Properties and Operations

When a property or operation is added to a type, old versions will raise the *undefined* error when a new program tries to access the property or operation in an old instance of the type. Conversely, when a property or operation is deleted from a type, the *undefined* error is raised when an old program attempts to access the property or operation in a new instance. For example, versions $Car_1$ and $Car_3$ would each raise the *undefined* error if a $P_2$ attempted to read the value of the `fuel` property from any of their instances.

## 4.2 Changing Property Constraints

When a change in a type alters the constraints on a property, the domain of legal values changes. The domain expected by a (new or old) program using the type may not match the domain defined on a given instance of the type. Consequently, the type may raise the *unknown* error when the program attempts to write a value to the property, since the value may be outside the defined domain. Conversely, a program may read an *unknown* value from the instance, since the domain defined for the instance may be wider than that expected by the program.

For example, a $P_2$ may attempt to write the value *10* to the `epa_mpg` property of a `car`$_3$, or a $P_3$ may attempt to write *50* to a `car`$_2$. Type versions `Car`$_3$ and `Car`$_2$, respectively, would raise the *unknown* error. Conversely, a $P_2$ may read an *unknown* value, such as *45*, from the `epa_mpg` property of a `car`$_3$, or a $P_3$ may read the *unknown* value *15* from a `car`$_2$.

## 4.3 Invalid Property Values

An error may also be raised by a type when a program uses an object of the type while expecting an instance of one of the type's supertypes. The error can occur when the type has *refined* a property defined by the supertype and the program writes a value to the object; the value may be outside the domain defined for the property by the type. On the surface the situation seems analogous to that encountered when constraints on a type are strengthened, and a program expecting an old instance of the type is applied to a new instance. However, the errors resulting from the two situations are different.

In the case of a type change that tightens the constraints on a property, the domain of the property is redefined and any value outside the new domain is *unknown* to the new type version. Values for `epa_mpg` outside the range $\{10 \,..\, 40\}$ are *unknown* to version `Car`$_2$, although values in the range of $\{41 \,..\, 50\}$ are legal in instances of version `Car`$_3$. Because we want instances of different versions to behave uniformly, our system supports the addition of handlers to cover the difference in domain definitions.

In contrast, a type that refines a property defined by a supertype does not redefine the domain. Rather, some of the domain values that are legal in the supertype are mapped to an *invalid* error in the type. If `Ford`$_1$ is a subtype of `Car`$_2$ and it refines the domain of `epa_mpg` to $\{20 \,..\, 40\}$, values in the range $\{10 \,..\, 19\}$ are *invalid* in `fords`. In this case we wish to preserve the tighter constraints of the subtype and not mask its behavior with handlers.

The *unknown* error is associated with values outside the defined value class of a property. The *invalid* error may be associated with certain values within the value class of the property that, because of other constraints, do not constitute legal values. If, for example, a program writes the value *NULL* to the `major` property of a `student` whose `year` is `jr` (cf. section 2), an *invalid* error will result. A type may choose to raise a more specific error when a program writes an illegal value to a property, but *invalid* is the default. Programs should be prepared to deal explicitly with this class of errors. Thus, the problem of substituting a subtype with stronger constraints for a supertype in a program is orthogonal to that of changing types. Although similar mechanisms could be used for both problems, we will only consider changing types in this paper.

## 4.4 Changing Operations

We manage changes in a type's operations by the same error handler mechanism. One kind of change involves enlarging or reducing the domains of an operation's input and output parameters.

The invocation of a type's operation may be thought of as writing to the input parameters and reading from the output parameters by a program. Thus, changing the domain of an operation's input and output parameters results in a situation quite similar to one in which the constraints on a type's properties have been changed. If the domain of an input parameter is enlarged, a new program may invoke the operation on an old instance with an input value outside the new domain. That is, the operation invoked on the instance receives an *unknown* value. If instead the domain is reduced, an old program may invoke the operation on a new instance with an *unknown* value.

When the domain of an output parameter of a type's operation is changed, programs may receive an *unknown* value upon invoking the operation. For example, the *unknown* error may occur when an old program uses the operation on a new instance where the output domain had been enlarged, or when a new program uses an old instance where the domain had been reduced.

Changes in the domain of an operation's input or output parameter can be managed by applying the same error handler mechanism as that used for managing changes in the domain of a property. Other kinds of change in a type's operation, such as changing the number of parameters or changing the effect of the operation, result in a new operation with a different name. When an operation defined on a type is changed in a fundamental way such that a differently named operation results, a new type version containing the new operation in place of the old is produced. Handlers are then added to the type versions as though a new operation had been added and an old one deleted from the type.

## 5. THE VERSION MODEL

Our database system includes a version control mechanism that is built on top of the basic system kernel [Zdo86d]. Much work has been done recently on incorporating time and version histories into databases [Kat82a,Lum84]. For the present discussion of our model, it is sufficient to understand that versions of an object are collected into aggregates called *version sets*. The elements of a version set are related to each other by an ordering relationship called *successor-of*. A linear version set is a total order and can only be added to at one end. All previous versions are read-only. It is also possible to have a branching version set for which the ordering of versions is a partial order. That is, a version might have several successors; multiple successors of a version are called alternatives. Alternatives correspond to the case in which two or more competing versions in a design coexist as most recent versions. Each alternative may have a subsequent independent version history of its own.

Because type definitions are objects in our database model, the general version mechanism can be applied equally well to type objects.

### 5.1 Type Versions

When a type $T$ is changed, a new version is created in the version set of the type. In addition, new versions of all subtypes of $T$ are also created. Each instance of a type is linked to the version of the type under which it was created. For operations on single objects, this scheme is sufficient. That is, if $t$ is an instance of the $i$th version of $T$, $T_i$, then an operation $f$ applied to $t$ will be executed by first finding the definition of $f$ on $T_i$. If $f$ is *undefined* on $T_i$ or if a parameter value is *unknown*, an error is raised by the type. Section 5 describes handlers that may be used for errors resulting from type changes.

Some modifications of a type $T$ do not result in a new version. Adding a subtype or creating a new version of a subtype does not generate a new version since instances of $T$ are not affected by the change. The addition of error handlers to a type version also does not result in a new version of the type. The behavior associated with handlers always supplements rather than diminishes the behavior defined by the type so that programs using the type version will never expect behavior that is no longer there.

### 5.2 Version Set Interface

We define the *version set interface* as the most general interface to a type. It is constructed as the disjunction of the type definitions for all versions of a type $T$. A type version $T_i$ is a triple $(op(T_i), pr(T_i), con(T_i))$ where $op(T_i)$ is a set of operations, $pr(T_i)$ is a set of properties, and $con(T_i)$ is a set of constraints. If a type $T$ has $n$ versions $T_1$ , ..., $T_n$, then the version set interface $V_T$ which has the form of a type definition is defined by:

$$\begin{aligned} V_T = (op(V_T), pr(V_T), con(V_T)) = \\ (op(T_1) \cup op(T_2) \cup \ldots \cup op(T_n), \\ pr(T_1) \cup pr(T_2) \cup \ldots \cup pr(T_n), \\ con(T_1) \cup con(T_2) \cup \ldots \cup con(T_n)). \end{aligned}$$

The version set interface contains all the properties and operations ever defined by some version of $T$ and every value ever declared valid for properties and operation parameters. If only one version of a type exists, the version set interface for that type is equivalent to the single type definition. We can compute the difference between the behavior described by a new version of $T$ and that described by the version set interface $V_T$ because we use the limited constraint language described in section 2 [Ska86,Zdo86b]. Consequently, the version set interface is useful in determining what handlers need to be created for a given type change.

## 6. TYPE VERSION HANDLERS

Error handlers are added to versions of a type in order to allow instances of different versions to be used uniformly. A version generally contains handlers to provide for behavior defined in the version set interface that is not defined in the version. The behavior defined by a type is comprised of properties, operations, and constraints, where a single constraint may be on the domains of one or more properties or operation parameters.

Errors occur when a property or operation referenced by a program is *undefined* for an object by its type version or when a constraint is violated with an *unknown* value supplied by a program or returned by an object. Handlers are added to a version for each *undefined* property or operation and for each *unknown* domain value that is defined in another version of the type and hence the version set interface.

An error handler is an executable object that acquires control when an *undefined* or *unknown* error occurs during a program's use of an object. Handlers are classified as either *prehandlers* or *posthandlers*. A prehandler is executed when the definition of a property or operation referenced by the program cannot be found for the object or when the program has sent an *unknown* value to the object for a property or as an operation parameter. A posthandler is executed when the action within the object has completed and the object is about to return a value *unknown* to the program. Handlers can perform arbitrary functions, but frequently they provide a mapping from one domain value to another. Figure 6.2 illustrates the difference between prehandlers and posthandlers with regard to the type version on which they are defined.

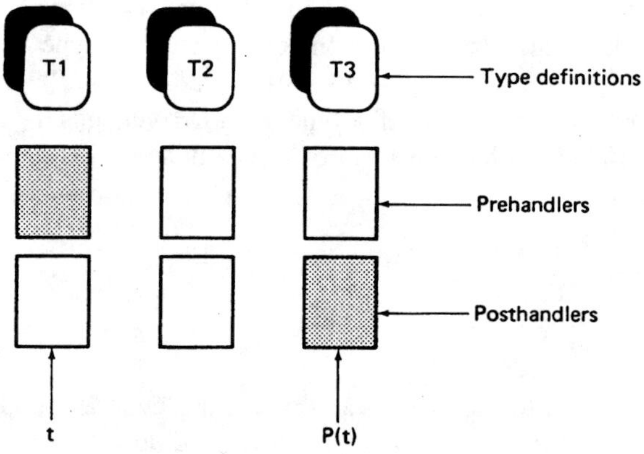


**Figure 6.2** An illustration of the difference between prehandlers and posthandlers. A program written under $T_3$ is using an instance of $T_1$. If an error occurs such that a handler is required, either a prehandler defined on $T_1$ or a posthandler defined on $T_3$ will execute.

The type version of an object manages the messages sent to the object by a program. When an object $t_i$ receives a message to which its type version, $T_i$, raises an *undefined* or *unknown* error, an appropriate handler executes if one has been defined on the version. Control passes to the handler before returning to the program. Moreover, if the object is returning a value to the program, be it from a property, operation, or a handler, the value is first passed to the type version, $T_j$, under which the program was written. The value is tested there for inclusion within the domain defined on $T_j$ and therefore expected by the program. If the returned value is outside the legal domain and if an appropriate posthandler has been defined on $T_j$, then the posthandler is executed in lieu of returning the value to the program.

Alternatively, it is possible for a program to receive control immediately upon an error condition in order to use a handler of its own. The integrity of the object is maintained by the type mechanism regardless of which handler is eventually executed. That is, a program's handler cannot circumvent the modularity of the data abstraction facility. For example, the following program fragment assigns the `fuel` of object `car` to variable $f$ and provides an explicit error handler to be executed in lieu of any default action imposed by the type's handler:

```
f := get_property_value (car, "fuel")
     except when undefined print ("Undefined property");
```

In this case, if the error *undefined* is raised by the type of object `car` the program fragment simply handles it by printing a message. If the program had not explicitly provided an error handler, then the handler defined on the type version of `car` would have executed.

For the following discussion we continue our vehicle example. Additional features appear in the type definitions, including error handlers and auxiliary supertypes, and are explained in the text. The handler section of a type definition $T$ contains specifications which, for property handlers, are of the form

```
for (t, p) :
  handler (t, p);
```

where $t$ is an instance of $T$, $p$ is a property defined on $T$, and *handler* is the body of the executable handler routine. $t$ is bound to the object whose property is being read or written. $p$ is the name of the property and is bound either to the object sent by a program as the value to be written to the property, or to the object returned by $t$ as a result of reading the property.

Figure 6.3 shows the three versions of type *Car* with handlers that manage the inclusion of the *fuel* and *epa_mpg* properties as well as the change in constraints on the latter. With the addition of $Car_3$ to the version set of *Car*, the version set interface contains the following properties and their domains:

```
color : Carcolors1
epa_mpg : {10 .. 50}
fuel : {leaded, unleaded}
```

The handlers added to a version of *Car* provide behavior present in the version set interface but lacking in the version. We see that it is not possible to cover all cases in all versions. For example, there are no EPA ratings for old cars.

## 6.1 Prehandlers

A type version carries prehandlers to cover situations in which a program using its instances references an *undefined* property or operation, or supplies an *unknown* value for a property or as an operation input parameter. A prehandler is executed on instances of the type version on which it is defined, much like any other operation defined on the type. If a new property or operation is added to a type $T$ a new version $T_j$ results, and the property or operation is added to the version set interface. A (possibly different) handler is added to each of former versions $T_1, T_2, \ldots, T_i$ to provide the new behavior. If

**Type Definitions**

```
Define Type Car1
 Supertypes
  Vehicle1
 Property Definitions
  color:Carcolors1

Prehandlers
Undefined Write
for (car, fuel):
 if value (fuel) = leaded
    return;
 if value (fuel) = unleaded
    raise invalid;
Undefined Read
for (car, fuel):
 return leaded;
```

```
Define Type Car2
 Supertypes
  Vehicle1
 Property Definitions
  color:Carcolors1
  epa_mpg:{10..40}
  fuel:{leaded, unleaded}

Prehandlers
Unknown Write
for (car, epa_mpg):
 if value (epa_mpg) ≤50
      and value (epa_mpg) > 40
    car.epa_mpg:=40;

Posthandlers
Unknown Read
for (car, epa_mpg):
 if value (epa_mpg) ≤ 50
      and value (epa_mpg) > 40
    return 40;
```

```
Define Type Car3
 Supertypes
  Vehicle1
 Property Definitions
  color:Carcolors1
  epa_mpg:{20..50}

Prehandlers
Undefined Write
for (car, fuel):
  if value (fuel) = unleaded
     return;
  if value (fuel) = leaded
     raise invalid;
Undefined Read
for (car, fuel):
  return unleaded;
Unknown Write
for (car, epa_mpg):
  if value (epa_mpg) ≥ 10
       and value (epa_mpg) < 20
     car.epa_mpg:=20;

Posthandlers
Unknown Read
for (car, epa_mpg):
  if value (epa_mpg) ≥ 10
       and value (epa_mpg) < 20
    return 20;
```

**Figure 6.3** The three versions of *Car* with the required handlers.

a property or operation is instead removed from the type, a new version $T_j$ also results. In this case the behavior remains in the version set interface but is *undefined* in $T_j$. Consequently, $T_j$ is the version that receives the handlers.

*Undefined* handlers are classified as either *write* prehandlers (i.e., executed when a program writes to an instance of the type) or *read* prehandlers (i.e., executed when a program attempts to read from an instance of the type). An *undefined* write handler may simply check that the values supplied by the program are valid and return a status object such as success or error. The action of the read handler may be to return a value that is true for all instances of the version even though the property or operation is not explicitly defined.

For example, version `Car`$_1$ does not define the properties `fuel` or `epa_mpg`. While no information exists on the EPA mileage ratings of old cars, it is known that they burned leaded gas. Handlers are added to the version to provide that behavior so that instances of `Car`$_1$ can be used by programs expecting an instance of `Car`$_2$. In contrast, the `fuel` property is also *undefined* in `Car`$_3$, but the handlers provide the unleaded gas behavior. In both cases the behavior of the handlers is such that when a correct value is written, a normal return occurs. If a program sends the wrong value for the property, the type raises an *invalid* error.

If a type $T$ is changed so that the domain of a property or operation input parameter is enlarged, a new version $T_j$ results and the new domain values are added to the version set interface. Former versions of the type then receive handlers for the new domain values that are *unknown* to the old versions. If the domain is instead reduced, a new version $T_j$ also results but the version set interface is unchanged. $T_j$ now defines a smaller domain for the property or operation parameter than does the version set interface; handlers then are required by $T_j$ for the *unknown* domain values. *Unknown* prehandlers are added to a type version only for the write case (that is, for the case in which a program writes to an instance of the version). Handlers for the read case are added to type versions as posthandlers, as discussed in the next section. The action of an *unknown* write prehandler may be to enter some default value into the property or operation input parameter.

For example, the constraints on the `epa_mpg` property differ in `Car`$_2$ and `Car`$_3$. Moreover, neither define the constraints to be the same as does the version set interface. Consequently, *unknown* handlers are required on both versions. `Car`$_2$ needs handlers to cover the domain $\{41 .. 50\}$; `Car`$_3$ needs handlers for the domain $\{10 .. 19\}$.

A version $T_i$ may have either an *undefined* or an *unknown* write prehandler for a given property or operation, but not both. We may explain by considering an example. Assume a property is added to a type $T$ that has a single version $T_1$. The new property is added to the version set interface, a new version $T_2$ is added to the version set, and $T_1$ may receive *undefined* read and write prehandlers for the property. Assume further that the domain of the property is then enlarged. The new domain values are added to the version set interface and $T_3$ is added to the version set. At this point, *unknown* write prehandlers should be required by both $T_1$ and $T_2$ for the new domain values. However, a domain is not explicit for the property in $T_1$ since the property is not even defined. The *unknown* error will never be raised by $T_1$ because the *undefined* error will occur instead. If an *undefined* prehandler has been supplied to the version, it will execute.

Consequently, an *unknown* write handler is not added to $T_1$. Rather, the *undefined* write handler is modified if necessary to include the possibility that some program may write the new domain values to the property in a $T_1$ instance.

## 6.2 Posthandlers

Posthandlers are executed by an object in lieu of returning a value that would result in the *unknown* error because it is outside the domain expected by the calling program. Values returned by objects may be from a property, an operation output parameter, or a prehandler from another type version. Control is passed to a posthandler in the final step before returning a value to the program. A posthandler acts like a filter for the program that is accepting a value from an object.

For example, assume a program expecting an instance of $Car_3$ reads the *epa_mpg* property from an instance of $Car_2$. $Car_2$ manages the messages received by its instances, so it finds the property and returns the value *15*. The value is then passed to version $Car_3$ since the program was written under that version. Because *15* is outside the legal domain for instances of $Car_3$, the posthandler for *epa_mpg* executes, and the program receives a value that is not *unknown*.

The value returned via $Car_3$ could have originated from a prehandler defined on the type version of the instance instead of from an actual property. Assume that it had been possible to add *undefined* handlers to $Car_1$ for *epa_mpg*. A read prehandler might have returned some default value, such as *18*. Assume further that a program expecting an instance of $Car_3$ attempts to read the *epa_mpg* property from an instance of $Car_1$. In this case, the *undefined* prehandler on $Car_1$ executes and returns the value *18* via $Car_3$. Again, the posthandler on $Car_3$ will execute since *18* is outside the legal domain of *epa_mpg*.

It is apparent from our examples that the posthandlers a type version carries are not used for errors involving its own instances. Rather, the posthandlers defined on a $T_i$ are used in response to an error involving instances of any other version of $T$ that are manipulated by programs expecting an instance of $T_i$. $T_i$ posthandlers never execute on $T_i$ instances because no instance of $T_i$ should contain a value *unknown* to a program expecting an instance of $T_i$. If instead posthandlers were written so that type versions carried the posthandlers for their own instances, the same posthandler would apply to all programs using the type regardless of the type version expected. The flexibility of posthandlers written in this way would be severely limited. We consider a type's versions to be views of the same conceptual type, and therefore it is not inconsistent to apply handlers defined on one version to instances of another.

Posthandlers then are added to $T_i$ for the domain values of properties and operation output parameters that are defined in the version set interface but are *unknown* to instances of $T_i$. When a domain is enlarged, posthandlers are added to those former versions of the type on which the property or operation is defined; when a domain is reduced, the new version gets posthandlers for the now *unknown* values. *Unknown* read posthandlers thus cover the same domain values as *unknown* write prehandlers in a given type version. $Car_3$ has both a write prehandler and a read posthandler for the *unknown* values of *epa_mpg* in the range $\{10 .. 19\}$. The prehandler executes on instances of $Car_3$; the posthandler executes on instances of $Car_2$ during use by a program expecting a $car_3$.

## 6.3 Inheritance

A major difference between a prehandler and a posthandler is that the latter is defined on one version of a type and is used on instances of another, while the former is defined by the same type version as the instances on which it is used. Both kinds of handlers are inherited by subtypes but with a characteristic difference. A prehandler defined on $T_i$ may execute when an instance of $T_i$ or one of its subtypes is used by any program. A posthandler may execute when a program expecting an instance of $T_i$ or an instance of a subtype of $T_i$ uses any object considered valid by the type checking mechanism.[1] A $T_i$ prehandler is inherited by instances of $T_i$'s subtypes, while a $T_i$ posthandler is inherited by programs expecting instances of $T_i$'s subtypes.

We expand our vehicle example to illustrate inheritance. Assume that at the time $Car_1$ was defined there was another type, $Chevy_1$, currently defined as a subtype of $Vehicle_1$. *Chevy* is made a subtype of *Car*, resulting in version $Chevy_2$. After some time and some radical design decisions, *Chevy* is removed as a subtype of *Car* to become again a subtype of *Vehicle*. Figure 6.4 shows the three development stages.

| Type Definitions | | |
|---|---|---|
| **Define Type** $Chevy_1$<br>**Supertypes**<br>$Vehicle_1$<br>**Property Definitions**<br>color: $Chevycolors_1$ | **Define Type** $Chevy_2$<br>**Supertypes**<br>$Car_1$<br>**Property Definitions**<br>**refine** color as<br>color: $Chevycolors_1$ | **Define Type** $Chevy_5$<br>**Supertypes**<br>$Vehicle_1$<br>**Property Definitions**<br>color: $Chevycolors_1$<br>epa_mpg: {20..40} |

**Figure 6.4** Three versions of *Chevy* illustrating the addition and deletion of a supertype.

The third version shown is $Chevy_5$, since a new version of *Chevy* resulted from each of the changes in *Car* described above. A change in a type generates a new version of the type and each of its subtypes.

A type inherits all of the properties, operations, constraints, and handlers of its supertypes. For example, each version of *Chevy* that is a subtype of *Car* inherits the behavior of its *Car* version supertype. A subtype may *refine* a property defined by its supertype by restricting the property to a narrower domain. The *color* property is defined in both *Chevy* and *Car* but is restricted to *Chevycolors* in *Chevy*. Not all *Carcolors* are valid as the color of a *chevy*.

[1]The type checking mechanism considers an object's *type* $T_o$ to match the type $T_p$ declared in a program when $T_o$ is equal to or a subtype of $T_p$. $T_o$ is a subtype of $T_p$ when the version of $T_o$ under which the object was created contains some version of $T_p$ as a supertype. $T_o$ is equal to $T_p$ if they are versions of the same type.

We stated earlier that type lattice changes, including the addition, deletion, and relocation of types within the lattice, can be managed by applying the mechanisms associated with type changes to each subtype affected. When a type $T$ is added or deleted from the lattice, subtypes effectively gain or lose the behavior of the type. If the behavior of $T$ is added directly to each subtype instead of making $T$ a new supertype, *undefined* prehandlers may be added to former versions of each subtype. In the same way, handlers may be added to former versions of subtypes when $T$ is added as a new supertype. If $T$ constrains a property defined by a supertype of $T$ and the subtypes, the effect is the same as constraining the property within each subtype. Consequently, the new versions of the subtypes receive a prehandler and a posthandler to cover the now *unknown* values of the property. The case of removing a supertype is treated symmetrically: a relocated type $T$ is cast as first removing a supertype from $T$ and its former subtypes and then adding a new supertype to $T$ and its new subtypes.

The addition of a new supertype results in a new version of each subtype. Consequently, some versions of a particular type may have type $T$ as a supertype while others do not. If the new supertype $T$ is modified, new versions of $T$ and its subtypes are generated, and handlers may be added to the new or to former version(s) of $T$ to maintain behavioral consistency. Versions of the subtypes that have $T$ as a supertype inherit the new handlers, but the remaining versions do not. Rather than adding handlers to all versions that do not have $T$ as a supertype, we declare a version of $T$ as an *auxiliary supertype* of each. The use of an additional inheritance path prevents a proliferation of handlers in subtypes when a type is changed. A type inherits only prehandlers from its auxiliary supertypes. Behavior defined as properties and operations is not inherited since auxiliary supertypes are not true supertypes. Also, posthandlers are not inherited because a posthandler is used for programs expecting an instance of the type version defining the posthandler or one of its true subtypes.

We conclude the vehicle example with a demonstration of managing type lattice change. With five versions in the `Chevy` version set, the version set interface contains the following properties and domains:

```
color : Chevycolors₁
epa_mpg : {10..50}
fuel : {leaded, unleaded}
```

Since *Chevy* adds no new properties, the interface is the same as that of `Car` except for the tighter constraints on *color*. Versions $Chevy_2$, ..., $Chevy_4$ inherit consistent behavior from $Car_1$, ..., $Car_3$, since changes in `Car` were managed with handlers. However, $Chevy_1$ and $Chevy_5$ are not consistent with each other or the other three versions. Both define an interface that is different from the version set interface. Figure 6.5 shows `Chevy` versions modified by handlers and auxiliary supertypes to manage the addition and removal of `Car` as a supertype.

Version $Chevy_1$ contains no handlers for the *undefined* properties `epa_mpg` and `fuel`, but the version $Car_1$ is added as an auxiliary supertype. Because $Chevy_1$ inherits prehandlers from $Car_1$, a $chevy_1$ will return the value leaded if the `fuel` property is read by a program. Just as there were no EPA ratings for instances of $Car_1$, there are

**Type Definitions**

```
Define Type Chevy1
  Supertypes
    Vehicle1
  Property Definitions
    color: Chevycolors1
  Auxiliary Supertypes
    Car1
```

```
Define Type Chevy2
  Supertypes
    Car1
  Property Definitions
    refine color as
      color: Chevycolors1
```

```
Define Type Chevy5
  Supertypes
    Vehicle1
  Property Definitions
    color: Chevycolors1
    epa_mpg: {20..40}
  Auxiliary Supertypes
    Car3

Prehandlers
Unknown Write
for (chevy, epa_mpg):
  if value (epa_mpg) ≤ 50
        and value (epa_mpg) > 40;
      chevy.epa_mpg:=40;
  if value (epa_mpg) ≥ 10
        and value (epa_mpg) < 20;
      chevy.epa_mpg:=20;

Posthandlers
Unknown Read
for (chevy, epa_mpg):
  if value (epa_mpg) ≤ 50
        and value (epa_mpg) >40
      return 40;
  if value (epa_mpg) ≥ 10
        and value (epa_mpg) < 20
      return 20;
```

**Figure 6.5** The three versions of *Chevy* with the required handlers and auxiliary supertypes.

no ratings for old *chevys*, so that it is not possible to add handlers to provide that behavior.

Versions $Chevy_2$, ..., $Chevy_4$ require neither handlers nor auxiliary supertypes, since they directly inherit or refine behavior from *Car* that is consistent with the *Chevy* version set interface. However, $Chevy_5$ defines a narrower domain for *epa_mpg* than that present in the version set interface. Consequently, *unknown* handlers are added to $Chevy_5$ to cover the domains $\{10 .. 19\}$ and $\{41 .. 50\}$. If a program expecting a $chevy_3$ attempts to write the value *15* to a $chevy_5$, the *unknown* write handler will execute. If a $car_4$ is about to return the value *45* to a program expecting a $chevy_5$, the *unknown* read handler will execute. If $Chevy_5$ had defined a wider domain for *epa_mpg* such as $\{10 .. 60\}$ instead of the narrower domain, prior versions of *Chevy* would have received the *unknown* handlers. Specifically, the versions on which `epa_mpg` is defined ($Chevy_3$ and $Chevy_4$) would have received handlers to cover the domain {*51* .. *60*}.

## 7. OTHER WORK

Several other recent efforts have addressed the problem of changing types. Ahlsen et al [Ahl84a] use mapping functions to compute a view of one type version from another. These functions are defined between pairs of types and are like temporary conversion functions. In order to view an instance of type $T_1$ as an instance of type $T_n$, the system must compose all of the pairwise translation functions between *1* and $n$ to get the appropriate mapping; the composed function is then applied to the $T_1$ instance. Our scheme allows the error to be trapped and the proper function to be called immediately. Moreover, with handlers, it is possible to specify different behavior depending on the two types involved.

Banerjee et al [Ban86] has considered the problem of type evolution in the context of an object-oriented type lattice. They analyzed the problem by defining basic categories of change. For each category, they then provide rules for keeping the lattice self-consistent and for converting existing instances to correspond to the new lattice. Our approach uses versions of types to maintain a consistent view of the type lattice and an exception handling mechanism that allows us to avoid converting old instances.

Borgida [Bor85b] has made use of exception handling mechanisms in a database context to deal with exceptional values. An object contains an exceptional value when the value does not match the constraints imposed by the type definitions. The value is flagged as exceptional and can be processed accordingly at some future time. This work takes a related approach but is somewhat different in its focus. Our focus is type level change, while [Bor85] focuses on instance level variation.

The problem of changing types arises from the strong notion of typing that is present in most object-oriented systems. A type enables the behavior of all of its instances. Changing the type requires a fairly complex analysis of the ways in which a type change can affect the environment that has been already defined. The notion of prototypes [Lie86] provides an alternative view in which there are no types. Any object can serve as a prototype for a new object. The new object uses the default behaviors defined on the prototype and redefines or adds behavior to take any differences into account.

At first, it might appear that this simplifies the problem of changing types since there are no types to change. However, a similar problem arises whenever a very long chain of prototypes occurs. Since any object can serve as a prototype, we can have $A$ as a prototype for $B$, $B$ as a prototype for $C$, and so on. If it is necessary to change $A$, then all of the other objects in the prototype chain may change as well if they are sharing behavior. The basis for the problem occurs whenever an object or objects depend on the state of some other object. It is possible to establish dependencies in both schemes.

We choose to adopt a typed scheme because we feel that for a database environment it offers benefits that outweigh the added flexibility of prototypes. Types provide guarantees about the behavior of a set of objects. We can exploit this in a database by, for example, computing indices to make retrieval faster. They also provide a unit of modularity for designing and building complex software systems.

## 8. SUMMARY

We have presented a model for management of change in type definitions. The mechanism presented maintains type change transparency so that instances of different versions of the same type behave uniformly. We categorize change as either change in a type lattice or change in a type. Types are changed by the addition, deletion, or modification of properties, operations, and constraints. Lattice changes, such as adding, deleting, or relocating a type, have an effect similar to the adding or deleting of properties, operations, and constraints to the type's subtypes.

Type change transparency is supported by the application of our version control mechanism to type objects and through the use of error handlers. A change in a type is manifested as the addition of a new version to the type's version set. Every instance of the type remains linked to the version under which it was created. Error handlers are added to a type version for behavior that is defined in the version set interface of the type but is not defined in the version. The version set interface is the most general interface to the type.

We saw in an example that it is not always possible to cover all versions of a type for the behavior expressed by the version set interface. There may not, for example, be values available for new properties in old instances of the type. However, for those changes in which compatibility can be maintained between different type versions, our model provides a systematic method for change such that minimal impact is felt by programs and other objects that are dependent on the type.

The modification of an arbitrary type lattice could well become quite complex. For this reason, we are in the process of building a database designers' workbench to assist type definers in writing type definitions and adding handlers. The handlers might be added to former type versions as well as the new changed version. The workbench environment would be able to prompt type designers for the handlers that are required whenever they modify a type definition.

# 7

# Integrating an Object-Oriented Programming System with a Database System

**Won Kim, Nat Ballou, Jay Banerjee, Hong-Tai Chou, Jorge F. Garza, and Darrell Woelk**

*Microelectronics and Computer Technology Corporation*
*Austin, Texas 78759*

## ABSTRACT

There are two major issues to address to achieve integration of an object-oriented programming system with a database system. One is the language issue: an object-oriented programming language must be augmented with semantic data modeling concepts to provide a robust set of data modeling concepts to allow modeling of entities for important real-world applications. Another is the computational-model issue: application programmers should be able to access and manipulate objects as though the objects are in an infinite virtual memory; in other words, they should not have to be aware of the

*Source*: Adapted from Kim, W., N. Ballou, H.-T. Chou, J. F. Garza, and D. Woelk, "Integrating an Object-Oriented Programming System with a Database System", Proceedings of the ACM Conference on Object-Oriented Programming Systems, Languages, and Applications, September 1988, pp. 142–152. 

existence of a database system in their computations with the data structures the programming language allows. This paper discusses these issues and presents the solutions which we have incorporated into the ORION object-oriented database system at MCC.

# 1. INTRODUCTION

In the Advanced Computer Architecture Program at MCC, we have built a prototype object-oriented database system, called ORION. Presently, it is being used in supporting the data management needs of PROTEUS, an expert system shell also prototyped in the Advanced Computer Architecture Program at MCC. In ORION we have directly implemented the object-oriented paradigm [Gol81,Gol83,Bob83,Sym84,Bob85], and added persistence and sharability to objects. We have two versions of ORION: a single-user, multi-task system called ORION-1; and a multi-user, multi-task system called ORION-1S, in which a single server provides persistent object management on behalf of several workstations. ORION is intended for applications from the AI [Ste86a], multimedia documents [Ahl84b,Iee85,Woe86], and computer-aided design domains [Afs85b], implemented in the object-oriented programming paradigm. Functions supported in ORION include versions and change notification [Cho86,Cho88], composite objects [Kim87], dynamic schema evolution [Ban87b], transaction management [Gar88], associative queries [Ban88], and multimedia data management [Woe87].

ORION has been implemented in Common LISP[Ste84b] on a Symbolics 3600 LISP machine [Sym85], and has also been ported to the SUN workstation under the UNIX operating system. ORION extends Common LISP with object-oriented programming and database capabilities. (In contrast, the proposed Common LISP Object System (CLOS) [X3i88] is only an object-oriented language extension to Common LISP.)

The objective of integrating a programming language system with a database system has provided much impetus to research in both the programming language and database communities. This has been motivated by the desire to enhance programming language systems with the benefits of database systems, such as persistent and sharable storage, database integrity control, and associative access to the database. One of the major objectives of ORION was the integration of a programming language (Common LISP) with a database system. To achieve this, we had to address two major issues. One is the language issue. Programming languages in general do not have the primitive semantic data modeling concepts which are necessary to model real-world entities. These include instantiation (an object is an instance of a class), aggregation (an object consists of a number of attributes), and generalization (a class can have a number of subclasses), composite objects (an object consists of a number of exclusive component objects), versions (an object may have a number of versions), and so on. Object-oriented programming languages embody some of these concepts, namely, instantiation, aggregation, and generalization; and as such, one may say that the gap between object-oriented programming languages and databases is substantially narrower than that between other programming languages (except the logic programming language, whose concepts subsume the relational model of data) and databases. The semantic data modeling concepts that programming languages do not have necessarily require language extensions. The traditional solution is to define a database language (such as SQL [Sql81]), and have the application programmers embed database-language statements in the application programs (typically written in FORTRAN, COBOL, PL/1, C, etc.). The trouble with this approach is that the programmers must learn to program in more than one language, and program the mapping between the data structures supported in the programming language and those supported in the data model [Cop84]. Clearly, database extensions to programming languages must not introduce new or conflicting language paradigms, and require unproductive mapping of data structures.

Another issue is the computational model that programming languages in general, and object-oriented programming languages in particular, imply. Programming language systems assume that all objects are in virtual memory, and computations are performed by chasing memory pointers and storing and referencing objects in data structures supported in the programming languages. In applications that require a large amount of data to be extensively accessed and manipulated, such as simulation of a complex assembly of mechanical parts or a design of an electronic device, computations cannot be offloaded to any traditional database system. This is because of the excessive overhead of crossing the boundary between the application and the database system. One of the important shortcomings of conventional database systems is that they are not designed to support navigational access over a large set of objects in virtual memory. The cost of fetching a single object is prohibitively high, especially in relational database systems (compared to a few memory lookups that it takes an application program manipulating objects in virtual memory). If the compute-intensive applications are to use the conventional database system simply as a repository of persistent objects, and copy objects out of the database into the application's address space for computations, it is entirely up to the application to manage consistency of the objects in its address space and to map the data structures to and from the database.

The objective of this paper is to present our approaches to addressing these two major issues in integrating a programming language system with a database system. In particular, we will outline our approach to integrating the object-oriented concepts with a programming language, further augmenting them with additional semantic data modeling concepts. Further, we will describe the architectural concepts and data structures we use in ORION to give the application programmers the illusion and the performance of an infinitely large virtual memory for their objects.

## 2. DATABASE EXTENSIONS TO A PROGRAMMING LANGUAGE

In this section, we will outline the ORION object-oriented extensions to Common LISP. First, we will describe the syntax for capturing the basic object-oriented programming concepts. Then we will augment the basic syntax with a number of database concepts, including associative access to objects and application-related data modeling concepts such as versions and composite objects. The objective of this section is to outline our approach to integrating these database concepts into the basic object-oriented programming paradigm, and demonstrate that the extensions are fairly simple. Therefore, we will not provide the full syntax and semantics of the ORION interface. The syntax, as presented in an abbreviated form in this paper, is similar in principle to that of a number of other object-oriented languages, such as Flavors [Sym84] and LOOPS [Bob83].

## 2.1 Basic Object-Oriented Extensions

The following message creates the definition of a new class.

```
(make-class  Classname :superclasses  ListofSuperclasses
                       :attributes  ListofAttributes
                       :methods  ListofMethodSpecs)
```

Classname is the name of the new class. All keyword arguments are optional. The ListofSuperclasses associated with the **:superclasses** keyword is a list of the superclasses of the new class. The ListofAttributes associated with the **:attribute** keyword is a list of attribute specifications. An attribute specification is a list consisting of an attribute name and keywords with associated values, as follows:

```
(AttributeName [:domain  DomainSpec]
               [:inherit-from  Superclass])
```

A DomainSpec is a LISP data type, a class, or a set of LISP data types or classes; and is used to specify the type(s) of an attribute. If the keyword **:inherit-from** is specified, the associated value is the name of the superclass from which the attribute will be inherited. Otherwise, the attribute is inherited from the first superclass in the ListofSuperclasses.

The ListofMethodSpecs associated with the **:methods** keyword is a list of pairs (MethodName SuperClass). The MethodName is the name of a method to be inherited from the SuperClass. The SuperClass is a class name. If the keyword **:methods** is not specified, methods are inherited from superclasses, and conflicts are resolved on the basis of superclass ordering.

An instance can be created by sending a **make** message to the class to which the instance will belong.

```
(make  Classname :Attribute1  value1
                 ...
                 :AttributeN  valueN)
```

## 2.2 Database Extensions

In this section we outline some important extensions to the basic object-oriented concepts. The extensions include associative access to objects, semantic data modeling concepts, and database control functions.

**2.2.1 Associative access.** Once the database size exceeds the virtual memory size, it is obviously important to bring into virtual memory only those objects which the application will need. Programming languages in general have traditionally not been concerned with queries which will return from the database a small subset of the database that satisfies search conditions. To select all instances (or any one instance) of a class that satisfy a given query expression, we use a **select** (or **select-any**) message. A *set object* (possibly an empty set) containing these instances is returned. The messages for selection have the following format, where QueryExpression is a Boolean expression of predicates:

```
(select  Class    QueryExpression)
(select-any  Class    QueryExpression)
```

An example query is to select the instances of a class Vehicle whose weight is over 5000 lbs.

```
(select  'Vehicle  '(>  Weight  5000))
```

To delete all instances of a class that satisfy a given query expression, a **delete** message is used.

```
(delete  Class    QueryExpression)
```

To delete a specific object, a delete-object message is used.

```
(delete-object  Object)
```

where Object is the object identifier.

Similarly, a change message is used to replace the value of an attribute of all instances of a class that satisfy a given Boolean expression.

```
(change  Class    [QueryExpression]    AttributeName   NewValue)
```

**2.2.2 Semantic data modeling concepts.** ORION supports two semantic data modeling concepts which are not part of the conventional object-oriented paradigm.

***Composite Objects.*** The conventional object-oriented paradigm, although powerful, does not capture the IS-PART-OF relationship between objects; that an object *is a part of* another object. In [Kim87], we define a *composite object* as an object with a hierarchy of exclusive component objects. The classes to which the objects of a composite object belong are also organized in a hierarchy. This hierarchical collection of classes is called a *composite object hierarchy.* A non-root class on a composite object hierarchy is called a *component class.* Each non-leaf class on a composite object hierarchy has one or more attributes whose domains are the component classes. We call such attributes *composite attributes.* A constituent object of a composite object references an instance of its component class through a composite attribute.

To support composite objects, we extend the **make-class** message as follows.

```
(AttributeName [:composite  TrueOrNil])
```

The keyword **:composite** declares whether an attribute is a composite attribute.

An instance can be made a part of a composite object only at the time of creation of that instance. This is done by extending the **make** message with a **parent** argument:

```
(make  Classname :parent  (ParentObject  ParentAttributeName)
                 :Attribute1  value1
                 ...
                 :AttributeN  valueN)
```

The keyword **:parent** is associated with a pair (ParentObject ParentAttribute-Name), where ParentObject with an attribute ParentAttributeName is to reference the instance being created. The **make** message, without the **:parent** keyword, is used to create root instances of composite objects.

***Versions.*** The ORION model of versions and its implementation are presented in [Cho88]. Here we will outline (not fully explain) some of the messages we support for versions.

An object is either *versioned* or *non-versioned.* A versioned object is an instance of a class which the application declares to be *versionable.* The **make-class** message was extended with an additional keyword argument, versionable, as follows.

```
(make-class  Classname :versionable  TrueOrNil)
```

The keyword **:versionable** can have a value true or nil, indicating whether versions can be created for instances of the class.

Our model distinguishes *transient versions* (temporary versions) from *working versions* (stable versions). A transient version may be created from scratch or *derived* from an existing version. Any number of transient versions may be derived at any time from an existing version, giving rise to a *version-derivation hierarchy* for each versioned object. We use the term *version instance* to refer to a specific version, and *generic instance* to refer to the abstract versioned object. A generic instance maintains the history of derivation of version instances for a versioned object.

When the user issues a **make** message to a versionable class, ORION creates a generic object, as well as the first version instance of the versionable object. The new version instance is a transient version, and becomes the root of the version-derivation hierarchy for the versionable object. The optional keyword arguments of a **make-class** message supply attribute names and values for the version instance.

To derive a new version from an existing version, a **derive-version** message is sent to a VersionedObject, as follows.

```
(derive-version  VersionedObject)
```

The message causes a copy to be made of the VersionedObject. The copy becomes a new transient version, and is assigned a new version number and an object identifier.

In ORION, both the generic instance and a version instance of the generic instance have object identifiers. An object, either a version instance or a non-versioned object, may reference one or more other objects. If an object references a version instance, the reference may be the object identifier of a generic instance or that of a version instance. If the reference is to a generic instance, the system dynamically binds the object to a *default version instance.*

The **delete-object** message is used to delete a version instance or a generic object. If the message is sent to a generic object, the entire version-derivation hierarchy is deleted. In other words, all version instances of the versionable object, as well as the generic object, are deleted. If a **delete-object** message is sent to a version instance, the version instance is deleted. If the version instance is a transient version, or a working version from which no other versions have been derived, the history (or version descriptor) of the version instance is deleted as well. (The history of a version instance is maintained within the generic object of the version instance). If the version instance is the only version instance of the versionable object, the generic object is also deleted. If the **delete-object** message is sent to a working version that has other derived versions, however, the history of the version instance is not deleted.

To fetch, update, or delete version instances of a versionable class based on a QueryExpression, the **select**, **change**, and **delete** messages shown earlier can be used, without any changes in their syntax or semantics. These messages cause all version instances of the specified class to be examined.

**2.2.3 Database control functions.** ORION provides an extensive set of messages for the user to control the integrity and resources of the database, including physical clustering of objects, schema evolution (changes to the definition of a database), secondary index management, and so on. Because of space limitations, we will indicate only some of the messages for transaction management and schema evolution here.

Transactions [Gra78] are an important capability in database systems. A *transaction* is an atomic sequence of database operations that takes the database from one consistent state to another consistent state, and is a unit of concurrency control and recovery. If a transaction aborts, all database changes made by the transaction are backed out. A transaction is shielded from the effects of other concurrently executing transactions. If a transaction commits, all updates are safely recorded in stable storage. The messages to commit and abort transactions are as follows:

```
(commit  )
(abort   )
```

The schema of an ORION database is a class hierarchy (actually a directed acyclic graph); and as such two types of changes to the schema are meaningful: changes to the definitions of a class (contents of a node) in the class hierarchy, and changes to the structure (edges and nodes) of the class hierarchy. Changes to the class definitions include adding and deleting attributes and methods. Changes to the class hierarchy structure include creation and deletion of a class, and alteration of the IS-A relationship between classes (adding and deleting the superclass-subclass relationship between a pair of classes). The complete taxonomy of schema changes we allow in ORION is given in [Ban87b].

To append a class to the superclass list of an existing class, or to remove a superclass from the superclass list of an existing class, one can use the messages:

```
(add-superclass  Class  Superclass)
(remove-superclass  Class  Superclass)
```

where the arguments Class and Superclass are the names of classes.

The **change-attribute** message given below can be used to add a new attribute to a class, to change the inheritance of an attribute, or to change the properties of an attribute. All keyword arguments in the message are optional, and they indicate the types of change to be made to the attribute.

```
(change-attribute  Class  AttributeName
                                         [:recursivep  TrueOrNil]
                                         [:domain  DomainSpec]
                                         [:inherit-from  Superclass])
```

The keyword **:recursivep** has a default value T. If nil, it indicates that the change to the attribute definition is limited to the specified class, and must not be propagated to its subclasses. If non-nil, it indicates that the change must be propagated.

To add a new attribute as a locally defined attribute, the **:inherit-from** keyword is used with a nil value. If the attribute name was a previously defined attribute of the class, it is simply re-defined. To change the inheritance of an attribute, the **:inherit-from** keyword is used, and its associated value is the name of the superclass from which the attribute is to be inherited.

## 3. IN-MEMORY OBJECT MANAGEMENT

Conventional database systems allocate a buffer pool of page frames in an attempt to pin in virtual memory data likely to be accessed again soon [Tra82]. The pages in the buffer pool are accessed using a fix/unfix protocol [Tra82,Eff84]. That is, the caller (various components of a database system) must request the page buffer manager to pin down a page in memory before accessing it. Further, when the caller is done with the page, it informs the page buffer manager that the buffer page can be re-used. A page is thus guaranteed to stay in the same memory location during a fix/unfix period; that is, there is no danger that it is swapped out while the caller (access manager or storage manager) is still working on it. The page buffer manager typically uses an LRU replacement algorithm or its variants [Cho85]. A buffer with a positive fix count, that is, a buffer which is still being worked on, is exempt from replacement decisions. The page buffer manager keeps track of all the pages in the buffer pool through a page table.

The buffering scheme used in conventional database systems is not adequate for supporting a programming language environment. One problem with this approach is that it tends to force the application programmers to map the data structures between the application and the database system. In a programming language environment, for storage and retrieval efficiency, the objects need to be stored on disk in one format (the disk format); however, the applications must be able to manipulate the objects in their in-memory format, the format supported by the programming language. A somewhat related problem is that, as we discussed in Section 1, database techniques for maintaining database consistency do not extend to the objects in virtual memory which the applications directly access and manipulate. Another problem with the conventional buffering scheme is memory utilization. As many important applications need to cache a large number of objects in virtual memory to perform extensive computations on them, it is often undesirable to keep page frames in the database buffer pool which contain many unneeded objects.

To solve the above problems, we have adopted a dual-buffer management scheme, in which the available database buffer space is partitioned into a page buffer pool and an object buffer pool. The *workspace* discussed in the context of the GemStone database system [Mai86] is similar to the object buffer pool in ORION. To access an object, the page that contains the object is brought into a page buffer, and then the object is located, retrieved, and placed in an object buffer. ORION supports data structures for efficiently managing objects in the object buffer pool, and addresses issues that arise from the fact that the object buffer pool and the database may contain different copies of the same object during a transaction (a sequence of read and write requests against the database; this sequence is treated by the database system as an atomic action for purposes of recovery). Applications can directly access the objects in the object buffer pool, and the transaction management feature of ORION ensures database consistency (concurrency control and crash recovery) for these in-memory objects. In this section, we describe the data structures ORION has implemented to manage in-memory objects, that is, objects in the object buffer pool. The impacts of dual buffering on the architecture of a database system, and the solutions we have implemented in ORION, will be discussed in Section 4.

## 3.1 Object Buffering

Figure 7.1a shows a high-level block diagram of the ORION architecture. The message handler receives all messages sent to ORION objects. The object subsystem provides high-level functions, such as schema evolution,version control, query optimization, and multimedia information management. The storage subsystem provides access to objects on disk. It manages the allocation and deallocation of pages on disk, finds and places objects on the pages, and moves pages to and from the disk. The transaction subsystem provides a concurrency control and recovery mechanism to protect database integrity while allowing concurrent execution of multiple transactions. As in conventional database systems [Gra78], concurrency control uses a locking protocol, and a logging mechanism is used for recovery from system crashes and aborts.

The storage subsystem consists of the access manager and the storage manager, as shown in Figure 7.1b. The storage manager manipulates objects in their disk format and performs the transformation between the disk format and the in-memory format. The access manager controls the transfer of objects between the object buffer pool and the page buffer pool.

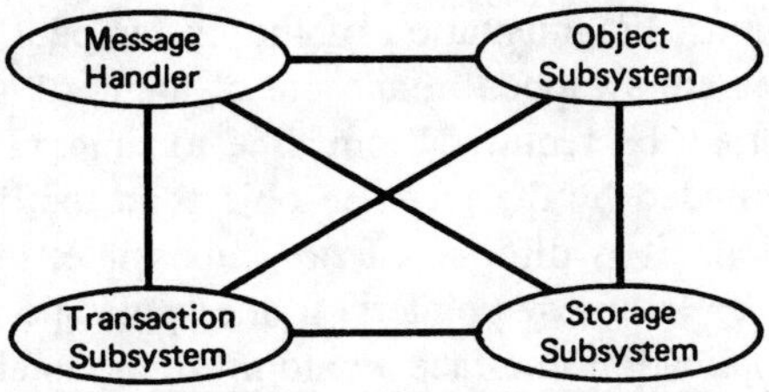


**Figure 7.1a** ORION architecture.

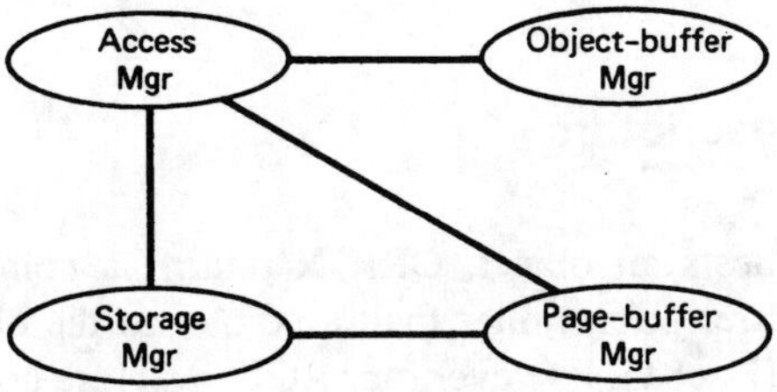


**Figure 7.1b** ORION storage subsystem.

The ORION page buffer manager is similar to the buffer manager in conventional database systems [Tra82]. It manages a pool of page frames and implements a page replacement algorithm. The page buffer pool serves as a staging area for regular (small) objects as well as the buffer area for caching portions of long multimedia objects.

The object buffer manager performs two major functions: it manages the object buffer pool; and maintains a virtual-memory address table (*resident object table or ROT*) for objects in the object buffer pool. There is a single physical object buffer pool, and multiple applications may concurrently access objects in the buffer pool. An application can accumulate objects in the object buffer pool by creating new objects or sending object requests to ORION.

A request to access an object through its system-wide unique identifier (UID) is directed to the access manager. It calls the object manager to first search the ROT. If the object is not registered in the table (i.e., an object fault occurs), the access manager calls the storage manager to retrieve the object from the database, and have the object buffer manager register it in the table and place the object in an object buffer.

The most frequent operation to the ROT is looking up the location of an object. Since the ROT can grow to a substantial size, a hash table is used to speed up associative searches based on UIDs. The key of the hash table is the UID, and the value is a pointer to the descriptor for the object associated with the UID (to be discussed shortly). Insertions and deletions of the ROT entries are two other frequent operations that are necessary for supporting object swapping. Sometimes a collection of objects in the buffer pool must be accessed: for example, when the modified objects need to be flushed to the database to commit a transaction, or when the contents of the object buffer pool are invalidated because of changes to the database schema (we will discuss these in more detail in Section 4).

Buffer management for objects in the object buffer pool is inherently more complex than that for pages because of the variability of object sizes. Placement of a newly retrieved object is a nontrivial task, since a free block of memory with at least the size of the object must be found. Fragmentation of the buffer pool becomes more severe as objects of different sizes are swapped in and out of memory. Expensive compaction of the object buffer pool may be required from time to time. The difficulty of object buffering is further compounded by the fact that objects in the buffer pool are directly accessible to the application. It is difficult, if not impossible, to keep track of all the outstanding object references (memory pointers) in the application program. Adding the fix/unfix protocol to the application interface would make the interface too cumbersome. Therefore, we need to rely on a garbage collection technique to reclaim space occupied by inactive objects.

## 3.2 Resident Object Descriptors

When the application requests an object, ORION returns a pointer to a descriptor of the object in the object buffer pool, rather than a pointer to the object. This is also the approach taken in LOOM [Kae81]; however, our ROD structure consists of several fields in addition to those used in LOOM, because of our consideration for the performance and integrity of the database in a multiple concurrent-user environment. (The rest of this paper will make this clear.) The descriptor, called the resident object descriptor (ROD), is illustrated in Figure 7.2a. The ROD is an intermediate data structure between the ROT and the actual object. The pointer-to-object field in the ROD contains a pointer through which the contents of the object can be accessed. The UID field contains the UID of the object; the PID field contains the physical address of the object on disk; and the class-ROD is the pointer to the ROD of the class object of which the object is an instance. The status field is used to indicate if the object is changed. The registered field is used to indicate whether the ROT contains a pointer to the ROD. The other fields of the ROD, message-cache and lock-cache, are used to speed up message passing and concurrency control; their use will be discussed later.

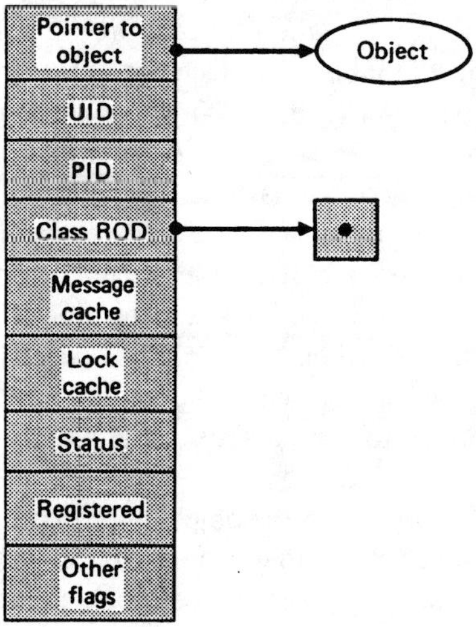


**Figure 7.2a** ROD structure.

We have introduced the ROD as a compromise between two somewhat conflicting goals that we need to satisfy for locating in-memory objects. On one hand, we would like to pass back the actual object (actually a pointer to the object) when a user requests it through a UID. On the other hand, we need to retain the ability to swap out any object in memory when such a need arises, for example, when the main memory is flooded with too many old objects. However, without direct hardware support, there is no easy way to catch a direct reference to a swapped-out object and take appropriate actions, as in a paged virtual memory system.

An object may be swapped out when it is not referenced in any active transaction, or when the object buffer pool becomes full. Then the pointer (to the object) in the ROD is changed to nil. The memory pointer to the ROD in the ROT is also removed, so that the ROD itself can be garbage collected when there are no more outstanding pointers to it. However, the ROD stays in memory so that the access manager can bring the object back in case the object is re-accessed through the ROD. There are situations where a ROD may be created before the object is brought into memory. For example, the result of a query is a set of RODs. There is no need to bring all the objects into memory since some of them may not be accessed at all. Under this situation, the access manager will create the RODs at query time, but fetch the objects only on demand. As shown in Figure 7.2b, some objects may have a ROT entry and a ROD that points to an in-memory copy of the object. Queried objects which have not been brought in have a ROT entry and a ROD containing a nil pointer. Swapped-out objects may have a ROD but no ROT entry. Finally, there are objects that reside only on disk and have no in-memory data structures associated with them.

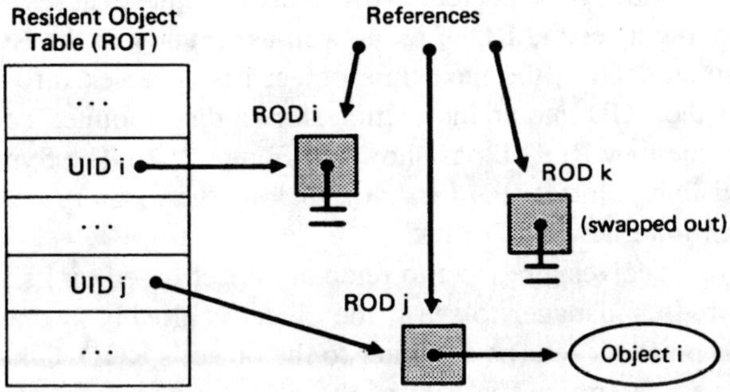


**Figure 7.2b** Object buffering.

The ROT is initially empty. The first time an object is accessed by a user, the object buffer manager detects that the object is not in the table and the access manager brings it in from the database. The access manager creates a ROD for the object and has the object buffer manager register it in the ROT with the UID as the key. The access manager passes a pointer to the ROD to the user, who can then directly access the contents of the object through the ROD. When another request comes in for the same object, the object buffer manager will locate the ROD (through the ROT) and pass back a pointer to the ROD. As shown in Figure 7.3, object y is referenced by both objects x and z through the same ROD.

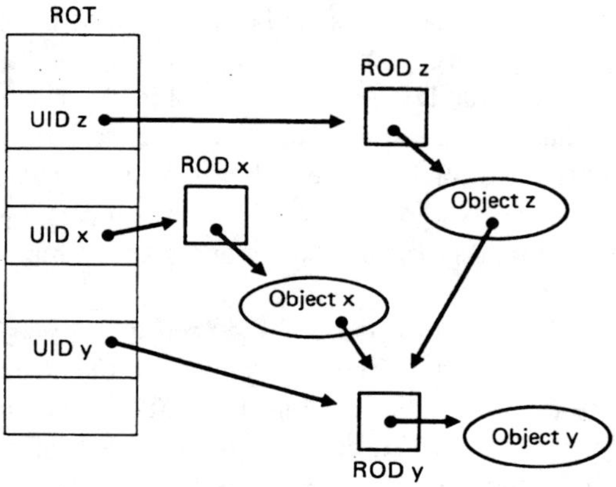


**Figure 7.3** Concurrent references to an object.

The object buffering and ROD manipulation discussed above are all transparent to ORION users. An ORION user simply sends a message to an object and expects a return message as in any object-oriented system. The objects that a user sees are actually pointers to RODs. To process a message sent to an object, the ORION message handler first examines the ROD and has the object read in from the database, if necessary.

Under our scheme for managing objects in the object buffer pool, it is possible for an extraneous ROD to be created for the same object while a ROD for the object already exists. Figure 7.4a illustrates this situation. Object i is swapped out, and its ROD, i1, is "de-registered" from the ROT; however, the ROD i1 is still being pointed to by a memory pointer, and is thus not garbage collected. Now another request causes object i to be swapped in (again), creating a second ROD, i2, as well as an entry in the ROT. To minimize the number of obsolete RODs, the next time object i is accessed through the old ROD i1, ORION converts the ROD into an indirection (forwarding) pointer, called an *invisible pointer* [Sym85], to the new ROD i2, as shown in Figure 7.4b. The Symbolics machine garbage collects invisible pointers (Figure 7.4c), making the memory pointer to the old ROD a direct pointer to the new ROD.

When the access manager receives a request to fetch an object based on its UID or ROD, it calls first the object buffer manager to see if the object is already in the object buffer pool. If it is, the access manager returns a pointer to the object's ROD. Otherwise, it directs the storage manager to determine the PID of the object by hashing into UID-PID table for all objects in the database (this is different from the ROT), fetch the page containing the object, isolate the object within the page, and transform the object from its disk format to the in-memory format. Finally, the access manager calls the object buffer manager to place the transformed object in the object buffer pool, and returns a pointer to the object's ROD. The PID of the object is recorded in the PID field of the ROD, shown in Figure 7.2a. This is to avoid the UID-to-PID translation overhead, when the object has to be flushed (written) to disk, or fetched again after it has been swapped out. To insert new objects, the storage manager determines the PIDs of the objects so as to cluster instances of the same class in the same physical segment, registers the objects in the UID-PID hash table for all database objects.

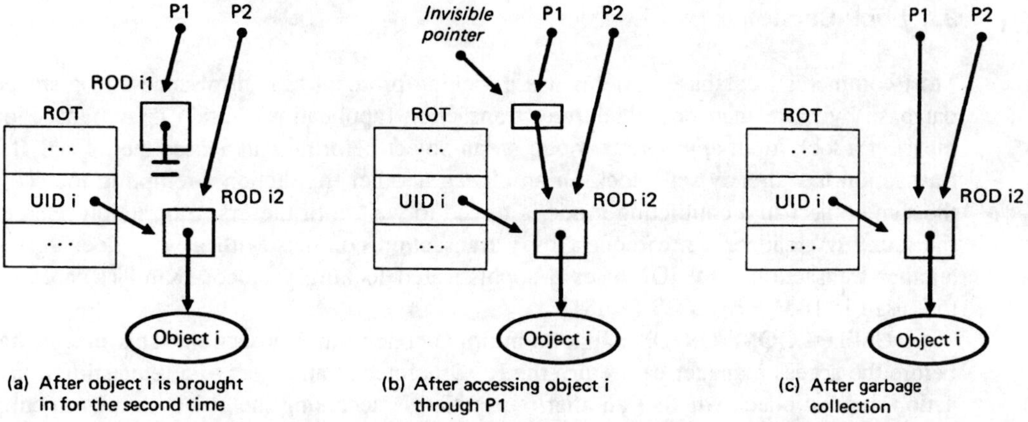


**Figure 7.4** Handling duplicate RODs.

### 3.3 Message Cache

ORION supports four types of messages: instance attribute messages, class attribute messages, instance method messages, and class method messages. We will use the term attribute messages to stand for both instance and class attribute messages, and the term method messages for both instance and class method messages. The function that is placed in the function cell of a message symbol in the LISP system is called a message function (this is called a discriminating function in CommonLoops, and a generic function in Flavors). A message function simply dispatches a message: it contains no knowledge of how the message is implemented.

The main data structure of the message handler is the message cache. The *message cache* consists of two arrays. The first array is the instance message cache: the instance message cache holds instance attribute messages and instance method messages. The second array of the message cache is the class message cache: the class message cache holds class attribute messages and class method messages. Each entry in the message cache contains a vector that holds either class messages or instance messages for a particular class. The entries in the message cache are called *class caches*. There are exactly two class caches for any class; one for class messages, and another for instance messages.

When a message is sent to an ORION object, the message-cache field in the ROD (Figure 7.2a) is first checked to see if the class cache has already been checked for the object. If the class cache is present, the message is dispatched on the cache. If it is not, the message handler looks up the object's class cache in the appropriate message cache. That is, if the object is a class, the class message cache is used; if it is an instance, the instance message cache is used. If the cache entry is found, it is recorded in the ROD for the object, and the message is dispatched. If it is not found, a cache entry is created, recorded in the appropriate message cache, and placed in the ROD for the object.

### 3.4 Lock Cache

Most commercial database systems use a locking protocol to control access to a shared database by more than one concurrent transaction (application) [Gra78]. A transaction must set a lock in an appropriate mode on an object before it can access the object. If a transaction has already set a lock on an object, another transaction attempting to access the same object in a conflicting mode is forced to wait until the first transaction releases the lock. (A read or write request by a transaction conflicts with a write lock set by another transaction.) ORION uses a sophisticated locking protocol [Kim87] based on that used in IBM's SQL/DS [Sql81].

Unlike LOOM, ORION supports multiple concurrent transaction. This means that before the access manager can return the ROD pointer of an object to a requesting transaction, it must check whether another transaction is accessing the object in a conflicting mode. This check is relatively expensive, since the access manager must call the lock manager in the transaction subsystem, and the lock manager must search the lock table.

To avoid this overhead whenever possible, when the access manager first creates or retrieves an object from the database, it encodes in the lock-cache field of the object's ROD the mode of the lock which is set on the object. In this way, the access manager needs to call the lock manager only the first time the object must be locked, and when a read lock on the object must be upgraded to a write lock (i.e., the object was first retrieved from the database with a read lock, and now object must be updated). In all other situations, calls to the lock manager may be avoided.

## 4. CONSEQUENCES OF OBJECT BUFFERING ON THE DATABASE SYSTEM ARCHITECTURE

Dual buffering has significant consequences on the architecture of a database system. These have to do with the fact that an object may have two different copies during a transaction: one in the object buffer pool and another in the database. One consequence is obviously the need for a translator to transform an object between its disk format and the in-memory format. A second consequence is the need to invalidate the in-memory objects, when certain types of changes are made to the database schema. A third consequence is the need to screen the database copy of an object from the result of a query, if the object has an in-memory copy.

### 4.1 Object Format Translation

To support efficient storage and retrieval, an object has to be packaged into a form that is suitable for disk storage. An object transformer is a part of the storage subsystem in ORION. The storage format for disk-resident objects is as shown in Figure 7.5.

The uid consists of two parts: the unique identifier of the class to which the object belongs, and the unique identifier of the object within the class. The object-length and attribute-count record the total length of the object and the number of attributes stored in the disk format. The attribute vector consists of the identifiers vi of all attributes for

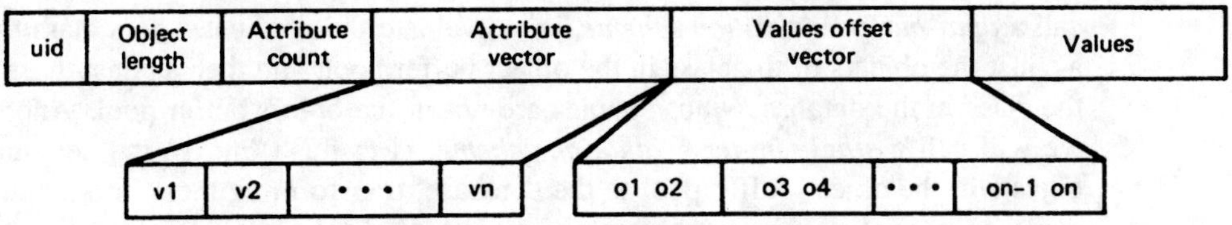


**Figure 7.5** Storage format for disk objects.

which the object has explicitly specified values. The values-offset vector consists of the offsets oi, in the values part of the object storage format, of the values of the attributes vi. A value can be a primitive value (such as an integer, string, etc.), or a reference to another instance, namely, the uid of the referenced object.

## 4.2 Object Buffer Flushing

Applications accumulate objects in the object buffer pool by creating new objects, fetching and updating objects from the database. The new objects and updated copies of objects need to be written to the database when the transaction which has created or updated the objects commits (successfully finishes). Of course, the objects are transformed to their disk format before being written to the database. New objects are registered in the UID-PID hash table for database objects, and updated objects replace their old copies in the database.

Further, when changes are made to the database schema (i.e., class definitions and the structure of the class hierarchy) which add or drop an attribute from a class, instances of the affected class which reside in the object buffer pool become invalid and must be purged from the object buffer pool. Of the 20 or so schema change operations ORION allows, the following invalidate objects in the object buffer pool.

1. Add a new attribute to a class
2. Drop an existing attribute from a class
3. Change the inheritance of an attribute (if any previously inherited attributes are lost)
4. Make a class S a superclass of a class C
5. Remove a class S from the superclass list of a class C
6. Drop an existing class

## 4.3 Query Processing

The access manager applies search predicates specified in a query to instances of a class. Our dual-buffering scheme complicates the implementation of a predicate-based access of objects. The two copies of the same object have the same identifier, but may differ in contents. Under an architecture which supports dual buffering, there are two fundamental approaches for processing a predicate-based access. One, which we will call a *dual-buffer evaluation scheme*, is to evaluate the predicates on a class twice: once against the objects of the class in the object buffer pool, and then against those objects of the class in the database whose copies are not in the object buffer pool. Another, which we will call a *single-buffer evaluation scheme*, is to flush (move) the new and updated objects in the object buffer pool to the database, transforming them into the disk format, and then to evaluate the predicates against the database.

Let us discuss the two options in more detail. Consider the situation shown in Figure 7.6. Objects X, Y, and Z, all of which are instances of the same class, have been placed in the object buffer pool, and X and Y have subsequently been updated and a new instance V created. We can see that predicates should not be evaluated against X and Y in the database, since updated copies of the objects, X' and Y', exist in the object buffer pool. Also if Z satisfies the predicate, it should not be brought into the object buffer pool, since a copy already exists in the object buffer pool. Further, in the case of a deletion, if X' or Y' satisfies the predicate, its older copy, X or Y, must also be deleted.

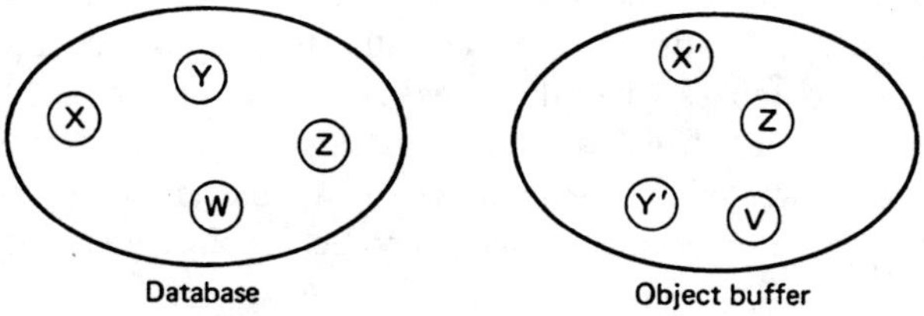


**Figure 7.6** Dual-buffer query evaluation.

The dual-buffer evaluation scheme may proceed in a number of different ways. One reasonable algorithm is as follows, assuming that the access request is confined to a single class C.

1. Evaluate the predicates against the instances of class C in the object buffer pool, generating a set O of object identifiers that satisfied the predicates.
2. Evaluate the predicates against the instances of class C in the database, generating a set D of object identifiers that satisfied the predicates. On this step, instances with copies in the object buffer pool are not evaluated again.
3. The result of the access request is the union of steps 1 and 2.

We note that on step 2 above the predicates need be evaluated against only those objects in the object buffer pool that have been marked as new or updated, since objects that have not been updated after their retrieval from the database have already been evaluated on step 1. When objects get flushed to the database, copies of the updated objects are sent to the access manager and applied to the database. The update flags for the new or updated objects in the object buffer pool are then reset (cleared).

The single-buffer evaluation scheme proceeds as follows, again assuming that objects that satisfy predicates on the attributes of a single class C are to be determined and retrieved.

1. Select those objects of class C in the object buffer pool that have been marked as new or updated since their retrieval from the database, and force copies of them to the database. This will make the two copies of each new or updated object identical.
2. Evaluate the predicates against objects of class C in the database, generating a set D of object identifiers that satisfied the predicates. D is the set of all objects to be retrieved.
3. Eliminate from D those objects of class C that are in the object buffer pool. Retrieve into the object buffer pool only those objects in the resulting set D'.

One major problem with the dual-buffer evaluation scheme is that the objects in the object buffer pool are in a different storage format from that used for objects in the database. As such, we need two different implementations of object search and predicate evaluation algorithms. We also need to support efficient access paths for the objects in the object buffer pool, so that we may avoid sequential searches of all objects. The shortcoming of the single-buffer evaluation scheme is of course that updates must be flushed to the database, and that the objects must be transformed from their in-memory format to the disk format for predicate evaluation. The overhead incurred in object transformation in a LISP environment led us to adopt the dual-buffer evaluation scheme for ORION: under a different environment, the single-buffer evaluation scheme may be superior.

## 5. SUMMARY

In this paper, we discussed two major issues in integrating a programming language system with a database system, and presented the solution we have implemented in integrating an object-oriented extension to Common LISP with the ORION object-oriented database system. One is the language issue. A programming language does not provide the primitive semantic data modeling concepts which are necessary to model real-world entities and the relationships among them. Database extensions to a programming language must not introduce a new or conflicting paradigm, or force the programmers to map between data structures in the programming language and those understood by the database system. Another issue is the computational model. A database system must support the illusion (along with adequate performance) that an application program has at its disposal an infinite virtual memory, in which it may access and manipulate the objects in the data structures supported by the programming language.

# 8

# Overview of the Iris DBMS*

**D. H. Fishman, D. Beech, J. Annevelink, E. Chow, T. Connors, J. W. Davis, W. Hasan, C. G. Hoch, W. Kent, S. Leichner, P. Lyngbaek, B. Mahbod, M. A. Neimat, T. Risch, M. C. Chan, W. K. Wilkinson**

*Hewlett-Packard Laboratories*
*Palo Alto, California 94304*

## 1. INTRODUCTION

The Iris database management system is a research prototype of a next-generation DBMS being developed at Hewlett-Packard Laboratories. We are exploring new database features and functionality through a series of increasingly more capable prototypes. In this paper, we present a snapshot of the current system and discuss its capabilities and those we are exploring for future implementations.

Iris is intended to meet the needs of new and emerging database applications [Fis87] such as office information and knowledge-based systems, engineering test and measurement, and hardware and software design. These applications require a rich set of capabilities that are not supported by the current generation (i.e., relational) DBMSs. In addition to the usual requirement for permanence of data, controlled sharing, backup, and recovery, the new capabilities that are needed include: rich data modeling constructs, direct database support for inference, novel data types (graphic images, voice, text,

**Source*: Adapted from Fishman et al, "Iris: An Object-Oriented Database Management System", in *Object Oriented Concepts, Databases and Applications*, edited by W. Kim and F. Lochovsky, ©1989, Addison-Wesley Publishing Co., Inc., Reading, Massachusetts. Reprinted with permission of the publisher.

vectors, matrices), lengthy interactions with the database spanning minutes to many days, and multiple versions of data. Data sharing must be provided at the object level in the sense of both concurrent and serial sharing, allowing a given object to be accessed by applications that may be written in different object-oriented programming languages. The Iris DBMS is being designed to meet these needs.

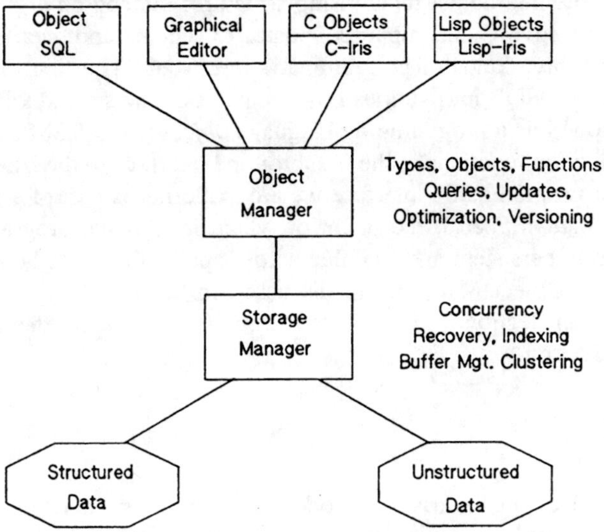


**Figure 8.1** Iris system structure.

Figure 8.1 shows the layered architecture of Iris. Central to this architecture is the Iris Object Manager [Lyn87a], the query and update processor of the DBMS. The Object Manager implements the Iris Data Model [Der85,Der86] which falls into the general category of object-oriented models that support high-level structural abstractions such as classification, generalization/specialization, and aggregation [Ham81,Smi77,Abr74,Che76,Shi81] as well as behavioral abstractions [Bro81,Myl80a,Kin82]. The query processor translates Iris queries and functions into an extended relational algebra format that is optimized and then interpreted against the stored database. Rather than inventing a totally new formalism upon which to base the correct behavior of our system, we rely on the relational algebra as our theory of computation [Lyn87b]. This has proven very convenient in terms of coexisting with, and migrating from, existing database applications.

The Iris Storage Manager is (currently) a conventional relational storage subsystem. It provides associative access and update capabilities to a single relation at a time and includes transaction support.

Like most other database systems, Iris is accessible via stand-alone interactive interfaces or through interface modules embedded in programming languages. Interface modules, such as those labeled C-Iris and Lisp-Iris in Figure 8.1, facilitate access to persistent objects from various programming languages. Construction of interfaces is made possible by a set of C language subroutines that defines, indeed *is*, the Object Manager interface.

Currently, three interactive interfaces are supported. One is simply a driver for the Object Manager interface. Another interactive interface, Object SQL (OSQL), is an object-oriented extension to SQL. We have chosen to extend SQL rather than invent a totally new language because of the prominence of SQL in the database community, and because, as we explored the possibility, the extensions seemed natural. A third interactive interface, the Graphical Editor, allows the user to interactively explore the Iris metadata (type) structures as well as the interobject relationship structures defined on a given Iris database. It is written in Objective-C and supports updates to schema and data.

We are also exploring three kinds of programmatic interfaces. The first kind is a straightforward embedding of OSQL into various host languages. The second kind is an encapsulation of the Iris DBMS as a programming language *object* [Cox86,Str86,Sny86] whose methods correspond to the functions in the C subroutine interface to the Iris Object Manager. The third kind of programmatic interface we are exploring is part of a longer-term investigation into *persistent objects*, the intent of which is to make programming language objects transparently persistent and sharable across applications and languages.

The capabilities of the Object Manager are discussed in Section 2. The various Iris interfaces are discussed in Section 3. Our plans to modify and extend the Storage Manager are discussed in Section 4.

## 2. IRIS OBJECT MANAGER

The Iris Object Manager implements the Iris data model by providing support for schema definition, data manipulation, and query processing. The data model, which is based on the three constructs, *objects, types* and *functions*, supports inheritance and generic properties, constraints, complex or non-normalized data, user-defined functions, version control, inference, and extensible data types. The roots of the model can be found in previous work on DAPLEX [Shi81], the Integrated Data Model [Bee83], the DAPLEX extension [Kul83], and the Taxis language [Myl80a].

### 2.1 Objects

Objects represent entities and concepts from the application domain being modeled. They are unique entities in the database with their own identity and existence, and they can be referred to regardless of their attribute values. For example, each object has an assigned, system-wide, unique object identifier, or OID. This supports referential integrity [Dat81a], and is a major advantage over record-oriented data models in which the objects, represented as records, can be referred to only in terms of their attribute values [Ken79].

Objects are described by their behavior, and can only be accessed and manipulated by means of functions. As long as the semantics of the functions remain the same, the database can be physically as well as logically reorganized without affecting application programs. This provides a high degree of data abstraction and data independence.

Objects are classified by type. Objects that belong to the same type share common functions. Types are organized into a type hierarchy with inherited functions. Consequently, an object may have multiple types. Objects serve as arguments to functions and may be returned as results of functions. A function may be applied to an object only if the function is defined on a type to which the object belongs.

By a *property* of an object we mean a function of one argument that returns a value when applied to that object. Thus, we model properties of Iris objects with functions. Functions that can be defined include predicates and functions of multiple arguments, providing direct support of binary or n-ary relationships.

The Iris data model distinguishes between *literal objects*, such as character-strings and numbers, and *non-literal objects* such as persons and departments. Non-literal objects are represented internally in the database by object identifiers. Literal objects have no user-accessible object identifier and are directly representable. As such, they cannot be created, destroyed or updated by users.

The Object Manager provides primitives for explicitly creating and deleting non-literal objects, and for assigning and updating values to their functions. Referential integrity is supported: when a given object is deleted, all references to the object are deleted as well.

## 2.2 Types and Type Hierarchies

Types are named collections of objects. Objects belonging to the same type share common functions. For example, all the objects belonging to the Person type have a Name and an Age function. Functions are computations defined on types (see Section 2.3); they are applicable to the instances of the types. In effect, therefore, types are constraints; that is, a type constrains the permissible functions that can be applied to an object of that type.

Types are organized in a type structure that supports generalization and specialization. A type may be declared to be a subtype of another type. In that case, *all* instances of the subtype are also instances of the supertype. It follows that functions defined on the supertype are also defined on the subtype. We say that the functions are *inherited* by the subtype. In Iris, a subtype inherits all functions defined on its supertypes. This is different from other object systems in which the functions of a supertype may, *optionally*, be inherited by a subtype. Of course, an Iris supertype may have instances that do not belong to any of its subtypes.

The Iris type structure is a directed acyclic graph. A given type may have multiple subtypes and multiple supertypes. Figure 8.2 illustrates a type graph with five types, each having a number of properties. The Employee type is a direct subtype of the Person and Taxpayer types, and the Employee type itself has two direct subtypes, Manager and Engineer.

Instances of type Employee also belong to the Taxpayer and Person types. The functions defined on Person and on Taxpayer are inherited by Employee. Thus, Employee objects have all six functions: Salary, Withholdings, Name, Age, Social-Security-Number, and Dependents. We may create a new type, Consultant, as follows.[1] All supertypes of the new type are listed in such a declaration.

[1]The examples in this section are presented in OSQL (see Section 3.1).

```
Create type Consultant subtype of Person, Taxpayer;
```

Functions do not actually "belong" to types. For display purposes, as in Figure 8.2, functions defined on a single argument are grouped with that argument type. A function of multiple arguments would not be so grouped (e.g., a function between Manager and Consultant that returns a consultant's date-of-hire).

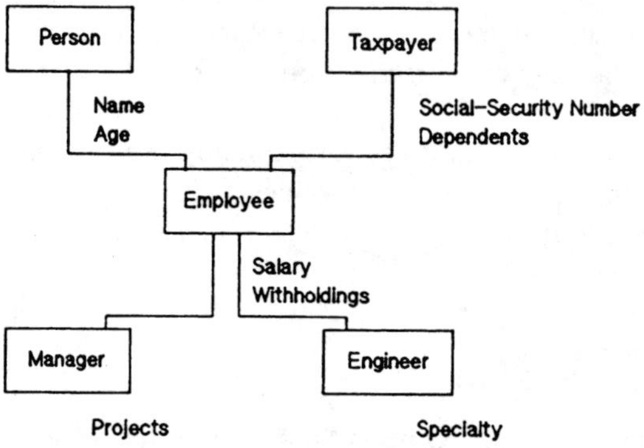


**Figure 8.2** A type graph.

Functions names may be *overloaded*, that is, functions defined on different types may have identical names even though their definitions may differ. Thus, a database designer can introduce a function in its most general form by defining it on a general type and later refine the function definition for the more specialized subtypes. For example, the Employee type may have a general Salary function whereas the Manager and Engineer types have Salary functions that are specific to the two job categories. This approach to design is called stepwise refinement by specialization [Myl80a].

When an overloaded function is applied to a given object, a single specific function must be selected at the time of application. The specific function is determined by the type of the object to which it is applied. If the object belongs to several types which all have specific functions of the given name, the function of the most specific type is selected. If a single most-specific type cannot be found, user-specified rules for function selection will apply. These rules are specified for families of functions that share the same names. These concepts also apply to functions taking several arguments.

The type Object is the supertype of all other types and therefore contains every object. Types are objects themselves, and their relationships to subtypes, supertypes, and instances are expressed as functions in the system [Lyn86].

In order to support graceful database evolution, the Object Manager allows the type graph to be changed dynamically. For example, new types may be created, existing types deleted and objects may gain or lose types throughout their lifetime. For example, an existing consultant object (bound to the variable "mohammed") may become an employee.

```
Add type Employee to mohammed;
```

However, new subtype/supertype relationships among existing types currently cannot be created. Thus, we could not make the type Consultant a subtype of the Employee type. Such operations will be supported in the future.

## 2.3 Functions and Rules

An Iris function is a computation that may or may not return a result. Functions are defined on types and are applicable to the instances of the types. Iris distinguishes retrieval functions from update functions. Thus, a retrieval function may not have side-effects. Updates are discussed in Section 2.3.5. Iris supports user-defined functions that are compiled, stored and executed under the control of the database management system. The specification of an Iris function, logically, consists of two parts: a *declaration* and an *implementation*, as discussed below. Note that OSQL also allows both specifications to be combined into a single **create function** statement.

**2.3.1 Function declaration.** A function declaration specifies the name of the function and the number and types of its parameters and results. For example:

```
Create Function Marriage(Person p) -><Person spouse,
Charstring date> forward;
```

creates a function called Marriage. The **forward** clause declares that the function implementation will be specified later. As a convenience, if **forward** is omitted, by default the function is given a *stored* implementation (see Section 2.3.2.1).

A function may return a compound result, as in the above example, where the result of the function contains both the spouse and the date of the marriage. Given an implementation, the Marriage function can be invoked as follows (assume "bob" is a variable bound to a Person object):

```
Select s, d for each Person s, Charstring d
    where <s, d> = Marriage(bob);
```

This statement may be abbreviated as:

```
Select each Person s, Charstring d
    where <s, d> = Marriage(bob);
```

or more simply:

```
Select Marriage(bob);
```

The function declaration is also used to specify participation constraints on the number of occurrences of each parameter and result value. For example, the interface has mechanisms for declaring function results to be *required* or *unique*. A required result means that a result value must exist for each possible parameter value in the database. A unique result means that distinct parameter values will be mapped onto distinct result values. We also distinguish between *single-valued* functions and *multi-valued* functions. Single-valued functions are functions that return only one result value for each invocation. In contrast, multi-valued functions may return many result values. For example, a function that returns all the children of a person would be a multi-valued function. A function that returns the mother of a person would be a single-valued function.

A database designer may wish to conceptually group together database functions in either of two ways:

1. Grouping according to argument types. For example, collecting together all of the functions on persons. This gives the sense of defining the properties of objects. This is the traditional object-oriented approach. We note that functions of multiple arguments do not fit into such a grouping.
2. Grouping by relationships. For example, collecting together functions and their inverses. This gives the sense of defining families of semantically-related functions.

Either of these ways of grouping functions together is valid in its context and the Iris data model does not insist on one or the other.

Information about objects is modeled in Iris using (Boolean) *predicate functions.* For example, the fact that a person has a name is represented as a predicate connecting the person object and the name object. This approach is different from that of the Entity-Relationship (E-R) Model [Che76] which allows objects to have attributes. The attribute concept is modeled in Iris by using functions whose values are derived from the predicates. Thus, a predicate, Person_Age, that connects persons and their ages could be defined as follows:

```
Create function Person_Age(Person p, Integer a) forward;
```

where Person_Age(john, 31) is true if the person specified has the age specified. Once Person_age has been implemented, we may then derive the functions

```
Age(Person) = Integer;
Person_with_Age(Integer) = Person;
```

which are inverses of each other. The Age function can be regarded as a property of Person. In this way, most simple functions are easily invertible since they are derived from predicates.

Relationships can be n-ary; for example, a relationship between mother, father and child can be represented as a predicate function with three parameters. An n-ary predicate can be used to derive a family of related functions; for example,

```
Father(Person) = Person;
Child(Person) = Person;
Parents(Person) = (Person mom, Person pop);
```

and so on. In general, an n-ary predicate has $2^n$ related functions. The related functions may be derived using the **`create function`** operation described in Section 2.3.2.2.

**2.3.2 Function implementation.** Iris functions may be implemented in one of several ways. These methods are outlined, below. Separating the function declaration from its implementation supports data abstraction, allowing users to change the implementation dynamically without affecting application programs.

*2.3.2.1 Stored Functions.* One way to implement a function is to store it as a table mapping input values to their corresponding result values. Such a table may be implemented and accessed using standard relational database techniques. The **cluster** operation allows the user to specify that a function is to be implemented in this way. Thus:

```
Create Function Marriage(Person p) ->
    <Person spouse, Charstring date> forward;
    Cluster Marriage;
```

causes the creation of a table with, in the case of the above declaration, three columns for person, spouse and date. The table can then be populated by applying an update operation to the Marriage function as described later. As mentioned earlier, the default implementation is to store all functions. Thus, removing the **forward** clause would make the cluster statement unnecessary.

The mappings of several functions may be stored together in a single table. For example, given Name and Address functions defined on Person:

```
Cluster Name on Person, Address on Person;
```

would create a table containing person OID's with their names and addresses. Restrictions have been introduced to ensure that such a table is in first normal form.

*2.3.2.2 Derived Functions.* The definition of a function may be specified in terms of other functions. For example:

```
Create function Emp_Manager(Employee e) -> Manager as
  select m for each Manager m
    where m = Department_Manager(Emp_Department(e))
```

This simple definition specifies how the manager of an employee may be derived from other functions using a **select** statement. Section 3.1 contains more examples of the use of the **select** statement.

In general, function definitions may contain arbitrary queries and include calls to any implemented function. In the following example, function Important_Manager calls a derived function, Emp_Manager, two stored functions, BirthDate and Salary, and a foreign function, DateCompare (described below).

```
Create function Important_Manager () -> Manager as
  select m for each Manager m, Employee e
    where Salary(e) > 10000 and m = Emp_Manager(e) and
      DateCompare(BirthDate(e),BirthDate(m)) > 0;
```

Note that the BirthDate function may apply to both Employee and Manager types since they are subtypes of Person (assuming BirthDate is defined on Person). The definition for the derived function is compiled by the Object Manager into an internal relational algebra representation. The relational algebra expressions for the called functions are merged into this relational algebra expression with selections and joins added where appropriate. The complete expression is optimized and then interpreted at execution time. Derived functions may be arbitrarily complex.

As a performance enhancement, Iris supports *materialized derived functions*. This is similar to the notion of materialized views in relational systems. Iris can precompute a derived function and store the results in a table. Subsequent invocations of the function are satisfied from the table. Updates invalidate the table. Currently, the table is not regenerated automatically.

***2.3.2.3 Foreign Functions.*** A third type of function implementation is to implement the function in some general-purpose programming language, such as C. We call these *foreign* functions because they are written in a language that Iris does not understand, and hence cannot optimize. For the class of applications Iris intends to support, it is desirable to be able to easily extend Iris's capabilities in unanticipated ways (e.g., to allow access to specialized storage managers, or to permit specialized operations as may be associated with new, user-defined data types such as vector and matrix operations, etc.). We have explored this capability by providing foreign functions in Iris for access to non-Iris databases. As an example, the foreign function, DateCompare, mentioned above, may be defined as follows.

```
Create function DateCompare (Charstring date1, Charstring date2)
        -> Integer as link 'date_cmp';
```

The file, `date_cmp`, should contain the machine object code for implementing DateCompare. Typically, it is produced by the language compiler for whatever language is used to write the foreign function. `date_cmp` is presumed to contain certain subroutine entry points for implementing the function (e.g., `open`, `get_next`, etc.). At execution time, when DateCompare is invoked, Iris transfers control to those entry points to evaluate and return results for the function call.

We emphasize that, although Iris cannot optimize the *implementation* of a foreign function, it can optimize the *usage* of a foreign function. Since the query optimizer is rule-based, one only need add rules appropriate to the particular foreign function of interest. For example, given a foreign function that adds two integers, one might add an identity rule to eliminate the addition function call whenever one operand is a zero constant. In fact, the Iris Storage Manager, itself, might be viewed as a foreign function given the rules for table and index selection and join ordering. Of course, the system is not implemented in this way since performance dictates a tight coupling between the modules.

The invocation of foreign functions is facilitated by the simple, well-defined interface between the query processing system and the storage subsystem. Each foreign function appears to the query processor as a virtual data set in the storage subsystem.

Parameters (where required) are passed as if they were the key to an indexed lookup in a traditional data set. The query processor retrieves information by making a procedure call to the storage subsystem. If the referenced data set is a foreign function, a dynamic loader is invoked to retrieve the foreign function from the file system and control actually transfers to the body of the foreign function (in the future, foreign function bodies will be stored in the database). Foreign functions return data in the same format used by the storage subsystem for traditional data sets. Any language can be used to write a foreign function so long as the object code can be linked with the query processor. The query optimizer knows which functions are stored in the storage subsystem as traditional data sets so that standard optimizing techniques may be applied.

As previously mentioned, complete optimization of queries involving foreign functions is impossible without a characterization of the function's behavior. Optimization "hooks" are a very interesting research topic. Currently, Iris is vulnerable to bugs in the body of a foreign function. Thus, at the very least, their implementation should be a privileged operation.

**2.3.3 Rules.** In Iris, rules are simply modeled as functions. For example, given a *Parent* function, we can define a *Grandparent* function as follows:

```
Create function Grandparent(Person p) -> Person as
 Select gp for each Person gp
   where gp = Parent(Parent(p));
```

A more complex rule may be defined as follows:

```
Create function Older_Cousin(Person p) -> Person as
 Select c for each Person c
   where c = Child(Sibling(Parent(p))) and Age(c) > Age(p);
```

We note that the nested-functions notation used in Iris' functional notation dispenses with the variables needed in logic programming languages, such as Prolog [Clo81], to carry results from one function call to the next. Variables can, however, be used in Iris function bodies, if required.

An important difference between C functions and Prolog rules (taking C and Prolog as examples of a traditional programming language and a rule-based language) is that a C function returns a single result, whereas a rule returns a stream of results. Iris functions can return multiple results, and a nested function call returns the concatenation of all the results obtained from calling the inner function. For example, the function call:

```
Children(Member(sales_dept))
```

returns all of the children of all of the members of the Sales Department.

Like Prolog, Iris makes the closed-world assumption—any fact which is not deducible from the data in the database is assumed to be false. The current Iris prototype supports only conjunctive, disjunctive, and non-recursive rules, but negation and recursion are being studied.

**2.3.4 Bags and aggregate functions.** The previous sections described functions defined on individual objects. There is also a need for functions over bags[2] of objects, such as *Average*. Bags in Iris are defined via nested **Select** statements. This is similar to the use of nested queries in SQL. For example, the following query computes the average salary of all employees.

```
Select y for each Real y
  where y = Average (Select Salary(x) for each Employee x );
```

The nested **Select** statement returns a bag of values which are then used as input to the Average function. Iris semantics are such that nested **select** statements and function calls are equivalent in retrievals. Thus, given a function, EmpSal( ), that returns the salaries of all employees, the above query could be rewritten by replacing the nested **select** statement by a call to EmpSal.

A nested **Select** statement may refer to variables defined outside its scope. Such variables are known as *correlated* variables and they, in effect, link the results of the nested **Select** statement to the outer query. For example, the following query computes the average salary of each department:

```
Select Dept_Name(d), y for each Real y, Department d
  where y = Average (Select Salary(x) for each Employee x
    where Emp_Department(x)=d );
```

We point out that bags are not Iris objects. They may not be stored directly in the database. If a bag must be preserved, the correct solution is to define a function and store the bag's elements as the results of the function. Also, note that Iris supports multiple bag definitions at any level in the query. SQL restricts users to, at most, one subquery per level.

Aggregate functions in Iris are implemented as foreign functions with bag operands. For example, Average might be created as follows:

```
Create function Average (bag of Real) -> Real
          as link 'avg_r';
```

where the file 'avg_r' contains the machine object code to implement Average. The **bag of** clause declares the argument to be a bag.

This approach of implementing aggregates as foreign functions simplifies query translation and query execution by reducing the number of possible operators. It also allows the user to implement new aggregate operations as needed. For example, by using a **distinct** clause to eliminate duplicates (see Section 3.1), true set operations such as union, intersection and difference could be implemented if an Iris application required them.

**2.3.5 Update operations.** An update operation changes the future behavior of a stored or derived Iris function. For example, the operation:

```
Set Department_Manager(sales_dept) = john;
```

[2]Bags are multi-sets (i.e., sets that may contain duplicates).

will cause future invocations of the Department_Manager function with the parameter sales_dept to return the object currently bound to the variable john. Iris also supports updates to multi-valued functions. The **add** operation can be used to add additional values. For example,

```
Add Member(sales_dept) = barbara;
```

adds "barbara" to the set of members of the Sales Department. More powerful updates may be accomplished, by operations of the form

```
Add Member(sales_dept) = p for each Person p
    where p = Member(toy_dept);
```

This causes all members of the Toy Department to also become members of the Sales Department. Values can be removed from single- and multi-valued functions using the **remove** operation. For example,

```
Remove Member(sales_dept) = sue;
```

removes the employee bound to variable sue from the Sales Department. More powerfully:

```
Remove Member(sales_dept) = e for each Employee e
    where e = Member(sales_dept) and Age(e) > 70;
```

removes from the Sales Department all employees older than 70, and

```
Remove Member(sales_dept);
```

drops all employees from the Sales Department.

Each function in Iris may have up to four compiled representations: one each for **select**, **set**, **add** and **remove**. If the **select** operation is a simple derived function,[3] the implementation of the update operations can be deduced by the system. But for more complex **select** operations, say one involving a join, it will be necessary for the function definer to specify the update implementations. Currently, Iris does not support these update specifications.

**2.3.6 Delete operations.** The **delete** operation can delete any user-defined object, type or function. The effect of a **delete** is propagated to all related information. For example, the operation:

```
Delete type Engineer;
```

will cause the type Engineer to be deleted. In addition, all functions with Engineer as an argument or result type are deleted. However, instances of the Engineer type are not deleted. Instead, those objects simply "lose" the Engineer type.

[3]A simple derived function is a select statement over a single predicate function.

**2.3.7 Procedures.** Update operations may be collected into a single parameterized function, known as a procedure. For example, the first two updates of Section 2.3.5 may be collected into a single, general-purpose procedure.

```
Create function Update_Dept (Department dept, Manager mgr,
             Employee emp) as
     begin
          Set Department_Manager(dept) = mgr;
          Add Member(dept) = emp;
     end;
```

Currently, update procedures have no return values.

## 2.4 Version Control

One of the goals of Iris is to support application areas that are not well-supported by existing database managers, such as computer-aided design, computer-aided software engineering and office automation. A common requirement of these applications is the desire to preserve alternative states for a particular entity. This necessitates the existence of an object versioning mechanism in order to provide controlled access to these values [Lor83,Kat85,Kat86,Lan86,Cho86]. A version control mechanism has been implemented as an integral part of the Iris Object Manager [Bee88a].

In Iris, as in other object systems, an object retains its identity throughout its existence although its state may change (i.e., its function values may be modified by **set**, **add**, or **remove**). Versions are like snapshots of an object in certain states, and are modeled by distinct objects. Thus, in Iris, separate objects correspond to each version and to the entity of which they are versions.

**2.4.1 Generic instance, specific and generic references.** One crucial aspect of version control in Iris is that it offers a form of indirect addressing, whereby objects can make *generic* references to other objects. The generic instance is an abstraction of the entity that may, itself, have properties (properties whose values are uniform over all versions). There is one generic instance per each *version set*, that is, the set of all versions of an object. Information about the version set and the predecessor-successor relationships that hold between members of the set are maintained by functions on the generic instance and version objects.

Any reference to a versioned object can be either a *specific reference* to a particular version of the object, or a *generic reference* to the entity's generic instance. A generic reference can at any time be coerced to refer to a specific version of an object.

**2.4.2 Transformation of non-versioned objects.** Iris provides the ability to create versions of what were originally unversioned objects. We feel this is important because it is not always possible to know beforehand which parts of a design to place under version control. The alternative is to treat all objects as versioned and this may impose undue overhead.

As an example, the following converts the unversioned object, "mod1", to a versioned object:

```
create version from mod1 instance mod1v1;
```

The result is that a new object, "mod1v1", will be created with the same user types as the original, unversioned, object. In addition, it will acquire the system type Version and it will be the first version of the version set. The original object, "mod1", will lose its system type Unversioned, acquire the system type Generic, and, retaining its original OID, it will act as the generic instance of the newly created version set. Thus, the generic instance serves as a place-holder for existing references to the original, unversioned, object.

**2.4.3 Version control operations.** Versions of an object are created explicitly by the user. A number of Iris commands, such as **checkin**, **checkout**, **lock**, **unlock**, allow for creation and manipulation of versions and for controlled sharing of versions among users. For example, the following command creates a successor version of "mod1v1":

```
checkout mod1v1 as mod1v2;
```

This creates a new version, "mod1v2", that can be modified and later checked back into the database with the request:

```
checkin mod1v2;
```

Since versions are objects, destruction of versions and schema modifications such as adding new types or removing existing types from version objects are performed with existing Iris operations. However, these operations on versioned objects are subject to additional constraints. For example, a type cannot be removed from a version unless it is removed from the entire version set.

Controlled sharing of versions among users is achieved through *version locks*, which are user-settable, long-term locks. As in RCS [Tic82a], objects may be locked at **checkout** and unlocked at **checkin**:

```
checkout mod1v1 key modkey1 as mod1v2;
```

The lock key is returned in variable "modkey1". The lock prevents other users from deriving a successor of "mod1v1". Given the key, the version may be unlocked at **checkin**:

```
checkin mod1v2 key modkey1;
```

## 2.5 Query Processing

Iris queries are expressed in terms of functions and objects. The Storage Manager deals with relational algebra and tables. The task of query processing in Iris is shared by two modules. The Query Translator compiles queries from their object representation to a relational algebra representation. The Query Interpreter evaluates the transformed query, invoking the Storage Manager to access the database and foreign functions to access other data sources. In this section, we provide a brief overview of the Query Translator and Query Interpreter modules.

**2.5.1 Query translator.** The Object Manager interface requires queries to be expressed in a tree structure, known as an *F-Tree*. The nodes of an F-Tree include function calls, comparison operators ($=$, $\neq$, $<$, $>$, $\leq$, $\geq$) the logical operators (**and**, **or**, **not**: negation is currently not supported) and variables and constants.

The query translation process consists of three main steps. First, the F-Tree is converted to a canonical form. This involves a series of tree transformations that are done to simplify subsequent transformations. For example, nested function calls are unnested by introducing auxiliary variables. The second step converts the canonical F-Tree to an extended relational algebra tree known as a *B-Tree*. This is a mechanical process in which function calls are replaced by their stored implementations (which are, themselves, B-Trees) and comparison and logical operators are converted to relational algebra selection and cross-product operators.

The resulting B-Tree consists of projection, selection, cross-product, and table nodes. The semantics of the tree are that results of a child node are sent to the parent node for subsequent processing. For example, a project node above a table node would filter out columns of the table.

The final, and most complex, step is to optimize the B-Tree. The optimizer is rule-based. Each rule consists of a test predicate and a transformation routine. The test predicate takes a B-Tree node as an argument and if the predicate evaluates to true, the transformation routine is invoked. The predicate might test the relative position of a node (e.g., selection node above a project node) or the state of a node (e.g., cross-product node has only one input). The possible transformations include deleting the node, moving it above or below another node, or replacing the node with a new B-Tree fragment. As in [Grd87], the system must be recompiled whenever the rules are modified.

Rules are organized into rule-sets which, together, accomplish a specific task. For example, one rule-set contains all rules concerned with simplifying expressions (e.g., constant propagation and folding). Optimization is accomplished by traversing the entire B-Tree for each rule-set. During the traversal, at a given node, any rule in the current rule set may be fired if its test predicate is true.

The optimization steps (i.e., rule-sets) can be roughly described as follows. There is an initial rule set that converts the B-Tree to a canonical form. The canonical form consists of a collection of query blocks. Each query block contains a project node, a selection node and a cross-product node. A second rule-set eliminates redundant joins which has the effect of reducing the number of tables in a cross-product. A third rule set is concerned with simplifying expressions. A fourth rule set chooses a join order. A fifth rule set handles Storage Manager-specific optimizations, for example, finding projection and selection operations that can be done in the Storage Manager.

The final (optimized) B-Tree is then sent to the Query Interpreter which processes the query and returns the result to the user. However, the B-Tree may not represent a query but may, instead, be the newly defined body of a derived function. In this case, the B-Tree is simply stored in the database system catalog for later retrieval when compiling queries that reference the derived function.

The Query Translator is quite flexible and can accommodate any optimization that can be expressed in terms of a predicate test on a node and a tree transformation. We expect to take advantage of this to optimize queries that call foreign functions.

**2.5.2 Query interpreter.** The Query Interpreter module evaluates a B-Tree and produces a set of tuples that may be returned to the user or stored back into the database (for example, to update the results of a function). The Query Interpreter treats each node in the B-Tree as a *scan object*. Each node in the B-Tree has 3 associated operations: *open-scan, get-next*, and *close-scan*. When the Query Interpreter is passed a B-Tree, it simply calls the open-scan operation for the root of the B-Tree, and then calls get-next until no more tuples are returned. Then close-scan is called.

An open-scan operation may call the Query Interpreter, recursively, to retrieve results from a sub-tree. For example, given a project node, the portion of the B-Tree below the project node represents the source of the tuples for the project operation. Thus, an open-scan on a project node must recursively open a scan on the sub-tree in order to get the tuples.

The get-next operation returns the next tuple in the scan. For example, get-next on a table node will request the Storage Manager to return the next stored tuple in the previously opened scan.

The Query Interpreter is fully re-entrant. It can handle B-Trees of arbitrary complexity, not just the simple project - select - cross-product trees mentioned earlier. In particular, nested queries can easily be processed.

## 3. IRIS INTERFACES

The Iris DBMS may be accessed via both interactive and programmatic interfaces. These interfaces are implemented using the library of C subroutines that define the Iris Object Manager interface. The library is intended to be a platform upon which stand-alone interfaces and interfaces to various programming languages are built. In addition, programmers may use this library directly. The following subsections discuss the design and functional capabilities of the existing interactive and programmatic interfaces to Iris.

### 3.1 Object SQL Interface

The initial Iris interfaces stayed quite close to the atomic level of the operations supported by the Object Manager. However, for more general use, it was decided to develop a higher-level interface that would take the primitive notion of an atomic object and combine it with the set of property (single-argument) functions that the user considered to be intrinsic to the nature of the object. This is much like the treatment of entities and their attributes in the E-R model, or like one use of the tables in the relational model [Cod70] where a row represents an object and each column represents a property. It is also close to the concept of an abstract type or class in an object-oriented programming language.

Given the definitions of two types of objects such as Person and Document, simple means are needed to create instances of these types, and to introduce relationships such as "is author of" or "has approval rights over" between persons and documents. This corresponds to the relationship-sets in the E-R model, and to the other usage of relational tables to relate objects (rows in other tables) by referring to their key values. Programming languages tend to lack high-level support for relationship-sets of this kind.

The functional emphasis in Iris suggests the use of a functional style of interface for expressing the relationships among interconnected objects. We therefore examined such languages as DAPLEX [Shi81], GORDAS [Elm81], and IDM [Bee83]. However, because of the strong similarities of these languages to a relational language such as SQL [Dat84], we also explored possible extensions to SQL to accommodate the object model and a more functional style. As a result of the study, we concluded that an Object SQL (OSQL) interface would be feasible and attractive.

The three main extensions we have made beyond SQL to adapt it to the object and function model are:

1. Users manipulate types and functions rather than tables.
2. Objects may be directly referenced rather than indirectly, through their keys. Interface variables may be bound to objects on creation or retrieval and may then be used to refer to the objects in subsequent statements. For example, see the variables "Jones", "Smith", "d1", etc., below.
3. User-defined functions and Iris system functions may appear in **where** and **select** clauses to give concise and powerful retrieval.

There are also a few keyword alternatives introduced into existing SQL. It is possible to mechanically reinterpret all existing keywords, but for human users some of the keywords would be found very misleading when applied to the object model.

A few examples should illustrate both the general similarity of OSQL to SQL, and the advantages of an object-based query language. Supposing that we wish to automate some office procedures for obtaining approvals for documents, some of the actions and corresponding OSQL statements could be as follows.

We need a type, Person, with property functions name, address and phone. Each Person object must have a value for the name function:

```
Create type Person
    (name Charstring required,
    address Charstring,
    phone Charstring);
```

Such creation of a type with properties is a syntactic shorthand for separately creating a type and each of the functions. Additional functions taking this type as an argument may be separately created and are semantically equivalent to properties created with the type. We also note that, since such properties can be multi-valued, a type may not correspond directly to a relational table.

To represent people with approval rights, we create a new type, Approver, as a subtype of Person. The type has a single property function, expertise, (we assume Topic has already been created as a type), in addition to the three properties inherited from Person. The new property function is multi-valued:

```
Create type Approver subtype of Person
    (expertise Topic many);
```

Some people will be authors of documents and we also need a document type:

```
Create type Author subtype of Person;
Create type Document
    (title Charstring required unique,
    authorOf Author required many,
    subject Topic,
    status Charstring required,
    approverOf Approver many);
```

Note that the document title is declared as unique so that duplicate titles are disallowed. Next, we need a stored function, grade, that, for a given document and approver, returns the grade assigned to the document by the approver:

```
Create function grade (Document, Approver) -> Integer;
```

Now, create three instances of the type Approver and assign values to the property functions name (inherited from the type Person) and expertise. Bind the interface variables Smith, Jones and Robinson to the objects created:

```
Create Approver (name, expertise) instances
     Smith ('Albert Smith', software),
     Jones ('Isaac Jones', (finance, marketing)),
     Robinson ('Alan Robinson', (hardware, marketing, manufacturing));
```

The expertise values (software, finance, etc.) are interface variables bound to Topic objects. Add the type Author to the two objects bound to interface variables Jones and Robinson. This shows objects being given multiple types:

```
Add type Author to
    Jones,
    Robinson;
```

Enter a document written by Jones:

```
Create Document (title, authorOf, status) instance
    d1 ('The Flight from Relational', Jones, 'Received');
```

Assign approvers to the document d1, and assign a grade to it:

```
Set approverOf(d1) = (Smith, Robinson);
Set grade(d1, Smith) = 3;
```

Make a type for approved documents, and approve d1:

```
Create type ApprovedDocument subtype of Document;
Add type ApprovedDocument to d1;
```

Get the title of document d1, the titles of all approved documents, and the titles of all documents of which Smith is an approver:

```
Select title(d1);
Select title(ad)
     for each ApprovedDocument ad;
Select title
     for each Document d
     where Smith = approverOf(d);
```

A **distinct** clause may be used in the result list to eliminate duplicate results. Find the names of all authors with some document awaiting approval:

```
Select distinct authorOf(d)
     for each Document d
     where status(d) = 'Received';
```

It is interesting to consider OSQL as a potential evolutionary growth path for SQL. Some of the new features of OSQL could be supported in a straightforward way on a relational system, while others would require a more ambitious object manager. Migration is never easy, but the OSQL approach could smooth the path for migration of both users and programs from SQL to the object world [Bee88b].

### 3.2 Iris Graphical Editor

The Iris Graphical Editor provides a graphical interface that enables a user to browse and update an Iris database. The type hierarchy is displayed as a directed, acyclic graph. For each type, one may display the functions defined on that type or the instances of that type. Each such type or instance may, in turn, be *inspected*, to examine its properties (i.e., functions of one argument defined on that type).

A given Iris object may have multiple supertypes through its immediate and transitive supertype relationships. The Graphical Editor produces property sub-lists for each type of an object. If the property function is single-valued, the Graphical Editor simply displays the result of the property function applied to the object. For multi-valued functions, an Iris query is generated and "<IRIS-SCAN>" is displayed. In this case, the user may request that the scan be evaluated, either in the same or a new window. The Graphical Editor supports both an indented textual view and a tree view. Function values may be updated using the Graphical Editor.

Schema updates, such as type and function creation and deletion, are supported in the Graphical Editor. Also supported are session control operations, such as commit and rollback. For schema update operations, users supply required information via mouse selections.

An Iris type tree is illustrated in Figure 8.3. Since the entire tree does not fit on the display, the subtree containing the user-defined types was placed in a separate window. Instances of type Programmer were selected and the Editor found and applied the *name* property to the Programmer instances.

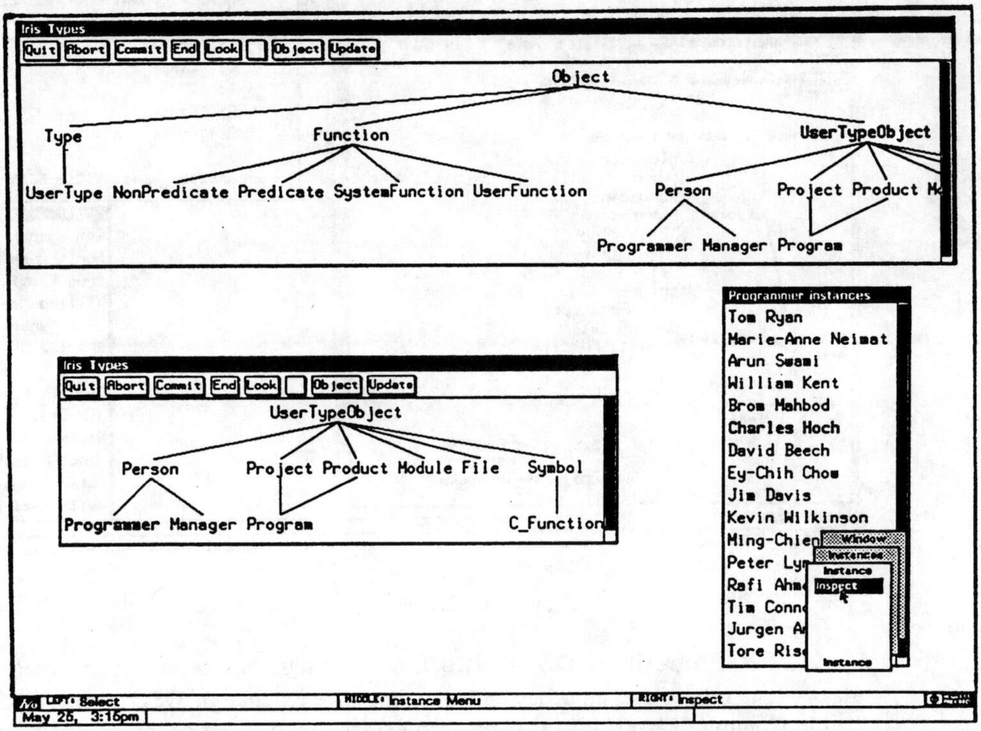


**Figure 8.3** Graphical editor - type tree.

Figure 8.4 illustrates a type creation window. In the display, note that `expertise` and `programmer_owns` are multi-valued functions represented by scans. The user has asked (via menu selection) for the values of `expertise`, but the values for `programmer_owns` have not yet been retrieved. In the New Type window, the type `Developer` is being created, which is to be a subtype of `Programmer`. One new function on `Developer` has been specified: `Responsibility`, which will return, possibly many, instances of `Program`.

### 3.3 Iris Programming Language Interface

In this section we will discuss the various Iris programming language interfaces, all based on the functionality provided by the Object Manager C subroutine library.

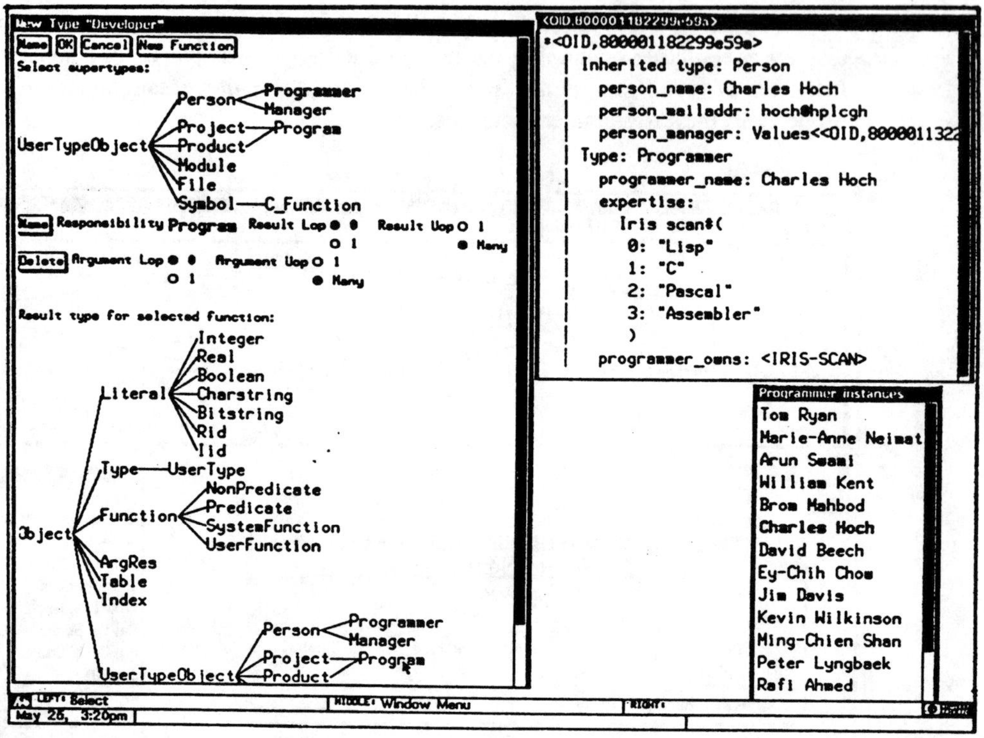


**Figure 8.4** Graphical editor - type creation.

**3.3.1 Embedded OSQL interface.** OSQL has been implemented both as a stand-alone interactive interface and as a language extension. OSQL is currently embedded in Common Lisp [Ste84a] via macro extension. A more general embedded interface is being provided for C that is based on the existing ANSI standard for SQL embedding. The traditional arguments for embedding query languages also apply to OSQL. In addition, the user-defined types provided by the object model should prove helpful in overcoming the "impedance mismatch" in passing information between host and embedded languages.

**3.3.2 Loosely integrated object-oriented interface.** Based on the functionality provided by the Object Manager library, we can define a layer of abstraction that exposes the Iris data model to a programmer. Following the object-oriented paradigm, this interface may be represented as a collection of object types (classes) and their associated operations. Instances of these classes represent the entities required to access and manipulate an Iris database. Typical classes might include: DataBase, Function, Type, Scan and Object.

For example, the class DataBase might support operations to start a new database, connect to an existing database, commit or abort a transaction, etc. Instances of the Function class might provide operations to create and/or update functions. A variety of programming languages may be used for such an interface and, depending on the constructs offered by the language, more or less of the implementation details may be hidden from programmers. A loosely-coupled interface to Iris has been implemented in Lisp.

**3.3.3 Tightly integrated object-oriented interface.** In order to support persistent object extensions, it is necessary to tightly integrate object-oriented programming languages with Iris. This requires a mechanism for object activation, that is, objects should be retrieved automatically when needed by an application program. An object-activation mechanism needs a schema or mapping that specifies how programming language objects are to be represented in the database and vice-versa. One advantage of an explicit schema is that there can be many such mappings: one for every application interface. This simplifies the sharing of objects between, otherwise heterogeneous, applications.

By retrieving an object from the database, an application program effectively caches the object. Subsequent changes to the state of the object are not automatically propagated back to the database. A tightly-coupled interface must ensure consistency between the cached object and the database object. Conventional transaction-oriented mechanisms do not appear suitable. Instead, we are investigating the use of both a versioning and a monitoring mechanism.

The versioning mechanism will be an interface to the versioning facilities described in Section 2.4. The monitor mechanism will allow an application to request that an Iris function be monitored for some specified argument objects. Iris will notify the application whenever the monitored function value changes. The application may then retrieve the new function value.

Persistent-CLOS (PCLOS [Pae87]) is one attempt at building a tightly integrated interface between Iris and an object language. It interfaces object-oriented programs to Iris by transparently mapping CLOS objects onto the database. CLOS is an object layer on top of Common Lisp that is evolving into a standard [Bob87]. PCLOS allows programmers to make objects transient or persistent by sending messages to them. Transient and persistent objects are semantically and syntactically equivalent, except for the effects of concurrency control and, of course, life span. State accesses to persistent objects are transparently intercepted and appropriate commands are sent to Iris for information update and retrieval. Transient objects are not known to Iris and cannot be accessed by other users.

The implementation of PCLOS is quite natural in that CLOS classes, instances and slots map into Iris types, objects and functions, respectively. The system automatically generates the appropriate Iris schemata from CLOS class hierarchies. Special care is needed when data of Lisp-specific types are stored in slots and therefore in the database. A CLOS converter object manages all mappings of such data items to formats storable in Iris or databases accessed through Iris. Whenever possible, PCLOS uses database literals. If there are no such appropriate primitives, the information is encoded in ASCII.

The system stores information about CLOS classes in the database to permit the reconstruction of in-memory class hierarchies at run-time before instances are accessed.

This includes mainly slot specifications that are not reflected in the database type hierarchy. We use this for consistency checks and expect to use the information to access our object bases from other object-oriented languages.

The default behavior of PCLOS is to leave all persistent data in the database, except when it is needed for processing. Modifications are immediately written back and committed to Iris. This mode of operation has the advantage of maximizing opportunities for concurrency. The disadvantage is very heavy database traffic and subsequent performance problems. All persistent objects respond to messages instructing them to cache or uncache themselves or to perform other functions needed for cache management. We are experimenting with the proper balance of caching in the database client versus server memory spaces.

## 4. IRIS STORAGE MANAGER

The Iris Object Manager is built on top of a conventional relational storage manager, namely that of HP-SQL [Hps].

HP-SQL's Storage Manager is very similar to System R's RSS [Bla79]. Tables can be created and dropped at any time. The system supports transactions with savepoints and restores to savepoints, concurrency control, logging and recovery, archiving, indexing and buffer management. It provides tuple-at-a-time processing with commands to retrieve, update, insert and delete tuples. Indexes and threads (links between tuples in the same table) allow users to access the tuples of a table in a predefined order. Additionally, a predicate over column values can be defined to qualify tuples during retrieval.

We plan to extend and modify this storage subsystem to better support the Iris data model and to provide capabilities needed to support our diverse set of intended applications. In this section, we discuss two planned extensions: support for foreign operators and long fields.

### 4.1 Foreign Operators

As discussed in Section 2, Iris functions can be implemented as stored tables, derived functions or foreign functions. Derived functions are defined in terms of other functions that, in turn, may be implemented as stored, derived or foreign functions. The initial step of the Iris Query Translator module is to (recursively) retrieve the definitions of all derived functions in the query. It is then left with an expression tree consisting of tables, relational algebra operators and calls to foreign functions. This tree is subsequently simplified and optimized. Part of the query optimization strategy is to delegate to the Storage Manager as much of the execution tree as possible. This reduces the number of calls to the Storage Manager as well as the amount of data passed between the Storage Manager and the Query Interpreter module of the Object Manager. Currently, operations involving multiple tables (joins), complex operations over a single table (aggregation) and foreign functions are all evaluated by the Query Interpreter, outside the Storage Manager.

One of the basic functions of the Storage Manager is the retrieval of tuples from tables. A retrieval request includes a table identifier and may include a selection predicate, a projection list and a preferred access method. The Storage Manager begins by opening a scan on the table. The scan specifies any projection list, selection predicate and whether the scan should be sequential or via an access method. The selection predicate is composed of conjunctions and disjunctions of operators applied to constants and column values. For example:

```
(Column6 eq "Smith") and
((Column3 neq 5) or
(Column2 gt Column1))
```

All operators known to the Storage Manager are binary and return a single boolean value.

Associated with each scan is a finite state machine that evaluates the selection predicate. The Storage Manager iterates through the scan by retrieving the next tuple and invoking the finite state machine to evaluate the predicate. If the output of the finite state machine is **true**, the tuple is returned. Otherwise, the tuple is dropped. Note that part of the predicate may be evaluated by an access method. For instance, in the example above, if an index exists on Column6, the open scan command may specify that the index should be used to retrieve tuples from the table. In this case, the term (Column6 **eq** "Smith") in the predicate is evaluated by the access method while the term, ((Column3 **neq** 5) **or** (Column2 **gt** Column1)), is evaluated by the finite state machine. Thus, prior to opening the scan, the Storage Manager may split the selection predicate into a subexpression for the access method and a subexpression for the finite state machine.

In the current version of Iris, the limited form of selection predicates recognized by the Storage Manager limits the portion of the query tree that the Query Translator may delegate to the Storage Manager. In particular, it may only delegate certain binary operators and the operands of those operators must be either a column and a constant or two columns of the same table.

As discussed in Section 2, we plan to support operator extensibility by implementing new operators as foreign functions. Thus, in its internal implementation, Iris will not understand the semantics of "factorial", for example, beyond the fact that it takes one operand of type integer and returns one value of type integer. To evaluate the function, the Query Interpreter will invoke the body of the foreign function.

The obvious next step is to delegate evaluation of foreign functions to the Storage Manager whenever possible. Thus, we plan to extend the Storage Manager so that it can evaluate any operator or foreign function so long as all column input parameters belong to the same table. This requires relaxing the Storage Manager assumption that all operators be binary and return boolean values. Even more interestingly, it implies that columns returned from the Storage Manager may not even be stored in the database (e.g., the result of an arithmetic operation). Note that a long-term goal will be to support operators over sets of tuples, such as aggregate operators. Just as the operator '=' can be executed directly by the finite state machine or indirectly by retrieval via a hashing access method or B-tree access method, foreign operators will be allowed to have several implementations and depending on their presence and estimated cost, the optimizer will decide which implementation to choose.

### 4.2 Long Fields

The Storage Manager is also being extended to support field lengths that exceed its maximum page size of 4K bytes. Each long field will be assigned a unique identifier by the Storage Manager. Tuples may use this identifier to reference the entire long field or some subset identified by a list of offsets and lengths. Long fields will be stored in a data structure similar to that used by EXODUS [Car86]. The basic operations on long fields will be retrieval and update. Retrieval of a long field will be allowed by reference (i.e., its unique identifier) or by value (i.e., the actual content of the long field) and may include a length. A retrieval request returns the requested bytes as a single byte stream. An update request similarly may be by reference or value and, essentially, replaces one byte sequence with another. This may cause the long field to expand or contract.

With each long field will be maintained a list of tuples which reference it. This list is needed to maintain some integrity in the management of long fields. For instance the addition or deletion of bytes to a long field may invalidate a reference to a subset of it. Types, such as "voice", "text", "bitmap", etc. will be associated with long fields. Foreign functions and operators will be allowed on long fields as on any other fields. Space efficient versioning facilities, similar to those in [Woe87] and [Car86], will be available for long fields to avoid nearly identical copies of large amounts of data.

## 5. CONCLUDING REMARKS

The Iris prototype is implemented in C on HP-9000/350 UNIX[4] workstations. These are MC68020-based computers. A port to HP's RISC architecture computers is being contemplated. The Storage Manager is the (still essentially unmodified) storage manager of HP's HP-SQL DBMS product. This is an RSS-like storage subsystem, augmented with parent-child links, to support both a relational and a network query processor.

The Object Manager is entirely new code. It consists of an implementation of the model discussed in Section 2, and its associated query processor. All features described in this paper have been implemented except recursive functions, negation, OSQL embedding in C and the extensions discussed in Section 4. All of these are in various stages of design and development.

The interfaces that have, thus far, been implemented for Iris include OSQL and the Graphical Editor, OSQL embedded in Lisp, and the PCLOS interface. An Objective-C - Iris integration has been prototyped and is being extended to provide a basis for integrating other object-oriented programming languages including C++. Of course, there is also the C subroutine library that *is* the Object Manager interface, the use of which is required to implement all Iris interfaces.

[4]UNIX is a trademark of AT&T Bell Laboratories.

## ACKNOWLEDGMENTS

Nigel Derrett was one of the initial investigators on the Iris project. He made many significant contributions, including the design and implementation of the query translator module. Thomas Ryan also made significant contributions to the original Iris prototype. David Beech designed and implemented the original OSQL interface.

Henry Cate adapted the HP-SQL Storage Manager for use in Iris. Andreas Paepcke designed and implemented the PCLOS interface and was an early and persistent Iris user.

Phillippe DeSmedt, Donald DuBois, Abbas Rafii and Robbe Walstra continue to provide performance analyses and modeling studies of Iris. Arun Swami has worked on various aspects of Iris including a detailed study of the Iris metadata. Diane Olsen has been supporting the Iris system test package. Mohammed Ketabchi has been providing valuable consulting on the functionality and usability of Iris.

# 9

# Development of an Object-Oriented DBMS*

**David Maier**

*Servio Logic Corporation and Oregon Graduate Center*

**Jacob Stein, Allen Otis**

*Servio Logic Corporation*

**Alan Purdy**

*Substantiations, Inc., Oregon*

## ABSTRACT

We describe the results of developing the GemStone object-oriented database server, which supports a model of objects similar to that of Smalltalk-80. We begin with a summary of the goals and requirements for the system: an extensible data model that captures behavioral semantics, no artificial bounds on the number or size of database objects, database amenities (concurrency, transactions, recovery, associative access, authorization) and an interactive development environment. Object-oriented languages,


The GemStone Object-Oriented Data Management system has evolved since the original publication of this paper [Bt].

*Source*: Adapted from Maier, D., J. Stein, A. Otis, and A. Purdy, "Development of an Object-Oriented DBMS", Proceedings of the ACM Conference on Object-Oriented Programming Systems, Languages, and Applications, September 1986, pp. 472–482. Copyright 1986, Association for Computing Machinery, Inc., reprinted by permission.

Smalltalk in particular, answer some of these requirements. We discuss satisfying the remaining requirements in an object-oriented context, and report briefly on the status of the development efforts. This paper is directed at an audience familiar with object-oriented languages and their implementation, but perhaps unacquainted with the difficulties and techniques of database system development. It updates the original report on the project (CM), and expands upon a more recent article [MDP].

## 1. INTRODUCTION

The GemStone database system is the result of a development project started three years ago at Servio. Our goal was to merge object-oriented language concepts with those of database systems. GemStone provides an object-oriented database language called OPAL, which is used for data definition, data manipulation and general computation.

Conventional record-oriented database systems, such as commercial relational systems, often reduce application development time and improve data sharing among applications. However, these DBMSs are subject to the limitations of a finite set of data types and the need to normalize data [Eas80,Sid80]. In contrast, object-oriented languages offer flexible abstract data-typing facilities, and the ability to encapsulate data and operations via the message metaphor. Smalltalk-80 is an example of a completely implemented object-oriented system [Gol83,Kra83].

Our premise is that a combination of object-oriented language capabilities with the storage management functions of a traditional data management system will result in a system that offers further reductions in application development efforts. The extensible data-typing facility of the system will facilitate storing information not suited to normalized relations. In addition, we believe that an object-oriented language can be complete enough to handle database design, database access, and applications. Object-like models have long been popular in CAD [Chu83,Emo83,Kat82b,Kat83,Lac81,Mcl83b,Spo86], and seem well suited to support programming environments [Pow83], knowledge bases [Dol84], and office information systems [Ahl84b,Zdo84]. Other groups are in the process of implementing object model database systems [Der85,Nie85,Zdo85b].

## 2. GOALS AND REQUIREMENTS

### 2.1 An Extensible Data Model

The system must have a data model that supports the definition of new data types, rather than constraining programmers to use a fixed set of predefined types. New types should also be indistinguishable from system-supplied types for the purposes of application programming: operations that apply to new types should be syntactically similar to the built-in operations on predefined types. The distinction between data types and data structures is important in achieving this goal of extensibility.

Data structures are made up of atomic values (integers, strings, etc.), plus constructors (record, relation, set, tree). A data type is really a collection of operators, the *protocol* , for operating on a particular structure. The underlying structure need not be the same as the appearance provided by the protocol. In conventional database systems, the types correspond to the structures. There is usually a fixed set of operations on atomic values, such as arithmetic and comparison operations. Each constructor has a fixed set of operations; for example, a record constructor has "set field" and "get field", and a relation constructor has "add record", "delete record" and "select record". It is not possible to add new operations that appear syntactically similar to the built-in operations. Thus the set of data types that are directly supported is the same as the set of data structures since nested application of the constructors is not supported.

Our goal is to model the *behavior*, not just the structure, of entities in the real world [Mor83]. Further, we must be able to package behavior with structure to create new data types. To get reasonable performance from such a system, the collection of constructors must be rich enough that most data types have fairly direct implementations. In particular, we should be able to capture many-to-many relationships, collections, and sequences directly. For an easily usable system, we should be able to nest the structuring operations to arbitrary levels, and use previously defined data types as building blocks for other types. GemStone must have system management functions for monitoring system performance, performing backups, recovering from failures, adding and removing users, and altering user privileges.

### 2.2 Database Amenities

GemStone is first a database system, so it must provide shared access to persistent data in a multi-user environment. It should support stable storage of data objects on disk, while providing location transparency to the application programmer on the movement of objects between main memory and secondary storage. GemStone must provide for ownership of data objects, and requests by the owner to authorize sharing with other users. Each database session should appear to have complete control of a consistent version of the database, even while users are running concurrently, and should be provided with a transaction mechanism to commit or abort a set of changes atomically. Users should be able to request replication of critical data to guard against localized media failure.

GemStone should support auxiliary storage structures that provide alternative access paths to data, and should give users some control over physical grouping of objects, to improve efficiency of specific access patterns. Bounds on the number and size of data objects should be determined only by the amount of secondary storage, not main-memory limitations or artificial restrictions on data definition. Thus, fields in a record should be variable-length, with no fixed upper bound. Collections of objects, such as arrays and sets, should not have a bound on the number of elements. Similarly, the total number of objects in a database system should not be arbitrarily limited. Finally, the system should handle both small and large objects with reasonable efficiency [Stem86].

### 2.3 Programming Environment

We feel that GemStone should provide at least the following tools and features for application development:

1. An interactive interface for defining new database objects, writing OPAL routines, and executing ad hoc queries in OPAL.
2. A windowing package upon which end-user interfaces can be built.
3. A procedural interface to conventional languages, such as C and Pascal.

## 3. ADVANTAGES OF AN OBJECT-ORIENTED MODEL

During the research stages of the GemStone project, we developed a mostly declarative query language that was deficient in procedural capabilities. Given the problems with providing procedural extensions and educating the marketplace to a completely new language, we decided to use an existing object-oriented language, Smalltalk-80 [Gol83], as the basis for product development. We have made extensions to Smalltalk in the areas of associative access support for queries, basic storage structures, typing and support for a multi-user environment. In the following subsections, we cover the advantages of an object-oriented approach as regards modeling and application development.

### 3.1 Modeling Power

GemStone supports modeling of complex objects and relationships directly and organizes classes of data items into an inheritance hierarchy. A single entity is modeled as a single object, not as multiple tuples spread amongst several relations [Has82, Joh83, Lor83, Plo84]. Properties of entities need not be simple data values, but can be other entities of arbitrary complexity. The address component of an employee object need not be just a text string. In GemStone it can be a structured object, itself having components for street number, street and city, and its own defined behavior. (See Figure 9.1.) GemStone directly supports set-valued entities, without the encoding required in the relational model. Furthermore, sets can have arbitrary objects as elements, and need not be homogenous. We provide the physical data independence of relational databases without the limitations on modeling power.

**3.1.1 Object identity.** GemStone supports *object identity* [Mac83]. A data object retains its identity through arbitrary changes in its own state. Entities with information in common can be modeled as two objects with a shared subobject containing the common information. Such sharing reduces "update anomalies" that exist in the relational data model. In the relational model, the properties of an entity must be sufficient to distinguish it from all other entities. For one entity to refer to another, there must be some fields that uniquely and immutably identify the other entity. (Some extensions to the relational model incorporate forms of identity [Cod79, Zan83].) Uniqueness and immutability are ideals seldom present in the real world. We may choose to refer to departments by name, but what happens if a department's name changes? (We note that all of our objects are assumed independent. Knowing that one object is owned by, or depends on, another could be useful for storage management [Gray84,Nie85,Wei85].)

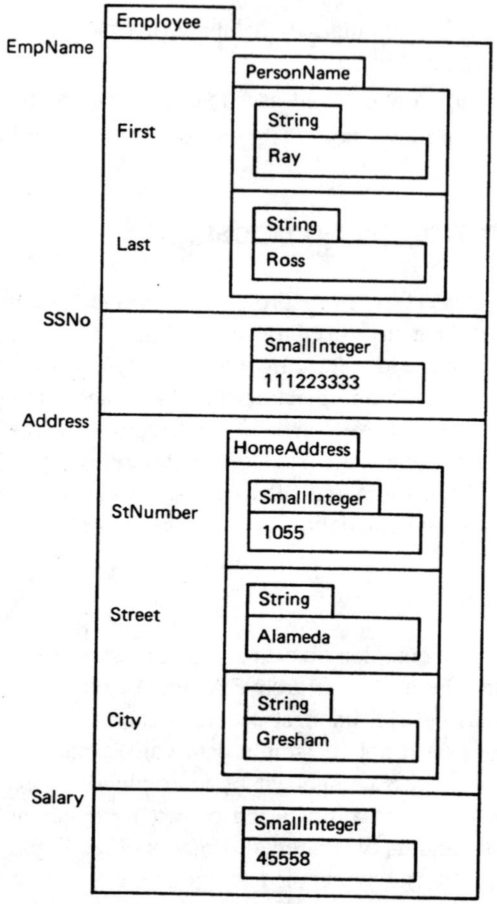


**Figure 9.1**

**3.1.2 Modeling behavior.** GemStone supports simulation of the *behavior* of real-world entities. Data manipulation commands in conventional systems are oriented towards machine representations: "modify field", "insert tuple", "get next within parent". For an office management system, several applications might reserve a room. In a conventional database system, each application would contain DML (data manipulation language) statements to test for room availability, insert or change a record to indicate the reservation, and perhaps create another record with a reminder to the reserver. Changes to the structure of the database may require locating and modifying every application that makes use of the database. In GemStone, a `reserveRoom` message can be defined that takes a date and a time as parameters, and performs all the necessary checks and updates to the database to reserve a room.

The OPAL method that implements a message can execute any number of database queries and updates, with many advantages. Applications are more concise: sending one message takes the place of many database operations. The code is more reliable, as every application that reserves a room uses exactly the same procedure – the method associated with the `reserveRoom` message. The scope of changes required by alterations to the structure of a type is limited to the methods for the type. Further, messages can protect the integrity of the database, by consistency checks in their methods. If all applications that enter an item in the room reservation list are required to use the `reserveRoom` message, double-booking of rooms can be forestalled.

**3.1.3 Classes.** The class structure of GemStone speeds application development in several ways. GemStone comes with a large complement of classes implementing frequently used data types. Class definitions are the analogue to schemes in other database systems, but classes also package operations with the structure, to encapsulate behavior. Thus the message definition facilities along with class mechanism meet the requirement of an extensible data model. GemStone includes a hierarchy of classes. Whereas a class helps organize data, the class hierarchy helps organize the classes. The subclassing mechanism allows a database scheme to capture similarities among various classes of entities that are not totally identic^1 in structure or behavior. Subclassing also provides a means to handle special cases without cluttering up the definition of the normal case [Myl80a].

**3.1.4 Associating types with objects.** Unlike most programming languages that support abstract data types, Smalltalk associates types with values, not the slots holding the values. Typing objects rather than names has liabilities for query processing, which we consider in the next section. We consider some advantages here.

We hope to enable database designers to model application domains they previously may have shied away from because of complexity or lack of regular structure. However, modeling an enterprise for the first time is a much different undertaking than building a database application for an area that has already been modeled, but has not yet been computerized. The basic modeling for financial record keeping was done thousands of years ago. The structure of the information involved is such that it readily fits into standard record-based data models. A development schedule based on scheme definition, application writing, database population and debugging is reasonable. Not so with a CAD task being modeled for the first time, or a database to support an expert system. The application area has not been modeled before, and there will be many iterations of the database scheme before the application is mature [Alb85,Alb84,Mai84]. Being able to start writing database routines without completely specifying the structure and behavior of every class of entities can be of great advantage. Later, when the model has stabilized, typing can be associated with fields for integrity or efficiency.

By not associating types with variables, unanticipated cases (a company car might be assigned to a department as well as an employee) can be more easily handled. A routine (method) makes assumptions about the protocol of its arguments, not their internal structure. Such routines are robust in the face of new classes. If every object responds to the `printString` message to return a string representing itself, then we can write an OPAL method for `Set` that prints a string representation of all its elements, regardless of their classes.

### 3.2 A Unified Language

OPAL is much more powerful than standard data manipulation languages. It is computationally complete, with assignment and flow of control constructs. Almost all the computation required in an application can be written within OPAL. This ability helps avoid the problem of *impedance mismatch*, where information must pass between two languages that are semantically and structurally different, such as a declarative data sublanguage and an imperative general-purpose language. GemStone stresses uniformity of access to all system objects and functions, using the same mechanisms as for regular data objects.

## 4. TURNING SMALLTALK INTO A DBMS

Smalltalk is a single-user, memory-based, single-processor system. It does not meet the requirements of a database system. While Smalltalk provides a powerful user interface and many tools for application development, it is oriented to a single user workstation. To meet the requirements of a database system the following enhancements have been added.

### 4.1 Support of a Multi-User, Disk-Based Environment

Being disk-based does not mean simply paging main memory to disk as it overflows. The database must be intelligent about staging objects between disk and memory. It should try to group objects accessed together onto the same disk pages, try to anticipate which objects in main memory are likely to be used again soon, and organize its query processing to minimize disk traffic.

Since GemStone data is shared by multiple users, the system must provide concurrent access. Each user should see a consistent version of the database, even with other users running simultaneously. Since a user may make changes that are not committed permanently to the database, GemStone must support some notion of multiple workspaces, in which proposed changes to the database can later be discarded or committed. A related requirement is management of multiple name spaces. Smalltalk assumes a single user per image, and so provides a single global name space. Several partially related or unrelated applications can be under development on a single database at one time. It is unreasonable to expect either that users share a single global name space, or, at the other extreme, that user name spaces are disjoint.

Current Smalltalk implementations use a single processor for both display processing and object management. We expect GemStone to support multiple, interactive applications. Hence, it does not seem wise to use the same processor for secondary storage management as for display processing at the end-user interface. We felt that the storage-management and user-interface functions in GemStone must be decoupled to run as separate processes on separate processors.

### 4.2 Data Integrity

Various kinds of failures (program, processor, media) and violations (consistency, access, typing) can compromise the validity and integrity of a database. A database system must be able to cope with failure by restoring the database to a consistent state while minimizing the amount of computation lost. It must also prevent violations from occurring.

By program failure we mean that an application program may fail to complete, say, because of a run-time error. If the program fails after some updates to the database have been made, the database can be left in an unexpected state. Database systems provide for multiple updates to be performed atomically (in an all-or-nothing manner) through the use of transactions. A transaction is used to mark a section of processing so that all its changes are made permanent (the transaction commits), or none are made permanent (the transaction aborts).

By processor failure, we mean that the processor handling GemStone storage management fails. For such failures, the database must be kept intact. Recovering from program and processor failure implies that master copies of objects on secondary storage must be updated carefully. Additionally, a good database system should be robust enough to tolerate additional failures during the recovery period.

By media failure we mean that damage or flaws in the secondary storage devices may cause committed data to be lost. No strategy can provide complete protection against media failure. We wanted GemStone to provide for both periodic backup and dynamic replication of sensitive information. By dynamic replication, we mean keeping multiple, on-line copies of a database, all of which are updated on every transaction.

Turning to violations, database consistency can be violated if transactions from multiple users interleave their updates. GemStone must support serializability of transactions: the net effect of concurrent transactions on the database must be equivalent to some serial execution of those transactions. The integrity of a database can also be violated if a user accesses data that he or she should not be permitted to see. In Smalltalk, all objects are available to the user. Gemstone must assign unique ownership to every object, and give the owner of an object the power to grant access to others.

Integrity constraints, such as keys and referential integrity, are assertions that a priori exclude certain states of the database. It is always a judgment call whether the database system should check constraints after each transaction, or whether the application programmer should be responsible for preserving consistency in each transaction. The former course is more reliable, but almost always more expensive. At a minimum, the database should support constraints that require subparts of an entity or collections to belong to a certain class. We note that referential integrity comes "for free" in GemStone. One object refers directly to another object, not to a name for that object. The reference cannot be created if the other object does not exist. Hence, there are no dangling references.

### 4.3 Large Object Space

Gemstone must store both large numbers of objects and objects that are large in size. The first Smalltalk-80 implementations had a limit of $2^{15}$ objects, $2^{15}$ instance variables in any object, and $2^{20}$ total words of object memory [Gol83]. More recent implementations raise these limits, but still use the same techniques to represent and manage objects

[Kae83]. Large disk-based objects require new storage techniques. Some objects will be too large to fit in main memory, and must be paged in.

While virtual-memory implementations page large objects, we felt we must get away from linear representations of long objects. Requiring objects that span disk pages to be laid out contiguously in secondary storage (or even virtual memory) will lead to unacceptable fragmentation or expensive compaction passes. In Smalltalk, to "grow" an object, such as an array, a new, larger object is created and the contents of the smaller object are copied into it. We want the time required to update or extend an object to be proportional to the size of the update or extension, *not* to the size of the object being updated. We also felt that Smalltalk's repertoire of basic storage representations was inadequate for supporting large unordered collections. Having to map such a collection into an ordered underlying representation imposes artificial restrictions. Thus, GemStone needs a basic storage type for unordered collections.

Finally, searching a long collection by a sequential scan will give unacceptable performance with a disk-based object. Searching for elements should be at most logarithmic in the size of the collection, rather than linear. Thus, GemStone should support associative access on elements of large collections: It should supply storage representations and auxiliary structures to support locating an element by its internal state. This requirement reinforces the need for typing on collections and instance variables. To index a collection `E` of employees on the value of the `salary` instance variable, the system needs assurances that every element in `E` has a `salary` entry. Furthermore, if that index is to support range queries on `salary`, the system needs a declaration that all `salary` values will be comparable according to some total order.

Along with storage-level support for associative access, OPAL must have language constructs that allow associative access.

### 4.4 Physical Storage Management

GemStone must provide features for managing the physical placement of objects on disk. Smalltalk is a memory-resident system, and so there is not much need to say where an object goes. The database administrator, or a savvy application programmer, should be able to hint to GemStone that certain objects are often used together, and so should be clustered on the disk. The administrator should be able to take objects off line, say for archiving, and bring them back on line later. Finally, as objects are never explicitly deleted, the system will be responsible for reclaiming the space used by unreferenced objects. (An alternative is to assume that a permanent object is never deleted, and that objects not referenced in the current state of the database should be shifted to archival storage.)

### 4.5 Access From Other Systems

While OPAL goes much further than conventional database languages in providing a single language for database application programming, we wanted to concentrate our initial efforts on storage management issues, rather than user interfaces. Thus, GemStone provides for access to its facilities from other programming languages. We want to support an application development environment for OPAL along the lines of the Smalltalk programming environment [Gol83], but we recognize that the application development environment may not be the same as the environment in which the finished application runs. However, we are committed to providing procedural interfaces to C and Pascal.

## 5. OUR APPROACH

This section addresses how we provided the enhancements needed to Smalltalk to make it a database system. We start with an overview of the architecture of GemStone.

### 5.1 GemStone Architecture

Figure 9.2 shows the major pieces of the GemStone system. Stone and Gem correspond roughly to the object memory and the virtual machine of the standard Smalltalk implementation [Gol83]. Stone provides secondary storage management, concurrency control, authorization, transactions, recovery, and support for associative access. Stone also manages workspaces for active sessions. Stone uses unique surrogates, called *object-oriented*

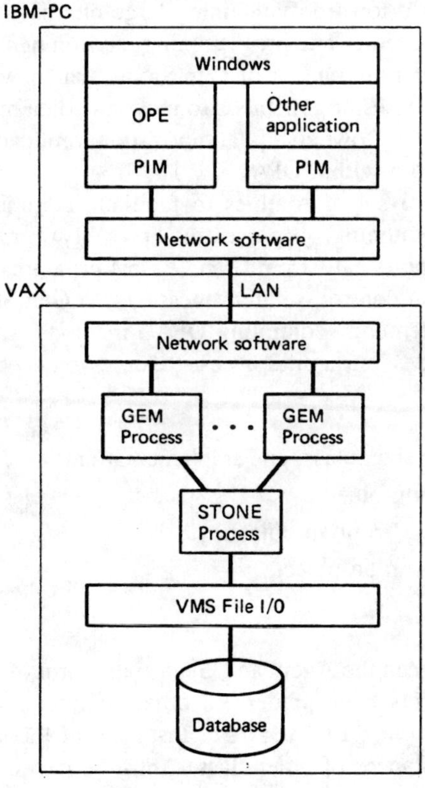


**Figure 9.2**

*pointers* (OOPs) to refer to objects. Stone uses an *object table* to map an OOP to a physical location. This level of indirection means that objects can easily be moved in memory. While the object table can potentially have $2^{31}$ entries, we expect that the portion for objects currently in use by various sessions is small enough to fit in main memory. Stone is built upon the underlying VMS file system. The data model that Stone provides is simpler than the full GemStone model, and provides only operators for structural update and access. An object may be stored separately from its subobjects, but the oops for the values of an object's instance variables are grouped together. Others have considered decomposed representations of objects [Cha82,Cop85].

Gem sits atop Stone, and elaborates Stone's storage model into the full GemStone model. Gem also adds the capabilities of compiling OPAL methods into bytecodes and executing that code, user authentication, and session control. (OPAL bytecodes are similar, but not identical, to the bytecodes used in Smalltalk.) Part of the Gem layer is the *virtual image*: the collection of OPAL classes, methods and objects that are supplied with every GemStone system.

Figure 9.3 shows the class hierarchy in the current GemStone virtual image. Comparing it to the Smalltalk hierarchy, we have removed classes for file access, communication, screen manipulation and the programming environment. The file classes are unnecessary, as we have persistent storage for all GemStone objects. Computation for screen manipulation needs to happen near the end user, and needs fast bytecode execution. GemStone is optimized toward maintaining large numbers of persistent objects, rather than fast bytecode execution. The programming environment classes are replaced by a browser application that runs on top of GemStone, which we describe in a later subsection. We have added classes and methods to make the data management functions of transaction control, accounting, ownership, authorization, replication, user profiles and index creation controllable from within OPAL.

The Agent interface is a set of routines to facilitate communication from other programs in other languages running on processors (possibly) remote from Gem. The Agent interface currently supports calls from C and Pascal programs running on an IBM-PC for session and transaction control, sending messages to GemStone objects, executing a sequence of OPAL statements, compiling OPAL methods, and error explanation. In addition, the Agent provides "structural access" calls, which perform the following functions:

1. determining an object's size, class, and implementation;
2. inspecting a class-defining object;
3. fetching bytes or pointers from an object;
4. storing bytes or pointers in an object;
5. creating objects.

Information passes between the Agent and Gem in the form of bytes and GemStone object pointers. Certain objects have predefined object pointers, such as instances of `Boolean`, `Character` and `SmallInteger`. Instances of `Float` and `String` are passed as byte sequences. Instances of other classes must be decomposed into instances

```
Object
   Association
      SymbolAssociation
   Behavior
      Class
      Metaclass
   Boolean
   Collection
      SequenceableCollection
         Array
            InvariantArray
            Repository
         String
            InvariantString
               Symbol
      Bag
         Set
            Dictionary
               SymbolDictionary
                  LanguageDictionary
            SymbolSet
            UserProfileSet
   Compiled Method
   Magnitude
      Character
      DateTime
      Number
         Float
         Integer
            SmallInteger
   MethodContext
      Block
         SelectionBlock
   Segment
   Stream
      PositionableStream
         ReadStream
         WriteStream
   System
   UndefinedObject
   UserProfile
```

**Figure 9.3**

of the classes mentioned, in order to pass their internal structure between the Agent and Gem. However, the identity of any object can be passed between the Agent and Gem, regardless of its complexity. The idea is to do the computation and manipulation of objects in Gem, and only pass data used for display through the Agent to the interface routines.

Gem, Stone and the Agent interface are structured as separate processes. Our current mapping of processes to processors has Gem and Stone running on a VAX under VMS. The Agent interface supports communication with Gem from an IBM PC. While a GemStone system has a single Stone process, it maintains a separate Gem process for each active user, and the Agent interface handles communication on a per-application basis.

## 5.2 Multiple Users

Stone supports multiple concurrent users by providing each user session with a workspace that contains a *shadow copy* of the object table derived from the most recent committed object table, called the *shared table*. Whenever a session modifies an object, a new copy of that object is created, and placed on a page that is inaccessible to other sessions. The shadow copy of the object table is updated to have the object's OOP map into the new page.

Conceptually, the shadow object table for a workspace is a complete copy of the version of the shared table when the session starts. Actually, we do not make a copy all at once. Object tables are represented as B-trees, indexed on OOPs. For a shadow object table, we need only copy the top node of the committed object table. As the objects arè changed by a session, the shadow object table adds new nodes that are copies of its shared object table with the proper changes. Figure 9.4 shows the state of a shadow object table after the alteration of a single object. Multiple paths have been copied since several objects may have been on the same page as the altered object.

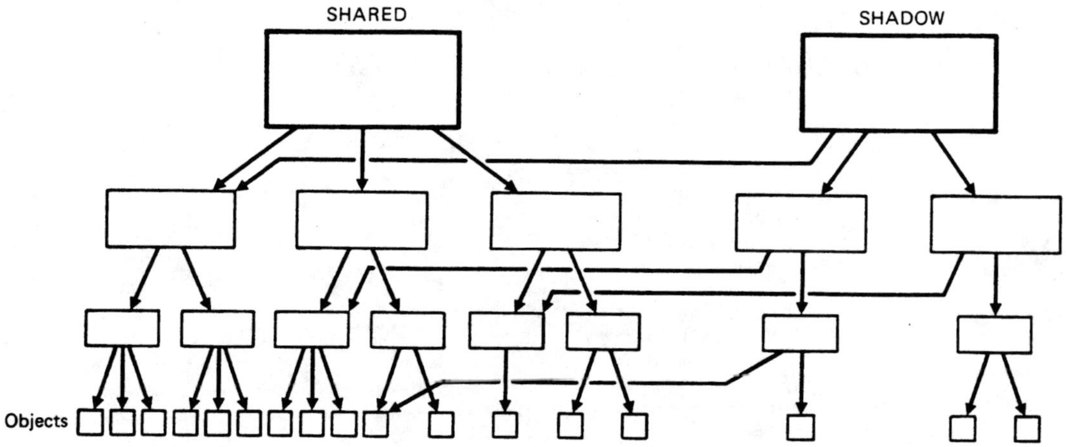


**Figure 9.4**

We chose an optimistic concurrency control scheme: one in which access conflicts are checked at commit time, rather than prevented from occuring through locking. For each transaction, Stone keeps track of which objects the transaction has read or written. At commit time, Stone checks for read-write and write-write conflicts with transactions that have committed since the time the transaction began. If there are no conflicts, the transaction is allowed to commit. For a commit, the shadow object table of the session is treated as if it were *transparent* on the entries that have not been modified, and is overlaid on the most recent version of the shared table. Thus, only entries in the shared table for objects that have been copied by the session are changed. In this way, the changes made by the committing session are merged with those of other transactions that committed after the committing session began. If the current transaction conflicts with a previously committed transaction (or is aborted by the application), the changes in its shadow table are discarded, after using the table to reclaim pages used for new copies of objects.

This optimistic scheme ensures that read-only transactions never conflict with other transactions. Such a transaction gets a consistent copy of the database state, does its reading, and has no changes to make to the shared table on commit. Only transactions that write can conflict with each other. This scheme never deadlocks, as a session experiences no contention with other sessions before a commit point. However, it is possible that an application that writes a large portion of the database may fail to commit any transactions for an arbitrarily long time. While shadowing has had some bad press, it seems a natural approach to us, given that we have an object table. It avoids some extra reads, makes commit and abort simple, and is a excellent candidate for write-once memory, since active pages are never changed in place.

### 5.3 Efficiency Considerations

One problem with recording all the objects a session reads or writes is that the list can grow quite long, and GemStone will spend a lot of time adding entries to such lists. One optimization is that certain classes of objects, such as `SmallInteger`, `Character`, and `Boolean` are known to contain only instances that cannot be updated. Thus, such objects need not be recorded for concurrency control. Even excluding these objects, single objects are just too fine a granularity for concurrency control. Thus, we introduced the notion of *segments*, which are logical groupings of objects that are the unit of concurrency control in GemStone, much like the segments of the ADAPLEX LDM [Cho81]. A segment may contain any number of objects. GemStone keeps a list of just the segments read or written by a session, rather than all objects. Also, at a physical level, pages respect segment boundaries. Thus the practice of copying all objects in a page when one is changed causes no additional conflicts. Segments are visible from within OPAL through the class `Segment`. Users can control placement of objects in segments, to group objects to try to avoid conflict. If an application has a group of private objects, all those objects and no others can be placed together in one segment. At the system level, system objects that are shared by many users, but are almost never updated (such as the class describing object for a system class) can be placed on a single segment, so that accesses to them never causes a conflict.

### 5.4 Name Spaces

Multiple name spaces are managed by Gem. The virtual image has a class `UserProfile` that is used to represent properties of each user that are of interest to the system, such as user Id, password, native language and local time zone. A `UserProfile` object also contains a list of dictionaries that are used to resolve symbols when compiling OPAL code for that user. When an identifier is encountered in OPAL code, and that identifier is neither an instance variable nor a class variable, the dictionaries are searched in order to find an object corresponding to that identifier. There may be any number of dictionaries for a user, to accommodate various degrees of sharing. For example, a programmer's first dictionary may contain objects and classes for his or her portion of a project, the second may be for objects shared with other programmers working on the same project, and the third could contain system objects. Note that symbol resolution can be performed at runtime, thus providing for dynamic symbol resolution during method execution.

## 5.5 Transactions and Recovery

Most of our approach to transactions has been covered in a previous section. To reiterate, every session gets a shadow copy of the shared object table when it begins, and installs its shadow copy as the shared copy when it successfully commits a transaction. Further, a session always writes changed and new objects into pages that are not accessible to any other transaction before commit time. Thus, aborting a transaction means throwing away its shadow object table, and committing means replacing the shared table with a shadow copy. The only issue that needs more elaboration is atomicity – that the changes of a transaction are made, seemingly, all at once. As object tables are trees, atomicity is not hard to provide. When a shadow table is to replace the shared table, and the shadow table differs from the table it is about to replace, the new table can replace the old by simply overwriting the root of the shared object table with the root of the new object table. (Actually, there is a "root of the database" above the root of the object table that gets overwritten. The database root references some other information besides the object table, such as a list of active transactions.) Rewriting the root is the only place where any part of the shared copy of the database is overwritten.

Recovery from processor failure does not require a great amount of additional mechanism over what we have for concurrency control. Our unit of recovery is a transaction. Changes made by committed transactions are kept, changes not yet committed are lost. Since the shared version of the database is never overwritten, we need almost nothing in the way of logs to bring the database to a consistent state, since it never leaves one. The only tricky part is a processor crash while writing a new database root. To handle that eventuality, we keep two copies of the root, which reside at a known place. To restore a consistent state of the database after the crash, we simply check those two pages. If they are different, we copy one that can be determined to be uncorrupted over the other. The real work on recovery is garbage collection: removing detritus of the transactions that had not committed before the crash.

To guard against media failure, we have introduced a structure called a *repository*. A repository is the unit of replication, and also the unit of storage that can be taken off line. Most of what we said before about the database actually pertains to repositories. Segments partition repositories, and all the objects in a segment are stored in the segment's repository. A repository may be taken off line, which means all its objects become inaccessible. `Repository` is an OPAL class providing internal representatives of repositories. A `Repository` instance can respond to a message `replicate`, which means two copies of the repository will be maintained (at increased cost in time and space), usually on separate external devices. The copies know about each other, and if the medium for one fails, the other is still available.

## 5.6 Authorization

Segments are also the unit of ownership and authorization. Every user has at least one segment, and when he or she creates new objects, they go in an owned segment. A user may grant read or write permission (write implies read) on a segment to other users or groups of users. Such grants must always come from the original owner. Read or write permission on a segment implies the same permission on all objects assigned to the segment. User identification is handled by Gem, using `userId` and `password` from a `UserProfile`.

There are some subtleties of read and write permission in an object model. First, having the identity of an object (its OOP) is not the same as reading the object. Second, having permission on an object does not imply having permission on all its subobjects. So, for example, an `Employee` object, along with the objects that are values for instance variables `empName,` `ssNo` and `address` could reside in one segment. By putting a `SalaryHistory` object in another segment, authorization can be granted to just a portion of an employee's personnel information. Third, name spaces are the first line of defense against unauthorized access. If a user cannot find an object, he or she cannot read the object.

## 5.7 Large Object Space

In designing GemStone, we have tried to always set limits on object numbers and sizes so that physical storage limits will be encountered first. A GemStone system can support $2^{31}$ objects ($2^{32}$ counting instances of `SmallInteger`) and an object can have up to $2^{31}$ instance variables. Segments have no upper bound on the number of objects they can contain, other than the number of objects in the system.

When an object is larger than a page, the object is broken into pieces and organized as a tree spanning several pages. To handle large unordered objects (instances of `Bag` and its subclasses), we have added a new basic storage structure called a *non-sequenceable collection* (NSC). This structure supports adding, removing and testing for membership, along with iteration over all the elements. However, NSCs have *anonymous instance variables*, which means their component objects may not be referenced by name or index. Large NSCs are also stored as trees, but ordered by OOP. In the next section, we show how content-based retrieval is supported for an NSC object.

A large object can be accessed and updated without bringing all the pages of an object into a workspace. The tree structure for large objects makes it possible to update pieces of them without rewriting the whole object, much as for the object table. Since pages of a large object need not be contiguous in secondary storage, such objects can grow and shrink with no need to recopy the entire object.

## 5.8 Associative Access and Typing

We briefly cover some of the language and typing issues relating to associative access, along with index structures and their maintenance. The fundamental language issue is being able to detect opportunities for using auxiliary storage structures. In a computationally complete language such as OPAL, it is neither necessary or desireable to consider using auxiliary structures for every database manipulation. Conceivably, we could analyze all OPAL methods to detect places where alternative access paths might be used. We felt that approach was too complex, and instead decided that the programmer must flag opportunities to use auxiliary structures.

OPAL supports the use of indices to speed the evaluation of expressions of the form

```
aBag select:  aBlock
```

The block has one variable and returns a `Boolean`. The result of the expression is the subset of elements of `aBag` for which `aBlock` returns `true`, and resembles the relational selection operator in the Cypress data model [Cat83]. This statement is evaluable in OPAL without indices, but at the cost of examining every element in `aBag`. Since a block can contain arbitrary OPAL expressions, indices are not useful in evaluating every expression in a block. Hence, for use with indices, we added *path syntax* to the OPAL language. For any variable, we can append to it a path composed of a sequence of pieces called *links*, which specify some subpart of an object. For example, **`anEmp.empName.last`** might access the last name of an `Employee` object. A question arises why sequences of unary messages do not suffice to the same thing, such as **`anEmp name last`**. The reason is that we want to support associative access at runtime without performing message sends, and so the support can come from the Stone level.

A selection block for associative access can contain a conjunction of *path comparisons*, where a path comparison is an expression of the form ⟨path expression⟩ ⟨comparator⟩ ⟨literal⟩ or ⟨path expression⟩ ⟨comparator⟩ ⟨path expression⟩:

```
anEmp.empName.last = 'Sanders'
anEmp.salary > anEmp.dept.manager.salary
```

Index use is requested by using set braces in place of brackets around the block in a `select:` message

```
empSet select:
  {:anEmp | anEmp.empName.lastName = 'Sanders'}
```

rather than

```
empSet select:
  [:anEmp | anEmp.empName.lastName = 'Sanders']
```

The two expressions give the same result, but the first one requests OPAL to use an index if available, while the second will *always* be evaluated by iterating through `empSet`. If no appropriate index exists, then the first expression might still be evaluated without the use of message sends if, as discussed below, the path is appropriately typed. Otherwise, the first expression evaluates using the same method as the second. We found it a great help in testing associative access processing to have a brute-force way to evaluate selection queries, as a kind of a "semantic benchmark" for checking index-based evaluation.

Another central decision in designing associative access was what to index, classes or collections? Many applications may use instances of the same class, and store them in different collections (like having several relations on the same scheme [Hay81]). Indexing on the class means that applications that do not use the index still bear the overhead for instances they use being in the index. Further, a classwide index presents authorization problems. No one user may have read access to set all the objects in the class, so no one is able to request the index be created. Also, indexing a collection allows the possibility that instances of subclasses be included in a collection that is indexed. Indexing on a class basis makes it easier to trace changes to the state of an object that could cause the object to be positioned differently within an index. We decided that minimizing cost for programs not using an index was the top priority, so we index on collections, but other systems have chosen class indexing [Zdo85b]. Additionally, if indexing by class, intersecting the result of a lookup with a collection may be time consuming with respect to the size of the collection. Note that a class can be implemented to keep a collection of all instances if desired, and that collection can be indexed.

Indices are created and abandoned by sending messages to a `Bag` or `Set` object, giving the path to index. For example, if `empSet` is a set of `Employee` objects, we can request an index on `empName.last`. There are two kinds of indices: *identity* and *equality*. An identity index supports searching a collection on the identity of some subobject of one of the elements, without reference to the subobject's state. An equality index supports lookup on the basis of the value or internal state of objects, and range searches on values.

The path syntax for associative selections and the kind of index desired dictate what typing information is required to support indexing. Referring back to the discussion in Section 4.3, to have an identity index on a collection using a particular path, we must know that the path expression is defined (leads somewhere) for every object in the collection. For an equality index, we must additionally know that the values of the paths for every element of the collection are comparable with respect to equality and the other comparisons supported by equality indices. OPAL provides typing for names and anonymous instance variables. For any named instance variable, the value of that variable can be constrained to be a *kind* of a given class. A value is a kind of a class if it is an instance of that class or of some subclass thereof. For example, we can declare that the `empName` instance variable of class `Employee` must have kind `PersonName`, which means the value can be a `PersonName` instance, or an instance of some subclass, say `TitledPersonName`. Subclasses of `Bag` and `Set` can be restricted in the kind of elements their instances may contain.

Both named and anonymous instance variable typing are inherited through the class hierarchy. Additionally, typing can be further restricted in a class's subclasses. If in `Employee` class instance variable `empName` is constrained to `PersonName`, then in a subclass of `Employee` `empName` can be constrained to `TitledPersonName`.

In order to create an identity index into `empSet` on `empname.last`, variable `empName` must be constrained to a class in which a variable `last` is defined. However, it would not be necessary for `last` to be be constrained within that class, for the comparisons supported by identity indices need not know the structure of employee's last names. In an equality index, employee's last names would need to be constrained to a class whose instances are totally ordered, in order to provide the comparisons supported by equality indices. The constraint on the last link of a path upon which an equality index is built is restricted to `Boolean, Character, DateTime, Float, String, Smallinteger` or subclasses thereof. For `Boolean, Character` and `SmallInteger`, there is no distinction between equality and identity indices.

In addition to supporting indexed associative access, typing of names can be used as an integrity constraint on named variables. In particular, it can be used to assure that the value of a named instance variable will understand a given protocol in all objects that are a kind of a given class.

Indices are implemented as a sequence of index components, one for each link in the path upon which the index is built. Each component is implemented as a B-tree. An index on `empName.last` into `empSet` would have two components, one from names to employees in `empSet` and one from last names to names of employees. Common prefixes of indexed paths share the index components that correspond to the common prefix. For example, an index on `empName.first` would share the index component from names to employees with the index on `empName.last`. Additionally, identity indices are implicitly created on the path prefixes of an indexed path. Creating an index on `empName.last` implicitly creates an identity index on `empName`.

Indexing is discussed in further detail elsewhere [Mai86b]. We here mention that the maintenance of indices is a problem that is related to that of maintaining *referential integrity constraints* [Dat83] in relational databases, and that Stone manages concurrent access to indexing structures since indices are maintained in object space.

## 5.9 Garbage Collection

Gem uses reachability information to remove temporary objects before a transaction commits. Objects that have been created during the current transaction and cannot be accessed transitively from the current state of some object present in the shared object table are temporary. Permanent objects, those that have previously been committed, are garbage collected off line using a mark-sweep algorithm. We believe this preferable to reference counting in that reference counting would require accessing an object every time a reference to it is added or removed.

## 5.10 Access From Other Systems

GemStone does not provide direct access to a human interface through OPAL. Applications manage the human interface through C modules running on a PC. These modules have complete access to OPAL through the *GemStone C Interface* (GCI), which is the interface to the agent. The role of the GCI in application development is depicted in Figure 9.5.

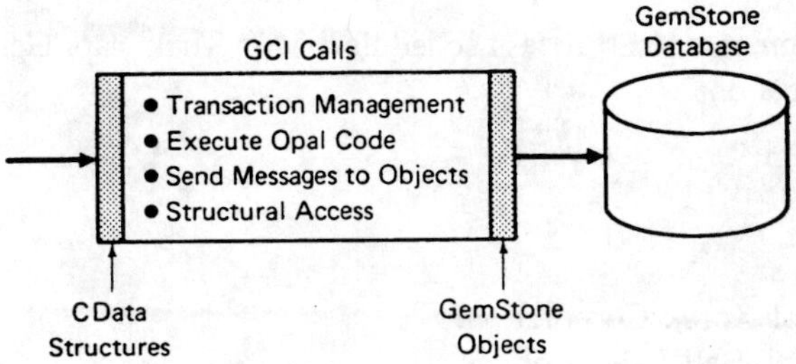


**Figure 9.5**

The *OPAL Programming Environment* (OPE) is a collection of Microsoft Windows-compatible applications for the creation of OPAL classes and methods. In addition, the OPE provides applications for the bulk loading and dumping of GemStone databases. The development of a GemStone application consists of two parts: first creating Gemstone classes and methods through the OPE and then developing a human interface on a PC that accesses OPAL through the GCI.

## 6. FUTURE DEVELOPMENT PLANS

As with all computer-based systems, performance efficiency is a perennial concern. We have two approaches to addressing GemStone's performance effciency: improving the execution model, and improving database functions. Research of Smalltalk virtual machines has demonstrated several techniques for improving their efficiency [Kra83]. Database systems spend most of their time in searching and sorting tasks. These functions can be improved by better algorithms and better buffer management.

We also plan to add several features to GemStone. We plan to add multiple repositories to allow users to dismount a portion of the database and either transport it to another site or preserve it off line. Support for distributed databases will allow multiple sites to share a collection of geographically distributed data. As our user population increases, we expect users to need increased performance efficiency in certain new classes. To support this need, we expect to add selected new classes to the set of predefined classes. GemStone currently supports only the IBM-PC workstation. We plan to offer interfaces to additional workstations such as Lisp and Smalltalk systems.

## ACKNOWLEDGMENTS

The authors would like to thank the following people for their contributions to the GemStone project: Ken Almond, quality and change control; Robert Bretl, Stone object manager; John Bruno, browser; Maureen Drury, virtual image; Jack Falk, documentation; Lynn Gallinat, virtual image; Larry Male, OPE editor; Daniel Moss, PC/VAX communications; Bruce Schuchardt, OPE implementation, bulk loader and dumper; Harold Willams, Gem implementation; Monty Williams, quality and support implementation; Mike Nastos, documentation and bug hunting; Rick Nelson, VAX system manager;

D. Jason Penney, Stone implementation, process scheduler; Mun Tuck Yap, Gem object manager, PC/VAX communications.

## TRADEMARKS

# 10

# The Vbase Object Database Environment*

**Timothy Andrews**

*Ontologic, Inc.*
*Burlington, Ma.*

## ABSTRACT

Object-oriented languages generally lack support for persistent objects—that is objects that survive a process or programming session. On the other hand, database systems lack the expressive capabilities of object-oriented languages. Both characteristics are necessary for production application development.

This paper presents a brief overview of Vbase, an object-oriented development environment that combines a procedural object language and persistent objects into one integrated system. Language aspects of Vbase include strong typing, a block structured schema defintion language, and parameterization, or the ability to type members of aggregate objects. Database aspects include system support for one-to-one, one-to-many, and many-to-many relationships between objects, an inverse mechanism, user control of object clustering in storage for space and retrieval efficiency, and support for trigger methods.

Unique aspects of the system are its mechanisms for custom implementations of storage allocation and access methods of properties and types, and its three layer, open architecture which enables efficient, extensible implementations without compromising the abstract interface.

**Source*: Adapted from Andrews, T., "The Vbase Object Database Environment", Ontologic Corp., 1989.

During the last several years, both languages and database systems have begun to incorporate object features. There are now many object-oriented programming languages. [Gol1983, Tes1985, Mey1987, Cox1986, Str1986]. Object-oriented database management systems are not as prevalent yet, and sometimes tend to use different terms (Entity-Relationship, Semantic Data Model), but they are beginning to appear on the horizon [Cat1983, Cop1984, Ston1986, Mylo1980]. Even less prevalent are systems which combine both language and database features in a single object-oriented development platform. This is essential since a system must provide both complex data management and advanced programming language features if it is to be used to develop significant production software systems. Providing only one or the other is somewhat akin to providing half a bridge: it might be made structurally sound, but it is not particularly useful to one interested in getting across the river safely.

Object-oriented languages have been available for many years. The productivity increases achievable through the use of such languages are well recognized. However, few serious applications have been developed using them. One reason has been performance, though this drawback is being eliminated through the development of compiled object languages. Another drawback, in our view, is the lack of support for persistence; the lack of objects that survive a processing session and provide object sharing among multiple users of an application.

Database management systems, in contrast, suffer from precisely the opposite problem. While having excellent facilities for managing large amounts of data stored on mass media, they generally support only limited expression capabilities, and no structuring facilities.

The traditional solution to this problem is to provide bridges between the systems. Thus the proliferation of 'embedded languages', such as SQL, allowing language systems to access database managers. These bridges are usually awkward, and still provide only restricted functionality. Both performance and safety can be enhanced through a tighter coupling between the data management and programming language facilities.

It is this lack of a truly integrated system which provided our inspiration at Ontologic, Inc. This paper reviews Ontologic's Vbase Integrated Object System and describes how it combines language and database functionality.

## 1. SYSTEM ARCHITECTURE

The single overriding consideration which drove the design and development of Vbase was to provide a complete development system for practical production applications based on object-oriented technology.

Two goals flowing from this motivation were:

1. To integrate a procedural language with support for persistent objects. This support should be as transparent as possible to users of the system.
2. To take maximum advantage of the strong typing inherent in object systems in both the language and database.

The system derives its heritage from many precursors. Probably the single most important language influence was the CLU programming language developed at MIT[Lis81]. Thus, Vbase is based around the abstract data type paradigm, rather than the object/message paradigm. This orientation manifests itself in many areas. For example, in typical object/message systems, all access to object behavior is through a uniform message syntax. In Vbase, object behavior is elicited by a combination of properties and operations. Properties represent static behavior; operations represent dynamic behavior. Property definition and access are syntactically differentiated from those of operations. This provides a more natural model of object behavior. It also saves the programmer from writing trivial code to get and set the values of properties. In Vbase, these operations are normally generated by the system, further increasing programmer productivity.

In fact, the fundamental emphasis on a strong separation between the specification of a system and the implementation of a system is common to abstract data type and object/message systems. Vbase uses this methodology at several levels to provide an extremely flexible architecture. (The overall architecture is shown in Figure 10.1.)

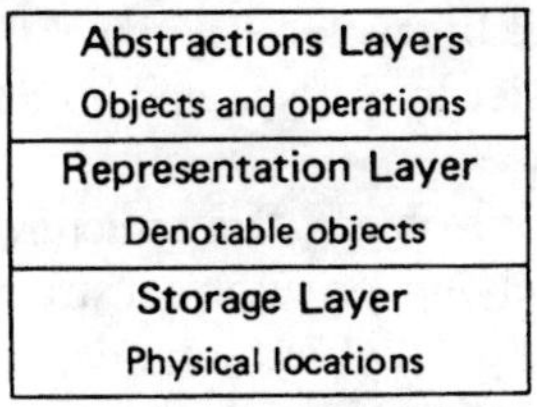


**Figure 10.1** VBASE architecture.

The abstraction layer implements the object meta-model, providing support for inheritance, operation dispatching, method combination, and property manipulation. This is where (it is hoped) most client interaction takes place. The representation layer is the locus of our reference semantics, translating the symbolic notation of the abstraction layer into denotable objects[Dam88a]. The storage layer is responsible for mapping the representation layer into physical storage[Dam88b].

Each layer of Vbase is implemented within Vbase itself. Thus each layer has a Vbase specification and a Vbase implementation. Consequently, we realize many of the advantages of the system in the implementation of the system itself. Chief among these has been the ability to implement the total system quickly and then tune performance by replacing or enhancing various implementations. As the specifications were unaffected, effort could be concentrated where it was needed, allowing a good deal of performance work to be completed on the system at an early date [Duh88].

As mentioned previously, support for persistent objects, or objects that survive process lifetimes and programming sessions was a key motivation. This requires 'database' support; that is, handling of storage on stable media such as disks. There are some further capabilities implied by 'database' support:

1. handling large numbers of objects and consequently handling a large object storage space.
2. sharing of object data among multiple processes/users, which further implies coordination (concurrency control) to avoid semantic corruption of the object database.

3. software stability so that the object space is maintained in a consistent state in the face of system or media failure (transactions).

We had a further desire: to provide 'seamless' support for persistent objects through a natural syntax. We particularly wished to avoid the 'embedded language' approach. The goal was to integrate persistent objects completely into the language as pseudo-standard variables. This makes the entire expression processing capability of the language available to the persistent objects.

The last of the primary motivations directing the design and development of Vbase was to build an object system that also provided strong typing. One drawback of the Smalltalk class of object systems is their lack of any notion of type specificity. There are simply objects. The benefits of strong typing are well known. There are three that are especially important in a system intended for commercial development.

First, strong typing resolves many more errors at compile time than weakly-typed systems. Since objects' main claim to fame is productivity gain, the resolution of errors at an earlier time in the software lifecycle is significant. It should also be noted that compile time errors are generally easier to analyze and correct than errors of type mismatch that occur at run time.

Second, strong typing of object data structures provides superior specification of the system. Rather than relying on user-constructed naming conventions to convey type information (aFruit, anApple, aCar, etc.), data structure type declarations provide a clear and exploitable specification since the type declarations are all part of the system specification. Thus, one can examine the declaration aFruit: Fruit, and then examine the Fruit definition for further information. This process can be applied recursively to any desired level of detail, and is not dependent on adoption of any conventions by the system implementors.

One final issue regarding strong typing is its effect on system performance. A strongly typed system allows the language processor to do far more analysis at compile time. This analysis can often reduce the need for runtime type checks, as well as allow methods to be statically bound. Our experience to date indicates that 90% of all type checking and method binding can be done at compile time. This eliminates the performance degradation frequently resulting from object systems' need to dynamically bind all method code to achieve object/message behavior. Thus Vbase exhibits the functionality of dynamic method binding based on a hierarchy of types, as do all object systems. However, it does so with performance comparable to a compiled, statically bound system.

There are, in fact, many more optimizations that the language processor can do based upon its knowledge of the semantics of the types and objects in the system, and the amount of work that can be done is proportional to the amount of information that is contained in the definitions. This is yet another argument for a strongly typed system.

Note, however, that Vbase's emphasis on typing is not done at the expense of polymorphism. Vbase is a fully polymorphic system, unlike C++ for example. While Vbase provides a high degree of static type checking—through the use of subtyping and parameterized types and operations—there are cases where static type checking is impossible or undesirable. Explicit run-time type checking can then be used to achieve the same expressive capability as an untyped object system. Thus, in Vbase, the trade-off between compile-time optimization and run-time flexibility is controlled by the application developer.

## 2. SYSTEM COMPONENTS

Vbase is currently implemented on top of Sun UNIX and VAX/VMS. There are presently two language interfaces: TDL (for Type Definition Language) and COP (for C Object Processor). TDL is used to specify abstract data types. That is, it is used to define data types and specify their associated properties and operations. COP is used in two roles. It is used to write the code to implement the operations. It is used to write the applications programs. There is also a set of tools to assist development. These include an integrated object browser, editor, and debugger, an SQL query interface with object extensions, and a verifier program that checks consistency of compiled images against an object database.

TDL is a proprietary language. It is block structured, with features in common with such languages as Pascal, Modula, and Algol. Types are the most common entities defined in TDL. A type serves as the nexus for behavior of its instances. It determines the properties for which its instances supply values and it defines operations which may be performed on its instances.

The current version of the system allows only one supertype to be specified; this supertype places the type definition in the type hierarchy. Behavior is inherited via the type hierarchy in the expected manner. A type is also a block scope in TDL, and consequently may contain other arbitrary definitions along with its central property and operation definitions.

COP is a strict superset of the C language as defined by Kernighan and Ritchie. Any program which compiles with standard C will compile with COP. It contains syntactic extensions to the C language to allow typed declarations of object variables, access to properties of objects, and invocation of operations on objects. COP is used to write the actual code that implements the operations and properties and other behaviors specified in TDL. It is currently implemented as a preprocessor which emits standard C code.

The debugger allows source line debugging of the COP source code. The object editor allows interactive traversal of type and object definitions, assignment of object property values, and invocation of operations. The verifier examines the object type references compiled into ".o" files and determines if they are in sync with a particular database.

## 3. BASIC ABSTRACTION MECHANICS

VBASE incorporates most of the standard object technology. There is a taxonomy of types, with subtypes inheriting both properties and operations from their supertype. Subtypes can add more specific behavior by specifying additional properties or operations, and can also refine existing behavior of inherited properties or operations. When an operation is invoked, it is dispatched according to the type of the object of the invocation. Thus in COP one writes:

```
Entity$print (someObject);
```

which means find the print operation of the type closest in the type hierarchy to the direct type of someObject. Of course, there is complete type extensibility, with the user being able to define and use whatever types are desired.

## 3.1 Strong Typing

The most important language influence-strong typing-is unusual among current object systems. The TDL definition in Figure 10.2 illustrates some of the typing aspects.

Note that all definitions are associated with a type. This applies at all levels. At the topmost level, the 'define Type Part' fragment says that Part is of type Type. In a similar manner, properties are defined in terms of their data type, as are operation arguments, return values, and exception specifications. The type information contained in the TDL specifications is then used to generate a schema for an object database. In practice, Vbase provides a substantial kernel schema. TDL is then used to augment this schema with user extensions. Thus TDL can be described as an incremental schema compiler.

After the datatypes are defined, COP code is written and compiled against the object database. The COP compiler is a database application, and uses the type information of the database to do what type checking is possible at compile time. When static type checking is not possible, the check is deferred to runtime.

Operations in the type definition are implemented by methods written in COP. Figure 10.3 shows the code to implement the Pipe_Connect method.

Note that all object variables are declared with the additional keyword obj. This allows the program variables to be associated with types in the schema, and COP can then do type checking based on the schema information. Therefore the assignment:

```
aPipe.leftConnection = toPipe;
```

is allowed since the leftConnection property of type Pipe is of type Part, and the declared type of the variable toPipe is Pipe. These are compatible since Pipe is a subtype of Part. All operation invocations and their arguments are similarly checked.

When it is not possible to determine type compatibility at compile time, the programmer uses the assert statement. The assert statement defers type checking until runtime. This allows handling assignment of a more general type to a more specific type without violating strict compile-time type checking in most cases, an invaluable productivity win in large, complex systems. In the method example in Figure 10.3, assert is used for two purposes.

First, this simple implementation assumes that pipes can only be connected to pipes; thus the assert does a runtime type check for the programmer, while allowing the code to be written for the more general case of connecting a pipe to any other part.

```
define Type Part
  supertypes = {Entity};

  properties = {
    partID: Identifier;
    name:  optional String;
    components:  distributed Set[Part]
      inverse componentOf;
    componentOf:  Part inverse components;
    }
  operations = {
    display (p:Part)
      raises (NoDisplayImage)
      method (Part_Display);

    isComponentOf (p1:  Part, p2:Part)
      raises (IsRootComponent)
      method (Part_isComponentOf)
      returns (Boolean);

    connect (p:  Part, to:  Part,
      keywords
        optional using:  Connector)
      raises (BadConnect)
      method (Part_Connect)
      returns (Part);

    iterator components (p:  Part)
      yields (p:  Part)
      method (Part_Components);

    refines delete (p:  Part)
      triggers (Part_deleteTrigger);
    };

 PRIVATE
    properties = {
      displayImage:  optional Image;
      isRootComponent:  Boolean :=False;
    };

 end Part;
```

```
define Type Pipe
  supertypes = {Part};

  properties = {
    length:  Integer := 0;
    diameter:  Integer := 0;
    leftConnection:  Part;
    rightConnection:  Part;
    threadtype:  optional ThreadType :=
      Threadtype$ScrewThread;
    isInsulated:  optional Boolean:= False;
  };
  operations = {
    refines connect (p:  Pipe, to:  Part,
      keywords
        optional usingConnector:  Connector)
      raises (ThreadtypeMisMatch,
        IncompatibleMaterials)
      method (Pipe_Connect)
      returns (Part);

    materialsCompatible(p1:Pipe, p2:Pipe)
      method (Pipe_MaterialsCompatible)
      returns (Boolean);

    refines delete (p:  Pipe)
      raises (CannotDelete)
      triggers (Pipe_deleteTrigger);
  };
end Pipe;

define Type ThreadType is enum (ScrewThread,
    PolThread);
```

**Figure 10.2** TDL code for two type definitions is shown. Type Part is a generic definition used for all parts in this hypothetical engineering design database. It is the supertype of type Pipe which inherits all the behavior of parts and adds behavior specific to pipes.

```
method
obj Part
Pipe_Connect (aPipe, toPart, usingConnector)
obj Pipe aPipe;
obj Part toPart;
keyword obj Connector usingConnector;
{
  obj Part connectedPart;
  obj Pipe toPipe;
  int j;
  if (hasvalue (usingConnector))
  {
   connectedPart = Pipe$Connect
     (aPipe, usingConnector);
   return (Part$Connect (connectedPart, toPart,
       using:  usingConnector));
  }
  toPipe = assert (toPart, obj Pipe);
  except (ia:  IllegalAssert)
  {
   PipeSystem$ErrorPrint (aPipe, toPart, "can only
     connect Pipes to Other Pipes");
  }
  if (aPipe.threadtype != toPipe.threadtype)
   raise (ThreadTypeMisMatch);
  if (!  Pipe$MaterialsCompatible (aPipe, toPipe))
   raise (IncompatibleMaterials);
  aPipe.leftConnection = toPipe;
  toPipe.rightConnection = aPipe;
  connectedPart = $$ (aPipe, aPart);
  return (connectedPart);
}
```

**Figure 10.3** COP code for the Pipe_Connect method. This method implements the operation defined in Type Pipe in Figure 10.2.

Second, the statement:

```
toPipe.rightConnection = aPipe;
```

will not compile if the declared type of toPipe is Part. This is because Part does not define the property rightConnection. rightConnection is defined by Pipe. Thus while it is quite possible that, since part is pipe's supertype, a given part is a pipe, it is not guaranteed by the declarations of the program. This is a very common type violation in object systems, and this is what Vbase prevents. The assert alerts the implementor that the actual type of the object toPipe must be pipe (or a subtype of pipe) in order for this assignment to be valid.

## 3.2 Inverse Relationships

Reviewing the TDL definition of the type Part (Figure 10.2) points out an important modeling mechanism in Vbase-the support for inverse relationships. Note the components and componentOf property definitions. These properties are declared as inverses.

This means that whenever a modification is made to one of these properties, the other property is modified accordingly. This construct solves one of the more vexing problems in database management systems, particularly relational database systems. One-to-one, one-to-many, and many-to-many relationships between objects can all be supported and maintained automatically using the inverse capability. Thus, such common relationships as Parts-Suppliers or Employees-Departments can be implemented directly with no additional definitions or code. This is a dramatic improvement over most current database systems, and is not available in current object systems.

## 3.3 Method Combination

Method combination in object systems results when a refining method invokes its refinee. In Smalltalk, for example, one uses the pseudo-variable 'super' for this purpose. Vbase uses '$$' for this purpose. This notation, rather than super or some derivative thereof, was chosen because of the novel view of operations behavior that Vbase takes.

Operations are viewed as being implemented by a series of executable code fragments. The number of fragments is arbitrary, and is the sum of all triggers and methods defined in the operation. Reviewing the TDL Figure 10.2, note that each operation definition can include a method clause, and a triggers clause. Each operation is therefore potentially associated with one method, called the base method, and an arbitrary number of trigger methods. The execution sequence begins with the first trigger in the triggers clause. The '$$' syntax transfers execution to the next code fragment: either the next trigger, or if no more are specified, to the method specified in the method clause. Once these fragments are executed, '$$' transfers execution to the refinee operation at the supertype level.

Thus, in the case where only a base method is defined, '$$' functions exactly as 'super' in Smalltalk. However, when triggers are used, this is not the case. Consequently, Vbase avoids the super syntax in favor of the '$$' syntax to avoid the impression of moving up the supertype chain. Rather, '$$' simply transfers execution to the next code fragment, whatever that may be.

Functionally, '$$' behaves like a function call. Thus, the placement of the '$$' in the code allows implementation of pre-processing, post-processing, or both: wrapper processing.

## 3.4 Triggers

The availability of triggers, discussed previously, can be considered both a language and a database influence. Their utility is obvious; they provide a robust mechanism for enforcing arbitrary dynamic constraints. Triggers can be attached to properties as well as operations to generate whatever behavior is desired. These behaviors include standard ones such as 'when my QuantityOnHand property falls under twenty, issue a new order for a hundred more', to more esoteric patterns such as keeping audit trails of property and operation access for security purposes.

In Vbase the triggers are often used to augment creation and deletion methods. The use of triggers can insure, for instance, that upon creation of an object, all important referent objects are created as well. Delete triggers reverse this to delete all referent objects. Consider the example in Figure 10.4.

```
method obj PipeConnector
PipeConnector_CreateTrigger
   (aType, numberOfBolts, boltSet)
obj Type aType;/* must always take a Type arg when
   doing a create */
obj Integer numberOfBolts;
obj List[obj Bolt] boltSet;
{
  obj PipeConnector newConnector; /* the result of
     the creation process */
  obj Bolt aBolt; /* range variable for bolt set */
  int j = 0; /* standard C variable */
  newConnector = $$ (aType);
    /* create the new object by invoking the
          standard system create operation */
  /* create the referent object */
  newConnector.bolts =
    $Array[obj Bolt]$[size:numberOfBolts];
  /* initialize the referent object */
  iterate (aBolt = boltSet)
     newConnector.bolts[j++] = aBolt;
  return (newConnector);
}
```

(a)

```
define Type PipeConnector
    supertypes = {Part};
properties = {
     bolts:  Array[Bolt];
    ...
    };
end PipeConnector;
```

(b)

**Figure 10.4** Triggers can add behaviors to a create operation. The trigger method is shown (a), and the type definition (b).

When a PipeConnector object is created, one would also like to create a List for the bolts property of the connector, perhaps initializing it from a set of Bolts passed to the Create operation. The use of a trigger on the standard create operation provides this functionality.

Two aspects of the system should be noted in passing. First is the arbitrary combination of C program variables with object variables. This, as stated, was an important goal: a truly integrated language. The language processor does all necessary conversion to assure a correct program is produced. The second factor is the iterate statement. Drawn from CLU, this statement processes all members of a database aggregate an element at a time without requiring the writing of a 'for' loop. This is yet another productivity gain of the system, as it is unnecessary to compute the boundaries for a for loop. More importantly, iterators provide access to the elements of an aggregate abstractly, without exposing (or requiring knowledge of) the underlying implementation.

## 3.5 Exceptions

In many languages, there are no specific exception handling mechanisms. Thus code to detect and handle exceptions must be explicitly inserted at each point in a program where an exception might occur. This not only forces the writing of a great many short, repetitive code fragments, it also places an additional burden on the establishment of extra-language applications conventions and creates numerous opportunities for lapses in programming discipline. The C language is notoriously deficient in this area.

In Vbase, we included a specific exception handling mechanism. Exception conditions detected during the execution of an operation raise an exception. That is, they transfer control to a pre-defined exception handling routine rather than return control to the caller.

Once again, referring to Figure 10.3, note the except and raise statements. These statements allow graceful handling of abnormal events that occur during processing, and are variations on a fairly standard theme. What is notable is that in Vbase, exceptions are types. This means that all of the behavior definition mechanisms available to types are available to exceptions. One consequence is that the implementor can define a hierarchy of exceptions. Thus exceptions can be generalized just like types are generalized. For example, a memory allocation operation might raise the exception OutOfMemory. A refinement of the operation, say one which allocates memory for strings, might raise a more specific exception, say StringSpaceFull. StringSpaceFull could be implemented as a subtype of OutOfMemory. As a subtype of OutOfMemory, it could be used in any context where OutOfMemory itself would be expected.

The second implication of exceptions as types is that one can define properties and/or operations of exceptions. Properties can be extremely useful. In the previous example, one could add the property AmountRequested to the exception type OutOfMemory. For example, assume the raising routine returned:

```
raise OutOfMemory (AmountRequested:  4000000);
```

The 'catching' program could then issue a meaningful error message or do something else appropriate. For example:

```
except (o:  OutOfMemory)
{
  printf ("The amount of memory:  %d, requested is
        not available\n", o.AmountRequested);
}
```

One can thus consider each actual raising of an exception as creating an instance of the exception type. This instance is available to the catching program, which can treat it like any other object, accessing its properties, etc.

# 4. ADVANCED SYSTEM FEATURES

## 4.1 Parameterization (Generic Types)

Another significant capability of Vbase is what is sometimes referred to as parameterization: the ability to specify the type of the objects contained inside aggregate objects. This ability is often not even available in procedural languages. Thus one can write:

```
obj Array[Animal] myZoo;
```

Vbase will type check all insertions into and assignments from the aggregate just as it checks standard types. The lack of such checking is a serious shortcoming of present systems as aggregates are widely used to store critical system information. Often this information is typed, but there is no way to enforce proper use short of writing expensive runtime checks of the elements of the aggregate. Thus:

```
{
  obj Array[Animal] myZoo;
  obj Fruit aKiwi;
  aKiwi = myZoo[3];
}
```

fails at compile time.

Once again, it must be emphasized that this does not limit the programmer. If the programmer actually wishes an 'untyped' Array:

```
obj Array[Entity] myUntypedArray;
```

will suffice. However, as most system implementors can testify, this is rarely the case. More often, the appropriate types cannot be defined within the confines of the chosen system, and the programmer must circumvent the system in order to accomplish the task with reasonable efficiency.

## 4.2 Constant & Variable Definitions in TDL

Another very useful capability available in Vbase is defining constants and variables. This allows user-customized constants and persistent global variables to be placed in the object database. For instance:

```
define Constant myDefault := Null;
define Constant No := False;
define Constant Yes := True;
define Variable background:  Color := Colors$Gray;
define Variable PartSerialNumber:  Integer := 0;
```

This capability provides two important advantages which are well illustrated by the PartSerialNumber example above. First, it provides an extremely convenient mechanism for defining global data that must be persistent, such as a serial number for generation of unique Part numbers. Applications making use of the variable reference it directly in COP:

```
nextNum = $PartSerialNumber++;
```

This is much simpler than is usually the case with a database management system, which would require the creation of an entire record type or relation with one field to store the serial number. The application would then have to open the record type and access the field—or perhaps issue a query—and then bind the result to a program variable. This variable could then be used as above, and the process reversed to store the updated serial number.

The second advantage here is that the overhead for storage is a function of the complexity of the variable. Again, in the serial number situation above, a single integer can be stored with minimal overhead (typically 64 bytes for a 32 bit integer). Defining an entire relation normally requires far more storage than this.

## 4.3 Enumeration, Union, and Variant Types

Along similar lines, TDL allows the definition of enumerations, unions and variants. Type definitions such as these are rarely supported in object systems or database systems. This is certainly unfortunate, as their uses are well known. For instance:

```
define type Day is enum (Monday, Tuesday, ...);
```

Unions and variants are especially important in object systems, particularly those which do not support multiple inheritance. These definitional abilities allow any type of polymorphism desired to be expressed without circumventing the type safety of the system. Rather than having to declare any variable that can potentially hold objects of types which are disjoint in the type hierarchy as Entity, one can restrict the set of types to only those which can actually occur:

```
define type BlockScope is union (Type, Module, Environment, Directory,
...);
```

This allows common mistakes to be ferreted out at compile time. Thus:

```
obj BlockScope scope;
....
scope = Day$Monday;
```

will fail at compile time. If, instead, the variable's scope had to be declared of type Entity (the root of the type hierarchy), this mistake would go unnoticed during compilation.

## 4.4 Clustering

Another database influence apparent in the system is the ability to cluster objects on disk and in memory. Every create operation allows the invoker to specify a previously-existing clustering object. The new object is then clustered according to the user's specification, usually in the same segment as the clustering object. Since segments are the unit of transfer to and from secondary storage in Vbase, whenever any one of the objects in the cluster is accessed, the segment is transferred to memory (if it is not already there). Thus any subsequent references to one of the clustered objects will not require a disk access.

This has numerous applications. For instance, objects contained within an array can be clustered with the array. It is also very useful for a-part-of, or component, hierarchies, which are extremely common in engineering and text management applications. In this case, all the component objects can be clustered. Therefore only one disk access is required to transfer the entire hierarchy into memory. Clustering also provides space saving benefits, as there is less overhead when objects are stored in one segment.

### 4.5 Access To Meta Level Information

Vbase is entirely self-describing: all system characteristics except the lowest layers of storage management are implemented using types. The properties and operations of these system types are freely available to programmers to use to their advantage. This makes system development easier, and allows implementors to create customized tools of their own while taking advantage of system tools already in existence.

### 4.6 Free Operations

Vbase defines free operations: operations that are not associated with a type, and consequently, are not invoked via the standard dispatching means. In object message systems, every message is dispatched; that is, the type of the object being sent the message is used to find the method which implements the message. Free operations in Vbase, in contrast, do not have a distinguished argument. They are simply procedures free of type association.

### 4.7 Overriding Property Implementations

Object systems are known for their ability to allow users to create customized abstractions. Vbase provides users with the unique ability to customize implementations as well. For properties, this ability is available at two levels.

In the simpler case, an implementor can provide customized access to a property by replacing the default get and set operations for the property by customized ones. For instance, the property 'age' in the following example has such customized operations specified.

```
define Type Person
  supertypes = {Mammal}
  properties ={
   age:  Integer define set
      method (Person_SetAge)
      define get
      method (Person_GetAge);
  };
end Person;
```

This specification will cause the user defined routines to be invoked whenever access to the age property occurs as in:

```
{
obj Person aPerson;
obj Integer theAge;
....
theAge = aPerson.age;
....
}
```

One notable difference here from most systems is that when both a get and set operation are specified, no storage is allocated. Thus the programmer truly takes over the implementation, including storage allocation. The user may choose to calculate the value (in the case of age, it is common to calculate the value as the difference between the person's birthdate and the current system date), in which case no storage is needed. If storage is necessary, the implementor may allocate it wherever he/she desires. For example, in a design application one might store large bitmap graphic images using a compression algorithm, and write customized code to read and write the image. In a similar vein, in a CASE system one might store fragments of source code in standard operating system files so that the various language processors will recognize the fragments. Finally, data from alien databases can be imported and exported transparently by using customized properties. The get and set operations are used to call the appropriate database routines on the foreign database to read and write the data.

## 5. TRANSACTION PROCESSING AND CONCURRENCY CONTROL

### 5.1 Overview

As a database system, Vbase provides a repository for a large number of objects which can be shared by multiple applications. An important requirement of such a system is maintenance of the integrity of the object database. This necessitates a mechanism which groups a number of operations and makes them appear as a single transformation to the object database: a transaction. Transactions allow the developer to assure that a set of semantically related changes appears atomic; either all of the changes occur or none of them occur (the classic example: transferring money from one account to another; the debit and credit must be treated as a unit). The transaction mechanism must work in the face of system or media failure as well.

A related matter is that Vbase is a multi-user database system, allowing several processes to access the object database simultaneously. This requires control mechanisms to avoid corruption of the object database when two or more processes access the same objects at the same time. This mediation mechanism is usually called concurrency control.

### 5.2 The Vbase Transaction Mechanism

The Vbase mechanism provides transactions and satisfies the two primary goals of integrity and invisibility. That is, all operations within the scope of a transaction constitute an atomic unit of change to the object database, and transactions proceeding simultaneously are unaware of each other. Vbase accomplishes this using an optimistic protocol. An optimistic protocol is so called because it is based on the assumption that most transactions do not interfere with each other by modifying the same object at the same time. Thus transactions are allowed to proceed unimpeded. When a transaction commits, or finishes, it is checked against any other concurrent transactions which finished earlier to determine if there was any interference, and if so, the transaction is aborted, which is to say the modifications made within the duration of the transaction are not made part of the object database.

This is in contrast to a pessimistic scheme, which assumes that there will be interference, and therefore prevents simultaneous access to an object via a locking protocol. A pessimistic scheme creates significant overhead during processing, but assures non-interference when a transaction commits. An optimistic scheme generates little runtime overhead, but has a longer commit time, and does not guarantee non-interference.

**5.2.1 Implementation.** Vbase implements the transaction mechanism by creating a separate work area for each transaction. All work is done by copying objects into the work area and operating on them there; no changes are made directly to the database:

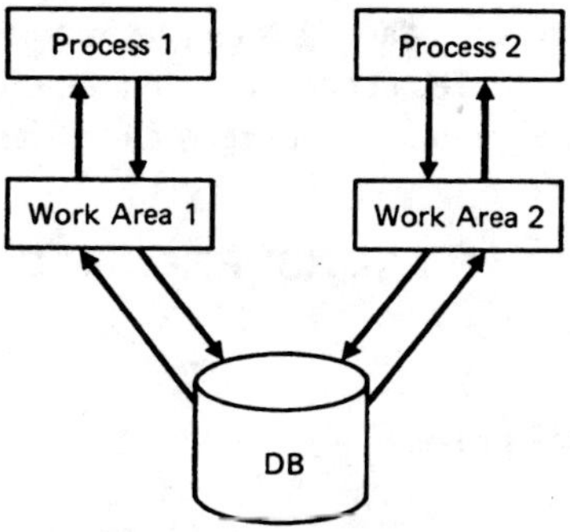


**Figure 10.5**

As the transaction proceeds, the reference of every object touched is kept in a list called the transaction set. If the transaction commits successfully, the references of those objects modified by the transaction are added to a list kept by Vbase in a special Vbase work area called the write set. The time at which the references were added to the write set is also retained.

This information is used by the interference algorithm to determine if there has been a collision between concurrent transactions. This algorithm runs as follows when a transaction attempts to commit:

1. Determine the start time and end time of the transaction.
2. Subset the write set to contain those objects added during the interval identified in (1).
3. Find the intersection of this subset of the write set and the transaction set.
4. If the intersection is null, commit the transaction, otherwise abort the transaction.

Aborting the transaction in Vbase is trivial since changes are buffered from the database. Aborting a transaction thus comes down to throwing away the buffered work area. Committing a transaction must make all changes appear atomic. Vbase assures this via an algorithm that reduces the issue to one forced write to the disk which is easily controlled.

### 5.3 Concurrency Control

The Vbase transaction mechanism provides a basic level of integrity, but is unacceptable when long transactions or transactions which would have high collision rates are necessary. In either case, the application may wish to assure that the transaction does not get aborted due to interference. The Vbase concurrency control capabilities can provide this assurance via a locking protocol.

**5.3.1 High level access.** Vbase provides a type called Lock with a very simple protocol as the easiest way to provide arbitration when two or more transactions desire access to the same object:

```
define Type Lock
 ...
  operations ={
    acquire (..)
    /* Obtain exclusive access to an object.  If
      another transaction has previously acquired
      the lock, place the invoker into a wait loop
      until the lock is released */

    release (..)
    /* release a previously acquired lock */
  };
end Type Lock;
```

An application can now guarantee that it will not interfere with other transactions by using the following algorithm:

1. Acquire locks on all objects used in the transaction.
2. Process the objects.
3. Commit the transaction.
4. Release the locks.

Since a lock can be used with any object, Vbase gives the developer a great deal of flexibility. The application can lock large composite objects, simulating a check in/check out facility, or small primitive objects, simulating a record locking facility.

**5.3.2 The base mechanism.** The high level concurrency control interface is synchronous in that an invocation of the acquire operation places the invoker into a waiting state until the lock is available. This can lead to deadlock, which occurs when transactions T1 and T2 both want objects A and B. If T1 locks A just as T2 locks B, then T1 will wait for B while T2 waits for A. In the synchronous situation above, deadlock now occurs as both transactions will wait forever for the lock on the second object. This is often tolerable in a small group using interactive applications: the author has had experience in such situations, and it is relatively simple for two users to realize they have deadlocked, and to agree to manually abort one of the applications and release the lock.

However, there are other situations (such as non-interactive applications) where the system must provide a deadlock resolution ability. Vbase does this by allowing the developer to access the base mechanism from which the Lock type is constructed. The base mechanism consists of two types: EventCount and Sequencer, and implements the model described in [Ree79]. It is often referred to as a deli-ticket system, as it is analogous to the way delis issue tickets and process orders at the counter.

The Sequencer type acts as the ticket dispenser, and the EventCount type plays the role of the number currently being served. The protocol is:

1. Get a ticket from the Sequencer.
2. Wait for the ticket number to come up on the EventCount.
3. Process.
4. Commit the transaction.
5. Advance the EventCount to the next ticket number.

The key difference here is that the EventCount type offers two interfaces to monitor the number currently being served. The await operation is used by the Lock type and is synchronous; the read operation, however, simply returns the current value without waiting. This allows the programmer, for example, to write an asynchronous loop which times out after a fixed period and releases any locks acquired. This solves the deadlock problem described earlier without human interaction.

## 6. REPRESENTATION AND STORAGE IN VBASE

### 6.1 Defining Open Architecture

As stated in the System Architecture description, the Vbase system consists of a three layer architecture: abstraction, representation, storage. In fact, this is one way of describing any linguistic system implemented on a computer. However, for most computer systems these three layers are not distinct. It is the author's contention that this three layer model provides a formal way of describing the term open architecture:

An **open architecture** is one in which the abstraction, representation, and storage layers of the system are distinct, explicit, orthogonal, and accessible to the programmer.

Making the layers explicit is an obvious requirement; making them distinct and orthogonal is what truly defines the openness of the system. This allows programmer access to any level of the system right down to the bits and bytes level. If the layers are orthogonal, the programmer only has to change what is actually necessary: any layer can be changed without affecting the other layers. For example, one could design a new storage manager for a database system which runs a compression algorithm on strings without changing the abstract language (typically a programming language or a query language) interface. In an object database system such as Vbase, this allows the developer to not only add new abstract types to the system, but also to provide new implementations for those types if desired.

This is a critical issue in database applications, where the underlying system generally cannot provide adequate performance in all aspects. Traditional systems are closed architectures, with a few limited tuning capabilities such as secondary indices. In traditional systems, adding an entirely different disk layout without changing the query interface is impossible without direct support from the vendor of the system.

## 6.2 Representation and Storage Layers in Vbase

In addition to the properties defined by an object's Abstract Type, every Vbase object inherits from type Entity properties referencing an Abstract Type, a Representation Manager, and a Storage Manager, each of which is another object:

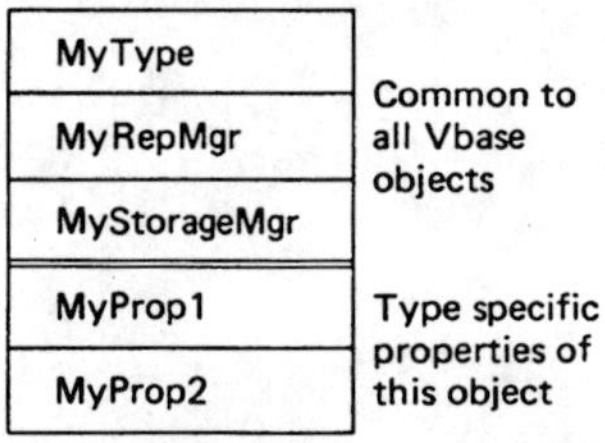


**Figure 10.6**

A developer has the option of specifying a representation manager or storage manager when instantiating an object; otherwise the system defaults are used. For a more complete description of these layers see [Dam88a] and [Dam88b].

The Vbase System defines RepManager and StorageManager abstract types which define the protocol for representation and storage managers. By creating new subtypes of these system types, developers can create new storage and representation managers. These can then be used to instantiate objects without altering the abstract type defining the properties and operations of the objects.

Vbase makes use of this subtyping capability to define many different representation managers when the default is inappropriate. The most obvious example is the Immediate representation manager, which allows an object to be stored directly in its reference. Vbase references are 64 bits, so this makes sense for Integer objects, Character objects, and the like.

Vbase also uses alternate storage managers to differentiate between temporary, or Process Local, objects, and persistent objects (persistent being the default). Storage managers also differentiate between transaction based objects and shared objects. Shared objects exist outside the transaction mechanism, and can thus be used for communication between transactions. This provides a natural mechanism for handling the write set and concurrency control objects described earlier. This is a significant advantage as the abstract interfaces (in Vbase the properties and operations) are identical so standard system Types can be used to implement the shared objects by instantiating them with a different storage manager.

## 7. SUMMARY

Vbase is a relatively complete development system with language processors and development tools. It is object based, strongly typed, and provides support for persistent objects. It has an open architecture which allows custom implementations for improved efficiency. It supports such standard database functions as transactions, concurrency control, and SQL, and also contains an object-oriented programming language for application development.

# 11

# SIM: Design and Implementation of a Semantic Database System*

**B. L. Fritchman, R. L. Guck, D. Jagannathan, J. P. Thompson, and D. M. Tolbert**

*Unisys Corporation*

## ABSTRACT

SIM is a fully featured, commercially available database management system based on a semantic data model similar to Hammer and McLeod's SDM. SIM has two primary modeling goals. The first is to narrow the gap between a user's real-world perception of data and the conceptual view imposed by the database system because of modeling presuppositions or limitations. The second goal is to allow, as much as possible, the semantics of data to be defined in the schema and make the database system responsible for enforcing its integrity. SIM provides a rich set of constructs for schema definition, including those for specifying generalization hierarchies modeled by directed acyclic graphs, interobject relationships and integrity constraints. It also features a novel, easy-to-use, English-like data manipulation language (DML) for retrieval and update operations. This paper describes the key modeling features of SIM, the architecture of the system and its implementation considerations.

**Source*: Adapted from Fritchman, B., R. Guck, D. Jagannathan, J. Thompson and D. Tolbert, "SIM: Design and Implementation of a Semantic Database System", Proceedings ACM SIGMOD Conference, 1989, pp. 46–55. 

## 1. INTRODUCTION

A data model consists of rules for defining the logical structure of data and associated operations. Expressive power, simplicity and freedom from implementation details are some desirable characteristics of a data model. The relational model was the first to emphasize both the structural and manipulative aspects of modeling as well as storage independence. It is built on mathematical foundations and its often-quoted advantages are the simplicity and completeness of its concepts. However, the principal weakness of the relational model is its lack of semantic expressive power—it does not have constructs which can directly capture application semantics known to the database designer [Ham81]. It requires that concepts of an application be fragmented to suit the model, forcing the resulting schema and queries on the database to lose their conceptual naturalness [Shi81]. Artificial steps in query formulations introduce a level of indirection and have procedural overtones.

Semantic data models address this weakness of the relational model. Their model of reality is usually based on abstract entities (objects) rather than records; they provide for interobject relationships and structural constraints. There is generally no consensus on what constitutes a semantic model and a number of them have been proposed. These include the binary relational model which views a database as objects and binary relationships between objects [Abr74], the entity-relationship model which treats the database as entities and n-ary relationships between entities [Che76], semantically enriched relational models [Cod79], the functional model which treats entities, attributes and relationships as functions with zero or more arguments [Shi81], the semantic model SDM [Ham81] and the object-oriented data models [Fis87,Ban88]. Many data definitional ideas of SIM are derived from SDM, while the DML is our own.

The SIM (Semantic Information Manager) project was initiated in 1982 at Unisys with the goal of producing the next generation of database management system (DBMS) tools. The semantic model was chosen because it is rich, expressive, conceptually natural and provides a path of growth and evolution for existing DMSII users. DMSII is a DBMS based on the network data model and runs on Unisys A Series machines. It has a large installed base of users and has been used to implement many large and complex applications. SIM has initially been built on top of DMSII and relies on DMSII for transaction, cursor and I/O management. However, the architecture of the system is designed such that virtually any data source, including other database systems, can be substituted in the place of DMSII. SIM forms the basis for the InfoExec[1] Environment which provides an array of database and application tools, including ADDS, IQF and WQF. ADDS is a data dictionary system which can be used for, among other things, defining a SIM database. IQF is a menu-based query facility and WQF is a workstation-based graphically-oriented query language. The InfoExec Environment also supports SIM database interfaces in COBOL, ALGOL and Pascal. The emphasis of this paper, however, is on SIM itself; details of the InfoExec Environment are not addressed here.

[1] InfoExec is a trademark of Unisys Corporation.

Our discussion of SIM begins with a brief review of the salient features of semantic data models in Section 2. Section 3 describes the data definition concepts of SIM used to capture descriptions of real-world application problems. The conceptual query language for accessing SIM databases is presented in Section 4 along with illustrative examples of both retrieval and update operations. Section 5 considers the objectives of SIM's internal architecture, and how they are addressed in the implementation of SIM on Unisys A-Series computers.

All examples in this paper are based on the schema of the University database appearing in Appendix A and graphically in Figure 11.3. This schema and examples based on it are described in the conceptual languages understood by SIM. Users, however, are not required to learn these languages and can instead use menu- based products. Readers are encouraged to make frequent comparisons of the examples in the text with the schema in Appendix A to better understand the feature content and power of SIM. In the text, items declared in the example schema begin with a captial letter.

We have attempted to provide an essentially complete description of SIM in a relatively short paper. Consequently, some readers may find the information density of this paper high. We hope that careful reading and liberal use of the example schema will help promote better understanding of the power and capabilities of SIM.

## 2. THE SEMANTIC DATA MODEL

Entities, relationships between entities, abstraction mechanisms and integrity constraints are the generally acknowledged key features of semantic models [Dat83,Ham81,Kin84a, Smi77,Tsi82b]. An entity is an abstract object that corresponds to some real or conceptual object in an application environment. A semantically meaningful collection of entities forms a class. Entities do not exist in isolation—they are related to each other in various ways, and the notion of attribute describes this relationship between entities. An attribute of an entity defines how it is related to other entities of another or perhaps the same class. Entities are represented by system-defined identifiers and their existence does not depend on any of their attributes. Attributes of an entity are said to be displayable if their range is one of a number of special, system-defined classes (for example, the class of all strings). Attributes can be single-valued or multi-valued.

Abstraction mechanisms allow complex information to be categorized and viewed in comprehensible ways. Classification, aggregation and generalization are the abstraction mechanisms normally used in semantic models. Classification represents a member/class relationship. Aggregation is a primitive that allows the relationship between entities to be treated by itself as an entity at a higher level [Smi77]. Generalization allows each member of a class to be related to a member of a more generic class, called its superclass. The notion of generalization can be applied successively, yielding a hierarchy of classes.

Data types, attribute options and assertion predicates are the principal techniques used for constraint specification in semantic data models. Semantic models provide strong typing features that can be used in a natural way to constrain the values of an attribute. Strong typing also discourages users from making meaningless associations between components of data. Attribute options like unique, required, distinct and maximum and minimum cardinality are used to specify the structural integrity of data. These options are sufficient to describe the usual one:one, one:many, and many:many relationships. Assertion predicates specify conditions that are to be satisfied by entities of a class. They are either stated as predicates that hold on the database at all times or as predicates tested after particular DML actions are executed. Assertions based on transitions [Dat83] are also allowed.

## 3. SCHEMA DEFINITION IN SIM

Most work on semantic data models has been concentrated on its utility as a logical database design tool. While some prototype database systems that implement a selected set of features of semantic models exist [Gol85,Tsu84,Myl80a,Shi81,Ban88], to the best of our knowledge, SIM is one of the first large scale, fully featured commercial implementations [Guc88, Jag88].

### 3.1 Entities

Entities are abstract objects that may represent a thing or idea in the real-world application problem. They play a role in SIM similar to records in conventional DBMSs or tuples in relational systems. However, entities are logical constructs and do not imply particular physical implementations as records and tuples often do. Entities and objects in object-oriented systems are similar in their structural aspects but differ in that objects may possess algorithmic descriptions (called methods) that SIM entities do not.

### 3.2 Classes

The primary unit of data encapsulation in SIM is a class, which represents a meaningful collection of entities. A class is either a base class or a subclass. A base class is defined independently of all other classes in the database, while a subclass is defined based on one or more classes, called its superclasses. In the example schema, Person, Course and Department are base classes, Student and Instructor are subclasses whose superclass is Person and Teaching-Assistant is a subclass whose superclasses are Student and Instructor. In this paper we will use the unqualified term class in any context where either a base class or a subclass is applicable. Interclass connections are usually represented as a directed graph whose nodes are the classes and whose edges denote superclass-to-subclass connections (Figure 11.3, for example). These graphs are called generalization hierarchies; SIM requires that they be acyclic and that the set of ancestors of any node contain at most one base class.

Every base class has a special system-maintained attribute called its surrogate. All subclasses eventually derived from a base class inherit its surrogate attribute. The surrogate value for every entity in a class must be unique, must not be null and cannot be changed once defined. In SIM, surrogates play a central role in the implementation of generalization hierarchies and entity relationships.

### 3.3 Attributes

In SIM, a distinction is made between data-valued attributes (DVA) and entity-valued attributes (EVA). A DVA describes a property of each entity in a class by associating the entity with a value or a (multi)set of values from a domain of values. Definition of DVAs in SIM and attributes in the E-R model [Che76] are similar. Values of DVAs may be displayed on a screen or printer. Name and Birthdate of the Person class are examples of DVAs.

An EVA describes a property of each entity of a class by relating it to an entity or entities of another class or perhaps to another entity in the same class. An EVA represents a binary relationship between the class that owns it (domain) and the class it points to (range). SIM uses EVAs to model relationships between entities. Hence, the "value" of an EVA cannot be displayed on an output device. In the example schema, Advisor is an EVA of Student whose "value" is an entity in the Instructor class.

Some readers may find the representation of relationships between entities as (entity-valued) attributes somewhat unusual. This approach is derived from the functional definition of attributes used by Hammer and McLeod [Ham81] and Shipman [Shi81] and has the desirable side effect of eliminating a temptation present in the relational model—viewing relationships as having an existence of their own, independent of the related entities. A SIM user cannot inadvertently create a relationship involving one or more non-existant entities.

A purist can avoid the distinction between DVAs and EVAs by assuming standard base classes of integers, strings, etc. We could get rid of explicit type declarations from the model by requiring that they be declared as (pre-enumerated) subclasses. For example, the ID-Number type can be represented by a subclass of the `INTEGER` base class with appropriate range conditions. While a purely functional definition of all attributes is aesthetically pleasing, we have observed that many users have difficulty understanding it. Explicit data types in SIM are more naturally imported into its host language interface programs. We feel that our approach is intuitive and more readily understood and we chose it because of historical considerations.

SIM provides full referential integrity by automatically maintaining the inverse of every declared EVA and guaranteeing that an EVA and its inverse will stay synchronized at all times. For example, when an entity is deleted, all of its references to other entities via EVAs are also automatically deleted (unless an integrity constraint would be violated). An inverse can also be explicitly named by the user. In the example schema, Advisees is the inverse of Advisor. In DML, the term `INVERSE`(Advisor) can be used in any context where Advisees is allowed.

A subclass inherits all the attributes of all its superclasses in its generalization hierarchy. In the example schema, attributes of Person are to be seen as an integral part of Student since every student must be a person. An attribute is said to be an immediate attribute of the base class or subclass it is declared in. In DML, an inherited attribute of a subclass can be used in any context where an immediate attribute is allowed and vice versa. For example, Student-id is an immediate attribute of Student while Name is an attribute of Student inherited from Person. SIM allows references to Name of Student, Name of Person, and Student-id of Student, but Student-id of Person is meaningless because only Students have Student-ids. Attributes are inherited by all subordinate levels in a generalization hierarchy; for example, Teaching-Assistant inherits Name from Person via Student (and Instructor, in this schema).

In SIM, every class that has subclasses must have a special attribute of subrole type declared with it (for example, Profession of Person). A subrole is a special case of enumerated types and its value set must contain the names of all the immediate subclasses of the class in which it is used. Subrole attributes are system-maintained and can only be read. They can be included in the target list of a retrieve query, provide a convenient method to retrieve symbolically all the roles an entity participates in, and provide a way to control (using attribute options) how entities may participate in generalization hierarchies.

Attribute types and options are used in combination to limit the values attributes may take and thus capture many of the structurally related integrity constraints in a SIM database. Non- structural integrity constraints can be captured by another construct described in Section 3.5.

**3.3.1 Attribute types.** For DVAs, SIM provides a type mechanism similar to that used in Pascal. Types may be declared in-line or declared globally and used throughout the schema. For example, Name of Person (Appendix A) is a character string of length 30 whereas Student-id of Student and Employee-id of Instructor are based on the globally declared type ID-Number. Types must be based on system primitive types and may be used to restrict the range of values a DVA may assume by applying appropriate range conditions as was done for ID-Number in the example schema. System-supplied primitive types include `INTEGER`, `CHARACTER`, `NUMBER` (packed decimal), `REAL` (floating point), `BOOLEAN`, `STRING`, `DATE`, `TIME`, and `SYMBOLIC` (an enumerated type). SIM's type mechanism provides more latitude when comparing types based on strings than is typically allowed by Pascal.

DVAs may be either simple or compound. Compound DVAs are made up of multiple constituent attributes. Constituents of a compound attribute must be single-valued DVAs and may themselves be compound. Multi-valued compound DVAs can be used to represent a "dependent" entity similar to the weak entity concept of the entity-relationship model [Che76]. For brevity, the example schema does not include a compound DVA, but the reader is encouraged to envision the redefinition of Name of Person as a compound DVA made of constituent `STRING` attributes First-Name, Initial, and Last-Name. The SIM DML permits the direct manipulation of both compounds (e.g., Name) and their constituent attributes (e.g., Last-Name of Name).

The name of a user-declared class or subclass in the schema is used to indicate the type of an EVA. Thus, the EVA Advisor declared in the Student class is said to be of type Instructor. EVAs may also be of the same type as the class in which they are declared. Such EVAs are called reflexive and reference another entity in the same class. For example, the Spouse of a Person is another Person entity.

**3.3.2 Attribute options.** `REQUIRED`, `UNIQUE`, `MV`, `DISTINCT` and `MAX` are the attribute options supported in SIM. `REQUIRED` implies that the value of an attribute cannot be null (a null is used to represent both "unknown" and "inapplicable" values

[Dat83]). UNIQUE implies that no two entities of the class can have a value in common. Null values are omitted from uniqueness considerations.

MV indicates that an attribute is multi-valued. By default, attributes are single-valued. The DISTINCT option on a multi-valued attribute implies a set of values as opposed to a multiset allowing duplicates. MAX limits the number of values an MV attribute can take, which by default is unbounded.

When specified appropriately on EVAs and their inverses, attribute options define the structural properties of data. The MV option can be used with EVAs to represent the classical types of relationships among entities. For example, suppose E1 is an EVA and Inv-E1 its inverse. If both E1 and Inv-E1 are single-valued, they define a one:one relationship. If E1 is multi-valued and Inv-E1 is single-valued, they define a one:many or many:one relationship, depending on the point of view. If both are multi- valued, they define a many:many relationship. Partial, total, or absence of dependency on the relationship can be defined by specifying the REQUIRED option appropriately on E1 and Inv-E1. Cardinality can be controlled by the MAX option. In the example schema, Spouse is a one:one relationship, Advisor:Advisees defines a many:one relationship between Student and Instructor with a limit of 10 advisees per instructor, and Courses-Enrolled: Students-Enrolled defines a many:many relationship between Student and Course.

**3.3.3 Class attributes.** Class attributes apply to all the members of a class taken as a whole. For example, Maximum-Salary is a class attribute of Instructor. Such attributes may have only one value and are normally used to capture statistical and other information common to all the members of a class. A different set of attributes can be associated with each class in the generalization hierarchy, and they obey normal rules of attribute inheritance. Values of a class attribute can be used as if they are constants in DML Retrieve queries. The initial implementation of SIM requires that class attributes be single-valued DVAs.

## 3.4 Views and Security

View definition in a semantic model poses challenging problems. In SIM, each class is a named type and classes are heavily interrelated. The output of DML queries follows a simple record structure and does not directly reflect the interconnections of entities. Hence, a view cannot just be defined as the output of a Retrieve query. We are currently designing extensions to DDL and DML to support views on a SIM database. However, SIM's security mechanisms and DML notions of perspective and extended attributes largely eliminate the need for views.

Names of classes and EVAs in SIM are of particular importance in making queries natural. We do not require a new named type (a view, for example) to be introduced just for the sake of a security specification. A user who is not allowed to see the SALARY attribute of instructors, for example, must still be allowed to use the class name Instructor. SIM provides a mechanism for security specification on a class C that does not create a new named class, does not affect C's role in its generalization hierarchy and does not affect EVAs whose range is C.

SIM Security has two components: Access and Permission. An access is specified in the form

```
ACCESS ⟨access name⟩ ON ⟨class name⟩ [( ⟨attribute list⟩ )]
       ⟨DML action⟩ [WHERE ⟨selection expression⟩].
```

⟨attribute list⟩ must be a subset of the class's immediate attributes and the selection expression must involve only constants or immediate attributes of the class. ⟨DML action⟩ indicates whether the class may be retrieved, inserted, deleted, or modified.

A permission assigns a particular access to a given user. A DML request will be rejected if it uses an attribute of a class not in the ⟨attribute list⟩ of the access selected for the user. For an entity of a class C to be visible to a user, it must satisfy the selection expression of C's access for his usercode as well as selection expressions of accesses associated with all ancestor classes of C in its hierarchy. This check will be performed by the system irrespective of how the class is accessed—whether directly, through role conversion or through EVAs. An access specification is a view definition in disguise. It does it in such a way that underlying classes are not disturbed and new types are not introduced.

### 3.5 Integrity Constraints

As mentioned before, the structural integrity of data in SIM is defined by judicious use of generalization and attribute types and options. Since all relationships are maintained by the system, SIM can guarantee full referential integrity and "dangling reference" problems do not exist.

SIM also allows the specification of non-structural integrity conditions with any class. An integrity condition can be any arbitrary DML selection expression with the class as perspective (see Section 4.1) and may even include quantifiers and aggregate functions. Full-Load and Valid-Salary are examples of integrity conditions in the example schema. Based on the terms of the integrity condition, SIM will determine all possible events that may cause this condition to be violated and will make sure it does not happen. Integrity constraints are handled by a trigger detection / query enhancement mechanism that works efficiently for a subset of constraints. In its most general form, maintaining integrity constraints not associated with explicit user-defined trigger events is an extremely difficult problem to solve efficiently, and we are experimenting with several algorithms. Currently, arbitrary integrity constraints have only been partially implemented.

## 4. DATA MANIPULATION IN SIM

SIM DML is a high-level, non-procedural language designed with a particular emphasis on its naturalness and ease of use. Constructs of the DML are a direct consequence of the features of the semantic model. It incorporates many ideas from GORDAS [Elm81] and DAPLEX [Shi81].

## 4.1 Perspective Class

The notion of perspective class is of fundamental importance in SIM DML. It is based on the assumption that when formulating a query (either retrieve or update), a user is primarily interested in entities of one class, called the perspective. Other classes in the database are viewed based on their relationship to the perspective class. Used in combination with other features of SIM, the notion of perspective class simplifies query formation and allows users with different interests to approach the database from points of view appropriate to their needs.

When combined with a syntactic process called qualification, immediate attributes of other classes in the database can be related to the perspective class of a query. This allows attributes of the other classes to be treated as if they were attributes of the perspective. Within the context of a DML query, attributes derived from the perspective (via its EVAs) by more than one level of qualification are called extended attributes. Derivation of values for extended attributes corresponds to the notion of directed outer join [Cod79] in relational systems and is a natural and direct result of the notion of perspective.

To better understand extended attributes, consider a query in which Student is the perspective class. Student-id of Student refers to an immediate attribute, Name of Student refers to an inherited attribute (from Person), Name of Advisor of Student refers to the name of his advisor (an Instructor entity), and Teachers of Courses-Enrolled of Student refers to the instructors who teach the courses he is enrolled in. The last two qualifications are extended attributes of Student for purposes of this query. Comparison with the example schema should make the relationships of these attributes to Student clear.

By choosing an appropriate perspective class, users may thus state their DML requests in terms relevant to their needs. For example, various users might interpret the value "Physics" differently. A user concerned with university departments might see "Physics" as a value for Name of Department, someone in the personnel department might interpret it as Name of Assigned- Department of Instructor, and a worker in the Admissions office might think of it as Name of Major-Department of Student. In fact, all three users are viewing the same piece of stored information but in ways that are "semantically relevant" to their intended use of the datum.

The notion of perspective class can be combined with generalization hierarchies to simplify query formation. For example, consider the request "print the name of each student and the name of his advisor, if any." In DML, this query is expressed as

```
FROM Student RETRIEVE Name, Name of Advisor.
```

Names of persons who are not students will not be printed. However, if a student does not have an advisor, SIM will still select and print his name with a null value for the advisor's name. The perspective of this query is Student and Name of Advisor refers to an extended attribute. The same information could be retrieved by choosing Person as the perspective class, but the query is more complicated:

```
FROM Person RETRIEVE Name, Name of Advisor AS Student
WHERE Profession = Student.
```

The AS and WHERE clauses must be added to exclude Persons who are not Students. The purpose of the AS clause is described in the following section.

Sometimes it may be necessary to form queries with more than one perspective class (for example, retrieve all pairs of students who are taking the same set of courses). SIM provides such a facility and queries so formulated are called multi-perspective queries. Multiple perspective classes are related to each other by value-based joins, which establish dynamic relationships between classes. We strongly recommend the use of EVAs over value-based joins since they represent a static, schema-defined, efficient and natural way of establishing relationships.

## 4.2 Qualification

As mentioned before, qualification is a syntactic process by which an attribute is connected to a perspective class as an extended attribute. Qualification of an attribute is usually of the form

```
⟨attribute name⟩ {OF ⟨eva name⟩ [AS ⟨class name⟩]}
OF ⟨perspective class name⟩ [AS ⟨class name⟩].
```

⟨attribute name⟩ can either be a DVA or an EVA. The 'AS' clause specifies role conversion from a class to another class in the same generalization hierarchy. It is normally used for converting the role of an entity from a superclass to a subclass and may be best thought of as "looking down" a generalization hierarchy (in the graphical sense of Figure 11.3).

The following are examples of qualification from Student: "Title of Courses-Enrolled of Student" represents the titles of all courses in which a student is enrolled, "Teaching-Load of Student AS Teaching-Assistant" returns a teaching load only if the student is also a teaching assistant (otherwise it returns null), and "Student-id of Spouse AS Student of Student" returns the student number of the student's spouse only if the spouse is also a student.

It is not necessary to qualify every attribute in a DML query to its perspective. Qualification can be cut short at any stage where the context is sufficient for the system parser (Section 5.3.3) to complete it unambiguously. For example, if Student is the perspective, "Name of Advisor of Student, Salary of Advisor of Student," and "Name of Advisor, Salary" will yield identical results. Qualifications of multiple target list items can also be parenthetically factored for syntactic convenience. Thus, "(Name, Salary) of Advisor" will also yield the same results.

## 4.3 Syntax of Retrieve Queries

A DML Retrieve query is expressed in the form

```
[FROM ⟨perspective class list⟩]
RETRIEVE [TABLE [DISTINCT] ! STRUCTURE] ⟨target list⟩
[ORDER BY ⟨order list⟩]
[WHERE ⟨selection expression⟩].
```

⟨perspective class list⟩ is the list of perspective classes for a query with optional associated reference variables. ⟨target list⟩ and ⟨order list⟩ are a list of expressions made up of constants, immediate, inherited and extended attributes of the perspectives, and aggregate and other functions applied on such attributes.

### 4.4 Binding and Range Variables

The semantics of SIM queries are understood in terms of nested iterative loops similar to DAPLEX [Shi81,Day82]. All occurrences of a perspective class name in a query are "bound" to one range (loop) variable. Similarly, all occurrences of an identically qualified EVA or multi-valued DVA are also bound to one range variable. Consider the following query:

```
RETRIEVE Name of Student,
   Title of Courses-Enrolled of Student,
   Credits of Courses-Enrolled of Student,
   Name of Teachers of Courses-Enrolled of Student
WHERE Soc-Sec-No of Student = 456887766.
```

For the Student with Soc-Sec-No 456887766, this query will print his name and for each course that he is taking, its title, credits and the name of the instructors who teach it. This is possible only because all five ocurrences of the literal "Student" and all three occurrences of the literal "Courses-Enrolled" are bound to their respective range variables.

Implicit binding of names is broken in a few special constructs such as aggregate functions, transitive closure and quantifiers. When needed, named range variables can also be explicitly established on a class, EVA or a multi-valued DVA with the CALLED construct. For example, the query

```
RETRIEVE Name of Instructor
WHERE Gpa of Advisees < 2.0 AND
      Gpa of Advisees CALLED GoodStudent > 3.5
```

returns the names of all instructors that advise students that are doing well AND students that are doing poorly. The named range vaiable is required because the normal binding rules ensure that the same selection expression without the CALLED construct will return no entities at all.

### 4.5 Semantics of Retrieve Queries

The qualification and binding rules of SIM, taken together, give rise to the concept of a query tree. The query tree generated for a particular query is converted into a series of nested loops that SIM uses to execute the query. Each nested loop is under the control of one range variable, and the outer-most loop is controlled by the range variable bound to the perspective class unless altered by the optimizer. The nesting sequence of these loops determines the order in which query results are returned to the user. These nested loops have the same logical structure as might a conventional application program written to accomplish the same result using a file system or record oriented DBMS.

Construction of query trees is considered in more detail in Sections 5.5 and 5.6. Appendix B contains a more detailed description of the structure of query trees intended for interested readers.

## 4.6 Aggregate Functions

In SIM, aggregate functions are specfied naturally by delimiting their scope in a qualification. Consider the following examples:

```
AVG(Salary of Instructor),
AVG(Salary of Instructors-employed) of Department,
COUNT(Teachers of Courses-enrolled) of Student.
```

The first gives the average salary of all instructors in the database, the second gives the average salary of instructor employed by each department (it's a dynamically derived attribute of Department) and the third gives, for each student, the count of teachers of all the courses he is enrolled in. Quantifiers (ALL, SOME, and NO) follow a similar syntax.

## 4.7 Transitive Closure

The transitive closure operation is expressed in syntax similar to that of aggregate functions. The following query will retrieve all the prerequisites of Calulus I:

```
RETRIEVE Title of TRANSITIVE (Prerequisite) of Course
WHERE Title of Course = "Calculus I".
```

The tree structure of a transitive closure will be preserved in a fully structured output, based on the notion of level numbers for output records. Transitive closure can be performed on any cyclic chain of EVAs (the single reflexive EVA in the example above is a cyclic chain one element long). The closure is computed in the depth-first order for interactive queries while in the host language interface special constructs can be used to traverse up and down the levels.

## 4.8 Update Statements

SIM provides the three usual update operations as separate statements. Syntactic examples of update statements may be found in Section 4.9.

An insert in SIM is of the form

```
INSERT ⟨class name1⟩
[FROM ⟨class name2⟩ WHERE ⟨boolean expn⟩]
[ ( ⟨assignment list⟩ ) ].
```

If the FROM clause is omitted, all superclass roles of ⟨class name1⟩ up to and including the root of the hierarchy will be inserted along with ⟨class name1⟩. For example, inserting a Student actually creates a corresponding Person entity that participates in the Student subclass. If a `FROM` clause is specified, ⟨class name2⟩ must be an ancestor of ⟨class name1⟩ in the hierarchy and all superclass roles of ⟨class name1⟩ up to but not including ⟨class name2⟩ will be automatically inserted as needed. The boolean expression selects the entity whose role is being extended. Immediate attributes of all the insert class and its superclasses can be assigned values in one `INSERT` statement. Thus, inserting a Student `FROM` Person causes a previously existing Person entity to assume the role of Student.

A Modify in SIM is of the form

```
MODIFY ⟨class name⟩ ( ⟨assignment list⟩ )
WHERE ⟨boolean expn⟩.
```

All immediate and inherited attributes of ⟨class name⟩ can be modified in one statement.

The keywords `INCLUDE` and `EXCLUDE` in an ⟨assignment list⟩ item define corresponding operations on multi-valued attributes. DVA assigments are straightforword:

```
⟨DVA name⟩ := [INCLUDE | EXCLUDE] ⟨data value⟩.
```

EVA assignments are particularly simple:

```
⟨EVA name⟩ := [INCLUDE | EXCLUDE]
              ⟨object name⟩ WITH ( ⟨boolean expn⟩ ).
```

⟨object name⟩ refers to a class name for single-valued EVA assignments and multi-valued EVA inclusions. It refers to the same EVA name for exclusions. If a class name is used, it must be the range class of the EVA.

A delete statement is of the form `DELETE ⟨class name⟩ WHERE ⟨boolean expn⟩`. When an entity is deleted, all its subclass roles will be deleted, while its superclass roles will remain unaffected. For example, if an entity of Student is deleted, it will continue to exist in class Person. However, if an entity of Person is deleted, it will also be deleted from Student, Instructor and Teaching-Assistant classes (if present). When an entity of a class or subclass is deleted, its immediate EVAs, if any, will be automatically deleted.

### 4.9 Miscellaneous

The DML also supports quantifiers, pattern matching and an array of operators and primitive functions. Null values are treated uniformly in expression evaluation, and SIM follows the three-valued logic (True, False, and Null). Examples below illustrate the power and ease of use of SIM DML.

**1.** Insert John Doe as a Student and enroll him in Algebra I.

```
INSERT Student(Name := "John Doe",
  Soc-Sec-No := 456887766,
  Courses-Enrolled := INCLUDE Course WITH (Title="Algebra I")).
```

2. Make John Doe an Instructor also.

```
INSERT Instructor
FROM Person WHERE Name = "John Doe"
  (Employee-Nbr := 1729).
```

3. Let John Doe drop Algebra I and let Joe Bloke be his advisor.

```
MODIFY Student (
  Courses-Enrolled := EXCLUDE Courses-Enrolled
                      WITH (Title = "Algebra I"),
  Advisor := Instructor WITH (Name = "Joe Bloke"))
WHERE Name of Student = "John Doe"
```

4. If an instructor teaches more than 3 courses and advises students from other departments, give him a 10% raise.

```
MODIFY Instructor (Salary := 1.1 * Salary)
WHERE COUNT(Courses-Taught) of Instructor > 3 AND
      Assigned-Department NEQ
         SOME(Major-Department of Advisees).
```

5. Find the minimum number of courses that must be completed before one enrolls in Quantum Chromodynamics.

```
FROM Course
RETRIEVE COUNT DISTINCT (TRANSITIVE(Prerequisite))
WHERE Title = "Quantum Chromodynamics".
```

6. Print the name of each instructor who advises some student from the Physics department and the courses he teaches, if any.

```
RETRIEVE Name of Instructor, Title of Courses-Taught
WHERE Name of Major-Department of Advisees = "Physics".
```

7. Print student, instructor pairs where the student is older than the instructor and the instructor is not a teaching assistant and is not the student's advisor.

```
FROM Student, Instructor
RETRIEVE Name of Student, Name of Instructor
Where Birthdate of Student < Birthdate of Instructor AND
      Advisor of Student NEQ Instructor AND
      NOT Instructor ISA Teaching-Assistant.
```

# 5. IMPLEMENTATION CONSIDERATIONS

## 5.1 Objectives

In addition to its functional objectives, SIM addresses specific implementation objectives which are summarized below.

**5.1.1 Environment.** SIM has been initially implemented on the Unisys A Series line of mainframes. All A Series systems are object-code compatible and range from entry-level systems to very large-scale mainframes. The principal data and software modules of a SIM database must reside on an A Series host, and data must be accessible by workstations as well as terminals connected to the host. Heterogeneous and distributed data access must also be addressed.

**5.1.2 Compatibility.** A major objective of SIM is to be completely compatible and integrated with Data Management System II (DMSII), a network DBMS which is used on almost all A Series systems. Existing DMSII databases must view SIM functionality as additional so that existing data and application code are preserved. Also, a migration path must be provided so that an existing DMSII database can be converted into a SIM database.

**5.1.3 Performance.** A Series systems primarily support commercial application systems that span a wide range of data processing needs. At the upper end of this range are systems that require high transaction rates (e.g., 100 transactions per second or more) and systems that access large quantities of data (e.g., 10 gigabytes of data or more). SIM must provide production-level performance for the full range of application systems found on the A Series, including those at the upper end.

**5.1.4 Data independence.** SIM is required to provide the highest degree of data independence possible so that physical database changes can be made with no impact on existing applications. Logical database changes must not affect programs whose queries are still relevant, and, when needed, query reparsing/reoptimization must be automatic.

**5.1.5 Heterogeneous data access.** SIM's initial objectives are to provide single-host access to data which resides in DMSII databases and simple data files. However, its architecture must accommodate other sources and types of data including complex data structures, transitory data such as process interfaces, and data residing on foreign hosts. The goal of this objective is to ensure that both the model and implementation architecture of SIM are flexible enough to allow an organization to use a uniform model with which it can represent and access all of its information.

These objectives form the basis on which SIM has been implemented. The most conflicting objectives are the need to address heterogeneous data access and to provide high performance. These objectives suggest an architecture which is highly modular yet highly efficient. These two criteria—modularity and performance—are considered to be the central issues for a successful implementation of a high-level DBMS. The next section presents the functional architecture of SIM, which addresses modularity requirements.

## 5.2 Functional Architecture

The basic functional architecture used for SIM is an enhanced version of the ANSI/SPARC three-schema approach [ANS75]. SIM employs the external and conceptual layers, but the proposed internal layer has been split into an interface layer and a physical layer. The resulting architecture is depicted in Figure 11.1.

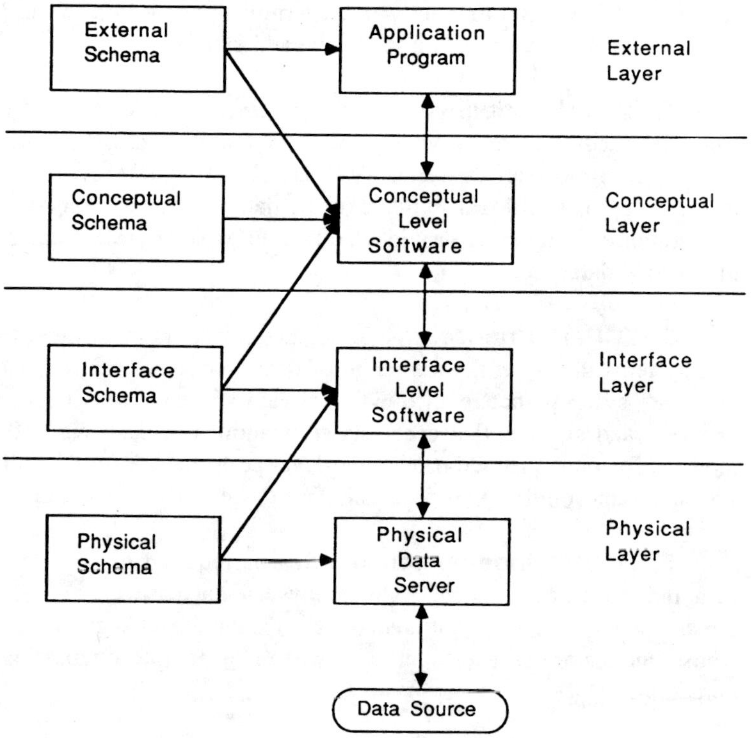


**Figure 11.1** SIM functional architecture is an enhanced version of the ANSI/SPARC three schema approach in which the lowest, internal layer has been split into an interface layer and a physical layer. Each layer possesses a schema and associated DBMS software components.

Each functional layer possesses a schema which defines the database from an increasingly lower level. Each layer also possesses certain DBMS software that is involved in creating, maintaining, or accessing the database. (Note that the ANSI/SPARC architecture defines "mapping" information which exists between each layer. This information exists within this architecture, but it is not shown here.)

The primary advantage of this architecture is that it allows an existing data server to provide as much functionality as it can for a particular data source. In many cases, the entire physical layer can be provided by an existing software system (e.g., a record-oriented database system). The external and conceptual layers of SIM are identical regardless of the type of data source used for a given database. Although SIM's interface software must be tailored for each type of data source, it need only implement the functionality not provided by the physical layer. This approach minimizes the amount of tailoring that must be performed for each type of data source that we wish to access as a SIM database.

**5.2.1 External layer.** The purpose of this layer is to provide end-user and application access to the database. Each user or application program accesses a SIM database relative to external schemas. With SIM, pre-declared external schemas are not needed for security purposes since the conceptual schema offers a declarative, predicate-oriented mechanism that causes proper security to be enforced automatically.

Instead, external schemas are dynamically defined by each submitted query. This is a result of the inherent properties (e.g., the query "perspective" and "extended" attributes) of the SIM data manipulation language. When using the InfoExec ad-hoc query products (IQF or WQF), external schemas are constructed graphically during query formation, and they may be saved in the data dictionary (ADDS) for later use. In the host language interfaces, external schemas are explicitly declared in the program source or imported from ADDS. Whether explicitly declared or imported, external schemas are defined in a language which is "tuned" to the flavor of the particular programming language involved. (The host language DML statements are also "tuned" to the flavor of each host language.)

**5.2.2 Conceptual layer.** At this level, the entire database is defined via a conceptual schema. A conceptual schema for a SIM database contains both structural definitions (e.g., generalization hierarchies, their attributes and relationships) and imperative definitions (e.g., security and integrity constraints). However, to provide data independence, the conceptual schema is completely devoid of references to record layouts or other physical storage details.

For accessing data, the conceptual level software includes query processing software. Its objectives are to parse and validate each submitted query, develop an optimized execution strategy, and control the execution of that strategy. These processes require access to the conceptual schema as well as to relevant external schemas. Note, however, that the same query processing software is used at this level regardless of the types or number of data sources used at the physical layer. Since meaningful query optimization must have some knowledge of physical details, the query processing software must attain this information from the software at the next lower level. This need to have "generalized" query processing software which yields efficient query execution regardless of data source is the prime justification for the interface layer.

**5.2.3 Interface layer.** At this level, an interface schema is generated for each database by the SIM utility program. The interface schema is defined in terms of a simpler, lower-level model than the semantic model used for the conceptual schema. The model consists of Logical Underlying Components (LUC) of which there are four types: records, record fields, indexes, and relationships. These LUC types were chosen because:

- Conceptual schema components are easily "mapped" into LUC objects of these types.
- LUC objects possess enough physical information to allow effective query optimization.
- Query processing software at the conceptual level only needs to generate operations on a limited set of structural components (i.e., limited when compared to the number of physical components that may be used).
- Collectively, these LUC types can describe—and therefore LUC objects can be mapped to—any record-oriented storage type.

The SIM utility maps each conceptual schema component into a LUC component and stores the mapping information so that it is obtainable by the interface level software. During query parsing and optimization, this information is accessible by the query processing software. The interface level software accepts commands oriented to each LUC type and translates them into appropriate commands on the appropriate physical data server.

A specific set of commands is assumed for each LUC type; hence, the interface software must know how to service each command for the data source type(s) to which it interfaces. For example, the query processing software assumes certain locking and transaction control commands. Where possible, the interface level software can exploit the presence of existing functionality from a given data server. In some cases, it must provide its own logic to supplement functionality missing from the physical layer.

**5.2.4 Physical layer.** As discussed above, this layer is provided by existing software systems wherever possible. Hence, the physical schema defined at this level is that required by the particular physical data server. The primary physical layer for SIM databases is provided by DMSII, whose physical schema is defined via a language called Data and Structure Definition Language (DASDL). The SIM utility generates the necessary DASDL source as well as other physical database components in the process of generating a DMSII- mapped SIM database. LUC-to-DASDL mapping information is stored so that it can be loaded and used by the appropriate interface software when needed.

The first release of SIM also provides access to simple data files. For this type of data source, any COBOL-like file description stored in ADDS can be used as a physical schema. The appropriate interface software dynamically translates this information into appropriate interface and conceptual schemas. The data server for this type of data source is actually the operating system's logical I/O routines.

This architecture allows a very flexible composition and distribution of a single database. What is viewed as a single SIM database at the external and conceptual levels can consist of data that is derived from multiple data sources. A single data server may distribute data within its own control, or data can be distributed at the interface level among multiple data servers, some of which may reside on foreign hosts. This architecture also allows a single query to access data within multiple databases.

## 5.3 Query Processing

The query processing architecture of SIM is derived directly from the functional architecture presented in the previous section. The software modules which comprise this architecture and their relationships are depicted in Figure 11.2. A description of the basic purpose and operation of each module is presented next.

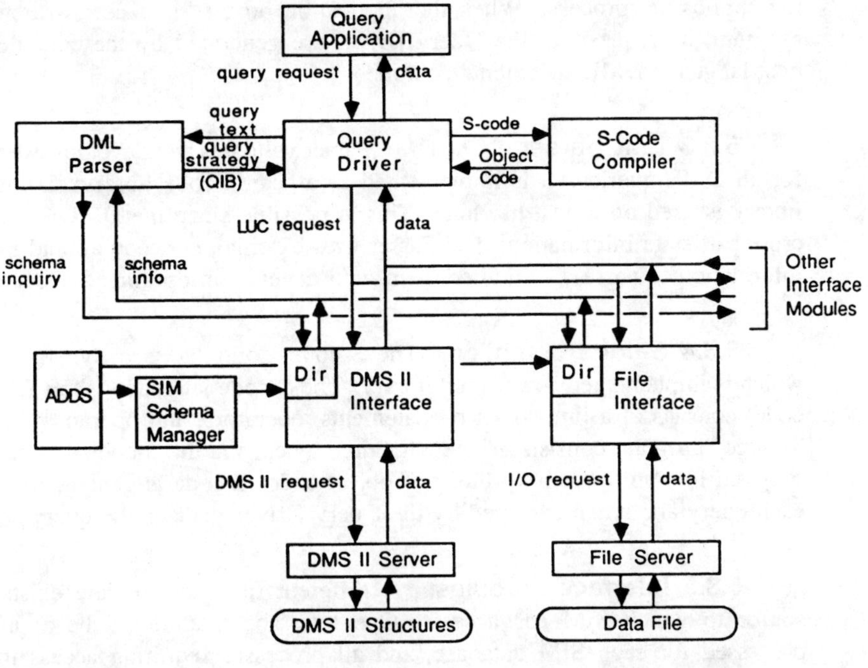


**Figure 11.2** Communication paths among software components of the InfoExec Environment. The Query Application comprises the External Layer of the Figure 11.1. The DML Parser, Query Driver, and S-Code Compiler reside in the Conceptual Layer. The Physical Layer is occupied by the DMSII DBMS software and the operating system's logical I/O functions acting as data servers.

**5.3.1 Query application.** A query application can be an ad-hoc query facility such as IQF or WQF, a host language compiler such as COBOL or Pascal, or a user-written host language program. Query applications submit separate requests to parse and/or execute DML queries, thus allowing the two processes to occur independently. Once a query is compiled, it can be executed multiple times, and multiple, simultaneous invocations (e.g., with different input parameters) are allowed.

**5.3.2 Query driver.** The Query Driver is the query application interface to SIM. It is implemented as a code library, which is the principal means of inter-program communication on A Series systems. Code libraries are similar to ADA "packages" except that they are highly efficient programs that, after initializing, "freeze" in memory and offer their services as procedural entry-points. Library services may be used by any process executing on the same host (including another library) by "importing" the library's entry-points and calling them much like a normal procedure call. A Series hardware has been designed to process these cross-program calls very efficiently.

One copy of the Query Driver is initiated for each query application process; hence, the Query Driver is private to that process. Its responsibility is to manage the query parsing and execution requests submitted by its corresponding application process. The Query Driver maintains state information for each database and query in use by the application process. When the application process is a user-written host language program, its requests to the Query Driver are generated by the compiler based on the host language DML statements compiled.

**5.3.3 DML parser.** The DML Parser validates and develops execution strategies for all DML queries. It is implemented as a shared code library: a single copy of the library is used on a host machine. This is possible since the DML Parser maintains no cross-call state information. The Parser uses external, conceptual, and interface schema information to parse a submitted query and develop an optimized execution strategy.

**5.3.4 S-code compiler.** The S-code Compiler is a dynamic code generator which is implemented as a shared library. The S-code language (short for semi-compiled code) consists of a limited set of statements, operators, and operands. A typical S-code "source" program consists of a few hundred bytes, and the S-code compiler converts this program into an in-memory block of object code. S-code is generated by the Parser for each query and when executed by the Query Driver realizes the query's execution.

**5.3.5 Interface modules.** A different Interface module exists for each data source to which SIM has access. One Interface module of the appropriate type is processed for each SIM database, and all processes requiring access to that database communicate with that Interface process. Hence, each Interface module is shared on a per-database basis. Each Interface module accepts LUC-oriented commands and translates them into appropriate calls on the underlying data server module. Each Interface module must also service schema inquiry requests from the DML Parser.

**5.3.6 Data server modules.** The Data Server modules with which Interface modules communicate are the processes which provide access to each physical data source. For DMSII-mapped databases, the DMSII Data Server is a shared-per-database library called the Accessroutines, which is a standard component of the DMSII software. For data file-mapped databases, the File Data Server is comprised of the operating system's logical I/O functions.

## 5.4 Physical Mapping Options

The high-level objects of the model are to be mapped into record-based LUC units for physical storage. SIM uses a carefully balanced set of rules to determine the mapping. The user can override the default and choose any access method or mapping supported by the underlying system. The default mappings are described below.

Classes in a tree structured generalization hierarchy are physically mapped into a storage unit with variable-format records based on record types. The number of record types needed will be equal to the number of nodes in the tree. This ensures that all immediate and inherited single-valued DVAs applicable to a class will be in one physical record. It is also efficient in terms of space. A class defined as the subclass of two or more immediate superclasses is mapped into a separate storage unit with one:one subclass links connecting it to its parent LUCs.

Multi-valued DVAs without the MAX option (unbounded) are mapped into a separate storage unit. Those with the MAX option are stored as arrays in the same physical record with their owner.

One:one EVAs are mapped based on foreign-keys. Many:many and one:many EVAs are mapped into a storage unit termed the Common EVA Structure. This structure has records of the form ⟨surrogate1⟩ ⟨relationship-id⟩ ⟨surrogate2⟩. The surrogates can be direct keys (record number), random keys (based on hashing) or index sequential keys. Separate Common EVA structures are created for Distinct and non-Distinct EVAs. This default mapping for EVAs was chosen to avoid additional index structures that will be needed with a foreign-key based mapping. There are a variety of ways in which EVAs can be mapped, including absolute addresses and embedded structures. The mapping of EVAs is the key factor in determining SIM's performance.

User-declared attributes which are Unique and Required can be defined to be the surrogate of a class. By default, the system will create its own surrogate attribute.

## 5.5 Parsing and Optimization

A query application submits a DML query in the form of a free- form command string to a parse-DML entry-point in the Query Driver. The query is assigned a unique query number used to identify it. The DML text is passed to the DML Parser along with a database table that indicates which databases are currently opened by the program, query options such as formatting requirements particular to the program, and security information relevant to the program. The database table allows a single SIM retrieval query to reference information in more than one database.

While parsing a query, the DML Parser retrieves conceptual and interface schema information by performing schema inquiry requests to the appropriate Interface modules. Schema information is used both to validate the query and to add LUC information to the query tree as it is built.

SIM optimizes a query by building a query graph (whose nodes are LUC objects), enumerating strategies, estimating the cost of processing for each strategy and choosing the one with the least cost. We have extended relational query optimization techniques to handle generalization hierarchies, EVAs and the perspective-oriented ordering and duplicate value semantics [Day82] implied by the DML. For example, when listing students and their courses, DML implies an implicit ordering of output based on student surrogates. Transformation of a query graph for a strategy is tested to see if it is semantics-preserving, and, if it is not, the cost of reordering/sorting output is added to the cost of a strategy. Cardinality of LUCs and relationships, blocking factors, indexes and the cost of accessing the first and subsequent instances of a relationship are some of the optimization parameters used. This technique enables the Optimizer to do its job without considering physical mapping details. For example, the I/O cost of accessing the first instance of a relationship will be 0 if the relationship is implemented by clustering and 1 block access if it is implemented by absolute addresses (pointers). Statistical optimization is not fully implemented yet.

S-code and other information generated by the Parser are returned to the Query Driver in a data structure called the Query Information Block (QIB). The Query Driver saves each QIB in local memory as it is generated. If the query application is an ad-hoc query facility, such as IQF or WQF, each query is normally executed immediately after it is parsed. In this case, QIBs are only saved for the duration of the query application process. However, if the query application is a host language compiler, all QIBs generated during the compilation are saved in the code file generated by the compiler. When the application program is executed, its QIBs are loaded from its code file into the local memory of its Query Driver.

### 5.6 Query Execution

To execute a query, the query application must first establish a query cursor by calling the open-cursor entry-point in the Query Driver. The query number of the desired query and any applicable input parameters are passed in, and the Query Driver passes back a cursor number which uniquely identifies the query cursor.

For retrieval queries, the query application then calls a retrieve-data entry-point, passing in the appropriate cursor number and a data buffer. For each retrieve-data call, the Query Driver constructs one record of data and returns it in the given data buffer. Each record is associated with some entity in the query's perspective. The query cursor's number can then be passed as an input parameter to some other query, thus providing a method of referencing the "current" entity of one query in another query.

For update queries, the query application calls a process- update entry-point passing in only the appropriate cursor number. The Query Driver then processes the query to completion, updating all relevant entities before returning back to the user.

To facilitate coordination between the Query Driver and the Interface modules, a cursor protocol is used similar to the query cursor protocol. The cursors used between the Query Driver and an Interface module are called LUC cursors and they operate on LUC objects. A specific set of commands is used to manipulate LUC cursors corresponding to each LUC type.

### 5.7 Integrity Checking

Integrity constraints are classified into three categories depending on when they are checked. Immediate constraints are checked as soon as the update is made. Range constraints on DVAs are examples of these. Constraints in the second category are invoked at the end of the update statement while those in the third are invoked at the end of the transaction. Unique constraint on a DVA and Required constraint on a reflexive EVA are examples of these, respectively.

The interface modules assure the structural integrity of data reflected in class interconnections. For example, when a record of a superclass is deleted, the module will automatically delete corresponding subclass records and delete instances of all EVAs the deleted records participate in. Structural integrity is maintained by the Interface Modules for performance reasons. For example, if class and subclass records are mapped into one physical record, the module will perform one delete instead of the two operations that may be needed otherwise. Integrity constraints specified by the user as ASSERTs are handled by the Parser/Optimizer using query augmentation techniques.

## 6. CONCLUSION AND FUTURE DEVELOPMENTS

We have described SIM, a database system based on the semantic data model. SIM provides a conceptually natural view of data by moving away from the notational simplicity of modeling with a minimally complete set of constructs. Entities, generalization hierarchies, schema-defined interobject relationships and integrity constraints are the key concepts of the model. The DML of this system is designed to take advantage of and directly support these features. The DML notions of perspective and qualification by EVAs are a natural complement to the system's schema definition features.

Our experience with a large number of test databases is testimony to the power and utility of the concepts mentioned before. The stand-alone data dictionary ADDS is itself a SIM database. It consists of 13 base classes, 209 subclasses, 39 EVA- inverse pairs, 530 DVAs and at its deepest, one hierarchy represents 5 levels of generalization.

We are currently working on several extensions to the model. Work under progress includes the design of a view mechanism, derived attributes, system-maintained ordering of classes and EVAs, temporal data, efficient algorithms for various categories of integrity constraints and experiments in quantifying the naturalness and ease of use of DDL and DML concepts.

## APPENDIX A - EXAMPLE SCHEMA

The example schema for the University data base is described below in SIM's conceptual data description language (called DDL) and presented graphically in Figure 11.3.

```
TYPE Degree              = SYMBOLIC (BS, MBA, MS, PHD);
TYPE ID-Number           = INTEGER (1001..39999,60001..99999);

CLASS Person
 (Name                   : STRING[30];
  Soc-Sec-No             : INTEGER, UNIQUE, REQUIRED;
  Birthdate              : DATE;
  Spouse                 : Person INVERSE IS Spouse;
```

```
  Profession                  : SUBROLE (Student, Instructor) MV;
);

SUBCLASS Student OF Person
 (Student-id                  : ID-Number;
  Gpa                         : NUMBER[4,2];
  Advisor                     : Instructor INVERSE IS Advisees;
  Instructor-Status           : SUBROLE (Teaching-Assistant);
  Courses-Enrolled            : Course INVERSE IS Students-Enrolled
                                MV (DISTINCT);
  Major-Department            : Department;
);
VERIFY Full-Load ON Student
  ASSERT SUM(Credits of Courses-Enrolled) ≥ 12
  ELSE "Student is taking too few credits";

SUBCLASS Instructor of Person
  CLASS-ATTRIBUTES (
    Maximum-Salary            : INTEGER;
    Instructor-Count          : INTEGER;)
 (Employee-id                 : ID-Number UNIQUE REQUIRED;
  Salary                      : NUMBER[9,2];
  Bonus                       : NUMBER[9,2];
  Student-Status              : SUBROLE(Teaching-Assistant);
  Advisees                    : Student INVERSE ID Advisor MV (MAX 10);
  Courses-Taught              : Course INVERSE IS Teachers
                                MV (MAX 3, DISTINCT);
  Assigned-Department         : Department INVERSE IS
                                Instructors-Employed;
);

VERIFY Valid-Salary ON Instructor
  ASSERT Salary + Bonus < 100000
  ELSE "Instructor makes too much money";

SUBCLASS Teaching-Assistant OF Student AND Instructor
  (Teaching-Load              : INTEGER (1..20);
  );

CLASS Course
 (Course-No                   : INTEGER (1..9999) UNIQUE REQUIRED;
  Title                       : STRING[30] REQUIRED;
  Credits                     : INTEGER (1..15) REQUIRED;
  Students-Enrolled           : Student INVERSE IS
                                Courses-Enrolled MV;
  Teachers                    : Instructor INVERSE IS
                                Courses-Taught MV (MAX 7);
  Prerequisites               : Course INVERSE IS Prerequisite-Of MV;
  Prerequisite-Of             : Course INVERSE IS Prerequisites MV;
);

CLASS Department
 (Dept-Nbr                    : INTEGER(100..999) REQUIRED UNIQUE;
  Name                        : STRING[30] REQUIRED;
  Instructors-Employed        : Instructor INVERSE IS
                                Assigned-Department MV;
  Courses-Offered             : Course MV;
  );
```

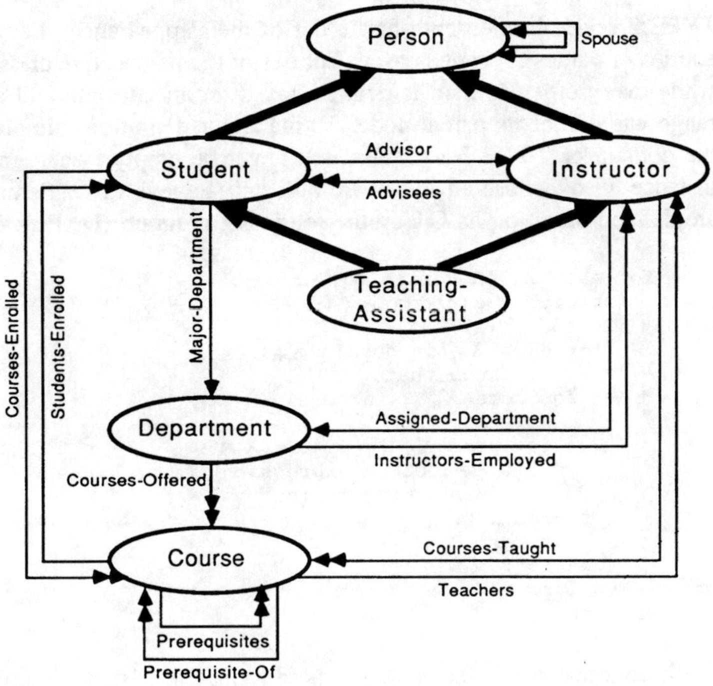


**Figure 11.3** Graphical representation of the University schema used throughout the text and described in Appendix A. Classes and subclasses are represented by ellipses, and the bold arrows show the generalization hierarchy relationships among them with arrowheads pointing to superclasses. Smaller arrows depict entity-valued attributes (EVAs) that model relationships between entities. Multi-valued EVAs are indicated by double arrowheads. Paired arrows represent declared inverse EVA pairs; inverses of single EVAs are available via the INVERSE function.

## APPENDIX B - SEMANTICS OF RETRIEVE QUERIES

This section presents a more in depth description of the query trees created by the SIM parser and is intended for more advanced readers.

Assume for the moment that queries are allowed to have only one perspective class. We can construct a tree QT such that its nodes, $X_1, X_2 ... X_n$, represent implicit or explicit range variables and its edges represent EVAs or multi-valued DVAs. The root of this tree ($X_1$) is the range variable of the perspective class. Qualification of every attribute in a query results in it being associated with one range variable in QT. Label each variable $X_i$ in QT as follows: label it "TYPE 3" if it and all its descendants are used only in the target list of the query and not in its selection expression; label it "TYPE 2" if it and all its descendants are used only in the selection expression of the query and not in its target list; label it "TYPE 1" otherwise. $X_1$ is always labeled TYPE 1. Without loss of generality, we can assume that $X_1, X_2 .. X_m, m <= n$, are either TYPE 1 or TYPE 3 nodes in the depth-first order of their appearance in QT and $X_{m+1} ... X_n$, are the

TYPE 2 nodes in the depth-first order of their appearance. Let domain($X_i$) denote the entities or values $X_i$ ranges over. Entities of the perspective class constitute domain($X_1$) while every other domain is defined based on an attribute and a given instance of the range variable of its parent node. To make our definitions simpler, we will assume that the domain of TYPE 3 variables will never be empty (when empty, adding a dummy instance all of whose attributes are null will achieve this). Semantics of a DML query are defined based on its QT by the following program (DAPLEX notation):

```
for each X1 in domain(X1)
  for each X2 in domain(X2)
        ...
    for each Xm in domain(Xm)
            such that
      for some Xm+1 in domain(Xm+1)
              ...
        for some Xn in domain(Xn)
          if ⟨selection expression⟩ is true then
            print ⟨target list⟩
        end for;
      end for;
    end for;
  end for;
end for;
```

Note that the order in which these loops are nested prescribes the order in which the output data is returned. Such an ordering is a direct consequence of the notion of perspective. The output of the program above is termed "fully tabular", in which one format describes every output record. SIM provides other forms of output that impose additional structuring on the output. They provide multiple record formats, and every output record is described by one of these formats. In the "fully structured" case, the number of different output formats is equal to the count of TYPE 1 and TYPE 3 variables in the query. Such forms of output are particularly useful in the host language interfaces to SIM (the details are omitted from here).

Multiple perspective classes can be handled as a cross product with minor extensions to the program above.

# 12

# Managing Change in Computer-Aided Design Databases*

**R. H. Katz and E. Chang**

*Computer Science Division*
*Electrical Engineering and Computer Science Department*
*University of California, Berkeley*

## ABSTRACT

Object-oriented concepts can make a design database more *reactive* to changes in its contents. By embedding change semantics in the database model, the design engineer can be relieved of managing the detailed effects of changes. However, mechanisms are needed to limit the scope of change propagation and to unambiguously identify the objects to which propagated changes should apply. We propose new mechanisms, based on group check-in/check-out, browser contexts and paths, configuration constraints, and rules, to support a powerful automatic change capability within a design database.

*Key Words and Phrases:* Object-oriented data models; Computer-aided design databases; Inheritance; Change propagation; Constraint propagation

*Research supported under N.S.F. grants ECS-8403004 and ECS-8352227, with matching support from the Microelectronics and Computer Technology Corporation.



*Source*: Adapted from Katz, R., and E. Chang, "Managing Change in Computer-Aided Design Databases", Proceedings of the International Conference on Very Large Databases, September 1987, pp. 455–462.

# 1. INTRODUCTION

Object-oriented [Gol83] concepts, as embodied in such systems as Smalltalk-80, LOOPS, and Flavors, are becoming pervasive throughout computer science. They provide an appealing way to structure applications and their data. An emerging consensus is that an object-oriented approach can simplify the applications that create and manipulate computer-aided design data. Several groups are using these concepts to structure a CAD database (e.g., [Atw85,Bat85a,Har86,Lan86]), as well as databases for office applications [Zdo84].

The elements of the object-oriented approach appear to include: (i) types (classes), in which operations (methods) on data are packaged with the data itself, (ii) inheritance, in which default procedure definitions and values are propagated from types to instances, and (iii) generic operation invocation, via message passing. For us, the first two concepts are the most important: "object-oriented" means abstract data types with inheritance.

*Inheritance* provides scoping for data and operation definitions through a taxonomic hierarchy of instances belonging to types, which in turn belong to supertypes (i.e., types of types). If a variable is accessed from an instance, and is not defined there, then its associated type is searched for the definition. If it is not defined in the type, the process recurses to the supertype and so on until the root of the lattice. More advanced models allow types to be instances of multiple supertypes (i.e., "mix-ins"), where one supertype's definition of a common variable must be specified to dominate the others.

In this paper, we are particularly interested in how object-oriented concepts can be used to manage change and constraint propagation in a design database. For example, inheritance provides an ability to define default values (for example, in a type) that can be locally overridden (in an instance). It can also be used to determine the constraints that apply to new versions. The goal is to embed change semantics within the database structure, so the system can react to changes automatically.

Most previous work has dealt with change *notification* rather than *propagation.* [Neu82] defined a transaction model for a database of independent and derived design objects. The database is not consistent until changes to independent objects are propagated to their associated derived objects, although the system does not propagate these itself. [Wie82] proposed a mechanism for flagging records that might be affected by a change in a CODASYL-structured design database. It works by traversing backwards from a changed record, recursively marking its ancestors up to the roots of any hierarchies that contain it. [Bat85b,Cho86] developed a more sophisticated change notification mechanism within an object-oriented data model. It uses time stamps to limit the range of objects to be flagged in response to a change. A related object is flagged only if it has an older timestamp. In these works, only very limited change propagation is supported. For example, a change propagates from a component to its immediate composite, but no further. There has been little discussion of how to handle ambiguity in the set of propagated changes. We concentrate on these new issues in this paper.

The rest of the paper is organized as follows. Section 2 contains an overview of a version data model, implemented in our prototype Version Server. In Section 3, we describe changes in a computer-aided design database in terms of default values, change propagation, and constraint propagation. An example demonstrating the interplay among these concepts is given in Section 4. Ways of disambiguating the required set of changes are given in Section 5. Section 6 discusses some implementation issues. Section 7 contains our summary and conclusions.

## 2. A VERSION DATA MODEL

The model described in this section has been implemented in a system called the *Version Server* [Kat86a,Kat86b]. It manages units of design called *design objects*, which roughly correspond to the named design files found in conventional design environments. In the following discussion, we call these "representation objects". They are uniquely denoted by *object-name[version#].type*. In addition, the Version Server introduces special "structural objects" with which to organize these representational objects, much as directories are used to organize files in file systems.

The Version Server recognizes three possible relationships among design objects: *version histories, configurations*, and *equivalences*. Version histories maintain **is-a-descendent-of** and **is-an-ancestor-of** relationships among version instances of the same real world object (e.g., ALU[4].layout **is-a-descendent-of** ALU[3].layout, both of which are versions of ALU.layout). A structural *version object* is associated with each collection of version instances. Structural *configuration objects* relate composite representational objects to their components via **is-a-component-of** and **is-composed-of** relationships. Finally, equivalences identify objects across types that are constrained to be different representations of the same real world object, e.g., ALU[2].layout **is-equivalent-to** ALU[3].schematic if these are different representations of the same ALU design. More generally, equivalences can denote arbitrary dependencies among representational objects. They are explicitly represented by structural *equivalence objects*. The Version Server relationships are summarized in Figure 12.2.1 and the associated data structure is given in Figure 12.2.2.

Operationally, the Version Server supports a workspace model. Designers *check-out* objects from shared archives into their private workspaces. Changes made in private workspaces are not visible to other designers until such objects are *checked-in* to a shared group workspace, where the changes can be integrated with other designers' work. Finally, the modified object is returned as a new version to the shared archive. The Validation Subsystem, invoked on object check-in, analyzes a log of verification events to ensure that the object has been successfully validated before it can be added to the archive. A Browser supports the interactive examination of Version Server databases.

## 3. REACTING TO CHANGES

### 3.1 Scope and Ambiguity

Database system implementors have always been reluctant to provide automatic change propagation, because users rarely understand the full (and potentially dangerous) effects of spawned changes. However, aspects of design databases can simplify these

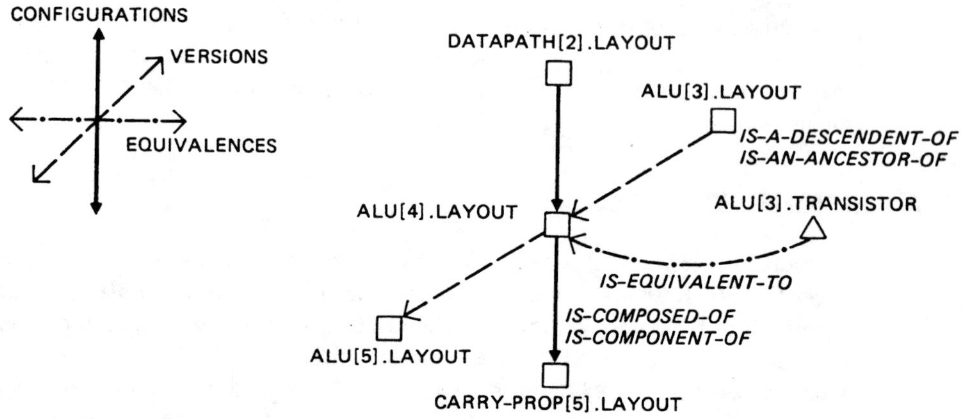


**Figure 12.2.1** *Version server logical data model.* Design data is organized as a collection of typed and versioned design objects, interrelated by configuration, version, and equivalence relationships. Only representational objects are shown. For example, ALU[4].layout is descended from ALU[3].layout and is the ancestor of ALU[5].layout. It is also a component of DATAPATH[2].layout and is composed of CARRY-PROPAGATE [5].layout. Additionally, ALU[4].layout is equivalent to other objects, such as ALU[3] .transistor.

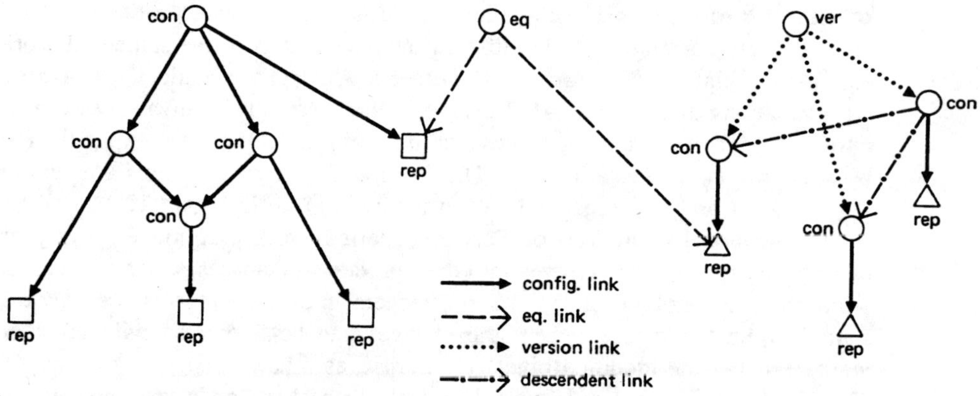


**Figure 12.2.2** *Version server physical data structure.* Circular objects are structural; square and triangular objects are representational. Relationships are actually implemented by interconnected structural objects, which indirectly reference representation objects. The structural objects are *con, ver,* and *eq,* for configuration, version, and equivalence relationships respectively.

problems. Since the design database is append-only, the correct response to change is to spawn new versions of related objects and to incorporate these into new configurations. Note that any new objects are created in private or group workspaces, never in an archive space. Since validation must be performed before these new versions are added to an archive, change propagation can never corrupt the "released" copies that reside there.

However, it is still possible to create a large number of useless intermediate versions. Mechanisms are needed to *limit the scope* of the propagation and *disambiguate* its effects. Ideally, the scope should be limited to the smallest set of objects "directly" affected by the change. Ambiguity is introduced if there is more than one way to incorporate the new versions into configurations. In the worst case, the cross-product of possible configurations could be added to the database, wasting both time and space.

### 3.2 Default Values

One of the simplest ways to change a design database is by adding to it a new version of an existing object. The designer can fill in its attributes and relationships at its creation time, but it is better if the system can fill these in automatically. Inheritance provides the necessary mechanism. For example, consider the "type" of ALU layouts. All instances of ALU layouts share much in common, perhaps their interface descriptions, or the operations (i.e., add, subtract, etc.) they support. This common data can be factored out of the instances and stored with the type. In creating new instances of the ALU layout, these common attributes can be inherited without being explicitly specified.

However, Smalltalk-style type-instance inheritance provides only one of many possible ways to propagate defaults to a new version. There are four different kinds of inheritance within the Version Server data model, which can conceivably vary on an instance by instance basis: (i) from version objects to version instances (i.e., the type-instance inheritance mentioned above), (ii) from ancestor to descendent (this is how the Version Server currently operates, since a new version begins as a copy of its ancestor), (iii) from composite object to component (where a version is used within the design hierarchy can determine the value of some of its attributes), and (iv) from equivalent to other equivalents. The propagation of information need not be limited to data; new object instances can inherit constraints, such as equivalence constraints, from their related objects.

### 3.3 Change Propagation

Once a new version instance is created, it must be incorporated into new configurations to be made part of the design. In most systems (including our prototype Version Server), these new configurations must be laboriously constructed by hand. *Change propagation* is the process that incorporates new versions into configurations automatically. Consider an object A that has been checked out from the archive to create a new version $A'$. At check-in time, new configuration objects could be created, that form a new configuration of the objects that formerly contained A as a component or subcomponent, but should now contain $A'$. If the propagations only go up a single level in the configuration hierarchy, then this is essentially the proposal of [Cho86].

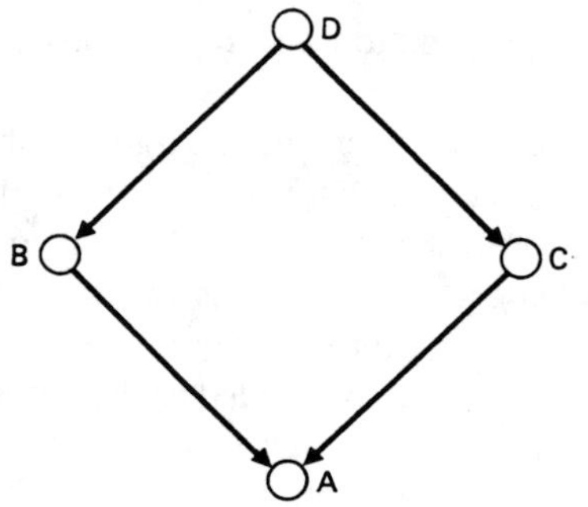


**Figure 12.3.1** *Configuration example.* Object D is composed of objects B and C. Both B and C use instances of A. Only configuration objects are shown to keep the figures simple. Note that each would contain a reference to a particular representation object.

However, it is desirable to propagate changes even further, but this requires additional mechanisms to limit the extent of changes and to keep them unambiguous. For example, consider the configuration of Figure 12.3.1. Object D is configured from objects B and C, which in turn share an object A (only configuration objects are shown). If a new version of object A is created, and changes are naively propagated along both paths, then there are two possible resulting configurations shown in Figure 12.3.2. This has been called the "multiple path problem" in [Mit86]. Either both paths of changes are merged into a single new configuration of D or two separate new configurations are spawned, one incorporating $A'$ in each of the two original uses of A (i.e., the use of A in B and in C respectively). In general, the former is to be preferred, but there are cases when the latter is what the designer intended. For example, some integrated circuit layout editors support editing in context, which allows a cell to be changed everywhere it is used, or alternatively, just within its current editing context. We will discuss mechanisms to disambiguate changes in Section 5.

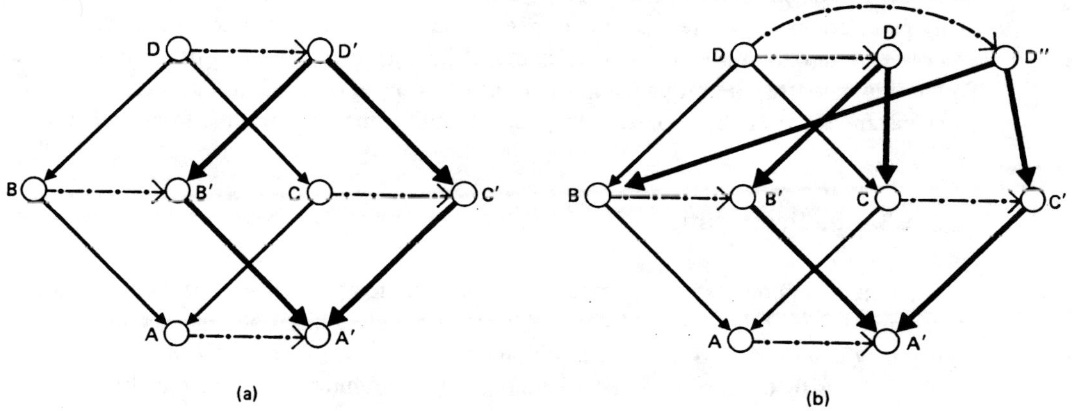


**Figure 12.3.2** *Ambiguous change propagation.* A new version of A, $A'$, causes new configurations of B and C to be created through change propagation. Configuration (a) has merged these new objects into a single new configuration of D. Configuration (b) has evolved separate configurations of D to incorporate the changed components B and C. $D'$ contains the new B and the old C, while $D''$ contains the new C and the old B. The broken arrows represent descendent linkages.

### 3.4 Constraint Propagation

Equivalence relationships model dependency constraints among objects, especially across representations. A new version inherits the equivalences of its ancestor at check-out time. Equivalence is interpreted in terms of the execution of a sequence of CAD verification programs whose success demonstrates that the objects are indeed equivalent. This condition is checked by the Version Server's validation subsystem [Bha86].

The system currently supports passive enforcement: object check-in fails if any equivalence constraints are left unsatisfied. The obvious extension is to support *active* enforcement by actually executing the validation script to create a new version of the constrained object. For example, if a schematic object and a netlist object are *actively constrained* to be equivalent, then equivalence is enforced by executing a netlist generator to create a new netlist version when the revised schematic is checked-in. The spawned netlist version becomes a descendent of the original netlist object. Changes to actively enforced constraints are the only kinds allowed to propagate to configurations of other representations. In other words, if the constraint between objects A and B is passively enforced, then a check-in of a new version of A will not spawn a check-out of B. Of course, the new version of A could not be checked-in unless its equivalence constraint with B had been satisfied.

## 4. A DETAILED EXAMPLE

The ideas presented above are developed more formally in the process of working through a specific example. Figure 12.4.1 shows initial configurations of square and triangle objects. These are used as icons for representational types, while circles stand for structural objects. Descendent linkages are not shown, to keep the figures uncluttered. The first step is for a designer to check-out A to create a new version $A'$. $A'$ will *inherit* certain attributes and relationships from its ancestor or objects related to it. Figure 12.4.2 shows that $A'$ has inherited the equivalence relationship between A and D. We will assume that this relationship represents an active constraint between square objects and triangle

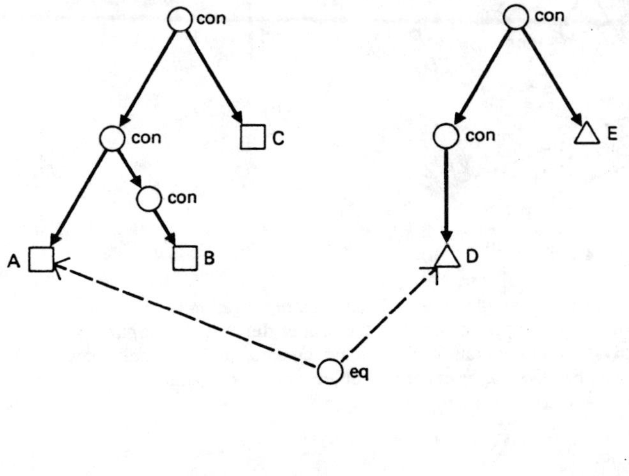


**Figure 12.4.1** *Initial conditions.* The initial condition has two simple configuration hierarchies, of square and triangle objects respectively, and a single *active* equivalence constraint between them.

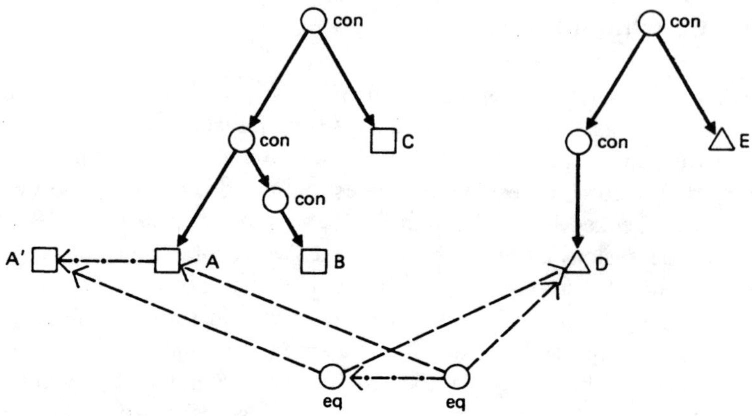


**Figure 12.4.2** *New version of object.* A new version of A is created, $A'$. Note how $A'$ *inherits* the equivalence constraint from its version ancestor.

objects, i.e., there is a procedure (or set of rules) that describes how to create a new triangle object from a changed square object.

The check-in of the new version $A'$ causes *change propagation.* New configuration objects are spawned to incorporate $A'$ and affect composites up through the root of the configuration hierarchy. The effects are shown in Figure 12.4.3. Since the constraint between $A'$ and D is actively enforced, a new version of D, $D'$, must be generated. The equivalence relationship is modified to reference this new version. The result is given in Figure 12.4.4. Finally change propagation must be performed for the configurations that contain D. This is shown in Figure 12.4.5.

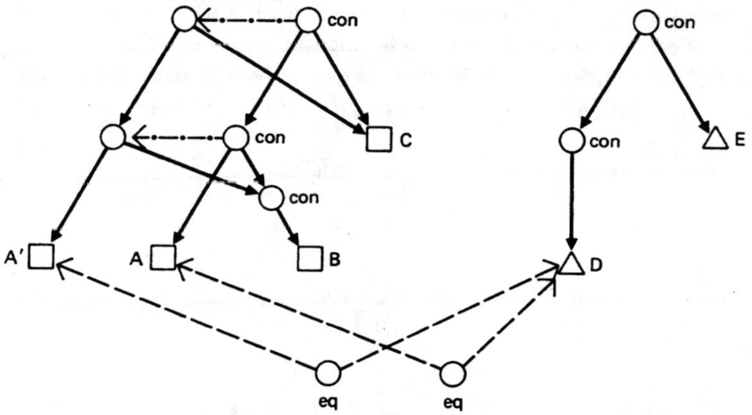


**Figure 12.4.3** *New configuration incorporating $A'$.* Change propagation is realized by spawning new configuration objects upwards towards the root of the square configuration hierarchy. Note that only new configuration objects are created, and that only new descendent links are shown. Existing representational objects are not modified.

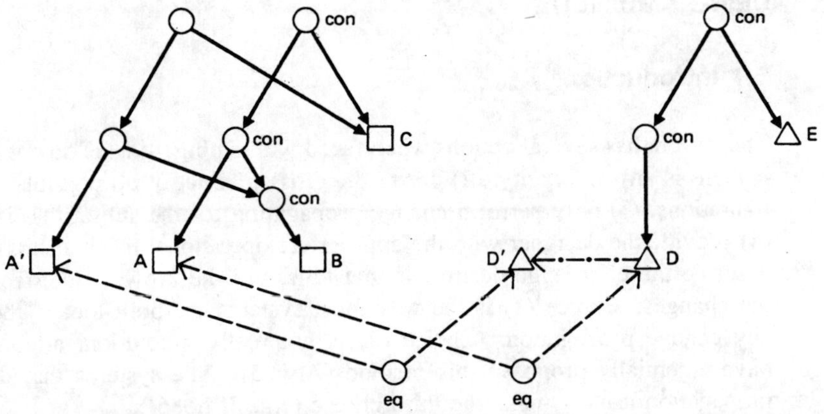


**Figure 12.4.4** *Constraint propagation to D*. Since the equivalence constraint is *actively* enforced, a new version of D must be spawned. Note how the equivalence object now points to $D'$. Only the new D -⟩ $D'$ descendent link is shown.

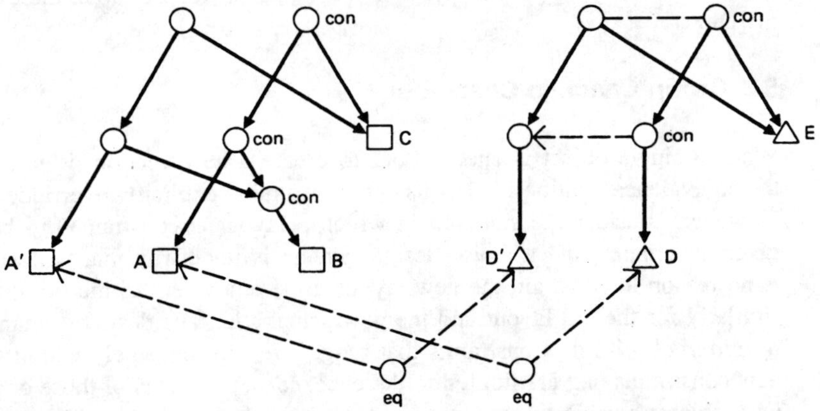


**Figure 12.4.5** *New configuration incorporating* $D'$. Finally, change propagation is once again invoked to spawn new configurations incorporating $D'$. Only the new descendent links are shown.

In addition to the multiple path problem already described, the interaction between change and constraint propagation can result in ambiguous configurations. Consider what would happen if object A and E are both checked out for update. If A′ and $E'$ are checked back independently, two new triangle configurations will be created: one containing the old D and the new $E'$ and another containing the new $D'$ and the old E. Note that the resulting configurations are independent of the order of the check-ins. However, if $A'$ and $E'$ are checked in as a group, then a single new configuration containing both $D'$ and $E'$ should be made. Group check-in as a method for disambiguating changes will be discussed in Section 5.2.

## 5. HANDLING AMBIGUITY

### 5.1 Introduction

The system has several options when faced with ambiguity: (1) do not propagate changes if there is any ambiguity, (2) create the cross product of all possible unambiguous configurations, (3) only perform change propagation for the subset that is unambiguous, or (4) provide the designer with the appropriate operational mechanisms to unambiguously describe the effect s/he desires; if that fails, use the browser interface to disambiguate the changes. Choice (1) is the way most systems are built today: they do not support any change propagation. Choice (2) is not really a solution, although some systems have essentially proposed this method [Atw85]. The systems that do support change propagation usually make the third choice (e.g., [Cho86]).

In this section, we examine the possible mechanisms for the last choice. Rather than propose a single general purpose approach, we concentrate on more specific "user-oriented" mechanisms. The idea is to provide change propagation effects that make sense to the designers who will be using the system. These may be implemented on top of the same underlying general purpose mechanisms, for example, the events and triggers of [Dit84].

### 5.2 Group Check-in/Check-out

When a single object is checked-out to create a new version, it automatically inherits the equivalence relationships of its ancestor, unless explicitly overridden by the designer. However, consider the situation in which a layout is constrained to be equivalent to a given schematic, and a major design change is underway that will affect both. There is no reason to constrain the new layout to be equivalent to the original schematic, and similarly for the old layout and the new schematic. The desired semantics are provided by *group check-out*. Constraints that range over objects solely within the group lead to new constraints that are limited to the checked-out versions of those objects. Constraints with objects outside the group are inherited in the usual way. Thus, a group check-out of the layout and schematic objects would yield an equivalence constraint between the new versions of the layout and schematic, but no constraints would exist between them and the original versions in the archive.

*Group check-in* is like a transaction, in that the objects in the group should be added to the database as an atomic unit. In effect, any spawned configurations should merge changes from all members of the group, rather than create new configurations for each. In other words, no more than one new version of a configuration object is created during group check-in, no matter how many change paths touch the configuration it is derived from. The difference between group and conventional check-ins is shown in Figure 12.5.1.

As long as there is at most one new version of each representation object being checked-in, group check-in is guaranteed to result in an unambiguous final configuration. The sketch of the proof is as follows. At most one new instance can be added for each

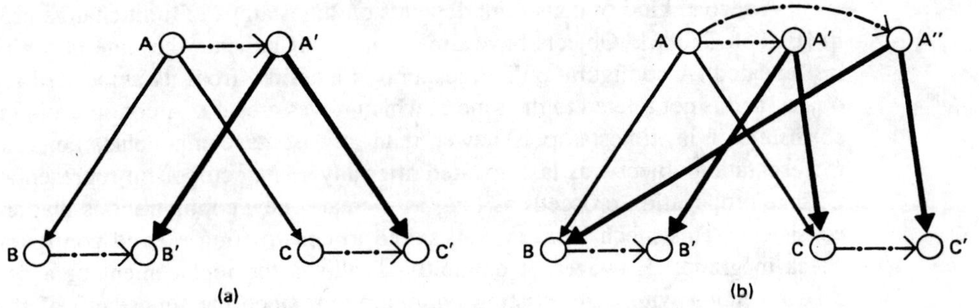


**Figure 12.5.1** *Group vs. non-group check-ins.* Configuration (i) illustrates the result of Check-in ($B'$, $C'$). Configuration (ii) shows what happens when Check-in ($B'$) is followed by Check-in ($C'$).

existing object, either as the result of change propagation (i.e., a new configuration object is spawned) or constraint propagation (i.e., a new representation object version is created as the result of an actively enforced equivalence constraint). It follows that the arcs out of new configuration instances can change at most once. There are two cases. At the time a new configuration object is first created, its arcs either point at old objects that may be superceded later or they already point at the new instances. In the first case, the arcs should change once the new instances are created. In the second case, they need never change during the duration of the check-in. Since each arc changes at most once, the order in which new instances are generated is irrelevant. The same final configuration is obtained.

## 5.3 Configuration Constraints

A mechanism for limiting change propagation is *configuration constraints*. Several kinds are possible: (1) dependency status constraints, (2) timestamp constraints, (3) interface constraints, and (4) containment and partitioning constraints. This list is meant to illustrate the kinds of constraints that are reasonable to associate with configuration objects. It is not meant to be exhaustive. Of course it is possible to associate more than one such constraint with a configuration object. We will discuss each kind in turn.

The simplest kind of configuration constraint relies on a simple status attribute associated with each configuration object. The value of this attribute can either be *dependent* or *independent*, not unlike independent and derived representations in [Neu82]. A dependent configuration is one that cannot exist outside another configuration. Change propagation proceeds through dependent configurations, stopping at the first independent configuration it encounters. The designers must incorporate new independent configurations into higher level composites by hand. The first instance of a configuration defaults to being independent, unless explicitly overridden by the designer. Spawned instances can inherit the value of their dependency status in any of the ways described in Section 3.2. Unless changed by the designers, the default inheritance is from their immediate ancestor configurations.

A second kind of constraint depends on timestamps to limit change propagation, as in [Bat85b,Cho86]. Objects have timestamps that indicate the time at which they were last updated. A configuration's timestamp is inherited from its associated representation object, and is not related to the time at which it was created. A configuration is *timestamp consistent* if its timestamp is newer than any of its components, i.e., the composite representation object was last updated after any of its component representation objects. Change propagation proceeds as long as it creates new configurations that are timestamp consistent. This mechanism is well-suited to constructing a valid configuration from a check-in group. However, it explicitly disallows the replacement of a component by a new version within an existing configuration, since the timestamp of the composite representation object will be older than the new version.

*Interface constraints* depend on the internal details of representation objects. We say that the interface of a new version is *compatible* with its ancestor's interface if it is possible to replace the ancestor in any existing configuration with the new version. The easiest way to ensure compatibility is for the designers to guarantee that the interface portion of the object has not changed across versions. This may be overly conservative since minor changes may not result in an incompatible interface. One can imagine representation-dependent programs that could determine the compatibility of a new version's interface. Change propagation stops when it would attempt to create a configuration from a version whose interface is incompatible with its ancestor.

The last constraint is *representation-dependent containment*. In general, a composite object's configuration is consistent if its components are properly contained within it. This is easy to verify if the representation type defines intersection operations: the intersection of each component with the composite should be the component itself. For example, consider a design type that associates a bounding box with each object, and defines an intersection operation on that box. If a component's bounding box is not properly contained within its associated composite, then the configuration is inconsistent. A related concept is a *partitioning constraint*, i.e., the pairwise intersection of each component is the empty set. Change can be propagated up the configuration hierarchy as long as these constraints are satisfied, and stopped as soon as a violation is detected.

## 5.4 Browser Paths and Contexts

The propagation of changes is unambiguous as long as each node along the path to the root of the configuration is not referenced from more than one place. When a node is used more than once, as for A in Figure 12.3.1, then information from the context in which the original was checked-out can be used to disambiguate the change propagation. *Check-in* ($A'$), without further specification, would result in configuration (i) of Figure 12.3.2. If A were checked-out along the path D → B → A, then a *Check-in* ($A'$) *along check-out path* would create the configuration rooted at $D'$ in configuration (ii). If the check-out had been along the path D → C → A, then the configuration rooted at $D''$ would be the result. A designer can specify a path explicitly or s/he can select it graphically by using the browser to choose the appropriate configuration arcs. Using the latter method, it is possible to check-in an object along multiple paths. This is particularly useful for

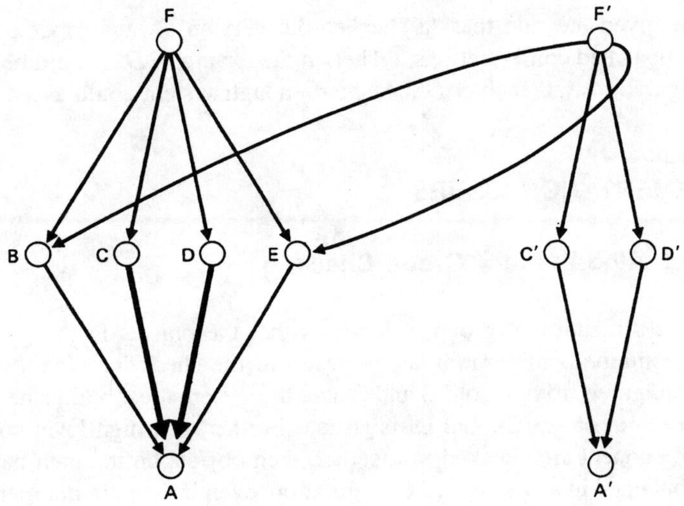


**Figure 12.5.2** *Check-in along selected paths.* Object A is used in four places in the configuration. A new version $A'$ is created, but is to be checked in along the selected paths, which are highlighted (it is possible to select these paths by interacting with the browser prior to check-in). The resulting configuration, rooted at $D'$, is shown on the right. Only the two middle uses of A have been replaced by $A'$.

objects that are used many places in the design, but the change should be propagated to only a portion of these. An example is shown in Figure 12.5.2.

Besides disambiguating the path of changes, browser information can limit the scope of changes through the *browser context.* The browser already implements mechanisms for pruning the complex design structure before presentation to the designer. Taking into account the structure of the configuration hierarchy, the browser heuristically determines the neighborhood of interest around an object being browsed. Change propagation can be limited to this neighborhood by issuing a *check-in within context* command.

Figure 12.4.5 demonstrates that the browsing context by itself is not enough to limit change propagation, because of the effects of constraint propagation across representations. In the figure, the triangle objects need not have been involved in any browser operations involving the original square object A. Mechanisms like configuration constraints must work with contexts to limit the propagation.

## 5.5 Rule-based Methods

There remains one case in which group check-in does not guarantee an unambiguous result. Consider the example of Section 4, and the case where A and D are checked-out for change, even though D is normally derived from A through an active constraint. A handcrafted version $D''$ will be created in parallel with the automatically propagated $D'$. Even if $A'$ and $D''$ are checked-in as a group, the system needs to disambiguate which of $D'$ or $D''$ to incorporate into the new configuration. For example, the system could be given the rule that "a checked-out version always supercedes a spawned version in propagated configurations". Then in the example, $D''$ would be incorporated in new configurations rather than $D'$. A smart enough system could avoid generating $D'$ altogether.

# 6. IMPLEMENTATION ISSUES

## 6.1 Algorithm for Group Check-in

The semantics of group check-in is that the objects in the group must be merged into a common configuration as the result of the check-in. Note that in Figure 12.6.1, A′ is configured from the old B and C, and the system must build a new configuration if a group check-in of A′, C′, and D′ is issued. Further, if a high-level component and a primitive component are checked-in together, then objects on the path between them must also be contained in any spawned configuration, even if they are not mentioned in the group. The group check-in algorithm from a source workspace to an archive proceeds as follows:

1. To keep the discussion simple, we assume each check-in group has a single object that dominates the rest, such as object A′ does in the check-in group A′, C′, and D′ in Figure 12.6.1. This dominating object forms the root of a minimum spanning graph that covers the ancestors of the remaining objects within the group (see Figure 12.6.2).
2. Any objects found in this subgraph that do not also have descendents in the check-in list should be marked (e.g., B).

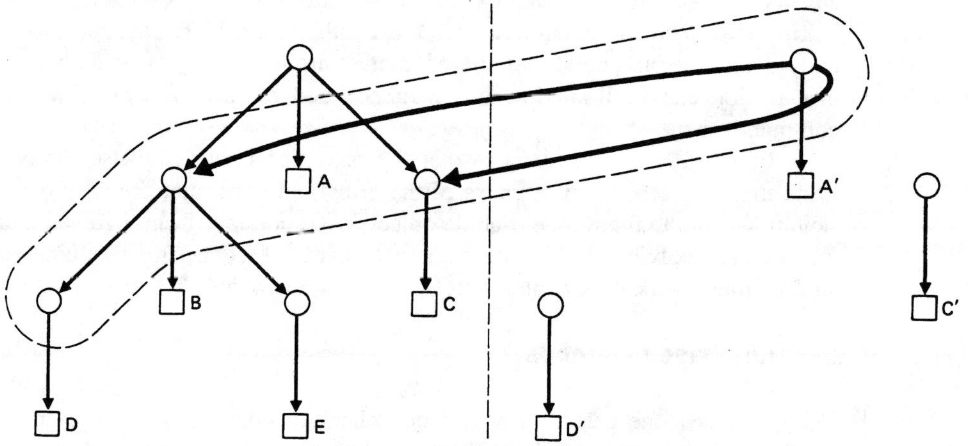


**Figure 12.6.1** *Before group check-in* (A′, C′, D′). The original configuration is shown on the left. Objects A, C, and D have been individually checked out into a workspace on the right, yielding the new versions A′, C′, and D′. The figure shows the configurations before the execution of *group check-in* ($A'$, $C'$, $D'$). The minimum spanning configuration subgraph that covers this check-in group is circled in the figure.

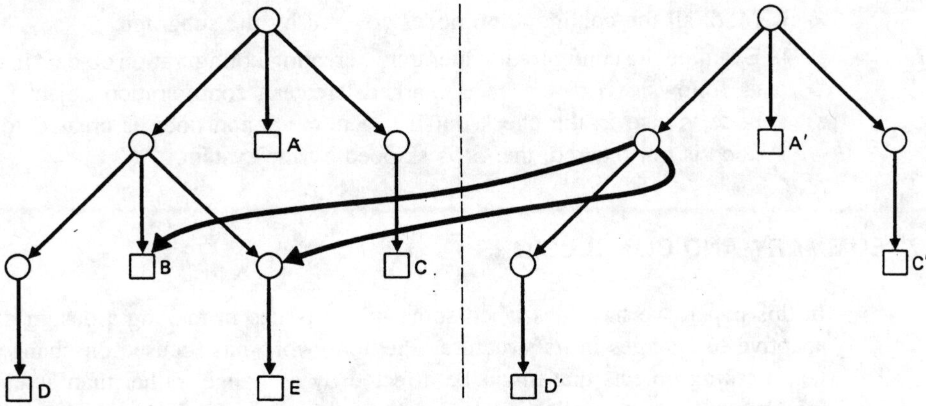


**Figure 12.6.2** *After group check-in* (A′, C′, D′). The configuration node associated with B is marked, because a new configuration node must be introduced into the workspace to complete the configuration. The final configuration is shown on the right.

3. Starting from the configuration of the root object (A′), recursively examine its components and subcomponents: (i) if a node is not marked and does not have a descendent in the check-in list, then the system can ignore the node and any of its components; (ii) if a node is marked, then the system creates a new configuration for it in the source workspace (even though it references a rep object in the archive); (iii) if a node's descendent is in the check-in list, the system will link its descendent's configuration to the configuration being formed in the source workspace.

If there are "holes" in the configurations that need to be filled in this way, then it is likely that the validation subsystem will veto the movement of the resulting configuration into the archive space. However, the full configuration is left in the source workspace, where it can be reverified, and successfully checked-in as a group at a later time.

If the browsing path is specified, the change algorithm is similar to the one above. However, the subgraph would cover only the paths among checked-in objects and the objects specified in the browsing path.

## 6.2 Algorithm for Group Check-out

The problem of rebuilding the configuration at check-in time can be avoided if the appropriate group of objects was checked-out together. Once again, the appropriate configuration relationships need to be constructed in the target workspace, even if there are "holes" in the group. The basic algorithm is described below:

1. Determine the root object within the check-out group.
2. Determine the minimum spanning subgraph that covers the configuration nodes of the checked-out objects and all the paths among them, starting with the configuration of the root object.

3. Mark all the configuration nodes covered by the subgraph.
4. Examine the configuration hierarchy, creating configuration objects in the workspace as follows: (i) if a node is marked, create a configuration object for it; (ii) if a node is also in the check-out list, a new version node is created for it; (iii) if a node is not marked, then it is skipped by the system.

## 7. SUMMARY AND CONCLUSIONS

In this paper, we have described some of the issues in making a design database more adaptive to changes in its structure. Previous work has focused on change notification, i.e., marking objects that might be affected by a change, rather than actually propagating changes automatically. To do so requires new mechanisms for disambiguating what changes are to take place, and for limiting the scope of change propagation. We described specific operational mechanisms that address these issues: group check-in/check-out and browser paths to disambiguate the effects of changes; configuration constraints and browser contexts to limit the scope of these effects. We are implementing these mechanisms in a second edition of the Version Server.

An object-oriented approach helps to limit much of the complexity of change propagation and design evolution. Inheritance makes it possible to identify default values and constraints. By having types with intersection operations, it is possible to support representation-dependent configuration constraints, such as containment and partitioning, without the system needing to know representation details.

We gratefully acknowledge the assistance of Rhajiv Bhateja, David Gedye, and Vony Trijanto, who as members of our research group contributed to the discussions that led to the work reported here. We also thank Thomas Atwood and the other referees for their constructive comments and suggestions.

# 13

# PICQUERY: A High Level Query Language for Pictorial Database Management

**Thomas Joseph**

*First Interstate Services Corporation*
*Los Angeles, California*

**Alfonso F. Cardenas**

*University of California, Los Angeles*

## ABSTRACT

A reasonably comprehensive set of data accessing and manipulation operations that should be supported by a generalized pictorial database management system (PDBMS) is proposed. A corresponding high level query language, PICQUERY, is presented and illustrated through examples. PICQUERY has been designed with a flavor similar to QBE as the highly nonprocedural and conversational language for the pictorial database management system PICDMS, designed and developed at UCLA. PICQUERY and a relational QBE-like language would form the language by which a user may access conventional relational databases and at the same time pictorial databases managed by PICDMS or other robust PDBMS. This language interface is part of an architecture toward data heterogeneity transparency over pictorial and nonpictorial databases.

*Index Terms:* Database management, heterogeneous data, pictorial data, pictorial data accessing and processing, pictorial query language.

*Source*: Adapted from Joseph, T., and A. F. Cardenas, "PICQUERY: A High Level Query Language for Pictorial Database Management", IEEE Transactions on Software Engineering, Vol. 14, No. 5, May 1988, Pages 630–638.

## 1. INTRODUCTION

Most of the data management systems that have been implemented to manage pictorial information (digitized images, drawings, etc.) were developed for use in specific application areas such as geographical applications, military reconnaissance, and medical applications. Very few generalized systems have been developed. Consequently the access or query languages developed for these systems are also largely application specific.

In this paper, we identify and propose a standard set of data manipulation operations that should be supported by generalized Pictorial Data Base Management Systems (PDBMS), and develop a high level query language (PICQUERY) which carries out these operations. PICQUERY has been designed to reside as a major software layer above a robust PDBMS such as PICDMS (Picture Data Base Management System) [Cho81], [Cho84], which is a PDBMS designed and developed at UCLA and now commercially available. PICQUERY is a query language with a flavor similar to QBE [IBM], and to QPE (Query by Pictorial Example) [Chan80a].

Architecturally, this effort is part of the UCLA Heterogeneous Distributed DBMS project, whose interest is the development of data heterogeneity transparency over pictorial and non-pictorial or conventional data (e.g., relational). As such, PICQUERY is intended to be the interface through which the user may access conventional relational data bases using QBE and at the same time pictorial data bases managed by PICDMS (or other robust PDBMS) using PICQUERY (See Figure 13.1). PICQUERY and QBE are seen as one single language by the user.

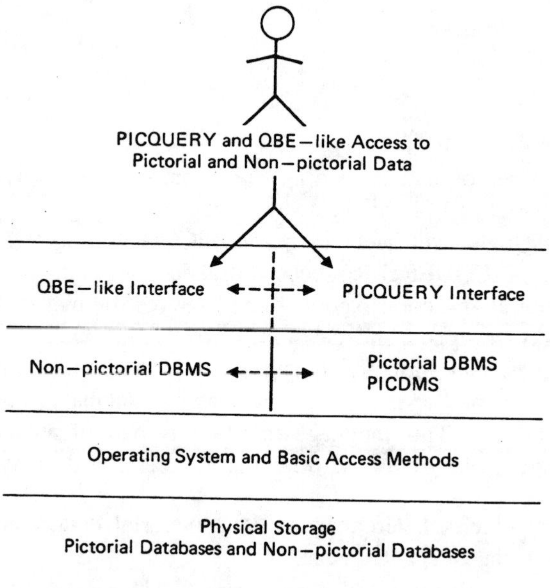


**Figure 13.1** Pictorial and nonpictorial database management architecture.

Section 2 summarizes the architecture and data manipulation capabilities of PICDMS. This section explains the motivation for the PICQUERY language and examines the architectural fit of PICQUERY with PICDMS.

Section 3 identifies the standard set of operations that should be supported by a PDBMS.

Section 4 focuses on the unique capabilities of PICQUERY and explains how various types of queries can be formulated.

Section 5 concludes this work.

## 2. DATA MODEL AND MANIPULATION IN PICDMS

PICDMS [Cho81], [Cho84] uses the gridded data representation scheme as opposed to the topological or polygonal subdivision scheme. Hence, it provides the generality to deal with pictorial or image data. It has a unique *dynamic stacked image logical data structure* as illustrated in Figure 13.2, which consists of two-dimensional variables or pictures registered to the same grid. All data values (one for each picture) for the same grid cell or pixel are stored in a conventional data record, but with the significant fact that the data record is of variable logical structure depending on the number of images stored. This allows flexibility and efficiency in the addition and deletion of pictorial data to the system, which is a crucial requirement. A new image is added as a new attribute in the data record, and not as a new instance of a fixed logical record. Conventional

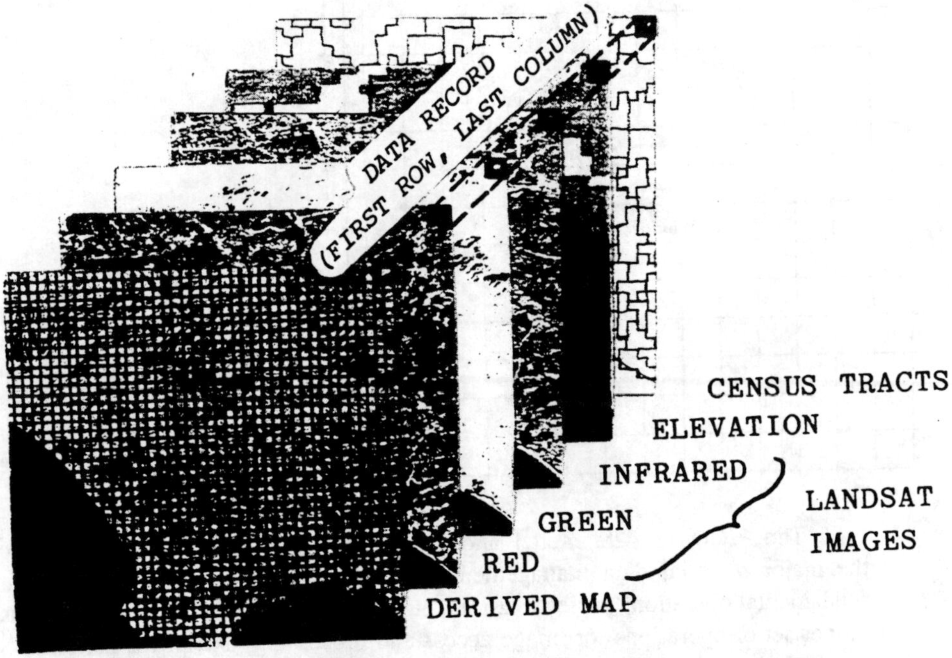


**Figure 13.2** *Stacked image database example.* Each (row, column) record contains one data item per image: an intensity for Landsat spectral band 4, 5, 6, and 7 brightness, an elevation, and a pointer to census tract.

DBMS do not support such schema dynamism. The PICDMS data dictionary keeps track of the current record structure(s).

The data access is through the use of a windowed raster scan control algorithm which runs a rectangular window over cells of the image stack in raster scan order (Figure 13.3). The PICDMS data access/manipulation language (DML) is a command oriented procedural language. The syntax of a PICDMS user language command is as follows:

```
⟨Command⟩::⟨Command Name⟩
            (⟨set of variable type statements⟩)
            ⟨set of data base assignment statements⟩,
            FOR ⟨ set of data base grid cells ⟩;
```

The command name specifies the action to be taken. The set of variable type statements define the variables to be used to perform the command. The set of data base assignment statements indicates the operations to be carried out on each grid cell belonging to the set of grid cells indicated in the fourth and last part of the command. The seven major data manipulation command names used to carry out data base operations are: `COMPUTE`, `LIST`, `DISTANCE`, `ADD`, `REPLACE`, `DELETE`, and `PRINT`. A large variety of PDBMS operations can be performed by the use of these commands.

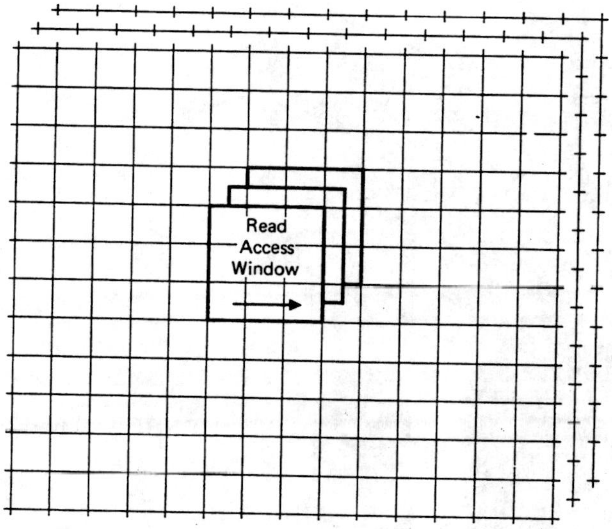


**Figure 13.3** Windowed-scan access to stacked images.

The PICDMS data model and access language have been designed to support the major pictorial data management needs as indicated in reference [Cho81]. The fundamental operations projection, join, etc. of conventional DBMS do not constitute the proper set of operations for image access and processing, except for perhaps topological oriented image handling (as in [Chan80a,Chan80b,Chan81]).

The PICDMS data manipulation language is procedural in nature in that the user specifies what is wanted as well as, to some extent, how to obtain it. As the operations become more complex, the queries in the PICDMS DML user language can be expected to become longer and more time consuming to formulate. (Nevertheless, with PICDMS DML any pictorial data management query not fulfilled by one command may be fulfilled by developing the proper procedure in the DML.)

Consequently, we have designed and are currently implementing the PICQUERY language as the non-procedural and highly Conversational language for non-programmer end-users (oceanographers, military analysts, medical analysts, etc.) to access and process pictorial data in PICDMS. PICQUERY is the high level end-user interface software layer above the PICDMS DML. (See Figure 13.1.)

We initially considered three types of languages for PICQUERY. A purely non-procedural, menu driven query language is good for on-line access. However, when the number of possible operations is very large, as is the case for PDBMS, the purely menu driven approach is cumbersome. Also, the purely menu driven approach is not entirely suitable for query formulation for PDBMS because of the large number of variable attributes that may be involved in A query. Similarly, a non-procedural SQL-like query language will be difficult to use by end-users.

A tabular form of query formulation provides a very efficient and easy means of query formulation to the user. The tabular format provides the user brief, easy to understand guidance in query formulation. Query by Pictorial Example (QPE) developed by Chang and Fu [Chan80a,Chan81] is a tabular query language for use with a PDBMS. The QPE approach adopts the QBE approach where the user formulates a query by entering an example of a possible answer in the appropriate location in a titled table, displayed on the screen by the query language interface. Each operation in a QPE-like query language is specified by using one or more tables, where each table is displayed on the screen with some parts being supplied by the system and the other parts by the user.

QPE and other similar pictorial interfaces designed for use on top of a conventional DBMS environment are practically suitable only for topological structures, that is, for pictures with well delineated objects. On the other hand, PICDMS and PICQUERY provide a native pictorial DBMS environment for arbitrary types of pictures, with the robust pictorial operations described in the following sections.

Thus, we propose PICQUERY as a new tabular query language beyond QPE for logically enhancing on-line access of PICDMS. PICQUERY has features of both a menu driven query language interface as well as that of a tabular query language. The PICQUERY language will be illustrated through examples in Section 4.

The PICQUERY language is being implemented as an interface to PICDMS. The PICQUERY queries may be translated into PICDMS DML to carry out the operations. (See Figure 13.1.)

## 3. MAJOR PICTORIAL DATABASE MANAGEMENT SYSTEMS OPERATIONS

Many areas of discourse and specialized pictorial data management systems were examined to gather the common denominator of pictorial data accessing and manipulation operations required [Cho81]. Figure 13.4 shows a sample of various pictorial data. Three

**Figure 13.4** Pictures with various objects.

major application areas to illustrate the spectrum of such common operations that would have to be available in a generalized PDBMS are: geographical, industrial and medical domains.

A PDBMS for *geographic* pictorial information systems needs to provide the following operations in the analysis of image data: capability of viewing images at different levels of detail (zooming), rotation of images by different angles, cross tabulation of data, identifying nearest object, statistical operations such as covariance measures or averages, geometrical or spatial operations, clustering and point classification, thresholding and edge detection.

*Industrial* PDBMS, in contrast to geographic PDBMS, tend to deal with smaller volumes of pictorial data and these systems may have to carry out complex computations on the basis of image data. Operations such as rotation of images, zooming, edge detection, template matching, texture measures, calculation of geometric and statistical measures, etc., are relevant for these systems.

*Medical* PDBMS, such as those used for storing X-ray pictures, also deal with large amounts of image data. The operations relevant for these systems include enhancement, rotation of images, contour extraction, and segmentation for automatic and semi-automatic diagnosis.

A general PDBMS should provide as many of these data manipulation capabilities (shared across several areas of discourse) as possible. The various data manipulation capabilities that should be provided by a generalized PDBMS can be classified into six categories. Sections 3.1–3.6 shall now outline major operations included in the six categories.

### 3.1 Image Manipulation Operations

Image manipulation operations perform certain transformations on the image to provide a different perspective of the image:

1. Panning or shifting operation to view different sections of an image.
2. Rotation of images to give a different view of the image.
3. Zooming operations. There are three types of zooming operations [Chan80c]: Vertical zooming, to enable the user to view and image at different levels of detail (microscopic or macroscopic); Horizontal zooming, to enable the user to view parts of an image selected on the basis of a selection criterion whose value can be varied continuously; Diagonal zooming, to enable the user to view parts of a picture A which is related to parts of another picture B selected on the basis of some selection criterion. Detailed examples, of these are given in Section 4.
4. Superimposing of one picture over another (one can think of it as a "pictorial" join).
5. Masking certain areas of a picture on the basis of some criteria.
6. Color transformation, to display a picture using different color combinations.
7. Projection operation on an image.

### 3.2 Pattern Recognition Operations

These operations involve recognizing and drawing (establishing) a pattern or searching the pictorial data base for objects that match an identified pattern:

1. Edge detection, to detect edges by measuring changes in light intensity along the picture.
2. Thresholding, to build a binary image which is white in the regions with light intensity less than a threshold limit and black elsewhere.
3. Contour drawing, to draw contour lines joining points on the picture associated with the same attribute value.
4. Similarity retrieval (or template matching) to identify or retrieve picture objects which are similar to a given picture using a certain similarity measure or which match certain template patterns. Similarity retrieval can be done on the basis of size, shape, texture, etc.
5. Establish the boundary or perimeter for a region.
6. Texture measure, to measure or quantify the texture of an image.

7. Clustering (or point classification), to cluster or group together objects or points which are close together in a picture.
8. Segmentation, to divide a picture on the basis of some criteria.
9. Interpolation, to interpolate scattered point values of any particular function.
10. Nearest neighbor, to identify and retrieve the nearest neighbor object (of a particular type).

### 3.3 Spatial or Geometric Operations

These operations deal with spatial relationships between objects within a picture. These operations often deal with computation of certain geometric attribute values. The objects referred to in classical spatial queries can be classified as points, lines, and regions. However, PICQUERY envisions that the user may define any arbitrary pattern in a picture as an object (e.g., river, tank, bad blood cell). Some of the spatial queries use set operators. The classical operations included in this category are:

1. Distance operation (point to point, point to line, point to region, line to line, line to region, region to region).
2. Length, center, slope of a line.
3. Area, centroid, perimeter of a region.
4. Operation to find the portion of a given line object similar to another region object.
5. Operation to find the portion of a given region object similar to another region object.
6. Intersection of a point and a line, a point and a region, two lines, a line and a region, and two regions.
7. Union of two region objects.
8. Difference between two region objects.

### 3.4 Function Operations

These operations are used with variables associated with an image or a picture:

1. Common functions (minimum, maximun, total value, count).
2. Statistical functions (average, standard deviation, covariance, histogram, range values, cross tabulation).

### 3.5 User Defined Functions and Programming Language Interface

A programming language interface should be provided to enable the user to define new functions and formulate queries using these functions.

### 3.6 Input/Output Operations

The Input/Output operations consist of:

1. Print or list tabular image information on paper.
2. Output operation to display/print a picture or object within a picture on a display screen or get a hard copy output.
3. Coloring operation to color parts of a picture on the basis of some criteria.
4. Change or update operation to change values of some picture variables.
5. Store operation to store some new information associated with an image in the pictorial data base.

The above list is a reasonably comprehensive (although not complete) list of operations that may be expected of a very general PDBMS. It is apparent that conventional DBMS (relational, CODASYL, hierarchical) do not provide the proper set of fundamental operations to support properly the majority of the pictorial operations.

## 4. THE PICQUERY LANGUAGE

PICQUERY language commands may operate on the whole pictorial database or a set of picture-object identifiers. A picture is a distinctly identified, independent image stored in the pictorial database. An object is a named region, line, point or part of a picture with which clearly defined features (variable values) are associated. Objects are identified to PICDMS/PICQUERY with the use feature extraction techniques/packages [Aya86,Tsa85,Meh,Meh85] and data base indexing (to identify picture-object relationships). If a picture or an object is identified in a command, the operation will be carried out on the identified picture-object set. If neither a picture nor an object is identified by the user in a command, the operation will be carried out on the entire pictorial database. Some commands require a picture-object set to be identified (eg., ROTATE) whereas others *may* be carried out on the entire database (eg., HORIZONTAL ZOOM). The syntax of the PICQUERY language is given in appendix A.

PICQUERY is built on top of PICDMS which is grid-oriented. Pictorial databases structured in vector or polygon formats may be handled by PICQUERY/PICDMS if they are converted to grid format accepted by PICQUERY. Such converters [Nag79] are available.

Since there are a large number of operations, the user will not be able to remember all the operations at any time. Hence, PICQUERY initially conveys to the user types in `OPERATIONS P.`, the system will print all the legal available operations with a brief explanation for each. If the user types in `IMAGE OPS P.`, `PATTERN OPS P.`, `FUNCTION OPS P.`, or `I/O OPS P.`, the system will list all the corresponding image manipulation operations.

Major elements of PICQUERY shall be now presented through a number of examples. A significant subset of the PICQUERY capability is illustrated. However, the following is not the complete definition of the language.

## 4.1 Image Manipulation Operations

**1.** *Panning or shifting operations.* A picture can be divided into a number of frames, each frame being the size of the display screen of the terminal. If a picture size is less than or equal to the screen size, the picture will be displayed at the center of the screen. When a picture is viewed whose size is greater than the screen, initially the top left frame will be displayed. Then, the picture can be shifted vertically or horizontally using the shift operation. There is a second shift operation. This involves repositioning an object within a picture. For both these operations, the same table will be displayed.

SHIFT

| Picture | Object name | Horizontal shift | Vertical shift |
|---|---|---|---|
| PIC | | −10 | 5 |

If the user wants to shift only the window over the picture, he/she should leave the object name column blank. The user has to enter the picture name in the first column, and the horizontal and vertical shifts in grid units in the third and fourth columns, respectively. A positive entry in the horizontal shift column indicates right shift and a negative entry indicates left shift. Similarly, a positive entry in the vertical shift column indicates shifting down whereas a negative entry indicates shifting up. If the user wants to carry out the second shift operation, he/she will have to fill in the column for object name. In that case, the identified object will be repositioned in the picture according to the entries in the last two columns. The entry in the table above indicates that the picture displayed is to be moved 10 grid units to the left and 5 grid units down.

**2.** *Rotation operation.* As in the case of the shift operations, there are two rotation operations. The first rotation operation involves rotating a picture, whereas the second rotation operation deals with rotating and repositioning an object within a picture. For both these operations, the same table will be used. When the user types in `ROTATE`, the following table will be displayed.

ROTATE

| Picture | Object name | Angle of rotation from vertical axis |
|---|---|---|
| PIC | STRIPE | −10° |

If the user wants to carry out the first rotate operation (i.e., rotation of the picture), he/she should leave the object name column blank. For the first operation, the user has to enter the picture name and the angle of rotation only. A positive value entered for angle indicates clockwise rotation relative to the vertical axis, and a negative value indicates anti-clockwise rotation. If the second rotate operation is to be done, then the user has to enter the value for the object name column too. The entries made in the table shown above indicate an operation where the line object, STRIPE (belonging to picture, PIC) is to be rotated by 10 degrees in the anti-clockwise direction and repositioned within the picture.

**3.** *Zooming operations.* For each of three different zooming operations provided, there is a different tabular format for constructing queries. There are two types of vertical zoom operations: one vertical zoom operation enables the user to zoom in/out on a picture, whereas the other vertical zoom operation allows the user to do the same on an object within the picture (the other parts of the picture remaining at the same level of magnification as before). For both these operations, the same table is used to formulate queries. When the user first types in `VZOOM` then the following table will be displayed.

VERTICAL ZOOM

| Picture | Object name | Degree of magnification |
|---|---|---|
| PIC | C1 | 3 |

The user has to enter only the first and the third columns for the first type of vertical zoom operation. For the second type of vertical zoom operation, the user has to fill in the object name column too. If the entry for the degree of magnification is greater than 1 then it is a zoom in operation, else it is a zoom out operation. The entry given in the table above indicates that the object, C1 is to be magnified by a factor of 3 and displayed.

For the horizontal zoom operation, the user has to first type in `HZOOM`. Then the following table will be displayed.

HORIZONTAL ZOOM

| Picture | Object name | Section condition | | | | |
|---|---|---|---|---|---|---|
| | | Variable | Relation operator | Value operator | Logical | Group |
| PIC | UTAH | elevation | .gt. | 1000 | .or. | 1 |
| | | elevation | .lt. | 1000 | .and. | 2 |
| | | rainfall | .gt. | 3 | | 2 |

The horizontal zoom operation may be performed on a whole picture or on only an object within a picture. If the user wants to do the former he should not fill in the column for object name. If the user wants to do the latter he/she has to fill in the column for object name. The query filled in the table above reads as follows: "Identify and display the places in UTAH (in picture, PIC) where (elevation is greater than 1000 ft.) or (elevation is less than 1000 ft. and rainfall is greater than 3 inches per annum)". Observe the use of the field, "Group" to be able to interpret the selection condition unambiguously. If the entry for "Group" in the second line in the table was 1 instead of 2, the query would have meant the following: "Identify and display the places in UTAH (in picture, PIC) where (rainfall is greater than 3 inches per annum)".

For the diagonal zoom operation, the user first types in DZOOM, to display the following format:

DIAGONAL ZOOM

| Picture 1 | Object name | Picture 2 | Section condition | | | | |
|---|---|---|---|---|---|---|---|
| | | | Variable | Relation operator | Value | Logical operator | Group |
| PIC1 | MISSILE SITES | PIC2 | Range<br>Speed | .gt.<br>.gt. | 5000<br>25000 | .and. | 1<br>1 |

Here, picture 1 and picture 2 are related pictures. Selection is first made on picture 2 and then those parts of picture 1 related to selected portions of picture 2 are identified and displayed. PIC2 contains prototypes of various kinds of missiles, whereas PIC1 contains missile sites. By this query, the user is trying to identify the points in picture PIC1 where missiles with range greater than 5000 miles and speed greater than 25000 mph are deployed.

**4.** *Superimposing.*

SUPERIMPOSE

| Picture 1 | Object name | Picture 2 | Object name |
|---|---|---|---|
| PIC1 | A1 | PIC2 | A2 |

Using this table, two pictures can be superimposed or two objects belonging to the same or different pictures can be superimposed. In the example query, the user wants to superimpose object A2 of PIC2 on object A1 of PIC1.

**5.** *Color Transformation.*

COLOR TRANSFORMATION

| Picture | Object name | Color | Section condition | | | | |
|---|---|---|---|---|---|---|---|
| | | | Variable | Relation operator | Value operator | Logical | Group |
| PIC | UTAH | Blue | Elevation | .gt. | 1000 | .and. | 1 |
| | | | Elevation | .le. | 2000 | | 1 |
| | | Red | Elevation | .gt. | 2000 | | 2 |

The following coloring scheme for the region object UTAH is requested: blue for those portions with elevation greater than 1000 ft. and less than or equal to 2000 ft., and red for those portions with elevation greater than 2000 ft. If the column for object name is left unfilled, then the coloring operation will be carried out on the entire picture PIC.

## 4.2 Pattern Recognition Operations

**1.** *Edge Detection Operation.* When the user types in `EDGE-DETECTION`, the following table format will be displayed.

EDGE DETECTION

| Picture | Object name | Edge name | Section condition | | | | |
|---|---|---|---|---|---|---|---|
| | | | Variable | Relation operator | Value | Logical operator | Group |
| PIC | | E1 | Band 7 | .gt. | 128 | .or. | 1 |
| | | | Elevation | .le. | 2000 | .and. | 2 |
| | | | Band 7 | .gt. | 64 | | 2 |

In this operation, the edges are detected on the basis of changes in light intensity between neighboring cells. So, when the user enters a spectral band variable in the column for "Variable", the relative value of the spectral band variable for a cell (compared to that of the 3 neighboring cells) is considered for carrying out the operation. In this example the edge E1 is to be created and displayed if the relative band 7 is less than or equal to 2000 ft. and the relative band 7 value is greater than 64.

2. *Contour Drawing.*

CONTOUR DRAWING

| Picture | Object name | Variable | Value |
|---|---|---|---|
| PIC | | Elevation<br>Elevation<br>Elevation | 1000<br>2000<br>3000 |

The contour drawing operation can also be done either on the whole picture or an object within a picture. If the operation is to be done on the whole picture, then the column for object name should be left unfilled. In the example given above, the user is requesting contours to be drawn for elevation equal to 1000 ft., 2000 ft., and 3000 ft.

3. *Similarity Retrieval.*

SIMILARITY RETRIEVAL

| Picture 1 | Object name | Basis | Picture 2 | Object name | Object type |
|---|---|---|---|---|---|
| PIC1 | C1 | Shape | PIC2 | P. | P. |

Similarity retrieval operations can be done on the basis of size, shape, texture, and any other user-defined, application dependent basis. The column for "Basis" in the table is for the user to indicate on what basis the operation is to be carried out. The purpose of this operation is to retrieve objects in "Picture 2" similar to the object identified in "Picture 1". A "P." entry in any column indicates that the values for the column are to be printed after the operation is carried out. In this example, the user is requesting identification and retrieval of objects in picture PIC2 similar in shape to object C1 in picture PIC1. As a result of this operation, the system will fill in the names of retrieved objects in the last two columns of the table.

4. *Segmentation Operation.*

SEGMENTATION

| Picture | Object name | Segment name | Section condition | | | | |
|---|---|---|---|---|---|---|---|
| | | | Variable | Relation operator | Value | Logical operator | Group |
| PIC | | SEG1 | Rainfall | .le. | 5 | | 1 |
| | | SEG2 | Rainfall | .le. | 10 | .and. | 2 |
| | | | Rainfall | .gt. | 5 | | 2 |
| | | SEG3 | Rainfall | .gt. | 10 | | 3 |

The user can use this operation to segment a whole picture or an object within a picture. If the user wants to segment an object within a picture, then the user has to fill in the column for object name. In this example, the user wants to divide the picture, PIC into 3 segments according to values for rainfall. SEG1 segment consists of areas with rainfall less than or equal to 5 inches per annum. SEG2 segment consists of areas with rainfall between 5 and 10 inches per annum and SEG3 segment consists of areas with rainfall greater than 10 inches per annum.

## 4.3 Spatial or Geometric Operations

**1.** *Distance Operation.* When user types in "DISTANCE", the system responds with the following table.

DISTANCE

| Picture | Object 1 name | Object 2 name | Distance |
|---|---|---|---|
| PIC | MAINE | NEVADA | P. |

The minimum distance between the two objects will be printed in the Column titled "Distance".

**2.** *Length of a Line.*

LENGTH

| Picture | Line name | Length |
|---|---|---|
| PIC | NILE | P. |

This example requests the length of the line NILE in picture PIC.

**3.** *Area of a Region.*

AREA

| Picture | Region name | Area |
|---|---|---|
| PIC | EGYPT | P. |

This example requests the area of the region EGYPT in picture PIC.

**4.** *Operation to Find the Portion of a Line Similar To Another Line.*

LINE SIMILARITY

| Picture 1 | Line name 1 | Picture 2 | Line name 2 | Basis similar portion |
|---|---|---|---|---|
| PIC1 | NILE | PIC2 | RHINE | ORIENTATION |

This operation involves finding the portions of line 1 similar to line 2. In this example, line RHINE is compared to line NILE. The portion in RHINE similar to NILE is to be identified and named RHILE. If the operation is successful, RHILE will be highlighted on the screen for the user.

**5.** *Operation to Find a Portion of a Given Region Object Similar to Another Region Object.*

REGION SIMILARITY

| Picture 1 | Region name 1 | Picture 2 | Region name 2 | Basis similar portion | Name for |
|---|---|---|---|---|---|
| PIC1 | EGYPT | PIC2 | FRANCE | TEMPERATURE | FRAPT |

Here the portion in FRANCE with similar temperatures to portions in EGYPT is to be identified and named FRAPT. If the operation is successful, FRAPT will be highlighted on the screen for the user.

**6.** *Set Operations.* This is a group of three operations: Union, Intersection and Difference.

| Picture 1 | Object 1 name | Picture 2 | Object 2 name | Function | Basis | Name of result object | Result null? |
|---|---|---|---|---|---|---|---|
| PIC1 | C1 | PIC2 | C2 | INTERSECTION | TEXTURE | C3 | P. |

In this example, those portions in objects C1 (of PIC 1) and C2 (of PIC 2) with the same texture measure are to be recognized and identified as C3. After the operation is over, the system will print "yes" or "no" to indicate whether there is any result or not. If the result is non-null, then C3 (the result object) will be highlighted on the screen.

In the following example, the area covered by objects R1 and R2 (of PIC1) will be identified as R3 and highlighted on the screen.

| Picture 1 | Object 1 name | Picture 2 | Object 2 name | Function name | Basis result object | Name of result null? | |
|---|---|---|---|---|---|---|---|
| PIC1 | R1 | PIC1 | R2 | UNION | AREA | R3 | P. |

## 4.4 Function Operations

**1.** *Generally Used Functions.* When the user types in "GENERAL-FUNCTION" the following table will be displayed.

GENERAL FUNCTIONS

| Picture | Object name | Variable | Function | Value |
|---|---|---|---|---|
| PIC | UTAH | Rainfall | MINIMUM | P. |

Possible functions are: MINIMUM, MAXIMUM, TOTAL, COUNT, AVERAGE, and STANDARD DEVIATION. After the operation is carried out, the value computed will be printed in the last column. In this example the user wants to know the minimum rainfall pertaining to the region UTAH.

**2.** *Histogram.*

HISTOGRAM

| Picture | Object name | Variable | Value range | | Frequency |
|---|---|---|---|---|---|
| | | | From | To | |
| PIC | UTAH | Tempera-ture | 32<br>41 | 40<br>50 | P. |

The number of points whose variable value falls within the value range will be printed in the frequency column. The user is requesting the frequency histogram on the basis of temperature values for the region UTAH in picture PIC.

3. *Range Values.*

RANGE VALUES

| Picture | Object name | Variable | Range values | |
|---|---|---|---|---|
| | | | Low | High |
| PIC | UTAH | Elevation | P. | P. |

Here, the range values are printed in the last two columns after the operation is carried out. The user wants to know the range of values for elevation for the region UTAH in picture PIC.

4. *Crosstabulation.*

CROSSTABULATE

| Picture | Object name | Crosstab variable | | | | | |
|---|---|---|---|---|---|---|---|
| | | Name | Value | Variable | Value | Variable | Value |
| PIC | | Population | P. | Census-Tract | 902<br>903<br>905 | School | Fran-klin<br>EDI-SON<br>MAD-ISON |

This operation will calculate and print the crosstabulation variable values for the new segmentation variable groups based on the figures for the old segmentation variable groups. In this example, the user is trying to estimate school district population from census tract population, given a picture of school districts and one of census tracts.

## 4.5 User Defined Functions

The programming language interface in PICQUERY allows the user to define his/her own functions to query the database. For this, the user will have to carry out the following tasks: (1) define the function to PICQUERY by writing a procedure in PICDMS DML and/or PICQUERY and a programming language like Pascal or C; (2) design and store a tabular format (to be associated with the query for this function) into PICQUERY. This feature allows for the extension of PICQUERY capabilities to satisfy the need of various users.

## 5. CONCLUSIONS

The motivation and justification for a highly interactive end-user language and environment for the increase and challenge of generalized pictorial data management has been presented. PICQUERY and a relational language like QBE would form the language by which a user may access conventional relational databases and at the same time pictorial data bases managed by PICDMS (or other robust PDBMSs). (See Figure 13.1.) A reasonably comprehensive set of pictorial data accessing and manipulation operations required of a PDBMS has been presented. The PICQUERY language designed provides support for the majority of these operations with few command entries. It is apparent that conventional PDBMSs (based on conventional relational, CODASYL, hierarchical DBMS) do not provide the proper set of fundamental operations to support properly the majority of pictorial operations.

A significant subset of PICQUERY has been illustrated through examples. The full definition of the language has not been included. It is clear, however, that the PICQUERY approach is such that it is a rather open ended language environment which can be extended to accommodate additional or new functions that maybe of particular interest to specific areas. In fact, the architecture of PICDMS, of the procedural-oriented PICDMS DML and of PICQUERY is such that they provide a fundamental shell on which further language operations for pictorial data management needs may be easily built.

Some of the operations cited in Section 3 and illustrated in Section 4 with PICQUERY can be done fully graphically with a mouse device and without keyboard intervention by means of a graphical interface such as Apple McIntosh, Microsoft Windows, or Digital Research's GEM. Examples are the movement of the window over a large picture, the rotation or shifting of objects within a picture, etc. This possibility is being currently addressed.

## APPENDIX-PICQUERY SYNTAX

The PICQUERY Syntax is defined as follows.

```
⟨Command⟩::          ⟨Command Name⟩
                      ⟨Set of Picture-Object Identifiers⟩
                      ⟨Set of Functional Variable Identifiers/Values⟩
                      ⟨Resultant Object Identifiers⟩
                      ⟨Set of Selection Conditions⟩
⟨Command Name⟩ ::     ⟨Command Name⟩
                      ⟨TABULAR FORMAT⟩
⟨Set of Picture-Object Identifiers⟩ ::
                      ⟨Picture Identifier⟩
                      ⟨Object Identifier⟩.....
                      ⟨Picture Identifier⟩
                      ⟨Object Identifer⟩
⟨Set of Functional Variable Identifiers/Values⟩::
                      ⟨Functional Variable Identifier⟩
                      ⟨Functional Variable Values⟩.......
                      ⟨Functional Variable Identifier⟩
                      ⟨Functional Variable Values⟩
```

```
Functional Variable values can be the result of an operation too.
⟨Resultant Object Identifiers⟩::
                   ⟨Object Identifier⟩
                   ⟨Presence of Resultant Object⟩
⟨Set of Selection Conditions⟩::
                   ⟨Selection Condition line⟩.....
                   ⟨Selection condition line⟩
⟨Selection Condition line⟩::
                   ⟨Variable Identifier⟩
                   ⟨Relation Operator⟩
                   ⟨Variable Values⟩
                   ⟨Logical Operator⟩
                   ⟨Group Identifier⟩
```

Group Identifier identifies the set of condition lines that are part of the same complex condition. For example, if the selection condition is (A or B or C) and (D), Condition lines A,B and C will have the same group identifier; whereas condition line D will have a different Group Identifier. The use of the Group Identifier removes any ambiguity in formulating selection conditions.

# 14

# Complex Entities for Engineering Applications*

**Klaus R. Dittrich, Willi Gotthard, Peter C. Lockemann**

*Forschungszentrum Informatik an der Universität Karlsruhe, Karlsruhe*

## ABSTRACT

The representation of complexly structured miniworld units can be made much more convenient and efficient if database systems for use in engineering applications (e.g., CAD/CAM, software engineering environments) offer data models that are more suited for that purpose than the classical ones. This paper introduces CERM, a data model that goes beyond the entity-relationship model by orthogonally extending it with complex objects, object versions and some other features. The paper presents the salient concepts and shows their usefulness by way of illustration with a major example chosen from a software development environment. Some related database system mechanisms and implementation issues are briefly sketched.

*Forschungszentrum Informatik an der Universität Karlsruhe Haid-und-Neu-Straße 10-14, D-7500 Karlsruhe 1

*Source*: Adapted from Dittrich, K. R., W. Gotthard, and P. C. Lockemann, "Complex Entities for Engineering Applications", Proceedings of the International Conference on the Entity-Relationship Approach, Elsevier Science Publishers B. V. (North-Holland), 1987, pp. 421–440.

# 1. INTRODUCTION

In business and government administration, database technology has been successfully used for more than a decade. It has been an important means for speeding up, standardizing and organizing the information flow, for eliminating much of the redundancy in data collection and data dissemination, and for increasing the quality and reliability of data management.

It is therefore small wonder that one would like to apply similar techniques to the large volumes of data arising from the engineering processes in enterprises. However, database technology for application in e.g., computer aided design (CAD) and manufacturing (CAM) in mechanical engineering, electronics, civil engineering, or in process automation and robotics is still in its infancy. This is mainly due to the fact that one cannot just take the existing technology and apply it to engineering applications, as the growing list of less than successful attempts to use existing, commercially available database management systems (DBMS) shows.

This observation has spawned a number of studies to examine whether the requirements for engineering databases, particularly CAD, differ from those for traditional commercial applications, and how they do (e.g. [Loc85]). These differences are by now well-known and understood, though by no means resolved. Many of the differences concern technical issues such as transaction management, synchronization, recovery and performance enhancement. Others have to do with data modeling facilities that are insufficiently oriented towards the needs of engineering applications. In fact, there is a close interrelationship between better-suited modeling concepts and the resolution of the technical issues—the latter cannot realistically be attacked without specifying the former. This paper, therefore, proposes a data model specifically suitable as a basis for design applications.

Engineers, particularly designers, deal in their world with what they perceive as clearly identifiable entities, such as mechanical parts, chips, or even software modules. Consequently, any data model reflecting the engineer's world of interest in a natural way should be distinctively **object-oriented** [Bat84]: it has to include concepts that allow for the representation of one miniworld entity—whatever its composition out of other entities may be—by exactly one database construct.

It is clear that the classical approaches such as the network or the relational data model [Dat81] are not object-oriented in this sense [Sid80] but need major extensions that at least provide an object-oriented view of network/relational structures. Through its notion of entity, the entity-relationship model (ERM; [Che76,Gri82]) provides a better basis, but still lacks—among others—a notion of object that explicitly accounts for the (possibly recursive) composition from other objects and a set of operators capable of dealing with these aspects. We will refer to objects with these properties as **complex objects** or **complex entities** as opposed to the usual, atomic entities. Obviously, with such a concept of entity, the concept of relationship will also have to undergo some extension.

**The complex-entity/relationship model (CERM)** proposed in this paper is a suitable extension of the ERM by the aforementioned properties, versioned entities, and some other features. Section 2 will give a brief introduction into the requirements of a design environment in order to motivate the extensions to the ERM in sufficient detail. On its basis, Section 3 will introduce and explain the necessary structural extensions to the ERM. Since the CERM forms the basis of a DBMS interface, it must include an appropriate set of operators; Section 4 will discuss these and point out in particular which ones are due to complex entities. Section 5 concludes by sketching some related DBMS mechanisms and implementation issues and by summarizing some first experience in using CERM.

## 2. MODELING REQUIREMENTS OF ENGINEERING DESIGN APPLICATIONS

A recent survey of design applications in mechanical engineering, VLSI design, and software engineering [Loc85] has clearly shown that they have much more in common than what separates them. Accordingly, we can afford to restrict ourselves to the discussion of one of these applications. We choose software engineering.

### 2.1 Objects in Software Engineering

The process of software development is divided into distinct **phases** according to a specific **software life cycle** (SLC), e.g., requirements analysis, functional specification, architectural design, component design, component implementation, component test, system integration and test, and maintenance. A **software engineering environment** (SEE) [Hen84] comprises a set of tools for the underlying SLC. Every tool supports one particular task resulting in one or more output documents (or **representations**) that form the input to other tools and/or contribute to the result of the design process. In their latter capacity they form a collection of descriptions of the software product, each from a particular point of view (e.g., specification, code, test cases, manuals).

Phases themselves are broken down into a number of **steps**, due to either the nature of the development process (take stepwise refinement as an example) or the need to parcel out work to several persons. The phase/step structure of software development is reflected (though not necessarily in a one-to-one fashion) in the object structure: the objects in SEEs are **structured objects** in which much of their information is carried by a set of subobjects and their mutual arrangement. As a further example for the need to structure objects, consider the compilation units of a piece of software that has been written in a programming language that provides for separate compilation. A syntax-oriented editor or the analysis phase of a compiler usually views a compilation unit as an attributed syntax tree. The structured object compilation unit thus consists of a set of nodes and their interconnections, with sets of attributes associated with each node. Not in all cases, however, the tree structure is of interest: to query for some global characteristics such as date of compilation, author, source, the "compilation unit" object has to be referenced as a whole.

To sum up, objects in SEEs may have both, **structural** properties reflecting their decomposition into subobjects, and **descriptive** properties associated with an object in its entirety. Which kind of property is of interest may vary. In consequence, a data model for SEEs should provide an object concept that includes operators allowing a structural and/or a descriptive view of objects.

## 2.2 Relationships in Software Engineering

Objects usually are not isolated units but are interconnected via numerous relationships [Loc83]. While some of them are rather specific for the design methodology or even for the individual software engineer, there are some general ones that merit explicit DBMS support:

- Software development is an iterative trial-and-error process where developers are continuously producing intermediate results, so-called **revisions** [Tic82]. Upon creation of a new revision of an object, the older ones cannot simply be discarded since it may prove necessary to return to one of them at some later time. The set of revisions is structured according to a predecessor-successor relation which in general forms a directed acyclic graph.
- The development of a large software system is a team effort. While revisions are usually private to one software engineer, so-called **releases** represent results that have been made public by their creators and thus may be used by others.
- Software production is often supposed to yield a program family [Par78,Tic82b] instead of a single product. For example, a program family may have members for different operating systems, with different functional user interfaces, or with optimizations satisfying different criteria. Hence, the data model should support **alternatives**. Obviously, for every alternative revisions and releases may exist.

Revisions, releases and alternatives are phenomena of what one calls **object versions** [Dit85a]. By supporting all these, the data model essentially deals with multiple instances of the same object that coexist in the database and represent different states of the same semantic entity.

- If several versions of parts of a software system exist, the designer has to choose among them when assembling the system from the individual parts. The resulting **configurations** have to be managed by the DBMS, too.

## 2.3 Further Requirements

In a team of software engineers working with a SEE, everybody must have a workspace of his own, his private database. The integration of developers' results must be done in databases that are public to at least a group of developers. As a consequence, the database system must manage multiple databases (private and public ones).

The performance of a DBMS for SEEs is crucial to the success of a SEE. If the data model provides concepts that are specifically geared to the application, i.e. that take note of the application semantics, performance can be enhanced if the implementation of the DBMS exploits the knowledge about these concepts to speed up processing.

One of the most important reasons for the application of a DBMS in a SEE is that it allows the integration of tools that otherwise would have to run in isolation. In consequence, the data model must be flexible enough to support different tools and different SLC models. Furthermore, since software technology is still an area of active research, novel tools and object structures are to be expected. Hence, the concepts in the data model must be general enough to provide the needed flexibility. Because general concepts normally are less efficient to implement than specialized ones, a data model for supporting SEEs should contain a good mix of both.

### 2.4 Related Approaches

A considerable amount of research has been spent to extend traditional data models for use in engineering applications. While this approach provides users that have previous database experience with environments they are familiar with, it also sets narrow limits for object-orientation. For example, extensions of the relational model (e.g., XSQL [Has82] and $NF^2$ [Sch84]) are usually restricted to purely tree-like structures. [Bat84] introduces a conceptual framework for so-called molecular objects that is suitable to address at least part of the requirements listed above.

Other approaches developed specifically for software engineering address only parts of the problem. For example, [Tic82b] and [Nar85] deal with the problems of version and configuration control, evolution control and maintenance. The latter approach uses a relational DBMS for the sole purpose of storing the global information associated with a (software) system. Both approaches cannot have the structural information managed by a DBMS efficiently because there is no concept of structured object.

## 3. STRUCTURAL PROPERTIES OF THE CERM

### 3.1 A Running Example

We shall use a simple example to illustrate the proposed data model. For the sake of better understanding, we summarize the underlying assumptions in this section.

Suppose that we plan to develop a piece of software in a manner determined by the system life cycle model of Figure 14.1. In the course of action a variety of documents are produced; furthermore, the software to be developed is broken down into a number of modules that are individually documented, designed and programmed. We assume further that each module can separately be compiled, with the necessary cross-checking of exported and imported interfaces as provided by programming languages such as Modula 2 [Wir82] or Ada [Ame83]. Take Ada in particular. The syntactic analysis generates a DIANA representation [Goo83] for each compilation unit which may roughly be viewed as a (parse-) tree structure, where each node is augmented by attributes during the semantic analysis phase. In reality, there are a number of types of

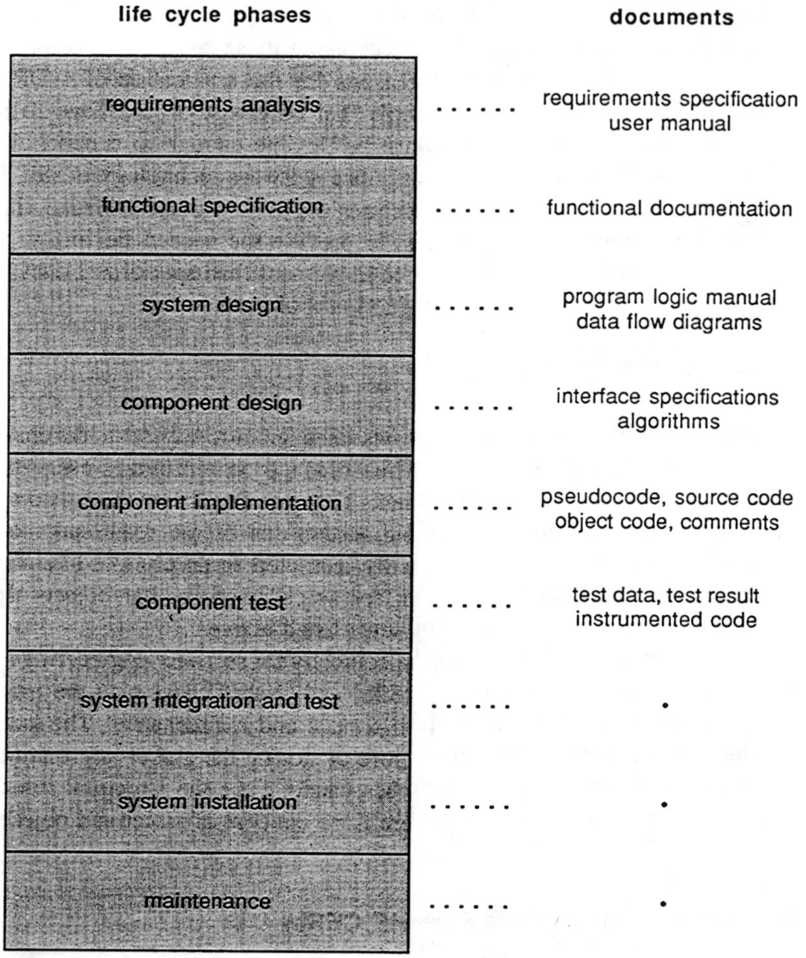


**Figure 14.1** System life cycle and documents.

DIANA nodes and relationships. For the sake of keeping the example simple we omit these details. Finally, we assume that all compilation units are maintained in a library.

## 3.2 Standard Features

As mentioned before, a data model for SEEs should include both general concepts to gain in flexibility, and specialized ones to gain in semantic expressiveness and related efficiency. Furthermore, in order to construct complex entities, one needs basic building blocks. For these reasons the CERM includes all concepts of the traditional ERM [Che76] together with several of its extensions [Gri82]: entities (together with entity types, entity sets), relationships (relationship types, relationship sets), and cardinalities.

Entities (called **objects** in the CERM) consist of a number of attributes with values taken from associated domains.

Relationships are n-place with $n \geq 1$, where each place is characterized by a role attribute; the relationship may have further attributes. The definition of cardinalities is restricted to minimum cardinalities 0 or 1, and maximum cardinalities 1 or $*$ (unlimited). Incidentally, the definition of cardinalities is associated with the object type declaration rather than the relationship type declaration.

Figure 14.2 shows the definition of a DIANA tree built from individual attributed nodes and introduces a simple graphical notation.

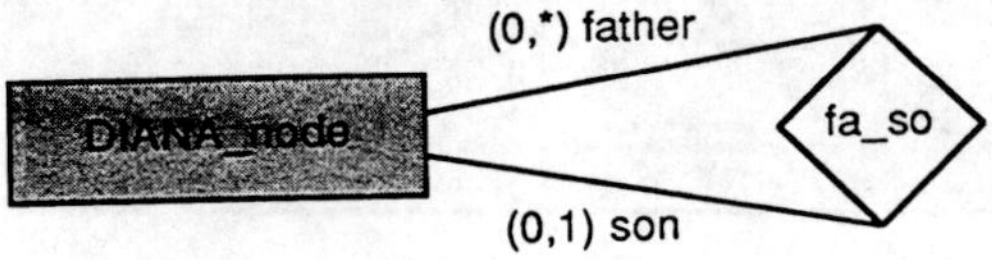


```
OBJECT TYPE DIANA_node
     ATTRIBUTES
        node_name          :    STRING [16]
        sem_attributes     :    STRING [8] ARRAY [10]
     AT MOST ONCE   (fa_so.son)
END DIANA_node

RELSHIP TYPE fa_so
     RELATES
        father        :    DIANA_node
        son           :    DIANA_node
     ATTRIBUTES
        no_of_siblings   :    INT
END fa_so
```

**Figure 14.2** Example of a CERM schema using standard features only.

There are no specific CERM-concepts for generalization and aggregation [Smi77]. Instead, they may be represented by somewhat more general concepts as will be demonstrated below.

### 3.3 Complex Entities

Complex entities or complex objects are collections of (atomic or again complex) entities and/or relationships that can be treated in their entirety. Consider Figure 14.3. It illustrates a schema where objects of various representation types of an SLC together with the connecting relationships have been collected into a complex object of type "design object" (dotted line). Hence instances of type "design object" may have attributes of their own that do not belong to any of their subobjects, and they may be referred to as a whole. The same is true for "compilation unit" (solid box) which is a complex object type comprising a DIANA tree as just modeled above, and for "documentation" (solid box; collects the textual - in a narrow sense - documents produced during the life cycle).

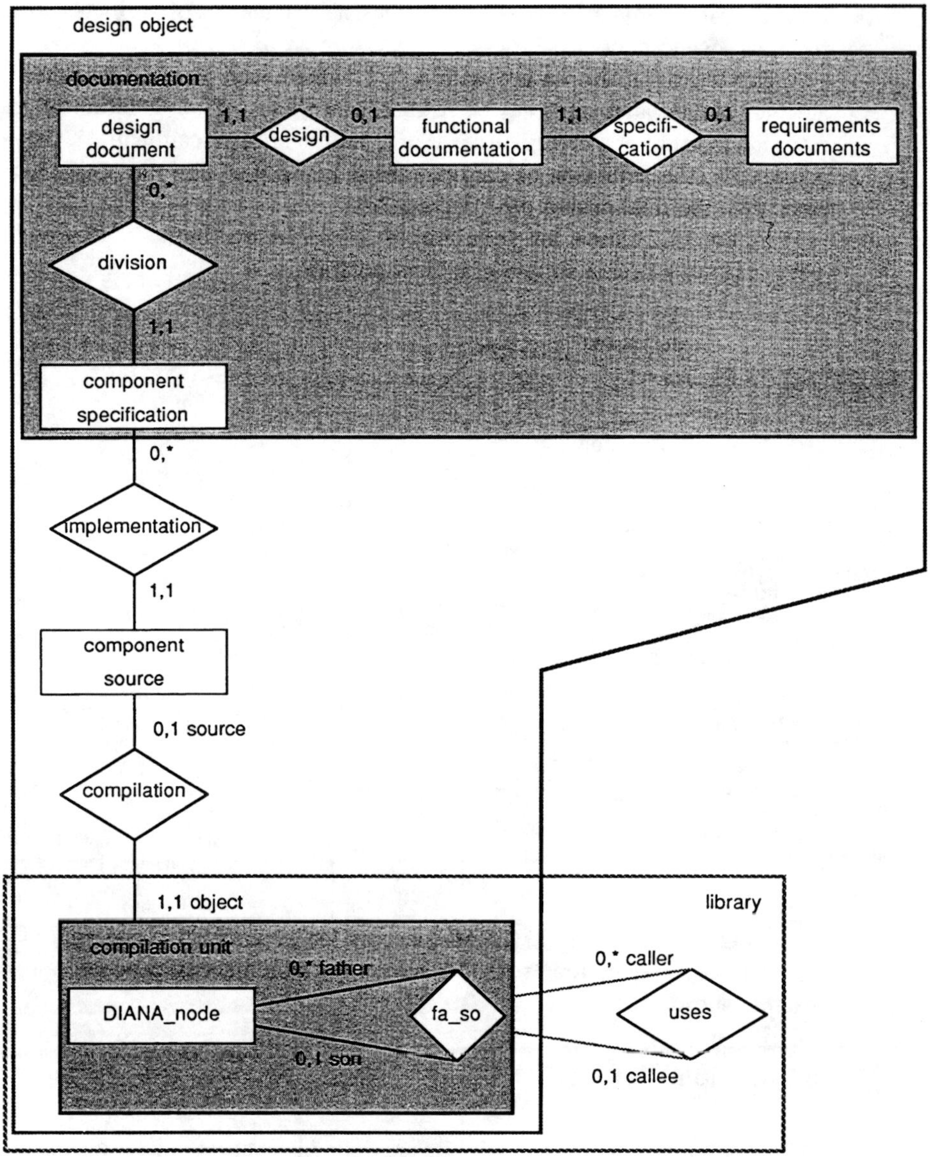


**Figure 14.3** A CERM schema for a software engineering database; solid, dashed and dotted boxes all represent (complex) objects.

Note that complex objects need not always be simple hierarchies of lesser objects. For example (Fig. 14.3, dashed lines) a compilation unit may not only be part of a design object, but independently be a member of a library. The "uses"-relationship is in this example considered part of the library, but not part of the design object representing the individual software product. Networks may also be encountered when one starts from a single node and comes across forks and joins.

Furthermore, a complex object could also be an arrangement of simpler objects that are not connected at all via relationships, i.e., an unstructured set of objects (sometimes called a grouping), or it may be a combination of both isolated and interconnected objects. Thus, the example of an instance of type "library" in Figure 14.4 and the (artificial; not related to software engineering) example of Figure 14.5 all are valid complex objects.

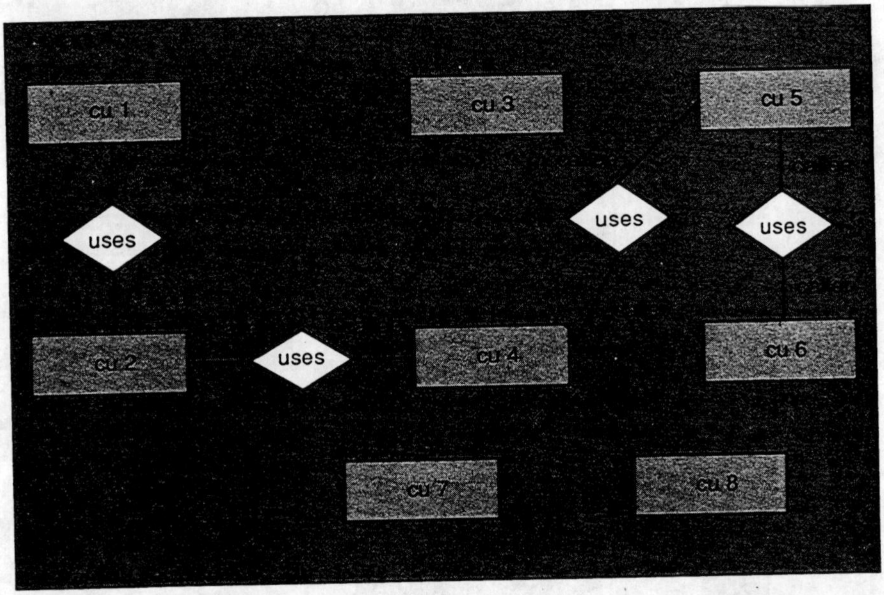


**Figure 14.4** Database instance of type "library" (of Fig. 14.3), consisting of several "compilation unit" instances (cu).

To sum up, a **complex object** is a set of—perhaps unconnected or only partially connected—objects. Correspondingly, a complex object type is simply a boundary line drawn around a set of objects and relationship types in the schema. The boundary line is expressed in the data definition language (DDL) via a structure clause that describes the composition of a complex object. For example, the definition of compilation unit (of Fig. 14.3) is:

```
OBJECT TYPE compilation unit
   ATTRIBUTES
      source_name :  STRING [256]
      compile_time :  TIME
   STRUCTURE IS DIANA_node , fa_so
   AT LEAST ONCE compilation.object
   AT MOST ONCE compilation.object
END compilation_unit
```

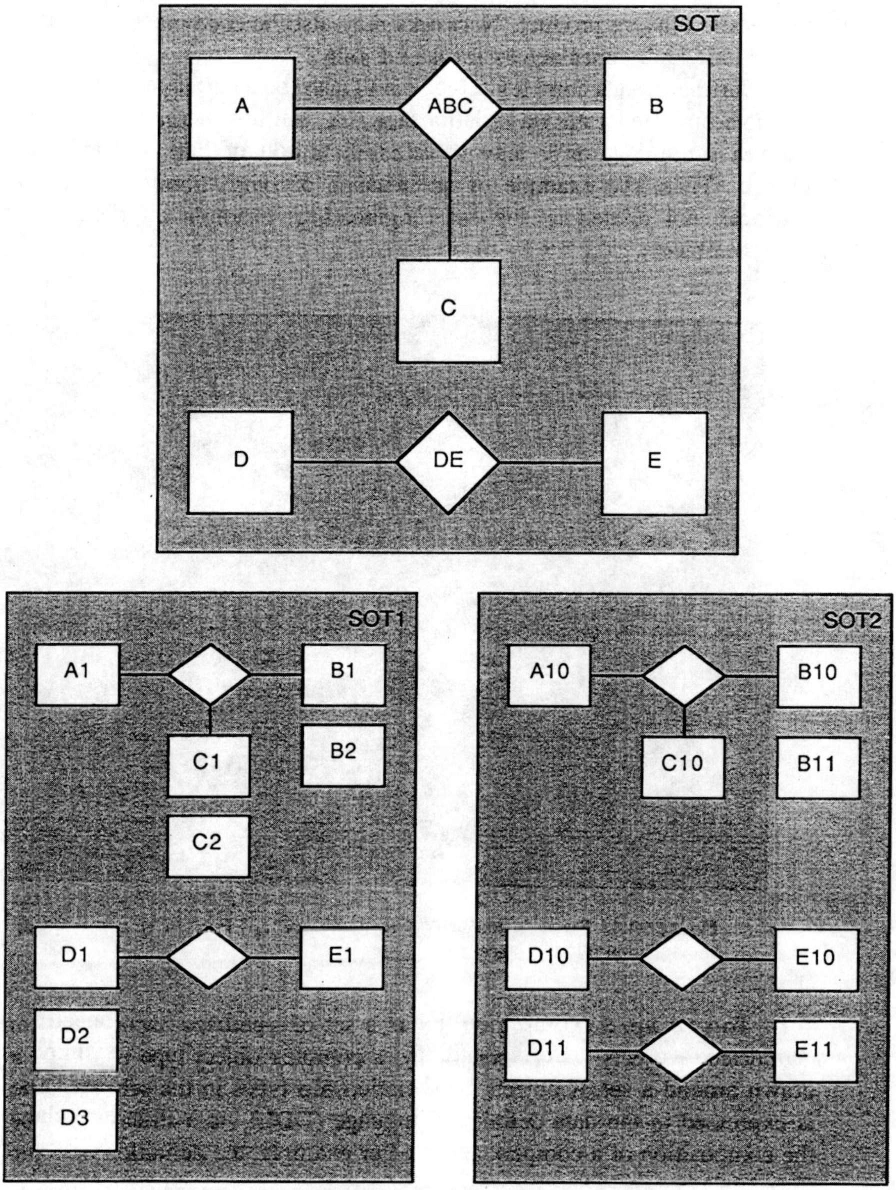


**Figure 14.5** Structured object type SOT with subobject.

As this example shows, complex objects may participate in relationships with other complex objects like any object (see also Fig. 14.3). The reader will have noticed that the structure concept is a generalization of the classical concept of aggregation (at least as far as structural aspects are concerned). By providing means for the definition of object types that are unions of other object types, the concept of generalization [Smi77] may also be modeled by using complex objects.

Object composition may involve recursions. Figure 14.6 shows two CERM solutions for a tree, one recursive, the other a non-recursive alternative.

```
OBJECT TYPE node
    ...
END node

RELSHIP TYPE f_s
    RELATES  father   : node,
             son      : node
    ...
END f_s

OBJECT TYPE tree
    ...
    STRUCTURE IS node, f_s
END tree
```

```
OBJECT TYPE node
    ...
END node

RELSHIP TYPE f_s
    RELATES  father   : node,
             son      : tree
    ...
END f_s

OBJECT TYPE tree
    ...
    STRUCTURE IS node, f_s, tree
END tree
```

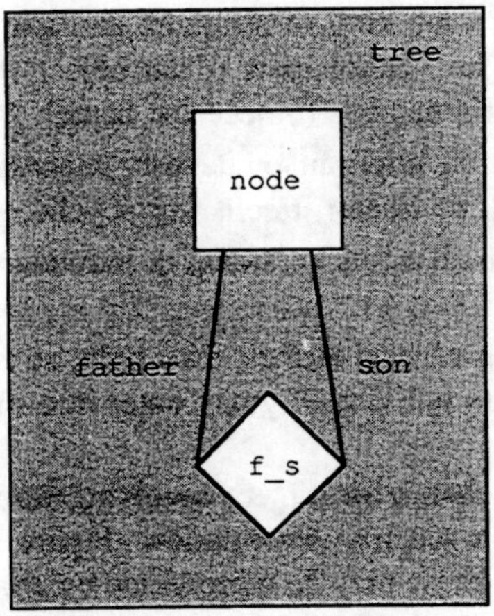


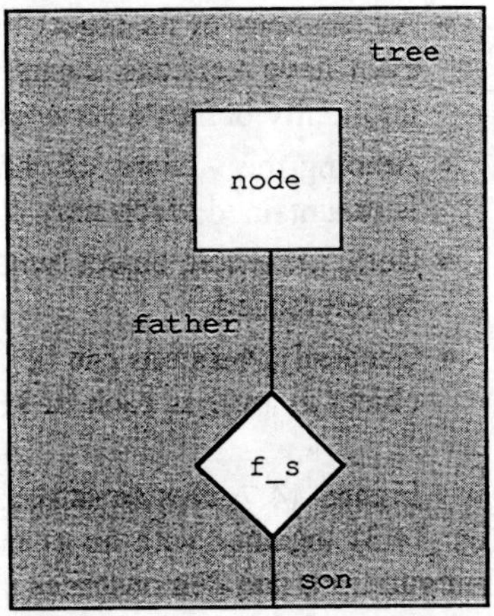


**Figure 14.6**

### 3.4 Special Relationships

In principle, complex objects might be expressed within the conventional ERM framework, e.g., by defining a relationship type "subobject". However, there are at least three good reasons that justify the introduction of a special concept instead of using the standard one:

1. Complex objects are very frequently needed to model the software engineering environment reality (the object-subobject relationship appears much more frequently than most other relationships);

2. It is much more convenient for the database designer to use the predefined concept than defining it all over again;
3. The system implementation can provide better performance for the special complex object concept than for the general relationship concept.

Screening the requirements of chapter 2, there are several other cases for which the same arguments hold, namely revisions, releases and alternatives. As already stated, we try to support the essential properties of all of them by providing **object versions** - multiple instances of the same object - in the data model. We maintain that this is preferable to supporting three distinct concepts that differ only slightly in their effects.

The CERM version concept has the following characteristics:

- Versions are associated with objects.
- Both, the objects as a whole ("generic" object) and its individual versions may have (descriptive and structural) properties; the object properties are supposed to be common to all its versions.
- All versions of an object have the same kind of structure and attributes and may even have versions themselves. The version part of an object type declaration implicitly defines a version type; it is named ⟨object type name⟩. `VERSION`.
- Among the versions of one object, an implicit predecessor-successor relationship is maintained which may optionally be linear, treelike, or acyclic.
- Both, the whole object (with or without all its versions) or individual versions may be referenced.
- Generally, versions can be treated as objects in their own right, so that a "generic" object as well as each of its versions individually may enter into relationships.

Figure 14.7 gives an (incomplete) schema for objects involving versions (based on Fig. 14.3) together with an example of a schema instantiation. Figure 14.8 illustrates configurations and demonstrates that even these may be represented by collecting specific versions into a complex "configuration" object.

We conclude as an important result that there are just two, albeit powerful, extensions to the ERM that according to our current experience suffice to account for the peculiarities of SEEs (and presumably of many other design environments): complex entities and entity versions.

### 3.5 Special Attributes

The ERM is a design tool emphasizing the modeling of entity and relationship types. If the same model (or its extension to CERM) is to serve as the basis of a DBMS interface, attribute domains (or value sets) are of central importance, too. Hence, we give a brief summary of the CERM attribute domains.

First, **predefined domains** for character, integer, boolean and time values are provided. Additional value sets may be constructed within the schema by using **con-**

```
OBJECT TYPE component_specification
  ATTRIBUTES
    name   :    STRING [32]
  VERSION       linear
    (ATTRIBUTES ...)
  AT LEAST ONCE division
  AT MOST ONCE  division
END component_specification
```

```
OBJECT TYPE design_document
  ATTRIBUTES
    name   :    STRING [32]
    author :    STRING [40]
  VERSIONS      tree-like
    (ATTRIBUTES ...)
END design_document

RELATIONSHIP TYPE division
  RELATES component_specification,
          design_component
END division
```

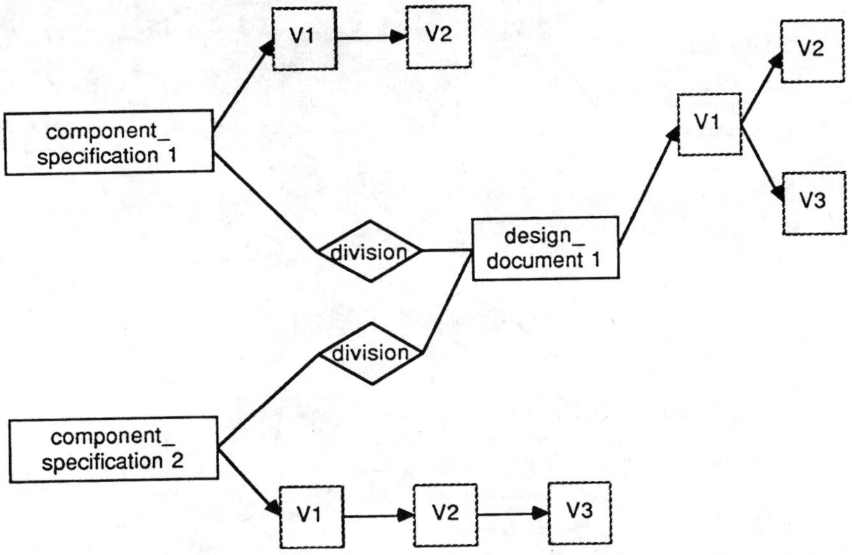


**Figure 14.7** Multiple versions (dashed boxes) of design document and component specification objects.

**structors** (similar to those found in programming languages) for character strings, byte strings, enumerations, subranges, arrays, records and type unions.

There is an additional predefined domain that merits some comments. LONG FIELD [Has82] defines a byte sequence of arbitrary and changing length. It may be compared to a file, and is accessible only by special operators similar to those found in file management. The idea is to allow design tools to store and access large volumes of data without communicating their structure to the DBMS. While the DBMS then is in no position to interpret the contents, to control its consistency, or to do an intelligent synchronization or recovery for it, the DBMS also avoids the concomittant overhead so that the application may gain in performance.

Consequently, by using long fields the designer has an option to waive typical database qualities and gain in performance instead.

```
OBJECT TYPE configuration
  ATTRIBUTES
     name    :    STRING [32]
  STRUCTURE IS component_specification.VERSION,
               design_document.VERSION,
               conf_div
END configuration

RELSHIP conf_div
  RELATES component_specification.VERSION,
          design_document.VERSION
  ...
END conf_div
```

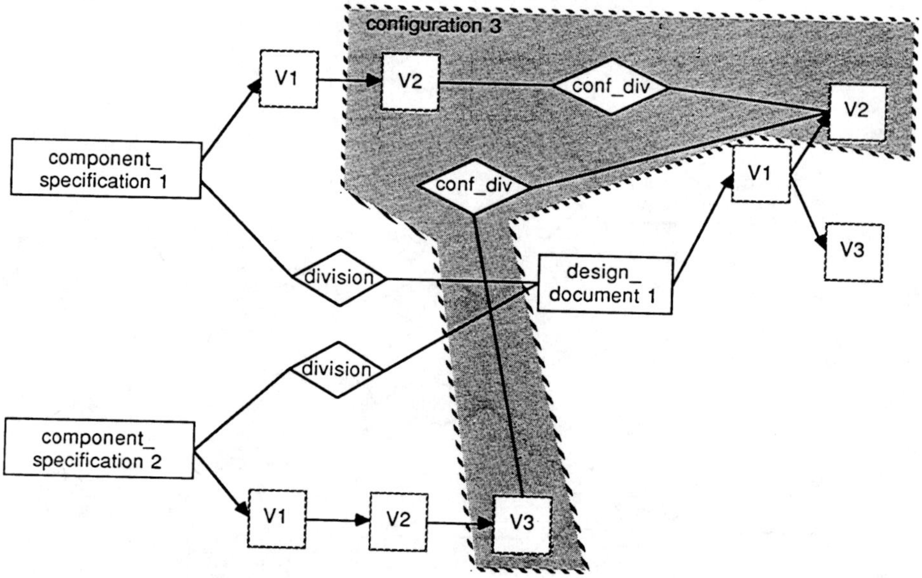


**Figure 14.8** A design document/component specification configuration (dotted lines); for ease of working with a configuration, the "conf_div" relationship has been introduced; its instances have to be consistently derived from the "division" instances.

## 3.6 Multiple Databases

The classical concept of a single integrated database is inappropriate for design applications. For one, design processes involve a high degree of trial and error, return to earlier stages, test of hypotheses, and they may extend over days, weeks or even months. Consequently, design data often tend to be transient, volatile, tentative, and tied to individual designers. Such data (remember the notion of revision) should be kept in the private databases of designers. Only design data that have been released should be transferred to public databases which may themselves be organized on two or three levels such as team databases, or a project database [Kla85]. Once designs have been completed and are not subject to further modification or even maintenance, they may be transferred to archives. Software objects that are suited for re-use in other projects or for separate marketing, or that have been acquired from outside sources, may be kept in separate library databases.

CERM handles multiple databases, subject to the following rules:

- An object is a member of exactly one database; however, copies are allowed in other databases.
- Relationships may be established between objects in different databases. However, the relationship attributes are confined to one of the involved databases (Fig. 14.9).
- The effects of operations are restricted to a single database; they do not automatically propagate to other databases.
- Long transactions [Has82,Kla85] are supported, based on checking out an object from one database to another and checking it back in when finished with its manipulation.

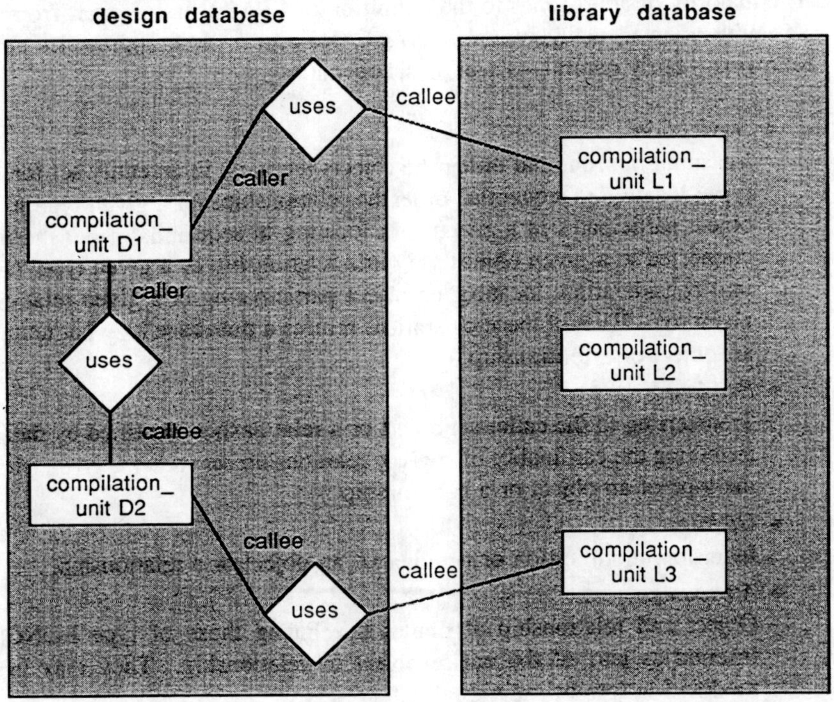


**Figure 14.9** Relationships extending across database boundaries.

## 4. OPERATORS OF THE CERM

DBMS interfaces have to provide users with facilities for creating, manipulating and accessing databases. As a data model comprises both structural and operational properties, data definition and data manipulation mechanisms are closely interrelated. This justifies the extreme caution taken in extending the ERM: the more concepts, the more database operators, and presumably the more confusion on the part of the user.

Unfortunately, there is no yardstick against which to hold the operational interface of the CERM. The ERM has by and large been used for semantic modeling, with the emphasis laid on structural aspects. Operations have been neglected because the ERM was never thought of as a DBMS interface. Only more recently attempts have surfaced that add operations to the ERM [Elm81,Mar83].

As a consequence, we divide the following discussion into a number of topics. We start by defining a set of basic ERM operators, extend it then by operators for dealing with complex objects and versions, and finally discuss operators for the attribute value sets.

## 4.1 Basic Operators

The majority of approaches to the definition of ERM operators start from the premise of an entity-oriented, navigational interface. We repeat these approaches and propose the following—fairly natural—set of basic operators.

- *Navigation.*
  Locating in sequential order the objects (entities) in an entity set for a given object type; locating in sequential order the relationships of a given type in which a given object participates in a given role; locating in sequential order the objects that are connected to a given object via some relationship of a given type, taking the roles into consideration; locating an object participating in a given relationship under a given role. Each of these operations returns a **database key** that uniquely identifies an object or a relationship.
- *Retrieval.*
  Transferring to the caller an object or a relationship identified by database key; determining the cardinality of a given relationship set under a given role; determining the type of an object or a relationship.
- *Update.*
  Insertion, modification or removal of an object or a relationship.
- *Attributes.*
  Object and relationship attributes (excluding those of type LONG FIELD) are inserted as part of the entire object or relationship. They may be retrieved or modified in toto or individually.

## 4.2 Operators on Complex Entities

A complex object may be considered as a boundary drawn around a set of (sub-) objects and relationships. Consequently, operators are needed that manipulate the object structure or exploit it: insertion or removal of a given object or relationship into/from a given structured (complex) object of known type, where all objects and relationships preexist and are known by their database keys; navigation within a structured object to the next subobject or relationship participates (remember that complex objects may overlap). The propagation of object deletion to subobject may be controlled in various ways.

Complex objects play a second major role: they are the units of transfer between different databases. The corresponding set of operators is: draw a copy of either the descriptive properties alone or of the entire object; transfer the object from one database to another or back into it.

### 4.3 Operators on Versions

The operators on versions are essentially extensions to the set of operators on objects: sequentially locating versions in the version graph for a given object where the order is determined by version number; locating the (complex) object that includes a given version object; insertion and removal of a version object into/from the version graph of a given object.

### 4.4 Cursors

It is often convenient to collect a number of otherwise distinct objects and/or relationships from the database and temporarily hold them as a unit for computation by an application program. We refer to such a dynamic arrangement as a **cursor**.

The contents of a cursor are determined by a complex search expression that may incorporate associative and structural criteria. Cursors can be introduced and dropped at will; they may be filled with database data determined by a search expression; the contents may subsequently be sorted on the basis of a sort expression; the cursor may be emptied of its contents. Usually cursors are lost after session termination. However, they may be saved across sessions and subsequently be restored; such "permanent" cursors must explicitly be removed.

The contents of cursors can be manipulated on an element-by-element or a set basis. Operators in the first class include those for inserting or removing an existing object or relationship into/from a cursor and for sequentially navigating through the cursor. Operators in the second class are the classical set operators of union, intersection and difference.

### 4.5 Long Field Operators

As we noted before, attributes are manipulated within the context of the basic object and relationship operators. Attributes of type `LONG FIELD` are an exception to this. Because long fields are kins to byte-stream-oriented files, their operators resemble the corresponding file operators: opening and closing of long fields; determining the length of or position within a long field; positioning within a long field; insertion, modification, deletion or retrieval of a given amount of bytes starting from a given position within the long field.

## 5. SYSTEM ENVIRONMENT, IMPLEMENTATION ISSUES AND FIRST EXPERIENCES

CERM has been developed for the DAMOKLES[1] database management system. DAMOKLES is used within UNIBASE, a cooperation project between a number of German commercial software companies and research institutions to develop a UNIX-based software engineering environment. The ultimate goal is to store all kinds of development data in DAMOKLES databases (probably distributed in a network of database servers and workstations) and thus to integrate software tools of various sources by means of the common database interface.

The full-fledged DAMOKLES system offers all salient database features like recovery, consistency control, access control, archiving and so on. Furthermore, **object-oriented main memory databases** [Kat85] will be provided that allow users to identify or assemble the objects they plan to work with in order for the system to fix the necessary structures in main memory until they are explicitly released. This mechanism overcomes deficiencies of traditional DBMSs which do not exploit the object-oriented way of accessing data.

The implementation of a comparatively complex data model like CERM is best achieved by devising a multilevel architecture [Dit85b]. One of the key differences to the implementation of conventional data models is the requirement to provide efficient operation on (possibly large) complex objects.

Our approach, therefore, introduces a lower level interface below CERM, represented by a so-called **Internal Object Data Model (IODM)**. Like CERM, the IODM is object-oriented but breaks down the complexity of structured objects. This is achieved by the IODM-concept of **logical clusters**. The mapping from CERM to IODM then places all subobjects and relationships directly contained in a structured object into one logical cluster. In this way, the complexity of implementing arbitrary hierarchies of objects and relationships is reduced to the problem of implementing sets of simple objects and relationships.

In a further step logical clusters (which obviously may overlap!) are split into disjoint ones which in turn lead to variable-size records. Lower modules are responsible for storage management in a way similar to conventional DBMS, but offer extensive physical clustering mechanisms. In summary, the information of what data should be clustered for efficient access is passed on from the top-most (semantic) level down to the (physical) storage management level.

A prototype system supporting the full CERM is scheduled for late 1986. However, the detailed specification of CERM itself has been frozen and accepted by all cooperating partners. First experience has been gained by some companies who developed CERM schemas for various software tools. Not surprisingly, it took some effort to teach the concepts to people that were not used to thinking in terms of data models (incidentally, something that has also been observed for the pure ERM concept!). However, the examples completed to date did not show any lack nor superfluity of CERM concepts, and after some training, engineers seem to do a good job in using the data model.

[1]Database Management System of Karlsruhe for Software Engineering Environments

## ACKNOWLEDGMENTS

K. Abramowicz, C. Eick, R. Langle, T. Raupp and T. Wenner together with the authors have been involved in determining the requirements and designing CERM. We are also grateful to our project partners in UNIBASE for their support and cooperation.

# List of References


[Abi87] Abiteboul, S. and Hull, R., "A Formal Semantic Database Model", *ACM Transactions on Database Systems*, Vol. 12, No. 4, pp. 525–565, 1987.

[Abr74] Abrial, J. R., "Data Semantics", *Data Base Management*, North-Holland, Amsterdam, pp. 1–59, 1974.

[Adi80] Adiba, M. E. and Lindsay, B. G., "Database Snapshots", *Proceedings of the 6th International Conference on Very Large Databases*, Montreal, Canada, pp. 86–91, October 1980.

[Afs84] Afsarmanesh, H. and McLeod, D., "A Framework for Semantic Database Models", *Proceedings of the NYU Symp. on New Directions for Database Systems*, May 16–18, 1984.

[Afs85a] Afsarmanesh, H., Knapp, D., McLeod, D. and Parker, A., "An Extensible, Object-Oriented Approach to Databases for VLSI/CAD", *Proceedings of the International Conference on Very Large Databases*, VLDB Endowment, August 1985.

[Afs85b] Afsarmanesh, H., Knapp, D., McLeod, D., and Parker, A., "An Object-Oriented Approach to VLSI/CAD", in *Proceedings of the International Conference on Very Large Data Bases*, Stockholm, Sweden, August 1985.

[Afs86] Afsarmanesh, H. and McLeod, D., "A Framework for Semantic Database Models", in G. Ariav and J. Clifford, editors, *New Directions for Database Systems*, pp. 149–67, Ablex Publishing Company, 1986.

[Ahl84a] Ahlsen, M., Bjornerstedt, A., Britts, S., Hulten, C. Soderlund, L., "Making Type Changes Transparent", University of Stockholm, SYSLAB Report No. 22, February 1984.

[Ahl84b] Ahlsen, M., Bjornerstedt, A., Britts, S., Hulten, C., and Soderlund, L., "An Architecture for Object Management in OIS", *ACM Transactions on Office Information Systems*, Vol. 2, No. 3, pp. 173–96, July 1984.

[Aik85] Aikens, J., "A Representation Scheme Using Both Frames and Rules", in *Rule-Based Expert Systems*, B. Buchanan and E. Shortliffe (editors), Addison-Wesley, pp. 424–40, 1985.

[Alb84] Albano, A. and Orsini, R., "A Prototyping Approach to Database Applications Development", *Database Engineering*, Vol. 7, No. 4, December 1984.

[Alb85] Albano, A., Cardelli, L., and Orsini, R., "Galileo: A Strongly-Typed, Interactive Conceptual Language", *ACM Transactions on Database Systems*, Vol. 10, No. 2, pp. 230–60, June 1985.

[Ame83] American National Standards Institute, Inc., *The Programming Language Ada Reference Manual*, ANSI/MIL-STD-1815A, 1983.

[And82] Andler, S., Ding, I., Eswaran, K., Hauser, C., Kim, W., Mehl, J., and Williams, R., "System D: A Distributed System for Availability", in *Proceedings of the 8th International Conference on Very Large Databases*, Mexico City, September 1982.

[And86] Anderson, T., et al., "PROTEUS: Objectifying the DBMS User Interface", *Proceedings International Workshop on Object-Oriented Database Systems*, Asilomar, CA, September 1986.

[And87] Andrews, T. and Harris, C., "Combining Language and Database Advances in an Object-Oriented Development Environment", *Proceedings of the Conference on Object-Oriented Programming Systems, Languages, and Applications*, pp. 430–40, ACM, 1987.

[Ans75] ANSI/X3/SPARC (STANDARDS PLANNING AND REQUIREMENTS COMMITTEE). Interim report from the study group on database management systems. *FDT (Bulletin of ACM SIGMOD)*, Vol. 7, No. 2, 1975.

[Atk83] Atkinson, M. P. and Kulkarni, K. G., "Experimenting with the Functional Data Model", Technical Report Persistent Programming Res. Report 5, University of Edinburgh, September 1983.

[Atw85] Atwood, T., "An Object Oriented DBMS for Design Support Applications", *Proceedings IEEE COMPINT 85*, Montreal, Canada, September 1985.

[Atz86] Atzeni, P. and Parker, D. S., "Formal Properties of Net-Based Knowledge Representation Schemes", *Proceedings of the Second IEEE International Conference on Data Engineering*, pp. 700–706, February 1986.

[Aya86] Ayache, N. and Faugeras, O.D., "HYPER: A New Approach for the Recognition and Position of Two-dimensional Objects", *IEEE Transactions Pattern Analysis Machine Intelligence*, Vol. PAMI-8, pp. 44–54, 1986.

[Bac77] Bachman, C. W., "The Role Concept in Data Models", in *Proceedings International Conference Very Large Databases*, Tokyo, Japan, October 1977.

[Ban86] Banerjee, J., Kim, H-J., Kim, W., Korth, H. F., "Schema Evolution in Object-Oriented Persistent Databases", *Proceedings of the Sixth Advanced Database Symposium*, August 1986.

[Ban87a] Banerjee, J., Chou, H., Garza, J., Kim, W., Woelk, D., Ballou, N., and Kim, H., "Data Model Issues for Object-Oriented Applications", *ACM Transactions on Office Information Systems*, Vol. 5, No. 1, pp. 3–26, January 1987.

[Ban87b] Banerjee, J., Kim, W., Kim, H. J., and Korth, H. F., "Semantics and Implementation of Schema Evolution in Object-Oriented Databases", in *Proceedings ACM SIGMOD Conference on the Management of Data*, San Francisco, CA, May 1987.

[Banc88] Bancilhon, F., Barbedette, G., Benzaken, V., Delobel, C., Gamerman, S., Lecluse, C.,

Pfeffer, P., Richard, P., and Velez, F., "The Design and Implementation of O2, an Object-Oriented Database System", in K. R. Dittrich, editor, *Advances in Object-Oriented Database Systems*, pp. 1–22, Springer-Verlag, 1988.

[Ban88] Banerjee, J., Kim, W., Kim, K. C., "Queries in Object-Oriented Databases", in *Proceedings 4th International Conference on Data Engineering*, Los Angeles, CA, February 1988.

[Bat84] Batory, B. and Buchmann, A., "Molecular Objects, Abstract Data Types and Data Models: A Framework", *Proceedings VLDB*, pp. 172–84, 1984.

[Bat85a] Batory, D. and Kim, W., "Modeling Concepts for VLSI CAD Objects", *ACM Transactions on Database Systems*, Vol. 10, No. 3, September 1985.

[Bat85b] Batory, D. and Kim, W., "Supporting Versions of VLSI CAD Objects", M.C.C. Technical Report, Austin, TX, 1985.

[Bat86] Batory, D., et al., "GENESIS: A Reconfigurable Database Management System", Technical Report, 86-07, Dept. of Comp. Sci., Univ. of Texas at Austin, 1986.

[Bati86] Batini, C., Lenzerini, M. and Navathe, S. B., "A Comparative Analysis of Methodologies for Database Schema Integration", *ACM Computing Survey 18*, Vol. 4, pp. 323–64, December 1986.

[Bee83] Beech, D. and Feldman, J. S., "The Integrated Data Model - A Database Perspective", *Proceedings of 9th International Conference on Very Large Databases*, Florence, 1983.

[Bee85] Beech, D., "Towards an Object Model of the Representation and Use of Information", Hewlett-Packard Technical Report, June 1985.

[Bee88] Beech, D., "A Foundation for Evolution from Relational to Object Databases", in Schmidt, J. W., Ceri, S., Missikoff, M. (Eds.), *Advances in Database Technology–EDBT 1988*, lecture notes in Computer Science 303, Springer-Verlag, 1988.

[Bee88] Beech, D. and Mahbod, B., "Generalized Version Control in an Object-Oriented Database", *IEEE 4th International Conference on Data Engineering*, February 1988.

[Bha86] Bhateja, R. and Katz, R. H., "A Validation Subsystem of a Version Server for Computer-Aided Design Data", submitted to ACM/IEEE 25th Design Automation Conference, Miami, FL, June 1987. Also available as UCB CSD Technical Report 87/317, October 1986.

[Bil78] Biller, H. and Neuhold, E. J., "Semantics of Databases: The Semantics of Data Models", *Inf. Syst.*, Vol. 3, pp. 11–30, 1978.

[Bla79] Blasgen, et al., "Architectural Updates to System R", IBM Res. Report RJ2654, June 1979.

[Bob83] Bobrow, D. G. and Stefik, M., *The Loops Manual*, Intelligent Systems Laboratory, Xerox Corporation, 1983.

[Bob85] Bobrow, D. G., Kahn, K., Kiczales, G., Masinter, L., Stefik, M., Zdybel, F., *CommonLoops: Merging Common Lisp and Object-Oriented Programming*, Intelligent Systems Laboratory Series ISL-85-8, Xerox PARC, Palo Alto, CA, 1985.

[Bob86a] Bobrow, D. G., Fogelsong, D. J., Miller, M. S., *Definition Groups, Making Sources First Class Objects*, ISL Report, Xerox PARC, 1986.

[Bob86b] Bobrow, D., Kahn, K., Kiczales, G., Masinter, L., Stefik, M., and Zdybel, F., "CommonLoops: Merging Lisp and Object-Oriented Programming", *Proceedings of ACM Conference on Object-Oriented Programming Systems, Languages and Applications*, pp. 17–29, March 1986.

[Bob86c] Bobrow, D. and Stefik, M., "Perspectives on Artificial Intelligence Programming", *Science*, Vol. 231, No. 4741, pp. 951, February 18, 1986.

[Bob87] Bobrow, D. G., et al., "Comon Lisp Object System Specification", ANSI Report 87-001, September 1987.

[Bor85a] Borgida, A., "Features of Languages for the Development of Information Systems at the Conceptual Level", *IEEE Software 2*, Vol. 1, pp. 63-72, January 1985.

[Bor85b] Borgida, A., "Language Features for Flexible Handling of Exceptions in Information Systems", *ACM Transactions on Database Systems*, Vol. 10, No. 4, December 1985.

[Bra85] Brachman, R. J. and Schmolze, J., "An Overview of the KL-ONE Knowledge Representation System", *Cognitive Science*, Vol. 9, pp. 171–216, 1985.

[Bro81] Brodie, M. L., "On Modelling Behavioral Semantics of Data", in *Proceedings of the 7th International Conference on Very Large Data Bases*, (Cannes, France), September 1981.

[Bro83] Brown, R. and Parker, D., S., "LAURA: A Formal Data Model and her Logical Design Methodology", *Proceedings 9th International Conference Very Large Data Bases*, pp. 206–18, 1983.

[Bro84a] Brodie, M. L., "On the Development of Data Models", in *On Conceptual Modelling*, M. L. Brodie, J. Mylopoulos and J. W. Schmidt (editor), Springer-Verlag, pp. 19–48, 1984.

[Bro84b] Brodie, M. L. Mylopoulos, J., and Schmidt, J. W., eds., *On Conceptual Modelling*, Springer-Verlag, New York, 1984.

[Bro84c] Brodie, M. L. and Ridjanovic, D., "On the Design and Specification of Database Transactions", in *On Conceptual Modelling*, Springer-Verlag, pp. 277-306, 184.

[Bro86] Brodie, M. and Mylopoulos, J. editors, *On Knowledge Base Management Systems*, Springer-Verlag, 1986.

[Bry86] Bryce, D. and Hull, R., "SNAP: A Graphic-Based Schema Manager", *Proceedings of the Second IEEE International Conference on Data Engineering*, pp. 151–64, February 1986.

[Bun77] Buneman, P. and Morgan, H. L., "Implementing Alerting Techniques in Database Systems", in *Proceedings COMPSAC'77*, Chicago, IL, November 1977.

[Bun79] Buneman, P. and Frankel, R. E., "FQL - A Functional Query Language", in *Proceedings ACM SIGMOD International Conference Management of Data*, Boston, MA, 1979.

[Bun82] Buneman, P., Frankel, R. E., and Nikhil, R., "An Implementation Technique for Database Query Languages", *ACM Transactions on Database Systems*, Vol. 7, No. 2, pp. 164–86, 1982.

[Car86] Carey, M., DeWitt, D. J., Richardson, J. E., and Shekita, E. J., "Object and File Management in the EXODUS Extensible Database System", *Proceedings of the 12th International Conference on Very Large Data Bases*, Kyoto, Japan, August 1986.

[Cat83] Catell, R. G., "Design and Implementation of a Relationship-Entity-Datum Model", Xerox CSL 83-4, May 1983.

[Cha75] Chamberlin, D. D., Gray, J. N., and Traiger, I. L., "Views, Authorization and Locking in a Relational Database System", *Proceedings AFIPS NCC*, Vol. 44, pp. 425–30, 1975.

[Cha75] Chang, C. L., "A Hyper-Relational Model of Databases", IBM Res. Report RJ1634, IBM, San Jose, CA, August 1975.

[Cha76] Chamberlin, D. D., "Relational Database Management Systems", *Comput. Surv.*, Vol. 8, No. 1, pp. 43–66, March 1976.

[Cha81] Chan, A., Fox, S. A., Lin, W.-T. K., and Ries, D., "Design of an ADA Compatible Local Database Manager (LDM)", TR CCA 81-09, Computer Corporation of America, November 1981.

[Cha82] Chan, A., Danberg, S., Fox, S., Lin, W. T. K., Nori, A., and Ries, D., "Storage and Access

Structures to Support a Semantic Data Model", *Proceedings 8th International Conference Very Large Data Bases*, pp. 122–30, 1982.

[Chan80a] Chang, N. S. and Fu, K. S., "Query-by-Pictorial Example", *IEEE Transactions on Software Engineering*, Vol. SE 6, No. 6, pp. 519–24, November 1980.

[Chan80b] Chang, N. S. and Fu, K. S., "A Relational Data Base System for Images", *Pictorial Information Systems*, Springer-Verlag, pp. 288-321, 1980.

[Chan80c] Chang, S. K., Lin, B. S., and Walser, R., "A Generalized Zooming Technique for Pictorial Data Base System", *Pictorial Information Systems*, Springer-Verlag, pp. 257–87, 1980.

[Chan81] Chang, N. S. and Fu, K. S., "Pictorial Query Languages for Pictorial Data Base Systems", *COMPUTER*, Vol. 14, No. 1, pp. 23–33, November 1981.

[Che76] Chen, P. P., "The Entity-Relationship Model–Toward a Unified View of Data", *ACM Transactions on Database Systems*, Vol. 1, No. 1, pp. 9–36, March 1976.

[Che78] Chen, P. P., "The Entity-Relationship Approach to Logical Database Design", Mono. 6, QED Information Sciences, Wellesley, MA, 1978.

[Cho81] Chock, M., Cardenas, A. F., and Klinger, A., "Manipulating Data Structures in Pictorial Information Systems", *IEEE Computer*, Vol. 25, No. 11, pp. 43–50, November 1981.

[Cho84] Chock, M., Cardenas, A. F., and Klinger, A., "Data Base Structure and Manipulation Capabilities of a Picture Data Base Management System (PICDMS)", *IEEE Transactions on Pattern Analysis and Machine Intelligence*, Vol. PAMI-6, No. 4, pp. 484–92, July 1984.

[Cho85] Chou, Hong-Tai and DeWitt, D., "An Evaluation of Buffer Management Strategies for Relational Database Systems", *Proceedings 11th International Conference on Very Large Data Bases*, August 1985.

[Cho86] Chou, H. T. and Kim, W., "A Unifying Framework for Versions in a CAD Environment", in *Proceedings International Conference on Very Large Data Bases*, Kyoto, Japan, August 1986.

[Cho88] Chou, H. T. and Kim W., "Versions and Change Notification in an Object-Oriented Database System", in *Proceedings 25th Design Automation Conference*, June 1988.

[Chu83] Chu, K. C., Fishburn, J. P., Honeyman, P., and Liem, Y. E., "Vdd - A VLSI Design Database", Engineering Design Application Proceedings from *SIGMOD Database Week*, May 1983.

[Clo81] Clocksin, W. F. and Mellish, C. S., *Programming in Prolog*, Springer-Verlag, New York, 1981.

[Cod70] Codd, E. F., "A Relational Model for Large Shared Data Banks", *Communications of the ACM*, Vol. 13, No. 6, pp. 377–87, June 1970.

[Cod71] Codd, E. F., "Further Normalization of the Database Relational Model", in *Database Systems*, Courant Computer Science Symposia 6, R. Rusin, ed. Englewood Cliffs, N.J.: Prentice-Hall, pp. 65–98, 1971.

[Cod79] Codd, E. F., "Extending the Database Relational Model to Capture More Meaning", *ACM Transactions on Database Systems*, Vol. 4, No. 4, pp. 397–434, December 1979.

[Cod81] Codd, E. F., "Data Models in Database Management", *ACM SIGMOD Rec.*, Vol. 11, No. 2, pp. 112–14, February 1981.

[Coda71] Codasyl Committee on Data System Languages, Codasyl database task group report, ACM, New York, 1971.

[Com79] Computer Corporation of America, DBMS - Independent CICIS Specifications, Technical Report CCA, Cambridge, MA, 1979.

[Cop84] Copeland, G. and Maier, D., "Making Smalltalk a Database System", *Proceedings 1984 ACM-SIGMOD International Conference on the Management of Data*, pp. 316–25, June 1984.

[Cop85] Copeland, G. and Koshafian, S. N., "A Decomposition Storage Model", *Proceedings ACM/SIGMOD International Conference on the Management of Data*, 1985.

[Cos84] Cosmadakis, S. S. and Papadimitriou, C. H., "Updates of Relational Views", *Journal of the ACM*, Vol. 31, No. 4, October 1984.

[Cox86] Cox, B. J., *Object Oriented Programming: An Evolutionary Approach*, Reading, MA: Addison-Wesley, 1986.

[Dad86] Dadam, P., et al., "A DBMS Prototype to Support Extended NF2 Relations: An Integrated View on Flat Tables and Hierarchies", *Proceedings ACM-SIGMOD International Conference on the Management of Data*, Washington, D.C., May 1986.

[Dam88a] Damon, C., "Data Abstraction and Objects: A Model of Representation", Ontologic, Inc., Billerica, MA, Submitted for Publication, 1988.

[Dam88b] Damon, C. and Landis, G., "Abstract Types and Storage Types in an OO-DBMS", *Proceedings of CompCon*, Spring 1988.

[Dat81a] Date, C. J., "Referential Integrity", in *Proceedings of the 7th International Conference on Very Large Data Bases*, Cannes, France, September 1981.

[Dat81b] Date, C. J., "Introduction to Database Systems", 3rd ed., Addison-Wesley, 1981.

[Dat82] Date, C. J., "An Introduction to Database Systems", Vol. 2, Addison-Wesley, 1984.

[Dat84] Date, C. J., *A Guide to DB2*, Addison-Wesley, 1984

[Day82] Dayal, U., Goodman, N., Katz, R. H., "An Extended Relational Algebra with Control over Duplicate Elimination", in *Proceedings ACM SIGACT-SIGMOD Symposium on Principles of Database Systems*, March 1982.

[Day84] Dayal, U. and Hwang, H. Y., "View Definition and Generalization for Database Integration in the Multidatabase System", *IEEE Transactions on Software Engineering SE-10*, Vol. 6, pp. 628–44, 1984.

[Day85] Dayal, U., et al., "A Knowledge Oriental Database Management System", *Proceedings Islamorada Conference on Large Scale Knowledge Base and Reasoning Systems*, February 1985.

[Dep86] Deppisch, U., et al., "A Storage System for Complex Objects", *Proceedings International Workshop on Object-Oriented Database Systems*, Asilomar, CA, September 1986.

[Der85] Derrett, N., Kent, W., and Lyngbaek, P., "Some Aspects of Operations in an Object-Oriented Database", *Database Engineering*, Vol. 8, No. 4, IEEE Computer Society, December 1985.

[Der86] Derrett, N., Fishman, D. H., Kent, W., Lyngbaek, P., and Ryan, T. A., "An Object-Oriented Approach to Data Management", in *Proceedings of Compcon 31st IEEE Computer Society International Conference*, San Francisco, CA, March 1986.

[Dit84] Dittrich, K. R., Kotz, A. M., and Mulle, J. M., "An Event/Trigger Mechanism to Enforce Complex Consistency Constraints in Design Databases", University of Karlsruhe Technical Report, Karlsruhe, West Germany, November 1984.

[Dit85a] Dittrich, K. R. and Lorie, R. A., "Version Support for Engineering Database Systems", Res. Report RJ 4769 (50628) 7/18/85. IBM Research Laboratory, San Jose, CA 95193 (to appear in *IEEE Transactions on Software Engineering*).

[Dit85b] Dittrich, K. R., Kotz, A. M., and Mulle, J. A., "A Multilevel Approach to Design Database Systems and its Basic Mechanisms", *Proceedings IEEE COMPINT*, Montreal, pp. 313-20, 1985.

[Dit86] Dittrich, K., Gotthard, W., Lockemann, P. C., "DAMOKLES - A Database System for Software Engineering Environments", *Proceedings of the IFIP 2.4 Workshop on Advanced Programming Environments*, Trondheim, Norway, June 1986.

[Dol84] Dolk, D. R. and Konsynski, B. R., "Knowledge Representation for Model Management Systems", *IEEE Transactions on Software Engineering*, Vol. 10, No. 6, November 1984.

[Dre] Drescher, *Object LISP User Manual*, LMI, 1000 Massachusetts Avenue, Cambridge, MA.

[Duh88] Duhl, J. and Damon, C., "A Performance Comparison of Object and Relational Databases Using the Sun Benchmark", in *Proceedings of ACM Conference on Object-Oriented Systems, Languages, and Applications*, San Diego, CA, 1988.

[Eas80] Eastman, C. M., "System Facilities for CAD Databases", *Proceedings IEEE 17th Design Automation Conference*, June 1980.

[Eff84] Effelsberg, W. and Haerder, T., "Principles of Database Buffer Management", *ACM Transactions on Database Systems*, Vol. 9, No. 4, pp. 560–95, December 1984.

[Ell82] Ellis, C. A. and Bernal, M., "Officetalk-D: An Experimental Office Information System", in *Proceedings of Conference on Office Information Systems*, Philadelphia, PA, pp. 131–40, June 1982.

[Elm81] Elmasri, R. and Wiederhold, G., "GORDAS: A Formal High-Level Query Language for the Entity-Relationship Model", in Chen, P. P. (ed.), *Entity-Relationship Approach to Information Modeling and Analysis*, ER Institute, pp. 49–70, 1981.

[Emo83] Emond, J. C. and Marechad, G., "Experience in Building ARCADE, A Computer Aided Design System Based on a Relational DBMS", *Engineering Design Application Proceedings* from SIGMOD Database Week, May 1983.

[Esw75] Eswaran, K. P. and Chamberlin, D. D., "Functional Specifications of a Subsystem for Database Integrity", in *Proceedings International Conference on Very Large Databases*, Framingham, MA, September 1975.

[Fag77] Fagin, R., "Multivalued Dependencies and a New Normal Form for Relation Databases", *ACM Transactions on Database Systems*, Vol. 2, No. 3, pp. 262–78, 1977.

[Far85] Farmer, D. B., King, R. and Myers, D. A., "The Semantic Database Constructor", *IEEE Transactions on Software Engineering SE-11*, Vol. 7, pp. 583–91, 1985.

[Fik85] Fikes, R. and Kehler, T., "The Role of Frame-Based Representation in Reasoning", *Communications of the ACM* , Vol. 9, pp. 904–20, September 1985.

[Fin79] Findler, N., ed., *Associative Networks*, New York: Academic Press, 1979.

[Fis87] Fishman, D., Beech, D., Cate, H., Chow, E., Connors, T., Davis, T., Derrett, N., Hoch, C., Kent, W., Lyngbaek, P., Mahbod, B., Neimat, M., Ryan, T. and Shan, M., "Iris: An Object-Oriented Database Management System", *ACM Transactions on Office Information Systems*, Vol. 5, No. 1, pp. 48–69, January 1987.

[Fla85] "Introduction to the Flavor System", in *Reference Guide to Symbolics Inc.*, 1985.

[Gar84] Garcia-Molina, H. and et al., "DataPatch: Integrating Inconsistent Copies of a Database After a Partition", Technical Report #304, Dept. Elec. Eng. and Comp. Sci., Princeton, NJ, 1984.

[Gar88] Garza, J. F. and Kim, W., "Transaction Management in an Object-Oriented Database System", in *Proceedings ACM-SIGMOD International Conference on the Management of Data*, June 1988.

[Gib83] Gibbs, S. and Tsichritzis, D., "A Data Modelling Approach for Office Information Systems", *ACM Transactions on Office Information Systems*, Vol. 1, No. 4, pp. 299–319, October 1983.

[Gol81] Goldberg, A., "Introducing the Smalltalk-80 System", *Byte*, Vol. 6, No. 8, pp. 14–26, August 1981.

[Gol83] Goldberg, A. and Robson, D., *Smalltalk-80: The Language and its Implementation*, Addison-Wesley, Reading, MA, 1983.

[Gol85] Goldman, K. J., Goldman, S. A., Kanellakis, P. C., and Zdonik, S. B., "ISIS: Interface for a Semantic Information System", *Proceedings ACM SIGMOD International Conference on the Management of Data*, 1985.

[Goo83] Goos, G., et al. (eds), *DIANA—An Intermediate Language for Ada*, lecture notes in Computer Science, Vol. 161, Springer, 1983.

[Gra87] Graefe, G. and DeWitt, D. J., "The EXODUS Optimizer Generator", *Proceedings ACM SIGMOD International Conference on the Management of Data*, San Francisco, CA, May 1987.

[Gray78] Gray, J. N., *Notes on Data Base Operating Systems*, IBM Res. Report: RJ2188, IBM Research, San Jose, CA, 1978.

[Gray84] Gray, M., "Databases for Computer-Aided Design", in *New Applications of Databases*, G. Gardarin, E. Gelenbe eds., Academic Press, 1984.

[Gri82] Griethuysen, J. J., ed., *Concepts and Terminology for the Conceptual Schema and the Information Base*, International Organization for Standardization, ISO/TC97/SC5/WG3, publication number ISO/TC97/SC5-N 695, 1982.

[Guc88] Guck, R. L., Fritchman, B. L., Thompson, J. P., and Tolbert, D. M., "SIM: Implementation of a Database Management System Based on a Semantic Data Model", *IEEE Data Engineering Bulletin*, Vol. 11, No. 2, June 1988.

[Gut77] Guttag, J., "Abstract Data Types and the Development of Data Structures", *Communications of the ACM*, Vol. 20, No. 6, pp. 396–404, 1977.

[Ham75] Hammer, M. and McLeod, D., "Semantic Integrity in a Relational Database System", in *Proceedings International Conference on Very Large Databases*, Framingham, MA, September 1975.

[Ham76] Hammer, M. and McLeod, D., "A Framework for Database Semantic Integrity", in *Proceedings 2nd International Conference Software Engineering*, San Francisco, CA, October 1976.

[Ham78] Hammer, M. and McLeod, D., "The Semantic Data Model: A Modelling Mechanism for Database Applications", in *Proceedings ACM SIGMOD International Conference Management of Data*, Austin, TX, 1978.

[Ham79] Hammer, M., "Research Directions in Database Management", in *Research Directions in Software Technology*, P. Wegner, ed., Cambridge, MA: M.I.T. Press, 1979.

[Ham80a] Hammer, M. and Berkowitz, B., "DIAL: A Programming Language for Data-Intensive Applications", Working Paper, M.I.T. Lab. Computer Science, Cambridge, MA, 1980.

[Ham80b] Hammer, M. and McLeod, D., "On the Architecture of Database Management Systems", in *Infotech State-of-the-Art Report on Data Design*, Berkshire, England: Pergamon Infotech Ltd., 1980.

[Ham81] Hammer, M. and McLeod, D., "Database Description with SDM: A Semantic Database Model", *ACM Transactions on Database Systems*, Vol. 6, No. 3, pp. 351–386, September 1981.

[Har86] Harrison, D., et al., "Data Management and Graphics Editing in the Berkeley Design Environment", *Proceedings ICCAD*, Santa Clara, CA, November 1986.

[Has82] Haskins, R. and Lorie, R., "On Extending the Functions of a Relational Database System", *Proceedings 1982 ACM-SIGMOD Conference on Management of Data*, Orlando, FL, June 1982.

[Hay81] Haynie, M. N., "The Relational/Network Hybrid Data Model for Design Automation Databases", *Proceedings IEEE 18th Design Automation Conference*, 1981.

[Hec81] Hecht, M. S. and Kerschberg, L., "Update Semantics for the Functional Data Model", Technical Report, Bell Laboratories, Holmdel, NJ, January 1981.

[Hei82] Heimbigner, D., "A Federated Architecture for Database Systems", Ph.D. dissertation, Univ. of Southern CA, August 1982.

[Hel75] Held, G., Stonebraker, M. R., and Wong, E., "INGRES – A Relational Data Base System", *Proceedings AFIPS NCC*, pp. 409–16, 1975.

[Hen84] Henderson, P. (ed.), *Proceedings of the ACM SIGSOFT/SIGPLAN Software Engineering Symposium on Practical Software Engineering Environments*, SIGPLAN Notices, Vol. 19, No. 5, May 1984.

[Hew84] Hewitt, C. and Jong, P. de, "Open Systems", in *On Conceptual Modelling: Perspectives from Artificial Intelligence, Databases and Programming Languages*, M. L. Brodie, J. Mylopoulos, J. W. Schmidt eds., Springer-Verlag, 1984.

[Hps] HPSQL Reference Manual, Part Number 36217-90001.

[Hud86] Hudson, S. E. and King, R., "CACTIS: A database system for specifying functionally-defined data", *Proceedings of the Workshop on Object-Oriented Databases*, Asilomar, Pacific Grove, CA, September 1986.

[Hud87] Hudson, S. E. and King, R., "Object-Oriented Database Support for Software Environments", *Proceedings of ACM SIGMOD International Conference on Management of Data*, San Francisco, CA, May 1987.

[Hul87] Hull, R. and King, R., "Semantic Database Modeling: Survey, Applications and Research Issues", *ACM Computing Surveys*, Vol. 19, No. 3, pp. 201–60, September 1987.

[Hun79] Hunt, H. B. and Rosenkrantz, D. J. "The Complexity of Testing Predicate Locks", *Proceedings of the ACM SIGMOD*, Boston, MA, May-June 1979.

[Ibm] "Query-by-Example, Program Description and Operations Manual", IBM Corporation, Form SH20-2077.

[Iee85] IEEE Computer Society, *Database Engineering*, Vol. 8, No. 4, December 1985, special issue on Object-Oriented Systems (edited by F. Lochovsky).

[Isr84] Israel, D. J. and Brachman, R. J., "Some Remarks on the Semantics of Representation Languages", in *On Conceptual Modelling*, Springer-Verlag, pp. 119–46, 1984.

[Jag88] Jagannathan, D., Fritchman, R. L., Guck, B. L., Thompson, J. P., and Tolbert, D. M., "SIM: A Database System Based on the Semantic Data Model", in *Proceedings of the ACM SIGMOD International Conference on Management of Data*, pp. 45–55, ACM SIGMOD, June 1988.

[Joh83] Johnson, H. R., Schweitzer, and Warkentire, E. R., "A DBMS Facility for Handling Structural Engineering Entities", *Engineering Design Application Proceedings*, from SIGMOD Database Week, May 1983.

[Kae81] Kaehler, T., "Virtual Memory for an Object-Oriented Language", *BYTE*, pp. 378–87, August 1981.

[Kae83] Kaehler, T. and Krasner, G., "LOOM - Large Object-Oriented Memory for Smalltalk-80 Systems", in Kra83.

[Kat82a] Katz, R. and Lehman, T., "Storage Structures for Versions and Alternatives", Computer Science Department, University of Wisconsin - Madison, Technical Report No. 479, July 1982.

[Kat82b] Katz, R. H., "A Database Approach for Managing VLSI Design Data", *Proceedings IEEE 9th Design Automation Conference*, 1982.

[Kat83] Katz, R. H., "Managing the Chip Design Database", *IEEE Computer*, Vol. 16, No. 12, December 1983.

[Kat85] Katz, R. H., *Information Management for Engineering Design*, Springer-Verlag, New York, 1985.

[Kat86a] Katz, R. H., Chang, E., and Bhateja, R., "Version Modeling Concepts for Computer-Aided Design Databases", *SIGMOD Conference Proceedings*, Washington, D.C., May 1986.

[Kat86b] Katz, R. H., Chang, E., and Anwarrudin, M., "A Version Server for Computer-Aided Design Databases", *ACM/IEEE 24th Design Automation Conference*, Las Vegas, NV, June 1986.

[Keh83] Kehler, T. P. and Clemenson, G. D., "An Application Development System for Expert Systems", *System Software*, Vol. 3, No. 1, pp. 212-23, January 1983.

[Ken78] Kent, W., "Data and Reality", North-Holland, Amsterdam, 1978.

[Ken79] Kent, W., "Limitations of Record-Oriented Information Models", *ACM Transactions on Database Systems*, Vol. 4, pp. 107–31, March 1979.

[Ker76a] Kerschberg, L. and Pacheco, J. E. S., "A Functional Data Base Model", Technical Report, Pontificia Universidade Catolica do Rio de Janeiro, Rio de Janeiro, Brazil, February 1976.

[Ker76b] Kerschberg, L., Klug, A., and Tsichritzis, D., "A Taxonomy of Data Models", *Systems for Large Data Bases*, North-Holland, Amsterdam, pp. 43–64, 1976.

[Kho86] Khoshafian, S. N. and Copeland, G. P., "Object Identity", in *Proceedings of Conference on Object-Oriented Programming Systems, Languages and Applications*, Portland, OR, pp. 406–16, September 1986.

[Kim87] Kim, W., Banerjee, J., Chou, H. T., Garza, J. F., and Woelk, D., "Composite Object Support in an Object-Oriented Database System", in *Proceedings of the Conference on Object-Oriented Programming Systems, Languages, and Applications*, pp. 118–25, 1987.

[Kim79] Kimbleton, S, R., Wang, P. S. C., and Fong, E., "XNDM: An Experimental Network Data Manager", in *Proceedings of Berkeley Workshop on Distributed Data Management System*, Berkeley, CA, August 1979.

[Kin82] King, R. and McLeod, D., "The Event Database Specification Model", in *Proceedings of International Conference on Improving Database Usability and Responsiveness*, Jerusalem, pp. 299–322, June 1982.

[Kin84a] King, R. and McLeod, D., "Semantic Database Models", in S. B. Yao, ed, *Principles of Database Design*, Englewood Cliffs, NJ: Prentice Hall, 1984.

[Kin84b] King, R., "Sambase: A Semantic DBMS", *Proceedings of the First International Workshop on Expert Database Systems*, pp. 151–71, October 1984.

[Kin84c] King, R. and McLeod, D., "A Unified Model and Methodology for Conceptual Database Design", in *On Conceptual Modelling: Perspectives from Artificial Intelligence, Database, and Programming Languages*, M. L. Brodie, J. Mylopoulos, and J. Schmidt, eds., Springer-Verlag, Frankfurt, 1984.

[Kin84d] King, R. and Melville, S., "The Semantics-Knowledgeable Interface", *Proceedings 10th International Conference on Very Large Data Bases*, pp. 30–37, 1984.

[Kin85a] King, R. and McLeod, D., "A Database Design Methodology and Tool for Information Systems", *ACM Transactions on Office Information Systems*, Vol. 3, No. 1, pp. 2–21, January 1985.

[Kin85b] King, R. and McLeod, D., "Semantic Database Models", in *Database Design*, Springer-Verlag, New York, pp. 115–50, 1985.

[Kla85] Klahold, P., et al., "Ein Transaktionskonzept zur Unterstutzung komplexer Anwendungen in integrierten Systemen", in *Proceedings GI-Fachtagung "Datenbanksysteme in Buro, Technik und Wissenschaft"*, Informatik Fachberichte, 94, Springer, S. 309–35, Marx 1985.

[Kra83] Krasner, G., ed., *Smalltalk-80: Bits of History, Words of Advice*, Reading, MA: Addison-Wesley, 1983.

[Kul83] Kulkarni, K. G., *Evaluation of Functional Data Models for Database Design and Use*, Ph.D. Thesis, University of Edinburgh, 1983.

[Kun84] Kung, R. and et al., "Heuristic Search in Database Systems", *Proceedings 1st International Workshop on Expert Data Bases*, Kiowah, SC, October 1984.

[Lac81] La Croix, M. and Pirotte, A., "Data Structures for CAD Object Description", *Proceedings IEEE 18th Design Automation Conference*, 1981.

[Lan86] Landis, G. S., "Design Evaluation and History in an Object-Oriented CAD/CAM Database", in *Proceedings of Compcon 31st IEEE Computer Society International Conference*, San Francisco, CA, March 1986.

[Lec88] Lecluse, C., Richard, P., and Velez, F., "O2, an Object-Oriented Data Model", *Proceedings ACM SIGMOD International Conference on the Management of Data*, June 1988.

[Lee78] Lee, R. M. and Gerritsen, R., "Extended Semantics for Generalization Hierarchies"", *Proceedings ACM SIGMOD International Conference Management of Data*, Austin, TX, 1978.

[Len87] Lenzerini, M., "Covering and Disjointness Constraints in Type Networks", in *Proceedings of IEEE Conference on Data Engineering*, Los Angeles, CA, pp. 386–93, February 1987.

[Lie86] Lieberman, H., "Using Prototypical Objects to Implement Shared Behavior in Object-Oriented Languages" *Proceedings of the ACM Conference on Object-Oriented Programming Systems, Languages, and Applications*, Portland, OR, September 1986.

[Lin80] Lindsay, B., "Object Naming and Catalog Management for a Distributed Database Manager", IBM Res. Report RJ2914, IBM Research Laboratory, San Jose, CA, August 1980.

[Lis77] Liskov, B., Snyder, A., Atkinson, R. and Schaffert, C., "Abstraction Mechanisms in CLU", *Communications of the ACM*, Vol. 20, No. 8, pp. 564–76, August 1977.

[Lis81] Liskov, B., Atkinson, R., Bloom, T., Moss, E., Schaffert, J. C., Scheifler, R. and Snyder, A., *Lecture Notes in Computer Science*, New York: Springer-Verlag, 1981.

[Lit81] Litwin, W., "Logical Design of Distributed Databases", Technical Report MOD-I-043, INRIA, Paris, July 1981.

[Loc83] Lockemann, P. C., "Analysis of Version and Configuration Control in a Software Engineering Environment", in C. G. Davis, S. Jajodia, P. A. Ng and R. T. Yeh, eds, *Entity-Relationship Approach to Software Engineering*, North Holland: Elsevier Science Publishers B. V., pp. 701–13, 1983.

[Loc85] Lockemann, P. C., et al., "Database Requirements of Engineering Applications—An Analysis", *Proceedings GI-Fachtangung "Datenbanksysteme in Buro, Technik und Wissenschaft"*, Karlsruhe, Marz 1985. Also available in English: Universität Karlsruhe, Fakultät für Informatik, Technical Report December 1985.

[Lor83] Lorie, R. and Plouffee, W., "Complex Objects and Their Use in Design Transactions", *Proceedings Engineering Design Applications Stream of ACM-IEEE Data Base Week*, San Jose, CA, May 1983.

[Lum84] Lum, V., Dadam, P., Erbe, R., Guenauer, J., Pistor, P., Walch, G., Werner, H., and Woodfill, J., "Designing DBMS Support for the Temporal Dimension", *Proceedings of the ACM SIGMOD*, Boston, MA, June 1984.

[Lyn82] Lyngbaek, P. and McLeod, D., "A Distributed Name Server for Information Objects", USC Technical Report TR-200, Univ. of Southern California, Los Angeles, CA, December 1982.

[Lyn83] Lyngbaek, P. and McLeod, D., "An Approach to Object Sharing in Distributed Database Systems", in *Proceedings of the 9th International Conference on Very Large Data Bases*, Florence, October 1983.

[Lyn84] Lyngbaek, P., "Information Modeling and Sharing in Highly Autonomous Database Systems", Ph.D. dissertation, Univ. of Southern California, 1984.

[Lyn86] Lyngbaek, P. and Kent, W., "A Data Modeling Methodology for the Design and Implementation of Information", in *International Workshop on Object-Oriented Database Systems*, Asilomar, Pacific Grove, CA, September 1986.

[Lyn87a] Lyngbaek, P. and Vianu, V., "Mapping a Semantic Database Model to the Relational Model", *SIGMOD Conference Proceedings*, San Francisco, CA, May 1987.

[Lyn87b] Lyngbaek, P., Derrett, N., Fishman, D. H., Kent, W., and Ryan, T. A., "Design and Implementation of the Iris Object Manager", in *Proceedings of a Workshop on Persistent Object Systems: Their Design, Implementation and Use*, Scotland, August 1987. Also available as HP Labs Technical Report STL-86-17, December 1986.

[Mac83] MacLennan, B. J., "A View of Object-Oriented Programming", Naval Postgraduate School NPS52-83-001, February 1983.

[Mai84] Maier, D. and Price, D., "Data Model Requirements for Engineering Applications", *Proceedings International Workshop on Expert Database Systems*, 1984.

[Mai85] Maier, D., Otis, A., and Purdy, A., "Object-Oriented Database Development at Servio Logic", *Database Engineering*, Vol. 18, No. 4, December 1985.

[Mai86a] Maier, D. and Stein, J., "Indexing in an Object-Oriented DBMS", Technical Report CS/E-86-006, Oregon Graduate Center, Beaverton, OR, May 1986.

[Mai86b] Maier, D., Stein, J., Otis, A., and Purdy, A., "Development of an Object-Oriented DBMS", *Proceedings of the Conference on Object-Oriented Programming Systems, Languages, and Applications*, pp. 472–82, September 29 - October 2, 1986.

[Mar83] Markowitz, V. M. and Raz, Y., "ERROL: An Entity-Relationship, Role Oriented EQuery Language", in C. G. Davis, S. Jajodia, P. A. Ng and T. Yeh, eds, *Entity-Relationship Approach to Software Engineering*, Elsevier Science Publishers B. V., North Holland: pp. 329–46, 1983.

[Mar86] Maryanski, F. and Peckham, J., "Semantic Data Models", Technical Report CSTR 86-15, Department of Computer Science and Engineering, University of Connecticut, 1986.

[Mcl77] McLeod, D., "High Level Definition of Abstract Domains in a Relational Database System", *J. Comput. Languages*, Vol. 2, No. 3, 1977.

[Mcl78] McLeod, D., "A Semantic Database Model and its Associated Structured User Interface", Technical Report, M.I.T. Laboratory Computer Science, Cambridge, MA, 1978.

[Mcl79] McLeod. D. and King, R., "Applying a Semantic Database Model", in *Proceedings International Conference Entity-Relationship Approach to Systems Analysis and Design*, Los Angeles, CA, December 1979.

[Mcl80a] McLeod, D., "A Database Transaction Specification Methodology for End-Users", Technical Report, Computer Science Dept., Univ. Southern California, Los Angeles, CA, 1980.

[Mcl80b] McLeod, D. and Heimbigner, D., "A Federated Architecture for Database System", in *Proceedings National Computer Conference*, Anaheim, CA, 1980.

[Mcl81] McLeod, D. and Smith, J. M., "Abstraction in Databases", in *Proceedings of the Workshop on Data Abstraction, Databases and Conceptual Modelling*, Pingree Park, CO, June 1980, SIGPLAN Not. 16, 1 January 1981.

[Mcl83a] McLeod, D., Bapa Rao, K. V., and Narayanaswamy, K., "Information Modelling for CAD/VLSI", in *Proceedings of the ACM SIGMOD International Conference on Management of Data*, San Jose, CA, May 1983.

[Mcl83b] McLeod, D., Narayanaswamy, K., and Rao, K. V. Bapa, "An Approach to Information Management for CAD/VLSI Applications", *Engineering Design Application Proceedings* from SIGMOD Database Week, May 1983.

[Meh85] Mehrotra, R. and Grosky, W. I., "REMINDS: A Relational Model-based Integrated Image and Text Data Base Management System", in *Proceedings IEEE Computer Society Workshop Computer Architecture for Pattern Analysis and Image Data Base Management*, Miami, FL, pp. 345–54, November 1985.

[Meh89] Mehrotra, R. and Grosky, W. I., "SMITH: An Efficient Model-based Two Dimensional Shape Matching Technique", in *Syntactic and Structural Pattern Recognition*, G. Ferrante, T. Pavlidis, et al., eds., New York: Springer-Verlag, 1989.

[Met76] Metcalfe, R. M. and Boggs, D. R., "Ethernet: Distributed Packet Switching for Local Computer Networks", *Communications ACM*, Vol. 19, No. 7, pp. 395–404, July 1976.

[Min84] Minsky, M. L., "A Framework for Representing Knowledge", in *The Psychology of Computer Vision*, P. H. Winston ed., New York: McGraw-Hill, pp. 211–77, 1984.

[Mit86] Mittal, S. J., Bobrow, D. G., and Kahn, K. M., "Virtual Copies: At the Boundary Between Classes and Instances", *Proceedings OOPSLA'86 Conference*, Portland, OR, September 1986.

[Moo86a] Moon, D. A., "Object-Oriented Programming with Flavors", *Proceedings of ACM Conference on Object-Oriented Programming Systems, Languages and Applications* pp. 1–8, March 1986.

[Moo86b] Moon, D. and Keene, S., *New Flavors*, Proceedings ACM 1986 OOPSLA Conference.

[Mor83] Morgenstern, M., "Active Databases as a Paradigm for Enhanced Computing Environments", *Proceeding Conference on Very Large Databases*, 1983.

[Mot81] Motro, A. and Buneman, P., "Constructing Superviews", in *Proceedings of ACM SIGMOD International Conference on Management of Data*, Ann Arbor, MI, April 1981.

[Myl78] Mylopoulos, J., Berstein, P. A., and Wong, H. K. T., "A Language Facility for Designing Interactive Database-Intensive Applications", in *Proceedings ACM SIGMOD International Conference Management of Data*, Austin, TX, 1978.

[Myl80a] Mylopoulos, J., Bernstein, P., and Wong, H.K. T., "A Language Facility for Designing Database-Intensive Applications", *ACM Transactions on Database Systems*, Vol. 5, No. 2, pp. 185–207, June 1980.

[Myl80b] Mylopoulos, J., "An Overview of Knowledge Representation", *Workshop on Data Abstract, Databases, and Conceptual Modelling*, Pingree Park, CO, pp. 5–12, 1980.

[Nar85] Narayanaswamy, K., Scacchi, W., and McLeod, D., "Information Management Support for Evolving Software Systems", Technical Report USC TR 85-324, University of Southern California, Los Angeles, CA, March 1985.

[Nav86] Navathe, S., Elmasri, R., and Larson, J., "Integrating User Views in Database Design", *IEEE Computer*, Vol., 19, No. 1, pp. 50–62, 1986.

[Neu82] Neumann, T. and Hornung, C., "Consistency and Transactions in CAD Databases", *Proceedings 8th VLDB*, Mexico City, Mexico, September 1982.

[Nie85] Nierstrasz, O. M., "Hybrid: A Unified Object-Oriented System", *Database Engineering*, Vol. 8, No. 4, December 1985.

[Opp83] Oppen, D. C. and Dalal, Y. K., "The Clearinghouse: A Decentralized Agent for Locating Named Objects in a Distributed Environment", *ACM Transactions Office Information System*, Vol. 1, No. 3, pp. 230–53, July 1983.

[Pae87] Paepcke, A., "PCLOS: A Flexible Implementation of CLOS Persistence", HP Labs Technical Report STL-88-13, April 1988. In the *Proceedings of the European Conference on Object-Oriented Programming*, Oslo, Norway, August 1988, published by Springer-Verlag.

[Pal78] Palmer, I., "Record Subtype Facilities in Database Systems", in *Proceedings 4th International Conference Very Large Databases*, Berlin, West Germany, September 1978.

[Par78] Parnas, D. L., "On the Design and Development of Program Families", *IEEE Transactions on Software Engineering*, Vol. SE-2, No. 1, pp. 1–9, March 1978.

[Pir77] Pirotte, A., "The Entity-Property-Association Model: An Information-Oriented Database Model", Technical Report, M.B.L.E. Res. Lab., Brussels, Belgium, 1977.

[Plo84] Plouffe, W., Kim, W., Lorie, R., and McNabb, D., "A Database System for Engineering Design", *Database Engineering*, Vol. 7, No. 2, June 1984.

[Pow83] Powell, M. L. and Linton, M. A., "Database Support for Programming Environments", *Engineering Design Application Proceedings* from SIGMOD Database Week, May 1983.

[Pur87] Purdy, A. Schuchardt, B., and Maier, D., "Integrating an Object Server with Other Worlds", *ACM Transactions on Office Information Systems*, Vol. 5, No. 1, pp. 27–47, January 1987.

[Rab82] Rabitti, F. and Gibbs, S., "A Distributed Form Management System with Global Query Facilities", in *Office Information Systems*, 1982.

[Ree79] Reed, D. P. and Kanodia, R. K., "Synchronization with Eventcounts and Sequencers", *Communications of the ACM*, February 1979.

[Ree82] Rees, J. A. and Adams, N. I. T.: A dialect of Lisp or, lambda: the ultimate software tool, *ACM Symposium on Lisp and Functional Programming*, 1982.

[Rot80] Rothnie, J. B., Bernstein, P. A., Fox, S., Goodman, N., Hammer, M., Landers, T. A., Reeve, C., Shipman, D., and Wong, E., "Introduction to a System for Distributed Database (SDD-1), *ACM Transactions Database System*, Vol. 5, No. 1, March 1980.

[Rou77] Roussopoulos, N., "Algebraic Data Definition", in *Proceedings 6th Texas Conference Computing Systems*, Austin, TX, November 1977.

[Rou84] Roussopoulos, N. and Yeh, R. T., "An Adaptable Methodology for Database Design", *IEEE Computer*, pp. 64–80, May 1984.

[Row86] Rowe, L. A., "A Shared Object Hierarchy", *Proceedings International Wkshop on Object-Oriented Database Systems*, Asilomar, CA, September 1986.

[Rud86] Rudmik, A., "Choosing an Environment Data Model", *Proceedings of the IFIP 2.4 Workshop on Advanced Programming Environments*, Trondheim, Norway, June 1986.

[Sch73] Schank, R. C., "Identification of Conceptualizations Underlying Natural Language", in *Computer Models of Thought and Language*, R. C. Schank and K. M. Colby, eds. W. H. Freeman, San Francisco, CA, 1973.

[Sch84] Schek, H.-J. and Scholl, M., "An Algebra for the Relational Model with Relation-Valued Attributes", Technical Report DVS I-1984-T1, Technische Hochschule Darmstadt, West Germany, 1984.

[Sch75] Schmid, H. A. and Swenson, J. R., "On the Semantics of the Relational Data Model", in *Proceedings of the ACM SIGMOD International Conference on the Management of Data*, San Jose, CA, 1975.

[Sen75] Senko, M. E., "Information Systems: Records, Relations, Sets, Entities, and Things", *Inf. Syst.*, Vol. 1, No. 1, pp. 3–14, 1975.

[Sen77] Senko, M. E., "Conceptual Schemas, Abstract Data Structures, Enterprise Descriptions", in *Proceedings ACM International Computing Symp.*, Belgium, April 1977.

[She84] Sheil, B., "Power Tools for Programmers", in Barstow, D., et al., ed., *Interactive Programming Environments*, McGraw Hill, 1984.

[Shi81] Shipman, D., "The Functional Data Model and the Data Language DAPLEX", *ACM Transactions on Database Systems*, Vol. 6, No. 1, pp. 140–73, 1981.

[Sib77] Sibley, E. and Kerschberg, L., "Data Architecture and Data Model Considerations", *Proceedings of NCC Conference*, pp. 85–96, 1977.

[Sid80] Sidle, T. W., "Weaknesses of Commercial Data Base Management Systems in Engineering Applications", *Proceedings IEEE 17th Design Automation Conference*, June 1980.

[Ska86] Skarra, A. H. and Zdonik, S. B., "The Management of Changing Types in an Object-Oriented Database", *Proceedings of the ACM Conference on Object-Oriented Programming Systems, Languages, and Applications*, Portland, OR, September 1986.

[Smi77] Smith, J. M. and Smith, D. C. P., "Database Abstractions: Aggregation and Generalization", *ACM Transactions on Database Systems*, Vol. 2, No. 2, pp. 105–33, June 1977.

[Smi78] Smith, J. M. and Smith, D. C. P., "Principles of Conceptual Database Design", in *Proceedings NYU Symp. Database Design*, New York, May 1978.

[Smi79] Smith, J. M. and Smith, D. C. P., "A Database Approach to Software Specification", Technical Report CCA-79-17, Computer Corporation of America, Cambridge, MA, April 1979.

[Smi81a] Smith, J. M., Bernstein, P. A., Dayal, U., Goodman, N., Landers, T., Lin, K. W. T., and Wong, E., "Multibase - Integrating Heterogeneous Distributed Database Systems", in *Proceedings of the National Computer Conference*, pp. 487–99, June 1981.

[Smi81b] Smith, J. M., Fox, S., and Landers, T., "Reference Manual for ADAPLEX", Technical Report, Computer Corporation of America, 1981.

[Smi83] Smith, J. M., Fox, S., and Landers, T., "ADAPLEX: Rational and Reference Manual", second ed., Computer Corporation of America, Cambridge, MA, 1983.

[Smi87] Smith, K. and Zdonik, S., "Intermedia: A Case Study of the Differences Between Relational and Object-Oriented Database Systems", in *Proceedings of the Conference on Object-Oriented Programming Systems, Languages, and Applications*, pp. 452–65, ACM, 1987.

[Sny86] Snyder, A., "CommonObjects: An Overview", *Sigplan Notices*, HP Labs Technical Report STL-86-13, June 1986.

[Sol79] Solvberg, A., "A Contribution of the Definition of Concepts for Expressing Users' Information System Requirements", in *Proceedings International Conference Entity-Relationship Approach to Systems Analysis and Design*, Los Angeles, CA, December 1979.

[Spo86] Spooner, D. L., Milican, M. A., and Fatz, D. B., "Modelling Mechanical CAD Data with Data Abstractions and Object-Oriented Technqiues', *Proceedings 2nd International Conference on Data Engineering*, February 1986.

[Sql81] SQL/Data System: Concepts and Facilities. GH24-5013-0, File No. S370-50, IBM Corporation, January 1981.

[Ste83] Stefik, M., Bobrow, D. G., Mittal, S., and Conway, L., "Knowledge Programming in LOOPS: Report on an Experimental Course", *Artificial Intelligence*, Vol. 4, No. 3, pp. 3–14, 1983.

[Ste84a] Steele, G. L., *Common Lisp: the Language*, Digital Press, 1984.

[Ste84b] Steele, G. L. Jr., Fahlman, S. E., Gabriel, R. P., Moon, D. A., and Weinreb, D. L., "Common Lisp", *Digital Press*, 1984.

[Ste86a] Stefik, M., Bobrow, D. G., Kahn, K., "Integrating Access-Oriented Programming into a Multi-Paradigm Environment", *IEEE Software*, 1986.

[Ste86b] Stefik, M. and Bobrow, D., "Object-Oriented Programming: Themes and Variations", *AI Magazine*, Vol. 6, No. 4, pp. 40–62, Winter 1986.

[Stem86] Stemple, D., Sheard, T., and Bunker, R., "Abstract Data Types in Databases: Specification Manipulation and Access", *Proceedings 2nd International Conference on Data Engineering*, February 1986.

[Sto74] Stonebraker, M. R., "High Level Integrity Assurance in Relational Database Management Systems", Electronics Res. Lab. Report ERL-M473, Univ. California, Berkeley, CA, August 1974.

[Sto76] Stonebraker, M. R., Wong, E. and Kreps, P., and Held, G. D., "The Design and Implementation of INGRES", *ACM Transactions on Database Systems*, Vol. 1, No. 3, pp. 189-22, 1976.

[Sto77] Stonebraker, M. and Neuhold, E., "A Distributed Database Version of INGRES", in *Proceedings of Berkeley Workshop on Distributed Data Management Systems*, Berkeley, CA, May 1977.

[Sto83] Stonebraker, M., Stettner, H., Lynn, N., Kalash, J. and Guttman, A., "Document Processing in a Relational Database System", *ACM Transactions Office Inf. Syst.*, Vol. 1, No. 2, pp. 143–58, October 1983.

[Sto84] Stonebraker, M. R. and et al., "QUEL as a Data Type", *Proceedings 1984 ACM-SIGMOD Conference on the Management of Data*, May 1984.

[Sto85] Stonebraker, M. R., "Triggers and Inference in Data Base Systems", *Proceedings Islamorada Conference on Large Scale Knowledge Base and Reasoning Systems*, February 1985.

[Sto86a] Stonebraker, M. and Rowe, L. A., "The Design of Postgres", *Proceedings of International Conference on the Management of Data*, pp. 340–55, June 1986.

[Sto86b] Stonebraker, M. R., "Object Management in POSTGRES Using Procedures", *Proceedings International Workshop on Object-Oriented Database Systems*, Asilomar, CA, September 1986.

[Sto86c] Stonebraker, M. R., "Inclusion of New Types in Relational Data Base Systems", *Proceedings Second International Conference on Data Base Eng.*, Los Angeles, CA, February 1986.

[Sto87] Stonebraker, M. R., "POSTGRES Storage System", submitted for publication, 1987.

[Str86] Stroustrup, B., *The C++ Programming Language*, Addison-Wesley, 1986.

[Sus79] Su, S. Y. W. and Lo, D. H., "A Semantic Association Model for Conceptual Database Design", in *Proceedings International Conference Entity-Relationship Approach to Systems Analysis and Design*, Los Angeles, CA, December 1979.

[Sus83] Su, S. Y. W., "SAM*: A Semantic Association Model for Corporate and Scientific-Statistical Databases", *Information Sciences*, Vol. 29, pp. 151–99, 1983.

[Sym84] *FLAV Objects, Message Passing, and Flavors*, Symbolics, Inc., Cambridge, MA, 1984.

[Sym85] Symbolics, Inc., "User's Guide to Symbolics Computers", *Symbolics Manual #996015*, March 1985.

[Tay76] Taylor, R. W. and Frank, R. L., "CODASYL Database Management Systems", *Comput. Surv.*, Vol. 8, No. 1, pp. 67–104, March 1976.

[Teo86] Teorey, T. J., Yang, D., and Fry, J. P., "A Logical Design Methodology for Relational Databases Using the Extended Entity-Relationship Model", *ACM Computing Surveys*, Vol. 18, No. 2, pp. 197–222, June 1986.

[Ter83] Terry, D. B. and Andler, S., "The Cosie Communication Subsystem: Support for Distributed Office Applications", IBM Res. Report RJ4006, IBM Research Laboratory, San Jose, CA, August 1983.

[Tic82a] Tichy, W. F., "Revision Control System", *Proceedings IEEE 6th International Conference on Software Engineering*, September 1982.

[Tic82b] Tichy, W. F., "A Data Model for Programming Support Environments and its Application", in H.-J. Schneider and A. I. Wasserman, eds., *Automated Tools for Information Systems Design*, North Holland, pp. 31–48, 1982.

[Tra82] Traiger, I., "Virtual Memory Management for Databases Systems", *ACM Operating Systems Reviews*, Vol. 16, No. 4, pp. 26–48, October 1982.

[Tsa85] Tsai, W. H., and Yu, S. S., "Attribute String Matching with Merging for Shape Recognition", *IEEE Transactions Pattern Analysis Machine Intelligence*, Vol. PAMI-7, pp. 453–62, 1985.

[Tsi76] Tsichritzis, D. C. and Lochovsky, F. H., "Hierarchical Database Management: A Survey", *Comput. Surv.*, Vol. 8, No. 1, pp. 105–24, March 1976.

[Tsi77] Tsichritzis, D. and Klug, A. C., *American National Standards Institute/X3/SPARC DBMS Framework: Report of the Study Group on Database Management Systems*, AFOPS Press, Arlington, VA, 1977.

[Tsi82a] Tsichritzis, D. C., "Form Management", *Commun. ACM*, Vol. 25, No. 7, pp. 453–78, July 1982.

[Tsi82b] Tsichritzis, D. and Lochovsky, F. H., *Data Models*, Englewood Cliffs, NJ: Prentice Hall, 1982.

[Tsi82c] Tsichritzis, D. C., Rabitti, F. A., Gibbs, S., Nierstrasz, O., and Hogg, J., "A System for Managing Structured Messages", *IEEE Transactions Commun. Com-30*, January 1982.

[Tsu84] Tsur, S., and Zaniolo, C., "Implementation of GEM - Supporting a Semantic Data Model on a Relational Back-End", in *Proceedings ACM SIGMOD International Conference on Management of Data*, May 1984.

[Ull82] Ullman, J. D., *Principles of Database Systems, 2nd ed.*, Potomac, MD: Computer Science Press, 1982.

[Ull87] Ullman, J. D., "Database Theory: Past and Future", *Proceedings of ACM SIGACT News-SIGMOD-SIGART Principles of Database Systems*, San Diego, CA, March 1987.

[Urb86] Urban, S. D., and Delcambre, L. M. L., "An Analysis of the Structural, Dynamic, and Temporal Aspects of Semantic Data Models", *Proceedings of the 2nd IEEE International Conference on Data Engineering*, pp. 382–89, February 1986.

[Ver82] Verheijen, G. and Bekkum, J. V., "NIAM: An Information Analysis Method", in *Information Systems Design Methodologies: A Comparative Review*, T. Otte, H. Sol and A. Verrijn-Stuart, eds., IFIP, 1982.

[Via87] Vianu, V., "Dynamic Constraints and Database Evolution", *Journal of the ACM*, Vol. 34, No. 1, pp. 128–59, January 1987.

[Wei85] Weisner, S. P., "An Object-Oriented Protocol for Managing Data", *Database Engineering*, Vol. 8, No. 4, December 1985.

[Wie77] Wiederhold, G., *Database Design*, New York: McGraw-Hill, 1977.

[Wie79] Wiederhold, G. and El-Masri, R., "Structural Model for Database Design", in *Proceedings International Conference Entity-Relationship Approach to Systems Analsys and Design*, Los Angeles, CA, December 1979.

[Wie82] Wiederhold, G., et al., "A Database Approach to Communication in VLSI Design", *I.E.E.E. Transactions on Computer-Aided Design*, V CAD-1, N 2, April 1982.

[Wil81] Williams, R., Daniels, D. Haass, L., Lapis, G., Lindsay, B., Ng., P., Obermarck, R., Selinger, P., Walker, A., Wilms, P., and Yost, R., "R*: An Overview of the Architecture", IBM Res. Report RJ3325, IBM Research Laboratory, San Jose, CA, February 1981.

[Wir82] Wirth, N., "Programming in Modula 2", Springer, 1982.

[Woe86] Woelk, D., Kim, W., and Luther, W., "An Object-Oriented Approach to Multimedia Databases", in *Proceedings ACM SIGMOD Conference on the Management of Data*, Washington D.C., May 1986.

[Woe87] Woelk, D. and Kim, W., "Multimedia Information Management in an Object-Oriented Database System", in *Proceedings Very Large Data Bases*, Brighton, England, September 1987.

[Won77] Wong, H. K. T. and Mylopoulos, J., "Two Views of Data Semantics: A Survey of Data Models in Artificial Intelligence and Database Management", *INFOR*, Vol. 15, No. 3, pp. 344–82, October 1977.

[Won82] Wong, H. K. T. and Kou, I., "GUIDE: A Graphical User Interface for Database Exploration", *Proceedings 8th International Conference Very large Data Bases*, pp. 22–32, 1982.

[Woo75] Woods, W. A., "What's in a Link: Foundation for Semantic Networks", in D. Bobrow and A. Collins, eds., *Representation and Understanding: Studies in Cognitive Science*, pp. 35–82, Academic Press, 1975.

[Woo81] Woodfill, J. Siegal, P., Randstrom, J., Meyer, M., and Allman, E., *INGRES Version 7 Reference Manual*, 1981.

[X3j88] X3J13 Standards Committee Documents 88-002 and 88-003, 1988.

[Zan76] Zaniolo, C., "Analysis and Design of Relational Schemata for Database Systems", Technical Report UCLA-Eng-7668, UCLA Dept. of Computer Science, July 1976.

[Zan83] Zaniolo, C., "The Database Language GEM", *Proceeding 1983 ACM-SIGMOD Conference on Management of Data*, San Jose, CA, May 1983.

[Zdo84] Zdonik, S., "Object Management System Concepts", in *Proceedings of the ACM-SIGOA Conference on Office Information Systems*, pp. 13–19, 1984.

[Zdo85a] Zdonik, S. B., "Object Management Systems for Design Environment", *Database Engineering*, Vol. 8, No. 4, December 1985.

[Zdo85b] Zdonik, S. B. and Wegner, P., "Towards Object-Oriented Database Environments", Brown University, RI, 1985.

[Zdo86a] Zdonik, S. B., "Version Management in an Object-Oriented Database", *Proceedings of the IFIP 2.4 Workshop on Advanced Programming Environments*, Trondheim, Norway, June 1986.

[Zdo86b] Zdonik, S. B., "Maintaining Consistency in a Database with Changing Types", *ACM SIGPLAN Notices*, Vol. 21, No. 10, pp. 120–27, October 1986.

[Zdo86c] Zdonik, S. B., "Why Properties are Objects or Some Refinements to is-a", *Proceedings of the ACM/IEEE Fall Joint Computer Conference*, Austin, TX, November 1986.

[Zdo86d] Zdonik, S. B. and Wegner, P., "Language and Methodology for Object-Oriented Database Environments", *Proceedings of the Nineteenth Annual Hawaii International Conference on System Sciences*, January 1986.